Themes in Jewish-Christian Relations

Edited by

Edward Kessler and Melanie J. Wright

First published in 2005 by Orchard Academic,
16 Orchard Street, Cambridge, England, CB1 1JT

Typeset and design: Siggi & Banjo

ISBN 1903283132 (paper)
ISBN 1903283140 (cloth)

Themes in Jewish-Christian Relations

Edited by

Edward Kessler and Melanie J. Wright

Orchard Academic

Contents

Contributors

Markus Anker
University of St Gallen
Hamutal Bar-Josef
Ben-Gurion University of the Negev
Maria Diemling
Trinity College Dublin
Eugene J. Fisher
US Conference of Catholic Bishops
Tomáš Halik
Charles University
David Herbert
Trinity College Dublin
Edward Kessler
Centre for the Study of Jewish-Christian Relations and
Cambridge University
William Klassen
University of Waterloo
John T. Pawlikowski
Catholic Theological Union, Chicago
Simon Rocker
The *Jewish Chronicle*
Marc Saperstein
The George Washington University
David C. Sim
Australian Catholic University
Isabel Wollaston
University of Birmingham
Melanie J. Wright
Centre for the Study of Jewish-Christian Relations and
Cambridge University

Introduction

Edward Kessler

The study of Jewish-Christian relations is a relatively recent development with its roots in the pioneering works of writers from the early 20th century such as the Jewish leader and theologian, Claude Montefiore, and the Anglican minister and scholar, James Parkes. Montefiore argued for a reassessment of Jewish attitudes towards Christianity, believing it was time for a Jewish reappraisal of Christianity and vice versa. His writings reached their climax in a call for a Jewish theology of Christianity. He was the first English Jewish writer to objectively present the New Testament to the Jewish community, controversially arguing that it was an entirely Jewish book with no Christian elements. He saw the teaching of Jesus, whom he regarded as a great teacher but in no sense God, as a revival of prophetic Judaism. Jesus 'started the movement which broke down the old barriers and brought about the translation of Judaism into the Gentile world… with many modifications, curtailments, additions both for the better and worse, good and evil'.[1]

For his part, James Parkes was a Christian scholar who was devoted to fighting antisemitism and seeking out its origins, which he found in the writings of the early Church, including the New Testament. Parkes argued that the Church bore much responsibility for the development of antisemitism, a view which was enormously controversial. He was courageously outspoken and wrote that he was 'completely unprepared for the discovery that it was the Christian Church, and the Christian Church alone, which turned normal xenophobia and normal good and bad communal relations between two human societies into the unique evil of antisemitism'.[2]

These writings, and those of a small number of other scholars in Europe and the USA, were generations ahead of their time. Many of the views of Montefiore and Parkes have now become accepted in mainstream Judaism and Christianity although their opinions can still engender conflict. Parkes' plea for Christians to abandon proselytising Jews and Montefiore's description of Judaism solely as a religion, rejecting the concept of peoplehood, remain contentious subjects.

Nevertheless, the pioneers of the modern study of Jewish-Christian relations provided the means by which the relationship between Judaism and Christianity began to be transformed. Indeed, this transformation is one of the few pieces of good news that can be reported in today's world of interfaith relations. However, before this transformation could become widespread, the trauma of the Holocaust and the creation of the state of Israel occurred. Both forever changed the Jewish-Christian encounter. Firstly, the murder of 6 million Jews, alongside 5 million non-Jews, during the years of 1933-45 in the heart of Christian Europe by people who called themselves – and were generally accepted as – Christians, threatened not only the future of Jews and Judaism, but also the moral integrity of Christianity. Secondly, a few years after the end of World War II, the state of Israel was declared, and the goal of the modern Zionist movement – which began around 70 years earlier – was achieved. A Jewish state in the Land of Israel had re-appeared after an absence of nearly 1900 years. These events have, unsurprisingly, had a huge impact on the study and practice of Jewish-Christian relations.

Particularly since the 1960s, scholarly and institutional contacts between Christians and Jews have increased, as is exemplified by the growing number of studies either co-edited by Jewish and Christian scholars or relating 'conversations' between Jews and Christians. (This book is the most recent example of this phenomenon.) Of all the events in the last 40 years of the Jewish-Christian encounter, the most well known is the publication of *Nostra Aetate* in 1965. Eugene Fisher's clear analysis of the fourth section of the Second Vatican Council declaration on non-Christian religions in this book, shows how it helped achieve a radical reversal of the Church's traditional teaching of contempt against Jews and Judaism. *Nostra Aetate* rejected anti-Jewish theological polemic, condemned antisemitism, and replaced them with the foundations for a renewed vision of the continuing role of the Jewish People in God's plan of salvation for all humanity. Fisher argues that most Protestant scholars engaged in Christian-Jewish relations attest to the positive impact of the Vatican Council's declaration on discussions within their own communions.

Although the Christian pioneers of Jewish-Christian dialogue were virtually all Protestant, the publication of *Nostra Aetate* began a process of mutual enrichment between Catholic, Protestant and Jewish scholars.

New Testament studies have benefited enormously from the contribution of late 20th century Jewish scholars such as David Flusser and Geza Vermes, as well as the earlier writings of Joseph Klausner. As Bill Klassen points out in his contribution to this volume, these scholars showed that (since Jesus was a Jew) his ministry could only be understood in the historical context of first-century Palestinian Judaism. David Sim's chapter on first century Christian Judaism demonstrates that Jesus' Jewish followers argued amongst themselves about the conditions under which Gentiles might be admitted to this new Jewish movement, and with other Jews over issues such as Torah observance and claims about Jesus. The New Testament bears witness to these disputes, which were vigorous and often bitter. Markus Anker, in his study of the polemical passages in John chapters 7-8, demonstrates that the author of the Fourth Gospel applies the approach of early Jewish polemics towards pagan philosophy his claim to offer readers 'true' interpretation of Judaism. Anker points out that it is essential to appreciate the significance of the Jewish festival of Sukkot in order properly to understand the Gospel, reinforcing the jointly-held view among these three contributors that it is no longer acceptable to ignore the fact that the New Testament arguments were between Jews, about a Jew or about 'Jewish issues'. Traditionally, polemical passages were read as if they were 'Christian' arguments against 'Jews'. To read them this way is to misread them. David Sim, for example, proposes that describing early Christianity as Christian Judaism will help ensure that Christian theology will not return to the classical teaching of contempt.

The study of polemic, and especially its modern manifestations – antisemitism and the Holocaust – are of central concern to the modern study of Jewish-Christian relations, as illustrated by continuing controversies over the war-time role of Pius XII. It is generally acknowledged today that Catholic and Protestant writers, such as Edward Flannery and Franklin Littell respectively, have studiously and honestly examined the history of Christian antisemitism. As far as the Holocaust is concerned, a number of Jewish thinkers, such as Richard Rubenstein and Emil Fackenheim, have been particularly influential on Jews and Christians. However, perhaps the most well known Jewish writer on the Holocaust, certainly in terms of popular recognition, is Elie Wiesel, who received the Nobel Prize for Literature. Isabel Wollaston's study of Wiesel's life and writings provide a striking insight into this 'Teller of Tales'. Only a first-class scholar with a deep understanding of her subject would have the courage, as well as the knowledge, to offer an essay with a highly unusual combination of breadth and depth. Wollaston's essay is based on a paper delivered at a conference organised by the Centre for the Study of Jewish-Christian Relations (CJCR) in Cambridge in 2003.

Maria Diemling offered a paper at the same conference and her chapter informs the reader about the comparatively unknown topic of medieval Jewish stories about Jewish conversion to Christianity. Jewish conversion remains a controversial topic in the Jewish-Christian encounter and the history of Jewish-Christian relations offers many examples of Jews being forced, under pain of death, to convert. Christians have been shocked to learn that Jews did not automatically acknowledge Christian truth-claims. Diemling shows that by examining storytelling we can better understand how Jews in the Middle Ages viewed conversion to Christianity. The existence of these stories and their evocative description of the terror surrounding Jewish conversion, she suggests, should be viewed as one strategy in the Jewish struggle for survival in Christendom.

The use of literature in the study of Jewish-Christian relations is also adopted by Israeli writer Hamutal bar-Yosef in her fascinating study of Jewish-Christian relations in modern Hebrew and Yiddish literature. Studies of medieval Jewish-Christian relations tend to show that the Jew was the 'other' in the eyes of the Christian but bar Yosef offers examples from Jewish literature which show the Christian as the 'other'. Marc Saperstein's paper also offers an unusual insight into the medieval period and he explores a number of examples of tolerance between the two religions. Anti-Jewish Christian teaching, as well as medieval expulsions and massacres, should not lead us to ignore the more positive moments and events in the history of Jewish-Christian relations. Indeed, as Saperstein shows, there is generally more than one story to tell.

It may now have become clear to the reader that one of the characteristics of the subject of Jewish-Christian Relations is that it should not simply be located in the category of Religious Studies. Saperstein is a historian and bar-Yosef a teacher of literature (and widely published poet). The multi-disciplinary nature of Jewish-Christian relations is reinforced by Melanie Wright's study of cinema. The relationships between history, theology, the cinematic text, and its reception, are complex. In her view, films do not simply reflect Jewish-Christian relations but actively constitute them. Wright's study is one of the few that explore the cinema's identity as a locus of Jewish-Christian relations. Another unexpected but insightful paper is offered by Simon Rocker, Senior Reporter at the *Jewish Chronicle*, the oldest English language Jewish newspaper in the world. Rocker discusses how events in the last 30 years have been reported by *The JC* and the reader is reminded that popular culture, and especially the media, are more often than not interested in controversy (such as that generated by Mel Gibson's film, *The Passion of the Christ*). The rousing of emotions, whether as a result of a film, the ongoing conflict between Israel and the Palestinians, or acts of antisemitism, indicates that Jewish-Christian relations is not only a subject of academic study but is an ongoing 'live' encounter, which has an impact on ordinary people's lives.

This is reinforced by Tomáš Halik's paper on Jewish-Christian-Muslim relations in Europe in the post 9/11 world. Halik, a Catholic priest and scholar from the Czech Republic, explores the place of Abraham in the three Abrahamic faiths, arguing that among the most important challenges of religion today is the need to reach out to the disenfranchised. Halik's call for a synthesis between faith and modern culture resonates with David Herbert's study on the place of Jewish-Christian relations in modern civil society. Herbert examines intergroup relations in contemporary society with particular reference to the Holocaust, and argues that religions can contribute positively to the establishment of a decent civil society, not by 'vertical' pressure but by developing 'horizontal' relations between and within faith communities.

The final papers in this book tackle the theological implications of Jewish-Christian relations in light of the changes since 1965. To what extent should Christians reshape fundamental church teachings on God, Jesus, Paul, covenant, scripture, and the nature of the church itself in light of Jewish-Christian dialogue? A number of Christian theologians have attempted to develop a systematic revision of Christian theology, the most detailed study perhaps being that of the late American Protestant scholar Paul Van Buren, who considered the implications that emerge within Christianity when the continuing validity of the covenant between God and the Jewish people is acknowledged. Van Buren's work has been continued by American Catholic scholar John Pawlikowski who has reflected on issues associated with covenant, mission and christology in the light of Jewish-Christian dialogue. Since the covenant between God and Israel is now viewed as 'irrevocable' (cf. Romans 9-11), christology needs to be revised. His contribution to this book considers the most recent developments in theological thinking on this topic in the USA.

For their part, a small but growing number of Jewish scholars have considered the theological implications of Jewish-Christian relations for Judaism. The Jewish community does not subject itself to the discipline of public statements like the numerous Christian statements of the Catholic and Protestant Churches. In part, this is because of the asymmetrical nature of the history of persecution of Jews by Christians and the teaching of contempt, and in part because of the distinctive nature of Jewish religious polity. However, the publication of *Dabru Emet* in 2000 attests to a growing awareness among Jewish theologians of the theological implications of Jewish-Christian relations. Edward Kessler offers a study of the problems raised for Judaism and Christianity by the existence of violent texts in their Scriptures. He points out that Jews and Christians share similar difficulties and can help each other in their search for solutions. By applying a combination of Jewish and Christian hermeneutical tools to this problem, Kessler shows that the contemporary Jewish-Christian encounter can lead to a mutually beneficial partnership (*chevruta*), which whilst based on commonality, does not lead to a loss of identity.

The editors would like to thank a number of people without whom this book would not have come into existence. Firstly, we are grateful to all the contributors, many of who delivered papers at conferences or seminars in Cambridge organised under the auspices of the Centre for the Study of Jewish-Christian Relations (CJCR) and have subsequently revised their work for publication. Secondly, we wish to thank our colleagues at CJCR (especially Deborah PattersonJones, Lucia Faltin, Maty Matyszak, Tunde Formadi and Eleanor Bass) for their support and encouragement. The logistics involved in planning conferences, organising seminars and providing hospitality to speakers and Visiting Fellows require a team effort. Thirdly, we are grateful to all our supporters and friends, especially those who have made financial contributions to CJCR. The Centre for the Study of Jewish-Christian Relations is dependent upon grants and donations and we are grateful for donations made towards our research and publications' programme, particularly to the John S. Cohen Foundation.

A number of these chapters have been written by International Visiting Scholars who have spent between two to three months at CJCR. They were awarded the Hugo Gryn Fellowship in Religious Tolerance, established in 2000 or the Sternberg Interfaith Fellowship, established in 2003. Numerous trusts and individuals – too many to mention by name – generously provided funds to establish these Fellowships. We hope that this publication will be seen as one small outcome of their support.

Notes

1. Claude Montefiore, 'The Synoptic Gospels and Jewish Consciousness', *Hibbert Journal* 3 (1904), p.779.

2. James Parkes, *Voyage of Discoveries* (London: Gollancz, 1969) p.123.

1

The Contribution of Jewish Scholars to the Quest for the Historical Jesus

William Klassen[1]

Introduction

Nearly one hundred years ago, Albert Schweitzer wrote his definitive work, *The Quest of the Historical Jesus*.[2] In it he described in exquisite detail the centrality of the scholarly search for the historical Jesus in Biblical studies and the contribution of German and French scholarship to this quest. Despite unlimited faith in historical research and the extreme diligence of well-disciplined German scholars, their quest had led to a dead end. The result of all their labour was that we were left with each scholar's own Jesus. Schweitzer's conclusion: 'He comes to us as One unknown, without a name, as of old, by the lake-side, He came to those men who knew Him not.' His words rang in our ears for ninety years and ring there still.[3]

Schweitzer's findings put a stop to the quest for the historical Jesus in continental European scholarship. However, in the English-speaking world throughout the 20th century, scholars have demonstrated a vigorous interest in the quest, as well as an awareness of popular ethics and of Jewish and Christian teachers in the 1st century. As a result, the search for the historical Jesus – even when not pursued under that name – goes on unabated.[4]

Dale Allison described the old consensus created by Johannes Weiss and made popular by Albert Schweitzer.[5] Weiss showed decisively that 'Jesus as a historical personage must be seen not as the founder of a new religion, but as the final product of the eschatological and apocalyptic thought of Late Judaism.'[6] Allison traced the rejection of the consensus in large part through C. H. Dodd's realised eschatology, a slight variation of which is currently represented by John Dominic Crossan.

One of the most remarkable features of the current quest is the genuine partnership that now exists in this vital area between Jewish scholars and their Christian colleagues in New Testament. Such a partnership has never before existed to this degree. Although scholars have posed questions attending efforts to write about 'Jewish contributions' to Biblical interpretation, Stefan Reif of Cambridge University has recently addressed some of them.[7]

One area in which a phenomenal change has taken place is in the contribution made to the historical quest by Jewish scholars, the topic of this investigation.

It should be noted that with such illustrious names as Jacob Neusner, Susannah Heschel, Jack Lightstone, Paula Fredriksen, Daniel Boyarin, Adele Rheinhartz, J. L. Kugel, Amy Jill Levine, and other Jews who have served or are now serving in North American Seminaries and departments of religion, one may be allowed to look with greater optimism than does Professor Reif at the prospects of fruitful collaboration between Jewish and Christian scholars.

Nevertheless, a quick survey of the major works on Jesus coming from the pens of Christian scholars - massive tomes some of them - provides little evidence that Christians, when questing for the historical Jesus, are reading their Jewish colleagues' work or taking their arguments seriously.

The subject matter of this paper covers vast ground which cannot, regrettably, be covered in one sitting. I wish to concentrate on the work of five scholars: Abraham Geiger, as seen in particular through the eyes of Susannah Heschel;[8] Martin Buber; Geza Vermes,[9] as seen through his autobiography and his own writings on Jesus;[10] David Flusser[11] and Paula Fredriksen.[12]

1. Abraham Geiger

Abraham Geiger was one of the founding figures of Reform Judaism and an influential thinker and writer of the 19th century. Although he did not write a 'Life of Jesus', he dealt with Jesus in several large sections of his history of Judaism (1864). He concluded that Jesus was a pupil of Hillel's: 'Jesus was a Pharisee, who walked in the ways of Hillel. He expressed no new ideas. Hillel, however, presents a picture of a genuine – the word does not denigrate him but ennobles him – reformer'.[13]

A number of scholars engaged Geiger in dialogue and signalled their respect for him.[14] Certainly, Delitzsch believes he is doing everyone a service by dealing with both Renan and Strauss. He challenges Geiger's statement that Hillel was a reformer, but what offends him most deeply is Geiger's statement that Jesus did not offer an original thought. Delitzsch thinks that bringing all the commandments into two (love God and love your neighbour as yourself) is original to Jesus and complains, 'never, surely has a statement been made which in such an offensive way denigrates the original cultural greatness of the founder of Christianity'.[15]

Susannah Heschel's book on Abraham Geiger is a model of research. It uncovers new sources, locates Geiger's work in the stream of theological work of the 19th century, and demonstrates how Geiger, in his history of Judaism, was able to break the taboos against dealing with Jesus. In fact, in his successful effort to establish what later became Reform Judaism, Geiger was in constant strife not only with his colleagues within Judaism but also with such Christian contemporaries as David Strauss and Ernst Renan.

According to Heschel, Geiger, as a good historian, wanted to find the place of Jesus in Jewish history. Inevitably, he also had to deal with the position of Jesus in early Christian history. Not only did his innate curiosity as a historian drive him to this quest for the historical Jesus, but the lamentable approach of Strauss with his mythological Jesus[16] and the romantic fantasies of Renan incited him to strive for a better job of tracing the history of Judaism and the Jesus of history. Both ignored the research of Jewish historians. Strauss, Geiger states, 'is imprisoned entirely in the old perspectives and with a truly vulgar fluency speaks the language of the old prejudices'.[17]

Judaism could then claim Jesus as one of its own, a Pharisee who lost his bearings. But what Jesus did himself was not nearly as pernicious, Geiger says, as what his followers did with their understanding of Jesus.

Geiger's encounter with Renan was an attempt to paint an accurate picture of Jesus, one that ran counter to Renan's efforts to convince the public to share his anti-Jewish sentiments.[18] In Renan's scheme, Jesus began as a Jew but soon overcame his Jewishness after visiting Jerusalem when Jesus no longer took his stand as a Jewish reformer, 'but as a destroyer of Judaism...Jesus is no longer a Jew'.[19] Renan then concludes: 'Fundamentally there was nothing Jewish about Jesus'.[20] Christianity would do well, Renan argued, to return to Jesus:

> The tendency of Christianity has been to move farther and farther from Judaism. It will become perfect by returning to Jesus, but certainly

11

not by returning to Judaism. The great originality of the founder remains then undiminished; his glory admits not to share it legitimately.[21]

Here he is attacking Geiger, who proposed that the genius of Jesus was simply a part of the collective religious genius of the Jewish people, so that an understanding of Jesus comes best through the faith of a Jew.[22] Is there an underlying claim here that one must be a Jew to understand Jesus fully?

According to Geiger, Judaism was unique, the only 'real' religion. He used his historical analysis to attempt to force Christians to admit that theirs was a religion about Jesus but not the faith of Jesus.[23] Many of the themes that have emerged repeatedly in Jewish-Christian discussions and in the debate about the Jewishness of Jesus were first broached by Geiger. Despite Geiger's agenda, it is important to note that much of the debate in recent years has been conducted in an atmosphere of mutual respect for the respective faiths and for their adherents.[24]

2. Martin Buber

Martin Buber, in numerous places in his writings, spoke of his profound respect for Jesus, the need to take his Jewishness seriously, and the implications this had for Israel and for Jewish-Christian relations. For if the centre of Judaism was its God-given role to unify or to unite, there were no better partners to work towards this goal in the Land of Israel than Jews and Christians. Although he was not a Biblical scholar, Buber's judgements about the history of the Jews and his analysis of what is at the centre of being a Jew have evoked considerable response.[25] But perhaps the most significant contribution he made was to call Jesus his 'brother' and in so doing, made it not only possible but necessary for both Jews and Christians to take another look at Jesus. No one is more responsible than Buber for the 'reclamation' of Jesus, or for treating Jesus as part of Jewish history by Jews. As seen above, here he built on the work of Geiger.

On the significance of Jesus for Judaism, he writes:

> ...to understand the relation of Judaism to the appearance of Jesus, one must descend into the depths of this faith...which can be shown from the testimonies.... Seen from the standpoint of Judaism he is the first in the series of men...who acknowledged their Messiahship in their souls and in their words. That this first one in the series was

incomparably the purest, the most legitimate, the most endowed with real Messianic power – as I experience ever again when those personal words that ring true to me merge for me into a unity whose speaker becomes visible to me – alters nothing in the fact of this firstness; indeed it belongs undoubtedly just to it, to the fearfully penetrating reality that has characterised this whole automessianic series.[26]

I firmly believe that the Jewish community in the course of its renaissance, will recognize Jesus; not merely as a great figure in its religious history, but also in the organic context of a Messianic development extending over millenia, whose final goal is the Redemption of the World. But I believe equally firmly that we will never recognize Jesus as the Messiah Come, for this would contradict the deepest meaning of our Messianic Passion...for us there is no cause of Jesus; only the cause of God exists for us.[27]

Following this path leads to a choice between considering Jesus a false Messiah or a 'failed' Messiah, a topic under vigorous discussion.

In an often overlooked section of a book published in 1918, Buber made another noteworthy contribution to this topic[28] when he outlined the three forms of responses to the destruction of Jerusalem in 70 C.E.:

1. Johanan ben Zakkai, who stood aside and rescued the Teaching (Torah).
2. The second response was to fight. It led to the bloodiest and the most hopeless war of liberation in all of history, led by the rebels from 70 to Bar Kochbah in 130.
3. The third response was to found a new community (*Gemeinde*), which grew in the body of the catastrophe (*Ungeheuers*) and sought to override it (wollte sie sprengen).[29]

In Buber's view, the West took over Jewish aspects in the teaching of Jesus but failed to appropriate the essential dimension at its heart: the tendency of actualising unity did not enter into the spiritual foundations of the life of the people.

'Let us not forget,' Buber wrote, 'that he [Jesus] was a Jew, a representative Jew. His work was a repristination [*aufbruch*] of Judaism in his transmission of Judaism to the nations. In order to understand correctly this powerful worker of the Spirit [*Gewalttater des Geistes*], we must first find the primal experience [*Urerlebnis*] of the Jew from which the tendency to actualise or realise grows eternally. This primal experience is an elementary feeling of that inner bifurcation which lives in all people, but in the Jew manifests itself in an especially strong energy and in the will to overcome through an actualisation of union'. Buber's comments became eventually a fertile debating ground between him and David Flusser.[30]

It is hard to measure the considerable contribution made by Buber to Jewish-Christian dialogue and to the study, by both Jews and Christians, of the historical Jesus. Countless numbers of Jews have written about their debt to Buber, whose books went through many translations and editions.[31] He saw the building of community as the central idea of Judaism – how barriers between people could be broken down – and he laid bare the mission of Judaism in the world. He also saw clearly that the divine mission to redeem the Gentiles had been achieved through the work of Jesus the Jew. As early as Paul, Christian distortions of the Jesus message began, and throughout the history of the church, the Jewish solution to attaining human community has been ignored. Caesar has been given what he demands and nothing, said Buber, has been left over for God.

It was no accident that a strong friendship nurtured by annual visits and correspondence existed between Buber and Schweitzer. It is also important to note that, like Geiger, Buber was on a quest to discover Judaism for his own day. In that quest, he came into a direct encounter with the historical Jesus.

The theme engages him at many points, nowhere more so than in his brilliant booklet, *The Holy Way*, which first appeared in a periodical, *Der Jude*, 1918, and clarifies what Christianity appropriated from Judaism. In a discussion of the role of the state in the contributions of Augustine and Thomas Aquinas, he argues that they lost the formation of genuine community and overlooked the unique contribution of Jesus to Jewish history.[32]

Buber compares the developments in the church after Constantine with the contribution of Judaism. Since it is in this context that he develops most fully his views on Jesus, we quote it at length. He writes:

> True community is no longer to be realized in the totality of human life with one another, in hallowed worldliness; it is to be realized in the Church, which as community of the spirit is separated from the community of the world, and as community of grace is separated from the community of nature.

Nor did Protestantism transcend this separation. For it, too, life is split into two separate realms, the realm of works and the realm of faith. Protestantism desires a co-existence of church and state, not a merging of the two into a higher unit, into true community. The perception of undivided being and consciousness of the conditionality of evil and the unconditionality of the human soul live on only in mysticism. But mysticism is wanting in the element of activity in the state of unconditionality, the tendency to realize undivided life in the world of humanity, in the world of being with one another.

Thus, though the peoples of the West took over Jewish teaching when they took over the teaching of Jesus, they did not take over its essence; the bent for realization did not become part of the spiritual foundations of these peoples' lives. Its flame did indeed flare up repeatedly in the passion of heretic and sectarian communities that wanted to initiate the Kingdom of God; but it was just as repeatedly extinguished by the air in which nations breathe, they breathe, the atmosphere of acquiescence in dualism. This atmosphere, which still obtains in our time, is an atmosphere of dualisms of truth and reality, idea and fact, morals and politics. It is the atmosphere in which Christianity rendered unto the Roman emperor what was Caesar's for so long a time that it had nothing left to deny him; the atmosphere in which Christianity did not oppose evil for so long a time that, when it finally did attempt to resist its most devastating excesses, it was forced to realize that it had become incapable of doing so.

We must not forget, however, that the man who, in transmitting Judaism to the peoples, brought about its 'repristination' [*aufbruch*] was also a Jew, a representative Jew. To understand fully this worker of powerful acts of the spirit [*Gewalttater des Geistes*], we must seek out in him that primal experience of the Jew from which the reaching for realization is generated eternally anew. This primal experience is an elemental perception of inner duality, inherent, to some degree in all people but especially in Jews; it is also the desire to overcome this duality by realization of unity.[33]

For Buber, the trouble began with Paul, the first major interpreter of the religion of Jesus, whom he credits with providing Christianity with the 'sweet poison' of rejecting the law. As he puts it:

Saul, the man from Tarsus, expressed the duality he found within him more unequivocally and more forcefully than any other man in the fateful words that ushered in the Christian era: 'For that which I work,

I understand not. For I do not that good which I will; but the evil which I hate, that I do' (Romans 7:15). To Paul, however, this terrible and paradoxical insight does not signify what it had once signified to the Jew and what it must once again signify to him: an overpoweringly strong incitement to dare the assault, no matter how impossible it seems; to break open the shell; and to realize God's will in the unification of one's own will. . . . [34]

Paul, according to Buber, summarises the great disappointment in reaching for realisation that Judaism was forced to suffer up to his own day. Adding up the national, as well as mankind's total, Buber notes that Paul declares that we ourselves can achieve nothing; that is, nothing by our own efforts but only by the grace of God or – and to him it is the same thing – by faithful adherence to the one in whom grace had visibly resided, the one who, as it is said, 'knew no sin' (II Corinthians 5:21). Buber writes:

The fact that at the time there was apparently no longer any reliable knowledge of Jesus' first thirty years, that even in the legend only the emblem of his threefold temptation (Matt 4:1-11) bears witness to the period of his struggles and his victories, so that the harmony of his spirit is, ostensibly, manifested without there having been any previous discord–this fact made it easier for Paul to develop his ideology. He transmitted Jesus' teaching, transformed by this ideology, to the nations, handing them the sweet poison of faith, a faith that was to disdain works, exempt the faithful from realization, and establish dualism in the world. It is the Pauline era whose death agonies we today are watching with transfixed eyes'.[35]

Thus Buber wrote in 1918!

3. Geza Vermes
Equally important to the quest for the historical Jesus is the work of Geza Vermes, who, with his first wife Pamela, more than any other scholar, must be credited for our access to the Dead Sea Scrolls in good English. In addition to the Qumran scholarship, he has been absorbed by research into the historical Jesus since 1970.[36]

In six books published between 1973 and 2003, he has produced some of the clearest writing available on Jesus. His books move us to an understanding of people such as Jesus' contemporary, Hanina ben Dosa, a charismatic leader and healer who has 'become a household name among NT scholars'.[37] In Vermes' first book on the historical Jesus,[38] to speak of Jesus the Jew was a radical idea, at least as radical as David Flusser's idea of producing a biography of Jesus. Flusser refused to speak of the 'Jewish background' of Jesus, while Vermes 'sought to portray Jesus against his genuine historical background.' As a historian, Vermes chooses Judaism as the context in which to learn about Jesus rather than 'the alien framework of Graeco-Roman culture and nineteen centuries of Christian elaboration.'[39]

Jesus the Jew was prompted by a single-minded search for fact and reality and undertaken out of feeling for the tragedy of Jesus of Nazareth. If, after working his way through the book, the reader recognizes that this man so distorted by Christian and Jewish myth alike, was in fact neither the Christ of the Church, nor the apostate and bogey-man of Jewish popular tradition, some small beginning may have been made in the repayment to him of a debt long overdue.

The purpose of *Jesus the Jew* was to rebuild the picture of the historical Jesus in the Palestine of the 1st century, especially in that of contemporaneous 1st century popular, charismatic Judaism of prophetic derivation. The hero of this type of Palestinian religion was not the King, the rabbi, or the priest, but the man of God, believed to be capable of working miracles and mastering the forces of evil and darkness, namely the devil and sickness. In the 1st century B.C.E., Honi the rainmaker was such a holy man and so was Hanina ben Dosa. His many wonderful interventions earned him the title of protector, saviour, and benefactor of human kind. The Galilean Jesus of the Synoptics is perfectly at home in such a company.[40]

After verifying this observation by reviewing titles used in the Gospels for Jesus, Vermes concluded that the historical Jesus could be situated best in 'the venerable company of the Devout, the ancient *Hasidim*.' In the postscript to the book, he puts it this way:

> The main finding of this exploration of the historical and linguistic elements of the Gospels....is that whereas none of the claims and aspirations of Jesus can be said definitely to associate him with the role of the Messiah, not to speak of that of *son of man*, the strange creation of modern myth-makers, everything combines....to place him in the venerable company of the Devout, the ancient *Hasidim*....[This] means that any new enquiry may accept as its point of departure the

safe assumption that Jesus did not belong among the Pharisees, Essenes, Zealots or Gnostics, but as one of the holy miracle workers of Galilee.[41]

Given that conclusion, one cannot help but wonder why recent scholarship has spent so much time on a 'Cynic' Jesus.

Vermes hastened to add that:

> 'Jesus stood out as incomparably superior' to the figures just mentioned, a verdict which at least one reviewer challenged as being inappropriate coming from a historian.[42] Vermes says of Jesus, 'second to none in profundity of insight and grandeur of character, he is in particular an unsurpassed master of the art of laying bare the innermost core of spiritual truth and bringing every issue back to the essence of religion, the existential relationship of [human] to [human] and [human] to God.'[43]

The reviews of this first bold attempt to treat *Jesus the Jew* were mixed from both Christian and Jewish scholars.

In the *Gospel of Jesus the Jew*, Vermes concluded:

> 'Jesus as a Jewish holy man nevertheless stands out as a teacher entirely inspired by the faith-trust (*emunah*) and dedicated to a call for repentance (*teshuvah*), preparatory to the coming of the Kingdom of God. He also appears uniquely aware of his filial relation to the Father in Heaven (*Abba*) and passionately to believe that his mission was to communicate the same sense of relationship to God among his fellow men and women'.[44]

While King and Father were the two dominant terms for God, Jesus appears never to have addressed God as King or indeed as God and King, as was common in Jewish prayers of the day, but preferred the term Father. Jesus died, said Vermes, because he was 'perceived' as a potential threat to the authorities. His action in the Temple, a 'temple tantrum' as the American scholar Paula Fredriksen calls it, led to a miscarriage of justice, representing 'one of the supreme tragedies in history'.[45]

He died on the cross for having done the wrong thing (caused a commotion), in the wrong place (the Temple), at the wrong time (just before Passover). Here lies the real tragedy of Jesus the Jew.

Agreeing with his critics that to do justice to Jesus, one had to deal also with the teaching of Jesus, Vermes wrote the book *The Religion of Jesus the Jew*. Vermes describes it as his favourite, calling it more mellow, mature, constructive and 'spiritual'. Jesus is portrayed as a faithful observer of Judaism and of the Jewish law, perceived primarily, essentially and positively not as a juridical, but as a religious-ethical reality, revealing what he thought to be the right and divinely ordained behaviour towards humans and God. Jesus, he says, was revered as prophet, inspired by the spirit of God. Vermes deals with three main radical topics: Repentance, confidence in God, and total self-dedication to the Kingdom of Heaven. Jesus never defined or spelled out the Kingdom of God. Candidates who might have been attracted to the Kingdom were the marginalised, 'those outside the fold of organized religion, the stray sheep of mankind, who yearn for a world of mercy, justice, and peace lived in as children of God'.[46] The real Jesus, Jesus the Jew, challenges traditional Christianity as well as traditional Judaism. 'Jesus cannot be represented as the founder of Christianity'.[47]

The impact of his books on Jesus scholarship are mentioned both in his autobiography[48] and also eleven years earlier in a speech opening a conference in Birmingham.[49] His important pioneering work, together with the changing climate of scholarship, helped bring about a sea-change in the way that people view Jesus. At the time of his first book, to use the title, 'Jesus the Jew,' seemed revolutionary. Now it is almost a cliché. An illustration of his influence may be cited.

Vermes tells the story of how the editors of the *New Shorter Oxford English Dictionary* asked him to advise them on all matters pertaining to Judaism.[50] A storm was evoked by a change he proposed which was adopted in the 'Jesus' entry. From 'Founder of Christianity' to 'the central figure of the Christian faith, a Jewish preacher ca 5 B.C.- A.D. 30, regarded by his followers as the Son of God and God incarnate'. Much hilarity was provoked by this turn of phrase in the pages of the *The Times*: 'Jesu, joy of man's defining' ran one front-page headline (Oct 9, 1993), which reported, among other things, that the Rev. Tony Higton, a senior evangelical and a member of the General Synod of the Church of England found the idea of Jesus as a Jewish preacher to be rather derogatory. As Vermes tells it, someone undoubtedly alerted the Rev. Higton to the possible antisemitic connotation of his statement. Higton sought to extricate himself from that by welcoming the fact that OED 'helpfully records for the first time that Jesus is Jewish' but objecting to the term 'preacher' (Letter to *The Times*, Oct. 13, 1993). A third interlocutor under the heading, 'The game of the name' (Oct. 9) came out firmly in support of Vermes: 'the *New Shorter Oxford English Dictionary* has defined the name of Jesus accurately and more economically than before.'

Vermes concludes that his 'best known and most lasting contribution to a better perception to the historical Jesus may be this dictionary definition which does not carry his name'.[51]

What qualifies Vermes for this discussion is that, in addition to his reputation as a Dead Sea Scrolls scholar, he has shown himself a master of textual analysis. Already in his book of 1961, *Scripture and Tradition in Judaism*, he demonstrated the gift of helping scholars approach New Testament texts through the door of the Qumran writings, Jewish and Old Testament texts. Like many of his contemporary Jewish colleagues, he was perhaps emboldened to declare his opinion of Jesus as a spiritual leader by the openness of Martin Buber. According to Rick Salutin in a column in the *Globe and Mail*, Dec. 24, 1999, a national newspaper in Canada, many Jewish young people visiting Israel before the Israeli occupation of the West Bank were inspired by Martin Buber to consider Jesus, as Vermes did, as their Jewish brother.

It is perhaps too early to assess the contribution of Geza Vermes to the quest for the historical Jesus. It is not too early, however, to express our gratitude to him for the courage he has shown in trying to find the Jesus of history and to record his results. He has caused scholars to look at their own biases and review their own presuppositions, providing a major impetus for both Jews and Christians to undertake further work in the quest of the historical Jesus and interfaith dialogue.

4. David Flusser

Since the late 1960s, one work in the area of Jesus research stands out above all others: David Flusser's *Jesus*. First published in German in 1968 by Rowohlt as an unassuming paperback, it remains in print (recently revised) in German and has continued to be in demand in various languages. Thankfully, however, it is no longer available in English in its 1969 version, which was poorly translated and deserved to go out of print.

The 1998 English translation and revision is long overdue and warmly welcomed. Today, the book is every bit as timely as it was when first published although it has, of course, been brought up to date. Prof. Flusser and Stephen Notley have produced a remarkable volume based on the earlier book but now almost double in length, with seven excellent articles dealing with such topics as the games the soldiers played with Jesus when he was in captivity, the character of Caiaphas, crucifixion and the weeping of Jesus over Jerusalem.

The author of this paper contends that Flusser's *Jesus* is the best book on Jesus published in the 20th century.[52] Noted scholars also give it high praise. When one considers the flood of books published on Jesus, especially since 1980, this is no mean accomplishment. Flusser believed it was possible to write a biography of Jesus and set out to do so. The book is deceptively brief and unassuming. That is part of its charm. The pertinent photographs do much to anchor the Jesus story concretely in history. The footnotes are kept to an essential minimum, but they are broad in scope and pertinent to the argument at virtually every point.

The range of Flusser's knowledge is impressive. As Edmund Wilson put it when he interviewed him in connection with the Dead Sea Scrolls:

> He seems to have simultaneously before him, in his mind, open texts for instant reference, both the Old and New Testaments, the Apocrypha and the Pseudepigrapha,...the Talmud and other rabbinic literature and the Fathers of the Church, as well as modern biblical scholarship and the philosophy and *belles-lettres* of classical and modern Europe.[53]

From Archilochus, the ancient elegiac poet of about 650 B.C.E., to Simon Kimbangu, the modern African charismatic leader, every reference to literature or historical persons is focussed on a better understanding of Jesus and his times.

Why did he write it? The answer is found in Edmund Wilson's description of an interview with Flusser in the second edition of his book on the Dead Sea Scrolls. Wilson's description of his encounter with Flusser before he revised his book, *The Dead Sea Scrolls*, in the late sixties captures the dynamism and passion of Flusser, besides providing a view into the pressure under which Israelis survive. Wilson's comments provide the highest tribute paid to Flusser. The background of his decision to write a book on Jesus is of direct interest to us. Wilson writes:

> 'It was very uncomfortable,' said Flusser, 'with a wife and two small children, to have something like this [international crisis] looming. What if this whole thing here should be wiped out! The prophets are

always right! They either say that the disasters have occurred because the Jews have been so sinful or that the Jews are being so sinful that disasters are going to occur. And the Jews are always sinful, so the prophet is always justified! Whom should we invoke now to intervene? Jeanne d'Arc? No, she might fight for Nasser. Thomas Aquinas, perhaps.'

I told him what Yadin had said about the attitude of Jesus toward the Romans. 'Yadin had been a soldier,' said Flusser, 'and he would naturally think in terms of weapons. The message of the teaching of Jesus was something entirely different.'

He then gave me the most eloquent disquisition on Jesus that I remember ever to have heard. (He told me that he was just about to write a book in German on the subject.)

'The Teacher of Righteousness and Jesus had completely different ideals and aims. The former wanted to create, in his isolated Dead Sea community, a little élite utopia. The members of the community were to be forbearing toward one another but to regard everyone else as their enemy; they denounced both the Romans and Jerusalem. But Jesus was out in the world, and he instructed his disciples not to resist authority; it would only make the civil authorities worse; they would very soon put you in prison. The Kingdom of God is within you.'

Yet Jesus was crucified, whereas the Teacher of Righteousness, as Flusser now believed, on the evidence of one of the Dead Sea fragments, was not, as had once been supposed, either executed or murdered by his enemies.

Mrs. Flusser, at the back of the house, had been listening to the radio news, and her husband now left the room to find out what was going on. 'Eshkol has appealed to de Gaulle,' he reported when he came back. 'Now, if Jesus were here and had heard this, he would say about Eshkol, 'Poor man!'– because Eshkol was appealing to authority. 'Wouldn't he,' I suggested, 'say the same thing about Nasser?' Flusser was silent a moment. 'Yes, he would say, 'Poor man' about Nasser, too, but he would not be particularly interested.' I did not think to make the point that Eshkol represented authority, too. I realized afterwards that Flusser, as a Jew, could put himself in Jesus's place and think he would not have behaved like Eshkol, but that he took it for granted that Nasser and de Gaulle belonged to the other side–the authorities of this world who would want to suppress the Jews. It seemed to me, too, that Yadin, when he had imagined the other Jews coming to Jesus and asking what attitude they should take toward the Romans, must have been interpreting this situation in terms of his own experience when he had doubtless, in the course of the armistice years, been consulted by his fellow-Israelis as to what they should do about the Arabs.[54]

The ease with which Flusser moves between Jesus and the first century problems and contemporary problems is evident from the preface of his book on Jesus dating from the late sixties. Then he wrote:

> This book does not set out to build a bridge between the Jesus of history and the Christian faith. With no axe to grind, but at the same time not pretending to submerge the author's own personality and milieu – for how can one do that when writing a biography? – it seeks merely to present Jesus directly to the reader. The present age seems especially well disposed to understand him and his interests. A new sensitivity has been awakened in us by profound fear of the future and the present. Today we are receptive to Jesus' reappraisal of all our usual values. Many of us have become aware of his questioning of the moral norm, which was his starting point. Like Jesus, we feel drawn to the social pariahs, to the sinners. If he says that one shall not oppose the wicked forces, he evidently means that by struggling against them one really only benefits the basically indifferent play of forces within society and the world at large (see e.g., Matt. 5:25-26). This, I believe, is the feeling of many today. If we free ourselves from the chains of dead prejudices, we are able to appreciate Jesus' demand for an all embracing love, not as philanthropic weakness, but as a realistic approach to our world.
>
> The enormity of Jesus' life also speaks to us today: the call at his baptism, the severing of ties with his estranged family and his discovery of a new, sublime sonship, the pandemonium of the sick and possessed, and his death on the cross. Therefore, the words which Matthew (28:20) places on the lips of the risen Lord take on for us a new, non-ecclesiastical meaning, 'Lo, I am with you always, to the close of the age'.[55]

Although written thirty-five years ago, the book fits neatly into modern research in at least two areas:

a. The Jewishness of Jesus

As noted above, the recognition that Jesus was a Jew and has to be understood in that context – although now widely held and almost a cliché – is not universally given its due. Not all scholars take this point seriously.

Many who do cannot bring to the topic the mastery of 1st century Judaism that both Vermes and Flusser display. Some prefer to ignore and others even to minimize the Jewishness of Jesus by categorizing Jesus as 'peasant' or as a 'Cynic.'

Flusser is not, of course, the first to recognize that Jesus was a Jew, nor even the first Jewish scholar to write about him as such (see, for example, the work of G. Lindeskog). But comparing Flusser with Klausner, Sandmel, Falk, Lapide, ben Chorin, Shalom Asch, Paula Fredriksen, or Amy-Jill Levine, all of whom have done impressive work in this area, makes it clear that Flusser stands in a class by himself. Reading this book helps modern readers comprehend 1st century Judaism, while it also introduces them to one of Judaism's most influential religious leaders.

Like Flusser, Josef Klausner recognized the 'sublimity, distinctiveness and originality of Jesus' ethical teaching as unparalleled in any Hebrew ethical code'. He continued: 'If ever the day should come and this ethical code be stripped of its wrappings of miracles and mysticism, the Book of the Ethics of Jesus will be one of the choicest treasures in the literature of Israel for all time.' Klausner wished only that his Messianic claims and its feverish apocalypticism could be split off from his teaching.[56] Flusser treats Jesus as a whole and credits Jesus for remaining aloof from the zealotism which destroyed the Temple and Jerusalem.

Flusser accepts Jesus fundamentally as he is portrayed in the Gospels (with some preference for Luke), recognizes him as a charismatic figure and respects his teaching and his extraordinary sense of mission. He invites his readers to listen to Jesus himself and wonders out loud whether the responses that Jesus gave in connection with human conflict may not still be the best that anyone has proposed.

Flusser has repeatedly disavowed any interest in interfaith dialogue. Yet the very force of his presentation, the solidity of his scholarship, and his fervour to have the church confront the historical Jesus, have made him a major figure in Jewish-Christian dialogue. He has been especially incisive in reminding Christians that neither Jesus nor Paul can be treated in terms of their 'Jewish background'. Judaism is not 'background' to them but their faith, life and culture. What we have made of Jesus or Paul needs to be tested by the documents of the 1st century.

Flusser is frank and bold in his confrontation with Christians. When told by a Christian professor that there is progress in interfaith dialogue because many Jews 'are coming closer to Christianity because many of them no longer live according to the Jewish ritual laws,' he replied: 'My dear professor, do you really think that a pork chop brings you closer to Christ?' He adds, 'I am sure that Paul would have agreed with my rejoinder'.[57]

b. The influence of Flusser's identity upon his research.
Flusser had a very clear identity: He was an Orthodox Jew committed to studying words and their meaning.[58] Spurred on by a Christian roommate in his university years to abandon the study of chemistry to explore his own Jewish faith, he gave his whole life to that quest. His dedication to Judaism was most clearly articulated in his article in the Gollwitzer *Festschrift*, 'The Experience of Being a Jew'.[59] With a delightful sense of humour, he contrasted the legalistic format of a Harvard Chapel service with a synagogue service and the way in which Christians welcome the food laws of Hindus but are critical of Jews who live by *kashrut*. But the strongest impression one gets from reading this piece is that the experience of being a Jew is one of joy. The law is anything but a burden.

Flusser devoured new discoveries such as the Dead Sea Scrolls and integrated them into his total understanding of the Jewish faith. Like Vermes, his exacting acquaintance with the Dead Sea Scrolls is brought to bear repeatedly in his interpretation of New Testament texts.

Flusser presents us with a wealth of materials in relation to early Christianity, and was particularly keen on noting a relationship between early Christianity and the Qumran community. Only those who had the opportunity to work with him directly could appreciate his passionate concern for doing serious historical research on Jesus and 1st century Judaism. His zeal for a correct understanding of Jesus came from a deep conviction that Jesus needs to be taken seriously as a teacher and spiritual leader by both Jews and Christians. Nor did he hesitate to invoke his credentials as a practising Jew to remind Christians that what he called the profound crisis which Christianity faces can be overcome only as Christianity becomes credible: '... only if it can rid itself of old and new anti-Jewish sentiments and sinks ever deeper roots into its Jewish heritage'.[60]

He claimed not to be a theologian; he was a linguist. As such, he had not been infected by the extreme scepticism with which so many Bible scholars approach the sources. Some considered him naive, but they are invited to consider the possibility that he was merely well informed and did not hesitate to cut his own path.

One does not always agree with his conclusions. For example, unlike Flusser, this writer cannot help but treat as genuine the report from Mark (3:21) that Jesus' mother and siblings considered him mad and wanted to take him away.[61] Such negative portrayals in official texts about people who have become famous, and especially founders of movements, are not usually invented. This one especially strikes me as genuine, since it serves no visible useful purpose in the narrative.

Flusser's book marks an important stage in Jewish scholarship on Jesus, and Christians have benefited enormously and can continue to benefit from the instruction that Flusser provided on Jesus. For Jews who are unaccustomed the 'high self-awareness of Jesus',[62] to be sure, also creates problems – but such problems are a necessary and indeed welcome part of the intellectual agenda of humankind.[63] Those who have never studied Hebrew and are unfamiliar with Second Temple Jewish sources may take exception to Flusser's statement that 'without a great deal of information about the Judaism of that time, nothing can be achieved' in historical Jesus research. 'Many wrong tracks were taken in the research on Jesus, his self-perception and his message' because they did not know the language and lacked 'essential Jewish learning.'[64] With the help of Jewish learning, he was confident that 'the historical fulcrum of the Christian faith' would be found. 'Faith in Christ cannot be in earnest unless that form of Jewish faith which stamped Jesus becomes a part of Christian faith and morality.'

Flusser's openness to discussion and his ability to provoke reflection based on analysis of evidence was a refreshing way to carry on dialogue. It is a remarkable fact that Flusser's following includes people as diverse as the passionate Palestinian Melkite priest, Elias Chacour, and the Baptist, Robert Lindsey.[65] Christian scholars have been the beneficiaries, consequently, of some superb studies of Jesus by excellent scholars, among whom Flusser ranks as first.[66] Pinchas Lapide notes '...while the Israeli books on Jesus of one or two decades ago merely expressed academic or historic curiosity, those of the late '60s, encouraged by Buber, show a growing self-identification of their authors with the life, thought and fate of their Galilean compatriot.'[67] Again Flusser's admiration of Jesus is an excellent example of that.

His desire to see Christianity strengthened is not selfishly motivated but genuinely driven by his desire to see Christians take Jesus' ethic seriously. He has particular concern for 'pulpit Christians' who have disdain for

Jesus' lofty self-perception. After participating in one of his seminars, Arnold Olson, an American writer, concluded that Flusser 'walks with Jesus, loves Jesus, but he is still an orthodox Jew'.[68]

After he suffered a severe heart attack and was resuscitated at the Hadassah hospital, Flusser remarked in personal conversation with typical humour and infectious joy: 'Now Jesus is not the only Jew who came back to life!'

The great writers of history have shown a degree of empathy for their subjects. What Flusser brings, however, is far more than merely empathy. He brings us a treasure of historical knowledge of the context in which Jesus lived. The superb blending of exquisite art, depictions of historical *realia*, and an understanding of the significance of the major events of the life of Jesus make this such an outstanding book.

Two high honours have been bestowed upon Professor Flusser: The Israel Prize for Literature and in May of 2000, the Rothschild Medal, bestowed by the Knesset.

5. Paula Fredriksen

In Paula Fredriksen's *Jesus of Nazareth, King of the Jews*, she enlivens her topic by imagining how Jesus could have responded the first time he went to the Temple. Some critics of her work are bothered by the way in which fiction and historical reporting overlap.[69] Others wonder whether attributing the death of Jesus mainly to his inability to control his crowd is not a bit too simplistic. It is doubtful that Fredriksen's attempts to refer to the Fourth Gospel as historical witness succeed. It is especially dubious that we do justice, as she suggests, to the 'Jewish life of Jesus' by ignoring the image of kingship in the mind of someone who boldly declared that God's kingdom (not his own) had now come.

Still, from every perspective, Fredriksen belongs in this survey. Without referring to them, she clearly stands in the tradition of Buber and Flusser. Like them, she is a practicing Jew, warm towards and affirming of both Judaism and Jesus as a Jew. Her first book was a well-received effort to trace historically how Jesus came to be seen as the Christ by early Christians and in an article which followed, she staked her claim to an interpretation of the Temple incident reported in all four gospels.[70] Arguing that Jesus and his followers had only appreciation for the Temple, she sought to establish that no devout Jew of the first century would have been critical of the Temple or of the Jewish cultus.

Her argument is somewhat blunted by the failure of her Jesus book to deal in more detail with the people of the New Covenant of the Dead Sea, who clearly held some distance from the Jerusalem Temple, criticised its leadership, took purity seriously, and looked forward in some measure to its cleansing. This 'cleansing' would not take place with whips (as John 2 suggests) or swords (murdering the High Priest, the Zealots of 66), but through an intense study of Torah and righteous living. Nor does Professor Fredriksen draw here from Philo, whose views of the Temple were less than admiring.[71]

In this connection and in preparing for her later book, *Jesus, King of the Jews, a Jewish Life and the Emergence of Christianity*, she began in public presentations to refer to the Temple incident as a 'Temple tantrum'. Although its origin is uncertain, the phrase was soon picked up by others. The expression 'Temple tantrum' does suggest 'an outburst or display of petulance, ill temper or a fit of passion' (OED). To some degree, this description is in line with the gospel accounts. At the same time, Mark asserts that what Jesus did in the Temple was a deliberate act, preceded by 'looking around at the whole scene in the Temple' the previous day (Mark 11:11 NEB). No indication of a 'fit' or impetuosity here. Likewise, in John 2:13-22, Jesus' action is described as deliberate, and he even braids a whip to control the animals as they leave the court (2:15), 'as he expelled them all, sheep, cattle and all'.[72] Although John introduces the element of 'zeal' in trying to understand the action, he clearly does not depict it as 'Jesus out of control'. Moreover, we cannot have it both ways, a tantrum and no critique of what was happening in the Temple. The one who throws a tantrum is usually upset about something!

Fredriksen follows Ed Sanders and most scholars in seeing a likely historical event here, a symbolic action along the lines of the prophets in which Jesus acts out his passion for the Temple. It is this passion that underlies his action on behalf of the Temple and his concern that it continue to be a place in which all people can pray. Fredriksen will have nothing to do with a 'cleansing of the Temple.' She deviates sharply from Craig Evans' detailed and careful study of this issue in his attempt to support the traditional 'cleansing' position and refers to it always as an action, albeit a 'violent disruption' and similar phraseology.

The anger and violence Jesus displayed here, obscured only by Luke, who prefers a more Stoic Jesus, has a long history in Jesus research. If we cite only one example, that of Renan's *Life of Jesus*, we find the following:

Renan saw the Temple action as an 'assault' on Jesus' attempt to destroy Judaism. Jesus had 'discomfort' in Jerusalem,[73] the Temple was a 'battle field of arguments:[74] 'The religious feeling of Jesus was wounded' by the 'careless and profane way' sacred matters were handled. The Temple action was 'an outburst of wrath'.[75] Pain and discomfort came from seeing 'these old Jewish institutions.' The Temple and Jerusalem are dismissed with the sentence, 'the place has always been unchristian!'.[76] The 'cold religious feeling and moral indifference … disgusted Jesus'.[77] He had so 'much disgust for it all he had to abrogate the Law and destroy Judaism'.[78]

Renan's account is astonishingly harsh, ignorant and insensitive, but, sadly, reflective of his times. By contrast, the second introduction to Fredriksen's Yale book demonstrates this scholar at her very best. She had hoped to avoid what she calls 'the tar baby of Jesus Research' but was drawn back into it by the invitation of a plenary address to AAR/SBL in 1990 and by her experience in walking the Temple area and discovering what a very big place it is. Her difficulty was to imagine the Temple action in either traditional terms or in the light of new evidence. It is out of this and her detailed review of the scholarship that the 'Temple tantrum' began to form and crystallise.

While the catchy term is helpful in getting us to think differently about the incident, it yields few long-range beneficial results. For example, are we to visualise Jesus as an immature brat or teenager throwing a tantrum? If Mark is right that his action had its roots in a detailed visit to the Temple the night before, what was it that grieved Jesus so deeply that he undertook the action he did? We do not know and are not told. Tantrums usually are thrown in the hope that they will be noticed and bring some results. What were those results in Jesus' case? Fredriksen surely is right when she says that, in such a huge place, the incident could not have attracted the attention of many people, nor could it have aroused the action of the Temple authorities.

Some scholars suggest that, along with the cursing of the fig tree, it was a reaction against the fierce desert winds that occasionally descend upon Jerusalem, especially in the spring, and cause everyone to be irritable and unpredictable. In other instances, the gospels report that Jesus was angered by illness or oppression (Mark 3:5). Perhaps the gospels are correct in seeing his anger as prompted by the blocking of the gentiles to this house of prayer, intended for everyone.

If there was a loss of control in the reaction of Jesus, it surely can be attributed to the stress under which he came into the city on this occasion. Momentous choices lay before him. The way forward was far from clear and would not open up before the moment of the arrest came.

Fredriksen's 'tantrum' theory deserves to be spelled out and analysed further. She surely is right in spurring us to reflect on this incident, and, as we study it, we can never again lose sight of the anger Jesus displayed on this occasion.

Critics who have assailed Professor Fredriksen for not being in conversation with modern methods of research (see below) must note that this same accusation has been made against Geiger, Buber and Flusser. It is an unjust and totally inaccurate accusation. It is well to remember that the approaches of some Jewish scholars to the New Testament texts are different, but that does not mean that they are not intellectually respectable or that others cannot learn from them. In Fredriksen's work we meet a mature scholar trained in all modern methods of research who is totally in command of her materials and deals with other people's positions gracefully but firmly. She engages the real issues and although not every position she advocates deserves acceptance, each one deserves careful study and serious consideration. Trained in a specific school, she is able to depart from it when the evidence invites her to do so. One of her strongest attributes is the ability to work within a specific religious framework and allow her position to be informed by it. We are all enriched by her presence there. Jewish and Christian scholars meet at the text, and our concern with the meaning of that text and its application to our wounded world keeps us together.[79]

Conclusion

Given the nature of the subject, there will always be a rivalry between Jewish and Christian quests for the historical Jesus. In part, this is true because Christians often confuse theological certainty with historical verification. In part, this is the case because Jewish scholars are clearly in the advantage if they know their tradition and history well. In a very thorough way, an old polemic book with a wide influence showed text after text of how Christians misused the Old Testament to prove that Jesus was the Messiah.[80] This is a time to return to the period when Jews and Christians saw each other as sisters and brothers in the same family, to carry on, if you will, a 'rivalry of genius';[81] a time for all of us to embrace the humility of true wisdom and seek to learn from each other without yielding to the temptation of trying to convince or convert.

Reimarus (1674-1768), the man who some credit as the initiator of the historical quest for Jesus, stated:

> We cannot in the least see that Jesus either intended to alter and abolish the Jewish religion and customs ordained in the law, or that he intended to preach new doctrines or mysteries in its place or introduce new ceremonies along with a new religion. Rather, it is much more evident that Jesus himself and his disciples were all full-fledged Jews and that for his own part he taught only that the Jews be truly converted and devote themselves to a better righteousness than the external and hypocritical righteousness of the Pharisees …. One part of his teaching may be summarized briefly in the single word, 'repent'.[82]

It is time for those of us who don't know Hebrew and Aramaic as well as we might and aren't particularly familiar with the Jewish literature of the time of Jesus to overcome our fear of being shown to be wrong by our Jewish colleagues who do.

N.T. Wright lists as one of the unfinished agenda items on the Quest of the Historical Jesus 'the exact interrelation between Judaism and Jesus', which, he concludes, 'is extremely difficult to plot and continual adjustments are to be expected'.[83] This writer suggests that as difficult as that may be, it is even more difficult when our Jewish partners in the quest are ignored or overlooked, a tendency even in Wright's own work.

The work that Buber, Flusser, Vermes and Fredriksen have done should encourage questers for the historical Jesus to take the Jewishness of Jesus seriously, which means to take his humanity earnestly but also to recognise that there are ways of doing serious historical study of Jesus other than the manner in which the Jesus Seminar adherents to a certain form of liberal Christianity do it. It is time to recognize the work our Jewish colleagues have done in trying to recover all we can know about the life of Jesus of Nazareth, for the time is past in which we either denied or denigrated the heritage, culture and religion, which nurtured Jesus of Nazareth. [84]

It is in the spirit of true dialogue that many Jewish historians and writers follow Martin Buber and embrace Jesus as their brother, and walk – with anyone who dares – the fascinating path of learning to discover the historical Jesus. The institution of the church is increasingly ready for such a partnership. Surely the academy and institutes like the Centre for the Study of Jewish-Christian Relations in Cambridge, which in its short life has made such a vital contribution to scholarly, lay and religious dialogue and understanding, will pursue that agenda.

Notes

1. I thank the Centre for the Study of Jewish-Christian Relations in Cambridge and its staff for inviting me to spend two months at the Centre in October and November, 1999. This paper, in an earlier form, was part of a seminar I offered there and at Birmingham University, Bristol University, and to a group of graduate students at Oxford University. In the last 5 years, much has been published on Jesus and his Jewishness, and Jewish scholars have continued to devote their talents to this topic. Cf. Beatrice Bruteau, ed., *Jesus Through Jewish Eyes: Rabbis and Scholars Engage an Ancient Brother in a New Conversation* (Maryknoll, New York: Orbis Press, 2001). An outstanding contribution to the place of Jesus as 'bridge figure' between Judaism and Christianity is a book written by numerous scholars and leaders, Tikva Freymer-Kensky, David Novak, et al., eds., *Christianity in Jewish Terms* (Boulder, CO: Westview Press, 2000). The main shift in this revision has been to deal with the omission of Martin Buber in the first edition, to note briefly the further works by Geza Vermes, and to touch on Paula Fredriksen's *Jesus of Nazareth, King of the Jews* (New York: Random House, 1999). Many colleagues have responded to the earlier edition, and I am grateful to all.

2. First German edition under the title, *Von Reimarus zu Wrede*. In 1906 it was translated by W. Montgomery and published in English in 1910 under the title, *The Quest of the Historical Jesus* (London: A. and C. Black, 1910).

3. This quote opens the last paragraph of the book, p. 401.

4. The effect of Schweitzer's work has been ably traced by Otto Piper, 'Das Problem des Lebens Jesu seit Schweitzer', in W. Foerster, ed., *Verbum Dei Manet in Aeternum, Fsft Otto Schmitz*. (Witten-Ruhr: Luther Verlag, 1953), pp. 73-93.

5. Dale C. Allison, 'The Eschatology of Jesus', in John Joseph Collins

ed., *The Encyclopedia of Apocalypticism Volume One: The Origins of Apocalypticism in Judaism and Christianity* (London: Continuum, 2000), pp. 267-302.

6. Schweitzer, *The Quest*, p. 23: 'Jesus as a historical personality is to be regarded, not as the founder of a new religion, but as the final product of the eschatological and apocalyptic thought of Late Judaism.' A similar view that Jesus is the last Jew based on the idea that Judaism 'as a historical religion had come to an end with Jesus' is attributed to Wellhausen, see Hans Dieter Betz, 'Wellhausen's Dictum 'Jesus was not a Christian, but a Jew' in Light of Present Scholarship', *Antike und Christentum, Gesammelte Aufsätze IV* (Tübingen: Mohr Siebeck, 1998), pp. 26-27.

7. Stefan C. Reif, 'Aspects of the Jewish Contribution to Biblical Interpretation' in John Barton, ed., *The Cambridge Companion to Biblical Interpretation* (Cambridge: Cambridge University Press, 1998), pp. 143-159. Reif, as one might expect, restricted himself to the Hebrew Bible and scholarship in that area, while this essay needs to confine itself to the quest for the historical Jesus. It is especially laudatory that Professor Reif did not shy away from treating his subject and, at another place and time, scholars need to reflect on some of the issues he raises in detail.

8. Susannah Heschel, *Abraham Geiger and the Jewish Jesus* (Chicago: Chicago University Press, 1998).

9. Geza Vermes, *The Changing Faces of Jesus* (London: Allen Lane, 2000).

10. Geza Vermes, *Providential Accidents – An Autobiography* (London: SCM, 1998), pp. 220-224.

11. David Flusser, *Jesus* (Hamburg: Rowohlt Taschenbuch Verlag, 1968). [E. T. 1969 (New York: Herder and Herder). Revised, 1997, 1998 2nd ed. (Jerusalem: Magnes Press)]. David Flusser, *Jewish Sources in Early Christianity* (Jerualem: Magnes Press, 1987).

12. Paula Fredriksen, *Jesus of Nazareth, King of the Jews. A Jewish Life and the Emergence of Christianity* (New York: Random House, 1999).

13. Franz Delitzsch, *Jesus und Hillel. Mit Rüksicht auf Renan und Geiger* (Erlangen: A. Deichert, 1879), p. 7.

14. Delitzsch, *Jesus und Hillel*, p. 8.

15. Delitzsch, *Jesus und Hillel*, p. 20.

16. Strauss 'does not recognize the reported actions as historical and true' (Heschel, *Geiger*, p. 109, citing from Geiger, *Das Judentum*, p. 187). See Ernest Renan, *Life of Jesus* (London: Walter Scott Ltd., 1897), pp. 131, 133.

17. Heschel, *Geiger*, p. 110.

18. Heschel, *Geiger*, p. 157.

19. Renan, *Life*, pp. 141-225; Heschel, *Geiger*, p. 157.

20. Heschel, *Geiger*, pp. 156, 277, note 127.

21. Renan, *Life*, p. 286.

22. Heschel, *Geiger*, p. 159.

23. Heschel, *Geiger*, p. 161.

24. Heschel also provides a brief survey of modern lives of Jesus and demonstrates a fine critical ability to weigh the various efforts. What is disappointing is her complete omission of Flusser's work. In my judgement he has more to teach us on the Jewishness of Jesus than her analogies to transvestism (Susannah Heschel, 'Jesus as Theological Transvestite', in Miriam Peshowitz and Laura Levitt, eds., *Judaism Since Gender* [London: Routledge, 1997], pp. 239-241). At the same time, it is perhaps my lack of understanding or dullness which causes me to miss the point.

25. Donald Berry, Mutuality: *The Vision of Martin Buber* (Albany: State University Press, 1985) especially chapter 3, 'The Brother', pp. 69-88.

26. The close ties Jews and Christians had in the earliest years and the impact of Jewish messianism on the Christians is clear from William Horbury's *Messianism and the Cult of Christ* (London: SCM Press, 1998).

27. Donald Berry, Memorial address for Leonard Ragaz as cited by Ernst Simon, *Jewish Frontier*, February 1948, p.69.

28. Martin Buber, *Der heilige Weg. Ein Wort an die Juden und an die Völker* (Frankfurt am Main: Ruetten und Loening, 1919). The English version followed here is edited and translated by Nahum Glatzer, Martin Buber, *On Judaism* (New York: Schocken, 1967), chapter 7, 'The Holy Way,' pp. 108-148. At some critical points, I have disagreed with his translation.

29. Glatzer, *Martin Buber*, p. 43.

30. Translation by William Klassen by permission of Cardun Verlag of David Flusser, Chapter 4, *Das essenische Abenteuer* (Winterthur: Cardun, 1994): 'Buber's Two Types of Faith', pp. 121-153. Text also appeared in *Postscript to M. Buber* (1994), *Zwei Glaubensweisen* (Gerlingen). The text here translated is from the former publication. Wherever identifiable, Flusser's quotes from Buber are taken from M. Buber, *Two Types of Faith: A Study of the Interpenetration of Judaism and Christianity*, trans. *Norman Goldhawk* (New York: Harper, Torchbook, 1961). Quite a few of Flusser's footnotes, e.g. most of the quotes from the Bible, have been incorporated into the text and the translation has attempted to be more literal than literary.

31. Margot Cohn and Rafael Buber, *Martin Buber, A Bibliography of His*

Writings, 1897-1978 (Jerusalem: Magnes Press, 1980).

32. Glatzer, *Martin Buber*, pp.126-128.

33. Glatzer, *Martin Buber*, pp.126-127.

34. Glatzer, *Martin Buber*, pp.126-127.

35. Glatzer, *Martin Buber*, pp.126-127.

36. See note 3 in the prologue of Geza Vermes, *The Authentic Gospel of Jesus* (Harmondsworth: Penguin, 2004).

37. Vermes, *Providential Accidents*, p. 210.

38. Geza Vermes, *Jesus the Jew* (London: SCM, 1973).

39. David Flusser, 'Reflections of a Jew on a Christian Theology of Judaism' in Helga Croner, ed., *A Christian Theology of Judaism* (New York: Paulist Press, 1980), pp. 14-15.

40. Vermes, *Providential Accidents*, p. 213.

41. Geza Vermes, 'Jesus the Jew: Christian and Jewish Reactions', *Toronto Journal of Theology* 4 (1988), p. 114, quoting from Vermes, *Jesus the Jew*, p. 223.

42. Vermes, 'Christian and Jewish', p. 118.

43. Vermes, 'Christian and Jewish', p. 118.

44. Vermes, *Providential Accidents*, p. 215.

45 The phrase 'temple tantrum' was coined by Paula Fredriksen in a 1990 SBL Seminar discussion.

46. Geza Vermes, *The Religion of Jesus the Jew* (London: SCM, 1993).

47. Vermes, *Providential Accidents*, p. 218.

48. Vermes, *Providential Accidents*, pp. 210-223.

49. Vermes, 'Christian and Jewish', pp. 112-123.

50. Vermes, *Providential Accidents*, pp. 223-224.

51. Vermes, *Providential Accidents*, p. 224.

52. 'One of the greatest studies on Jesus by a Jew', James Charlesworth, *Jesus Within Judaism* (New York: Doubleday, 1988), p. 229. More recently, Charlesworth described it 'as the finest book on Jesus that I have seen over the last 20-30 years' (Letter to W. Klassen, 01-14-98).

53. Edmund Wilson, *The Dead Sea Scrolls* (New York: Oxford University Press, 1969), pp 47, 78-83.

54. Used by permission of Farrar, Straus and Giroux, LLC, quoting from Wilson, *Dead Sea Scrolls*, pp. 251-255. Wilson then notes that Flusser's book has been published in German and proceeds to translate two paragraphs from the opening chapter. I reproduce instead the more accurate text from the 1998 English version by Notley (Flusser, *Jesus*, pp.

22-23).

55. Flusser, *Jesus*, pp. 2-23.

56. J. Klausner, *Jesus of Nazareth*. Transl. H. Danby (London: George Allen, 1929), p. 414.

57. Flusser, 'Reflections', p. 7.

58. He found it quite amusing that Wilson would describe him as 'an independent scholar not committed to any religion' (*Dead Sea Scrolls*, p. 82).

59. David Flusser, 'Das Erlebnis ein Jude zu Sein', *Richte unsere Füsse auf den Weg des Friedens. Helmut Gollwitzer zum 70. Geburtstag* (Munich: Kaiser Verlag, 1980), pp. 18-25.

60. Flusser, 'Reflections', p. 2.

61. John W. Miller, *Jesus at Thirty* (Minneapolis: Fortress Press, 1997).

62. Flusser, *Jesus*, p.176.

63. Daniel Harrington, 'The Jewishness of Jesus: Facing Some Problems', *Catholic Biblical Quarterly* 49 (1987), pp. 1-13.

64. Flusser, 'Reflections', pp. 15-16.

65. See his excellent critical review of the English version of Flusser's book: Robert Lindsey, *A Review of David Flusser's Jesus* (Jerusalem: Dugith Publishers, 1973).

66. Pinchas Lapide, writing in 1970, says: 'Israel's 20-some years of statehood have seen the writing, in Jerusalem alone, of more books about Jesus by Jews than world Jewry produced in all the 18 preceding centuries, and that in the past decade no fewer than 23 new Hebrew works had the Nazarene for their central subject.' 'Jesus in Israeli Literature', *Christian Century*, October 21, 1970, pp.1248-1253, this quote, page 1248.

67. Lapide, 'Jesus in Israeli Literature', p. 1253. For Flusser's place see pp. 1250-1252.

68. Lapide, 'Jesus in Israeli Literature', p. 1250.

69. Cf. Peter Richardson's 'press releases' on Herod's death in his book on Herod and my fictional suicide note of Judas in *Judas, Friend or Betrayer of Jesus* (Minneapolis: Fortress, 1996), pp. 205-207.

70. *From Jesus to Christ* (New Haven: Yale University Press, 1988). See the introduction to the second edition (2000) on her website. 'Jesus and the Temple, Mark and the War', *SBL Seminar Papers* (Atlanta: Scholars Press, 1990), pp. 291-310.

71. Compare Craig Evans, 'Jesus' Action in the Temple, Cleansing or Portent of Destruction?' *Catholic Biblical Quarterly* 51 (1989), pp. 237-270.

It should be noted that Fredriksen addresses these matters in other writings.

72. Fredriksen disavows being the source of this intriguing bon mot, but it surely must have originated with a parent. It cannot be seen as a praiseworthy term for someone like Jesus, who is thirty-three years old and 'King of the Jews'.

73. Renan, *Life*, p. 133.

74. Renan, *Life*, p. 135.

75. Renan, *Life*, p. 136.

76. Renan, *Life*, p. 137.

77. Renan, *Life*, p. 139.

78. Renan, *Life*, p. 141.

79. William Klassen, *Love of Enemies, The Way to Peace* (Eugene, Oregon: Wipf and Stock, 1998-99).

80. David Berger, *The Jewish-Christian Debate in the High Middle Ages* (Philadelphia: Jewish Publication Society, 1979).

81. Marc Hirschman, *A Rivalry of Genius. Jewish and Christian Biblical Interpretation in Late Antiquity* (Albany: State University of New York Press, 1996).

82. Charles Talbert, *Reimarus: Fragments* (London SCM, 1970), p. 123.

83. N.T. Wright, 'Jesus, Quest for the Historical', *The Anchor Bible Dictionary* (New York: Doubleday, 1992), p. 801.

84. Trude Weiss-Rosmarin, *Jewish Expressions on Jesus* (New York: KTAV Press, 1977). H. Falk, *Jesus the Pharisee. A New Look at the Jewishness of Jesus* (New York: Paulist, 1985); Samuel Sandmel, *We Jews and Jesus* (New York: Oxford University Press, 1965), pp. 44, 46-47; idem. *Judaism and Christian Beginnings* (New York: Oxford, 1978), pp. 393-398; Irving M. Zeitlin, *Jesus and the Judaism of his Time* (Cambridge: Polity Press, 1988). Also see G. Lindeskog, note 4 above. In addition, Israeli novelists have shown special interest in Jesus. Lapide considers Aharon A. Kabak, *The Narrow Path: The Man of Nazareth*, written in Hebrew in 1938 and then translated by the Institute for the Translation of Hebrew Literature and published in English in Tel Aviv (Massada Press) in 1968, the best. The theme grew out of an intense religious experience. In the novel, Jesus offers himself up in order to bring redemption to his people and all humankind. The narrow path of redemption, Kabak implies, 'leads through the fusion of intense humanity with a titanic heavenward thrust – a fusion such as few, too few, ever achieve.'

2

Christian Judaism: A Reconstruction and Evaluation of the Original Christian Tradition

David C. Sim

1. Introduction

I wish to begin this study by making an obvious but important point. When we use terms such as 'Jewish/Christian relations' or 'Jewish/Christian dialogue', there is an immediate acknowledgement that we are dealing with two distinct and independent entities. On the one side we have Jews and Judaism, and on the other we have Christians and Christianity. In the modern day these two categories are mutually exclusive; an individual is either a member of the Jewish faith or a member of the Christian faith, but one cannot be both. Their mutual exclusivity is reinforced by the fact that a Jew who wishes to be a Christian must leave the religion of Judaism to do so, and similarly, a Christian who wishes to embrace Judaism must leave the religion of Christianity to do so. Modern Jewish/Christian dialogue therefore works on the correct assumption that a gulf separates these two traditions, even though there are obvious points of contact as well. Such dialogue attempts to build bridges between them, emphasising mutual acceptance and understanding of their differences, without prejudicing the integrity of either. This is an important and necessary enterprise in a post-Holocaust world, and the Centre for the Study of Jewish-Christian Relations in Cambridge is an excellent example of work in this area.

But what holds true in the modern day, the mutual exclusivity of the Jewish and Christian traditions, has not always held true. In the distant past there were Jews who were Christians, and there were Christians who were Jews. These people were not one or the other, but both Jew and Christian. They lived in an age when the boundaries between Judaism and the Christian movement were far more fluid than they are today, and they represent an important historical and theological link between these great religious traditions. In this study I wish to focus on these Jews who were Christians (or Christians who were Jews). For reasons that will become clear later, I do not follow the usual convention of describing these people as Jewish Christians and their religious tradition as Jewish Christianity. I refer to them as Christian Jews and their religion as Christian Judaism. This terminological distinction is crucial.

I aim to answer a few important questions. What was Christian Judaism? What was its theological perspective? Who in the early Christian movement belonged within the Christian Jewish tradition? How defensible was their point of view by comparison with other Christian groups? Why did this version of the Christian tradition die out? Finally, I will reflect on the need within Christian circles to re-evaluate views concerning Christian Judaism, the original Christian tradition.

2. Defining and Reconstructing Christian Judaism

Christian Judaism can be simplistically defined as a tradition that accepted the messiahship of Jesus of Nazareth within the traditional parameters of Judaism. We can reconstruct its major theological themes and perspectives from a wide range of early Christian sources. Some of these sources are critical of this tradition or elements of it. These critical sources include the Pauline epistles, notably Galatians, and a number of Deutero-Pauline texts, in particular 1 and 2 Timothy, Titus and Colossians.[1] The slightly later epistles of Ignatius of Antioch, especially those to the Philadelphians and the Magnesians, are relevant as well for they contain a number of very uncomplimentary references to Christian Judaism and its adherents.[2] Other sources, however, provide a much more positive assessment of Christian Judaism, and were arguably written from a Christian Jewish perspective. Two such texts in the New Testament are the Gospel of Matthew[3] and the epistle of James.[4] A further important source, and one which is more neutral in its assessment of Christian Judaism, is the Acts of the Apostles. Despite the fact that all of these texts have their own biases and agendas, they convey a fairly consistent general picture of this early Christian Jewish perspective. They provide sufficient information for an objective reconstruction of its major themes.

The central claim of Christian Judaism was that belief in Jesus as the messiah was only legitimate within the established boundaries of the Jewish faith. It therefore maintained that the Christ-event – the life, death and resurrection of Jesus the Christ – involved no break whatsoever with the religion of Judaism. To put this another way, the revelation of the Christ was continuous rather than discontinuous with the earlier covenant between the God of Israel and the people of Israel, which was mediated through Moses at Mount Sinai. In accordance with this belief, the members of this Christian tradition argued that it was necessary for all followers of the Christ to observe the terms of that covenant, which meant essentially that they were to obey the Mosaic Law. In this respect these people were no different from other Jews of the time.

But these Jews were also quite distinctive, in that they also accepted that the Christ had come in the person of Jesus of Nazareth. The revelation of the Christ entailed a whole range of additional beliefs and practices. At the very minimum they accepted that Jesus was the Jewish messiah, that he fulfilled the prophecies of the Jewish scriptures, that God had raised him from the dead, that Jesus now sits at the right hand of God in heaven, that he would return soon to preside over the final judgement, and that Jesus the Christ is the key to salvation. These people performed baptism in the name of Jesus as the initiation rite into their Jewish movement, and they held specifically Christian meetings based upon a common meal.

These Christian Jews were therefore followers of Jesus, the one they believed to be the messiah, within the Jewish tradition. It is important to remember when reconstructing their viewpoint that they were both Jews and Christians. Because of this dual allegiance to the traditional Sinai covenant and the newer revelation of the Christ, they claimed that salvation was available only to those who were both Jewish and Christian. Simply being Jewish and observing the Torah was not enough to gain salvation, because the Sinai covenant was now supplemented by the revelation of the messiah. Thus one had to be a Christian as well as a Jew. Non-Christian Jews, those Jews who rejected the messiahship of Jesus, would be excluded from salvation (cf. Acts 4:12). By the same token, simply being Christian by professing Jesus as Christ and saviour was in itself not sufficient for salvation unless one did so within the terms of the Sinai covenant and observed the Torah as well. Thus one had to be a Jew as well as a Christian. Non-Jewish Christians would also be excluded from salvation. It was on account of this belief that Christian Jews attempted to convince Gentile Christians, in Antioch, Galatia and elsewhere, to convert to Judaism and observe the Jewish Law as a necessary component of their Christian existence (Acts 15:1).

The mention of Gentile Christians reminds us that Christian Judaism was merely one tradition within the primitive Christian movement. There were other Christian traditions that existed alongside Christian Judaism, but the most important of these was the alternative gospel preached by Paul and others. This point raises a crucial question. How did the Pauline gospel differ from Christian Judaism? There is no evidence in any of our sources that there were serious disagreements in christology. The major difference between them seems to have been the significance of the Christ-event, particularly in terms of its implications for the existing religion of Judaism.

Unlike Christian Judaism, which stressed continuity between the old covenant and the revelation of the messiah, Paul emphasised a decisive break with the Jewish tradition.[5] The old covenant between God and the people of Israel had been superseded by the coming of the Christ (2 Cor. 3:14). In the light of this new covenant brought by Jesus the messiah (cf. 1 Cor. 11:25; 2 Cor. 3:6), there was no longer any difference between Jew and Greek (Rom. 10:12; 1 Cor. 12:13; Gal. 3:28; cf. Gal. 6:15). Salvation now comes through faith in Christ alone and not through membership of the people of Israel and not through obedience to the Law (cf. Rom. 3:22, 30). The Torah, though given by God at Sinai, was intended merely as a temporary measure, a custodian until faith was revealed by the Christ (Gal. 3:23-5), and Christ has now brought the Law to an end (Rom. 10:4a).

Paul spells out his own break with Judaism in Gal. 1:13-14 when he differentiates between his current life as a Christian and his former life in Judaism. In Phil. 3:5-8 he even goes so far as to say that his Jewish heritage now counts for nothing. What this means in practical terms is that Paul is no longer bound by the Torah (1 Cor. 9:20-1). He therefore has no compunction in criticising the ritual elements of the Law that he himself had renounced - circumcision (Rom. 2:28-9; Gal. 5:12; Phil. 3:2-3), the sabbath and the Jewish festivals (Gal. 4:10), and the purity laws (Rom. 14:14, 20). It was this gospel, what we might call the Law-free gospel about the Christ, that Paul preached to the Gentiles, and it is obvious that it stood poles apart from the Law-observant gospel of Christian Judaism.

I want now to look a little more closely at the issue of terminology. In the past scholars referred to the Law-observant Christian tradition as 'Jewish Christianity'. This particular label, however, is misleading and inappropriate. The term 'Christianity' (Gr. *christianismos*) first appears in the letters of Ignatius of Antioch, written in the early second century.

When Ignatius uses this term, it is always contrasted with 'Judaism' (cf. Mag. 8:1; 10:2). Ignatius was a devoted follower of Paul, who also came into conflict with Christians who continued to observe the Torah, and he argued that one cannot practise Christianity (believe in Jesus as the messiah and saviour) and practise Judaism (observe the Jewish Law) (Mag. 10:3); for Ignatius the two traditions are mutually exclusive.[6] This definition of 'Christianity' as a religious tradition distinct from Judaism soon gained currency in the Christian church and is still in use today.

It stands to reason that the label 'Christianity' is not an appropriate term for those first- century Jewish believers in Jesus who continued to observe the Torah. Such a term implies separation from Judaism and is therefore entirely misleading in terms of the theological perspective of these people. This problem is not alleviated by using the term 'Jewish Christianity', because the all-important noun still suggests that the practitioners of this tradition, though Jewish by birth, stand outside Judaism. In my opinion the term 'Jewish Christianity' is a contradiction in terms. How can something that is by definition non-Jewish be qualified as Jewish in any meaningful sense? Scholars have wrestled with these terminological and conceptual difficulties.[7] But over and above this issue, the problematic nature of the label 'Jewish Christianity' is highlighted by the fact that scholars use it in a wide variety of ways. Most scholars employ this term to describe the tradition of ethnic and Law-observant Jews who followed Jesus, but there are some who use it to describe the Law-free tradition within the Christian movement.[8] Still others define this term in a very broad sense. All the early believers in Jesus as the messiah belong to Jewish Christianity, regardless of their obedience or otherwise to the Torah.[9] Such are the difficulties with this label that the scholarly discussion of the early Christian movement would be much better served if we consigned the term 'Jewish Christianity' to the dustbin of history, and found a more suitable and accurate replacement.

The label I prefer is 'Christian Judaism'. Since these Law-observant Christians emphasised rather than rescinded the fundamental elements of first century Judaism, it follows that their religion was Judaism. What they practised was a distinctive form of Judaism, a Judaism that proclaimed that a certain Jesus of Nazareth was the messiah. So just as we speak of other types of first century Judaism – Pharisaic Judaism, Essenic Judaism and so on – we can speak of Christian Judaism.[10] By the same token, just as we refer to Pharisaic Jews or Essenic Jews, so too can we refer to

Christian Jews.[11] The term 'Christianity', though perhaps coined in the early second century, can be used in a first century context to describe the Law-free Christian tradition that had broken with Judaism.[12]

3. The Relations Between the Law-Observant and Law-Free Christian Traditions

Christian Judaism was the original Christian tradition. The book of Acts and the epistles of Paul make clear that the earliest church in Jerusalem, which included the disciples and the family of Jesus (Acts 1:13-14), was still firmly within the sphere of Judaism. These Christians, in addition to their beliefs about Jesus as the Christ, continued to participate in the Temple cult (Acts 2:46; 3:1-2; 5:20) and to observe the Torah. Their theological position did not change in any major way over the ensuing decades. The alternative Law-free gospel that later came to dominate the Christian movement did not originate with these original Christians. This was a development that Acts attributes to a group of early converts known as the Hellenists.[13] The Hellenists were originally Greek-speaking Jews from the Diaspora who had settled in Jerusalem. For reasons which are not entirely clear, the Hellenists came to reject certain aspects of the Christian Jewish position by maintaining that the Christ event had rendered obsolete both the Jewish Temple and the Jewish Law (Acts 6:13-14). The Hellenists were persecuted by other Jews and driven from Jerusalem. They travelled to other parts of the Roman empire, and in Antioch they preached their Law-free message about Jesus to the Gentiles for the first time (Acts 11:19-20). This led to a very new and distinctive Christian community composed of Jews and Gentiles, who were bound together by faith in Jesus and not by the Mosaic Law. So distinctive was this community that it was in Antioch that the term 'Christian' was coined to describe them (Acts 11:26). Paul later travelled to Antioch and joined this Law-free, Hellenist Gentile mission (Acts 11:25-6; cf. Gal. 1:21).

What was the Christian Jewish response to these developments? Despite the testimony of Acts that there was close co-operation between the two churches during the 30s and 40s (Acts 11:22-4, 27-30), the reality was probably somewhat different. The Jerusalem church had certainly not accepted the validity of the Antiochene mission by the year 48, because it sent agents to Antioch with the message that the salvation of the Gentile Christians there depended upon the observance of the Torah (Acts 15:1). This incursion by the Jerusalem church led to the so-called apostolic council in the same year. The Christian community in Antioch sent a number of delegates to Jerusalem to defend their Law-free version of the gospel. Both Acts 15 and Paul in Gal. 2:1-10 refer to this meeting and each suggests, though in different ways, that the Antiochene delegates were successful; it was agreed that Gentile Christians were exempt from circumcision and the full demands of the Mosaic Law. There are, however, valid reasons for rejecting both of these accounts as they stand.[14] But even if we accept the Pauline version of events, as most scholars do, it is clear that any agreement reached in Jerusalem was short-lived. James, the brother of Jesus and by then the leader of the Jerusalem church, moved soon after to impose the Law-observant gospel on the Antiochene church. Paul refers to this event in Gal. 2:11-14, and there can no doubt that, despite Paul's best efforts, James was successful.[15] The defeated Paul then left Antioch to begin new Law-free Gentile missions in Asia Minor and Greece.

Paul was hampered in these missionary endeavours by Christian Jews who located Paul's Gentile converts and tried to convert them to Christian Judaism. This is most clearly described in Galatians, but some of the other Pauline epistles provide evidence of these people as well (cf. Phil. 3:2-20; 2 Cor. 10-13). It is a matter of scholarly debate as to whether these Christian Jewish missionaries were directly associated with the Jerusalem church, but the most plausible hypothesis is that they were. Their actions in attempting to convert Law-free Gentile Christians to the Law-observant gospel parallel exactly the actions of the emissaries sent by James to Antioch both before and after the apostolic council. James was therefore continuing to enforce the policy he implemented in Antioch. The opponents of Paul in Galatia and elsewhere were therefore not acting alone or without authority. They had the full backing of the Jerusalem church, and were acting under its instructions.[16]

4. In Defence of Christian Judaism[17]
When scholars examine this intra-Christian conflict, they almost always defend the position of Paul and criticise or denigrate Paul's opponents, who are often denounced as 'judaisers' or 'Jewish legalists'. Some scholars concede that they acted in good faith but misunderstood the true significance of the Christ event, while other scholars are less generous, and maintain that they deliberately misrepresented the implications of the Christ's appearance. On either view, scholars normally consider these Christian Jews to have been a significant threat to the nascent church, and

they declare that Paul was absolutely correct to stand up to them and their theologically false tradition. This defence of Paul and his gospel is entirely understandable, given that the modern Christian churches have inherited the Pauline Law-free perspective, but much of the discussion is hardly fair to those Christians who opposed Paul.

If we put to the side our inherent Pauline bias, and consider the position of Christian Judaism in a more objective manner, then we find that this tradition could mount a strong defence of its Law-observant position. One could even go so far as to state that, on the basis of the available evidence, Christian Judaism could present a stronger and therefore more defensible case than the alternative position embraced by Paul. This need not mean that Paul was wrong and his Christian Jewish opponents were right, since defensibility and truth are not the same thing. A better attested argument may not necessarily be true and a less convincing argument may not necessarily be false. This is especially so in the theological realm where matters of faith, revelation and the mysterious ways of God play a central role. Paul himself was aware of this distinction between truth and defensibility. In 1 Cor. 1:23 he states that his proclamation of a crucified messiah was a stumbling block to Jews and a folly to Gentiles. It was, in other words, a claim that was difficult to defend by arguments, evidence and logic. Yet there is no doubt that Paul was convinced of its truth. Similarly, Paul may have been hard pressed to defend his gospel against those Christians who demanded observance of the Torah, but his position may still have represented 'the truth of the gospel' (Gal. 2:5).

Readers will come to their own conclusions concerning the validity or otherwise of Paul's theological position. What I am concerned with here is the question of defensibility. How convincingly could each side of the debate defend its particular gospel? I will suggest that of the two alternatives the Law-observant gospel of Christian Judaism was more defensible than its Law-free Pauline equivalent. It was certainly not the demonstrably false tradition that many scholars depict it to have been. Once we understand the strengths of Christian Judaism, then we can at least understand why these Christian Jews believed what they did, and why they were so opposed to the Law-free gospel of Paul. It seems to me that Christian Judaism could defend its Law-observant gospel with three major arguments.

The first argument concerns the permanent nature of the Torah as it is represented in the Jewish scriptures. Paul argued that the Mosaic Law was intended to have a temporary custodial role until faith was revealed with the coming of the Christ (Gal. 3:23-5), but the Hebrew scriptures know nothing of this. On the contrary, they contradict this claim of Paul. For example, in Deut. 11:1 God stipulates that the commandments he gives at Sinai are to be observed always (cf. 12:1). After the giving of this Law, Moses addresses the people of Israel and acknowledges the eternal nature of the Torah. In Deut. 29:29 we read, 'The things that are revealed belong to us and to our children *forever*, that we may do all the words of this Law' (emphasis added). The Torah that God delivered to Moses is therefore a permanent obligation that God demanded of the people of Israel and not a temporary Law to be replaced at a later stage. Paul's Christian Jewish opponents could have pointed to this and other texts to validate their Law-observant version of the gospel. It is significant that when Paul refers to the temporary nature of the Torah, he cites no scriptural text in support.

It is certain that Paul's Christian Jewish opponents in Galatia appealed to the story of Abraham in Genesis 12-25 to convince the Gentile Christians that circumcision at the very least was necessary. Scholars are in agreement that these Christian Jews were depicting Abraham as the prime example of the pagan who turns to the true God. They emphasised the section in Gen. 17:9-14, where God delivers the rite of circumcision to Abraham and explains that this covenant in the flesh will be an everlasting covenant between God and the patriarch's descendants. Moreover, they identified just who were the true descendants of Abraham. Ishmael was born to Hagar, the slave of Abraham, and from him are descended the Gentiles. By contrast, God promised a son to Abraham and his wife, Sarah, and the fruit of the promise was Isaac. Isaac was the true heir of the patriarch, and it was through this legitimate line, the Israelite line, that the covenant was preserved (Gen. 17:15-21). Gentiles can share in this heritage of Isaac by submitting to circumcision and joining the covenant people of Israel.[18]

Paul responded to this challenge by providing a very different interpretation of the Abraham story. According to Paul, Abraham was justified by faith centuries before the giving of the Law, and those who will inherit the promises to Abraham will do so by faith rather than by the works of the Torah (Gal. 3:6-18, 27-9; cf. Rom. 4:1-25). Paul also provides an allegorical reading of Hagar and Sarah and their respective offspring (Gal. 4:21-31). Hagar the slave represents the Sinai covenant, and her children are enslaved to the Law (cf. 5:1), whereas the children or descendants of Sarah, like Paul and his Gentile converts, are the children of promise and therefore the legitimate heirs. Some scholars have suggested that Paul's exegesis of the Abraham story is both artificial and strained.[19] Certainly his allegorical interpretation of the descendants of Sarah and Hagar runs contrary to the plain sense of the text in Genesis. But more than this, there can be no doubt that Paul's explanation of the Abraham narrative is selective. He does not mention at all the crucial material in Gen. 17:9-14, which stipulates that circumcision has a permanent role within the terms of the covenant between God and Abraham's descendants. On any objective assessment of this issue, one would have to conclude that the Jewish scriptures, both in Genesis and elsewhere, favour not the argument of Paul but that of his opponents.[20]

The second argument that supports the position of Christian Judaism concerns the attitude of the historical Jesus to the Torah. This is a very complex question that is muddied by the inconsistent traditions in the Gospels.[21] While Mark presents a Jesus who either criticises the Mosaic Law or deliberately breaks its commandments (e.g. Mark 2:23-8; 3:1-6; 7:1-23), the Matthean Jesus demands that the Torah be obeyed in its entirety (e.g. Matt. 5:17-19). Each account clearly represents the Christian tradition of its author; Mark stands in the Pauline tradition,[22] while Matthew represents the Christian Jewish perspective.[23] Limitations of space preclude any assessment of the relevant Gospel traditions, but there is other important evidence, external to the Gospels and often neglected in historical Jesus research, that directly bears upon the question of Jesus' attitude to the Law. This evidence comes from the Pauline epistles and from the practice of the earliest church in Jerusalem, and suggests that the historical Jesus, true to the Jewish scriptures, honoured and obeyed the laws given to Moses.

While Paul is not much concerned with the teaching of the historical Jesus, he does implicitly acknowledge in three different ways that the Jesus of history observed the Torah. First, when he speaks of the origin of his gospel, the Law-free gospel, he does not say that it is based upon the teachings of the historical Jesus. On the contrary, he says explicitly that this gospel was revealed to him by the risen Christ (Gal. 1:11-12). In other words, the Law-free gospel did not come to Paul from church traditions about Jesus of Nazareth. Secondly, Paul seems to concede that the historical Jesus was faithful to the Torah when he remarks in Gal. 4:4-5 that Jesus was born under the Law to redeem those who were under the Law. Elsewhere in his writings Paul uses the phrase 'under the Law' to denote observance of the Torah (cf. Rom 6:14-15; 1 Cor. 9:20; Gal. 3:23; 4:21; 5:18), so this text presumably acknowledges that the historical Jesus, born under the Law, was an observant Jew.[24] Thirdly, when Paul presents his case against keeping the Mosaic Law, especially in Romans and Galatians, he produces a whole range of arguments in support of his view, but he never once appeals to the example of the historical Jesus. Surely he would have done so had he possessed information that Jesus had been a critic of the Torah, just as he was himself.

We may now turn to the evidence of the earliest church in Jerusalem. This church comprised to a large extent people who knew the historical Jesus intimately, his disciples and his immediate family. As I stated earlier, the Jerusalem church was Christian Jewish, and its Law-observant practice is important in terms of establishing the prior actions of Jesus. If Jesus had clearly and unambiguously criticised and broken the Mosaic Law, which is what Mark would have us believe, then we would expect those who lived with him and who knew him best to have followed suit. The fact that the disciples and the family of Jesus continued to obey the Torah is therefore a sure indication that Jesus had done so as well.[25] Christian Judaism therefore could point to the example of the messiah himself to justify its theological stance.

The third argument in defence of Christian Judaism concerns the revelations of the risen Christ. In Gal. 1:11-17 Paul claims that his Law-free gospel was imparted to him by the risen Christ, and he emphasises that there were no human intermediaries involved (Gal. 1:11-17). Paul's claim here is contradicted by Acts chs 6-7, which specifies that the Hellenists were the first to proclaim the Law-free gospel, but I do not wish to press this point. For sake of argument, let us assume that Paul was the first to receive the Law-free gospel. The evidence is clear that the leaders of the Jerusalem church simply did not believe Paul's claim that the risen Christ had appeared to him and had imparted to him the Law-free gospel. Apart from the fact that they tried to sabotage Paul's missionary efforts among the Gentiles in Antioch, Galatia and elsewhere, something they would never had done had they accepted the divine origin of his gospel, the Jerusalem church also omitted Paul from its list of resurrection witnesses. Paul refers to this traditional list in 1 Cor. 15:5-7. Jesus appeared first to Peter, then to the Twelve, then to more than five hundred, then to

James (the brother of Jesus) and then to all the apostles. The traditional list which Paul received ends at this point, but Paul then adds to it by referring to his own visitation from the risen Christ and describing it as the last of these revelations (15:8).

The significance of this Pauline addition must be correctly understood. The fact that Paul needed to append his own experience of the risen Christ indicates that he was not included in the list of authentic resurrection witnesses produced by the Jerusalem church. We must infer from this that the members of this church, who certainly knew of Paul's claim of a resurrection appearance, did not accept the veracity of that claim. Had they done so, then surely Paul would have been added to the list as a further important witness to the resurrection of the Christ. It is also clear from the traditional list that Paul was not considered to be an authentic apostle by this church, because it specifies that Jesus appeared to all the apostles, which effectively closes this office and excludes later claimants to this position. Paul of course was well aware of this, but he tried to include himself in this group by mentioning in 15:9 that he was the least of the apostles who was unworthy to bear that title.[26] This rejection of Paul's apostleship by those in Jerusalem provides further evidence for a close link between them and Paul's Christian Jewish opponents who infiltrated his churches. It is clear that in both Galatia and Corinth one of the major attacks on Paul concerned his status as a legitimate apostle (cf. Gal. 1:1, 11-17; 1 Cor. 9:1-18; 2 Cor. 10-13).

All of this prompts an obvious question. Why did the Jerusalem church reject these claims of Paul? I think its position is understandable once we examine carefully what Paul says of his conversion and his commission in Gal. 1:11-17. Here Paul sets out in detail the origin of his gospel and his mission to evangelise the Gentile world. He attests that his Law-free gospel is not a human gospel that he was taught. On the contrary, it came directly through a revelation of Jesus Christ. Paul stipulates that his gospel was entirely independent of the Jerusalem church by mentioning that he did not confer with 'flesh and blood' and he did not consult immediately with the apostles in Jerusalem. It is important to note that Paul takes pains to emphasise his exclusive claim on this gospel, which he does by stating that God had set him apart to take this Law-free message to the Gentile world. When we ask what the Jerusalem church found objectionable or unbelievable about this testimony of Paul, two points in particular present themselves.

The first is that the experience Paul describes is a private revelation. The revelation of the risen Christ was given to Paul alone and to Paul exclusively; no-one else was privy to it. How could those in the Jerusalem church be certain that Paul had experienced the risen Christ or even that he had interpreted the revelation correctly? The short answer is that they could not. Private revelations, by definition, are incapable of demonstration, and Paul could not prove in any definitive manner that the risen Christ had appeared to him and commissioned him. An interesting tradition in this respect appears in the third century Pseudo-Clementine literature, which has a clear Christian Jewish orientation. In the *Homilies* 18:13-19 we find a debate between the disciple Peter and a certain Simon, whom most scholars correctly identify as Paul. In this dialogue Peter questions Paul's legitimacy to speak for Jesus because his version of the gospel is based upon visions which are both unreliable and unprovable. Peter claims that he can speak for Jesus because he knew him intimately and was personally instructed by him. Although this story is apocryphal in its present form, it probably represents the sorts of issues that arose in the early church between Paul and his critics. Paul was treated with suspicion because his gospel was based upon revelations that he claimed to be true but which he could never prove conclusively.[27]

Paul did in fact try to demonstrate the reality of his encounter with the risen Christ in two ways. First, he points to his conversion (Gal. 1:13-17; cf. 1 Cor. 9:1; 15:9-10). Why would he, an enemy of Christ, suddenly become his chief defender if he had not received a revelation from the risen Lord? Secondly, Paul emphasises the hardships of his apostolic life (2 Cor. 11:23-28). Why would he endure beatings, imprisonments, shipwrecks and many other hardships if Christ had not called upon him to do so? These are significant arguments that must be given some weight. They certainly demonstrate Paul's radical change of heart and his absolute commitment to his new cause, but in the final analysis they do not constitute irrefutable proof that the risen Christ appeared to Paul and revealed to him the Law-free gospel.

This brings us to the second reason for the scepticism of the Jerusalem church. Paul's claim that he had been set apart by God and that his gospel was revealed to him alone means effectively that it was not revealed by the risen Christ to anyone else. Yet Paul acknowledges in 1 Cor. 15:5-7 that the resurrected Christ also appeared to the leaders of the Jerusalem church, and he mentions Peter and James by name. An obvious question arises from this. What precisely did the risen Jesus communicate to those in the Jerusalem church? It was certainly not the Law-free gospel, since Paul is adamant this was revealed to him alone. This is confirmed by the fact that Paul had to defend his Law-free gospel before the pillar apostles at the apostolic council. So, if the risen Jesus did not reveal the Law-free gospel to the leaders of the Jerusalem church, what did he reveal to them? We must assume that he revealed the gospel that they themselves proclaimed, the Law-observant gospel, the good news about Jesus the messiah which retained the observance of the Mosaic Law.

It is precisely this point that makes Paul's position precarious. The logic of his position is that the risen Christ was not consistent in his communications. On the one hand, he revealed the Law-free gospel to Paul alone, instructing him that the Torah was now no longer binding on Jew or Gentile. On the other hand, he communicated the Law-observant gospel to the leaders of the Jerusalem church, expressing his desire that all Christians, both Jew and Gentile, obey the Torah as a necessary mark of their Christian commitment. That the risen Christ acted in this unconventional way is not impossible and it might even be true, but it is entirely understandable that the Jerusalem church had problems accepting this proposition. Why should those who knew the historical Jesus personally, and who received particular and consistent messages from the risen Christ, believe that the very same heavenly mediator was delivering an entirely different message to someone else, especially when that individual acknowledged that only he received these revelations, and he could not provide proof of his claims?

Therefore, when we consider in objective fashion the position of Christian Judaism and the Law-observant gospel as opposed to the position of Paul and the Law-free gospel, its strengths become clear. It was consistent with the eternal nature of the Torah as attested in the Hebrew scriptures, it was consistent with the Law-observant example of Jesus their messiah, and it was consistent with the revelations of the risen Christ to the leaders of the Jerusalem church. On the other hand, the Law-free gospel was not unambiguously supported by the Jewish scriptures and it was not supported by the example of the historical Jesus. It may have been revealed by the risen Christ, but to argue in this fashion, it has to be accepted that this gospel was revealed to Paul exclusively and that it was inconsistent with the resurrection experiences of the Jerusalem church. In making this point, let me repeat that I am not suggesting that Paul was wrong and that the Christian church of today has inherited a false gospel. What I am suggesting is that Christian Judaism is much more defensible than most scholars allow. Those who followed this Christian tradition should not be viewed as deliberate distorters or misguided interpreters of the Christ event who preached a demonstrably false gospel. Whether right or wrong, they could provide strong arguments in favour of their position, and I for one can well understand why they so staunchly opposed the Law-free mission of Paul.

5. The Later History of Christian Judaism

Christian Judaism lasted as a powerful force for only a generation. Its demise began with the Jewish war of 66-70, which had a significant impact upon all forms of Second Temple Judaism. Despite the later Christian tradition that the Jerusalem church fled to Pella in the Transjordan prior to the war (Eusebius, *History*, 3:5), the probability is that these Christians remained in Jerusalem for the duration of the conflict.[28] When the city fell to the Romans in the year 70, the members of the Jerusalem church shared the same horrific fate as Jerusalem's other residents, and many were either killed or sold into slavery.[29] The fall and destruction of Jerusalem therefore witnessed the destruction of the Jerusalem church.

This event had a momentous impact upon the Christian movement in general and Christian Judaism in particular.[30] The demise of the authoritative and powerful Jerusalem church meant that there was a significant change in the balance of power in the Christian world. The Law-free Gentile churches, which were relatively unscathed by the Jewish war, were now free of the pressure that the Jerusalem church had previously exerted. In the decades that followed, these churches flourished and expanded their numbers. By contrast, the destruction of the Jerusalem church was a massive blow for Christian Judaism. This tradition continued to exist in isolated pockets in the eastern part of the Roman empire, but the loss of its major centre in Jerusalem left it leaderless and weak. The problems faced by these Christian Jews in the final part of the first century are well documented in the Gospel of Matthew. On the one hand, Matthew's Christian Jewish community came into conflict with a new force in post-war Judaism, formative Judaism, which was a coalition of formerly disparate groups led by the Pharisees.[31] On the other hand, the Matthean community encountered problems with a resurgent Paulinism, which now had little to fear from its Christian Jewish rival.[32] The Gospel of Matthew therefore provides a grim picture of the prospects of Christian Judaism at the end of the first century. It was no longer welcome in the Jewish world as formative Judaism took a hard-line approach to any Jewish minority groups that opposed it, and assimilation into the Christian world, dominated as it was by Law-free Gentiles, was unthinkable.

The remarkable tenacity of Christian Judaism is evident from the fact that this tradition continued to exist for many centuries in very precarious circumstances. Some of the church fathers refer to various Christian Jewish groups that existed in Syria and the surrounding regions - the Ebionites, the Elkesaites, the Nazarenes and others as well.[33] In addition, a number of later Christian Jewish texts have survived, notably the Pseudo-Clementine literature.[34] But while Christian Judaism survived over the centuries, it existed in complete isolation. It belonged neither to the wider Jewish world nor to the wider Christian world. In a rather ironic twist of fate, Christian Jews came to be regarded as heretical by both Rabbinic Judaism and the greater Christian church. Despite its tenacity to exist in the face of fierce and powerful opposition, Christian Judaism disappeared from history around the seventh century, probably as a result of the rise of Islam that spread so quickly across the middle east.

6. Conclusions and Reflections

In this study I have offered a reconstruction and evaluation of Christian Judaism, the original Christian tradition. Despite claims that this tradition was a clearly false version of the Christian gospel, I have argued that Christian Judaism was much more defensible than its critics, both ancient and modern, have conceded. This Christian tradition did not lose the battle with its Law-free competitor because it was false and discredited, but because of historical circumstances. Had the Jewish war of 66-70 not occurred, then Christian Judaism may well have won its struggle against the Law-free Gentile gospel. In that case the followers of Jesus the messiah would have remained a small sectarian group within the wider Jewish world. But the Jewish uprising did occur, and it changed definitively and forever the nature and destiny of both Judaism and the Christian church.

How should Christians today view Christian Judaism? In my opinion the polemic against this tradition which we find especially in the Pauline and the Deutero-Pauline writings has no place in the modern day. The polemical stance of these writers was occasioned by the very real threat they faced from Christian Jewish opponents, but this threat has long ceased to exist. In similar vein, the condemnation of Christian Judaism as heretical by the later Christian church should not dictate our appraisal of this tradition in the twenty-first century. In these days of ecumenism and inter-faith dialogue, where respect, tolerance and understanding have replaced polemic and intolerance, Christian Judaism deserves a fairer and more objective evaluation within Christian circles. If Christians can now approach other Christian denominations and even other religions in a spirit of genuine dialogue, seeking true understanding rather than offering value judgements and condemnation, then the representatives of the original Christian tradition deserve the same courtesy.

Notes

1. For a detailed statement of the view that the Pastoral epistles and Colossians were attacking Christian Jewish opponents, see D.C. Sim, *The Gospel of Matthew and Christian Judaism: The History and Social Setting of the Matthean Community* (SNTW; Edinburgh: T & T Clark, 1998), pp. 172-7.

2. See Sim, *Matthew and Christian Judaism*, pp. 272-82.

3. For evidence that the Gospel of Matthew is a Christian Jewish document, see Sim, *Matthew and Christian Judaism*, passim, esp. pp. 123-39, 188-211.

4. Sim, *Matthew and Christian Judaism*, pp. 178-81.

5. Sim, *Matthew and Christian Judaism*, pp. 21-4.

6. Sim, *Matthew and Christian Judaism*, pp. 275-8.

7. See R.A. Kraft, 'In Search of "Jewish Christianity" and its "Theology": Problems of Definition and Methodology', *RSR* 60 (1972), pp. 81-92; A.F.J. Klijn, 'The Study of Jewish Christianity', *NTS* 20 (1974), pp. 419-31; S.K. Riegel, 'Jewish Christianity: Definitions and Terminology', *NTS* 24 (1978), pp. 410-15; R. Murray, 'Jews, Hebrews and Christians: Some Needed Distinctions', *NovT* 24 (1982), pp. 194-208; G. Lüdemann, *Opposition to Paul in Jewish Christianity* (Minneapolis: Fortress Press, 1989), pp. 1-32 and J.E. Taylor, 'The Phenomenon of Early Jewish-Christianity: Reality or Scholarly Invention?', *VC* 44 (1990), pp. 313-44.

8. So B.J. Malina, 'Jewish Christianity or Christian Judaism: Toward a Hypothetical Definition', *JSJ* 7 (1990), pp. 46-57.

9. See H. Köster, 'Gnomai Diaphorai: The Origin and Nature of Diversification in the History of Early Christianity', in J.M. Robinson and H. Köster, *Trajectories Through Early Christianity* (Philadelphia: Fortess Press, 1971), pp. 114-57, esp. p. 115. For a similar view, see J. Daniélou, *The Theology of Jewish Christianity* (London: Darton, Longman & Todd, 1964), p. 9.

10. Sim, *Matthew and Christian Judaism*, pp. 25-6.

11. Despite claims to the contrary that the term 'Christian Jew' was coined only recently, it has existed for almost sixty years. It is found in G.D. Kilpatrick, *The Origins of the Gospel according to St. Matthew* (Oxford: Clarendon: 1946), p. 111. Kilpatrick does not, however, use the cognate term 'Christian Judaism'; he prefers 'Jewish Christianity' which is found throughout his monograph.

12. See Sim, *Matthew and Christian Judaism*, pp. 24-5.

13. For detailed discussion of the Hellenists, see Sim, *Matthew and Christian Judaism*, pp. 64-77 and literature cited there.

14. See Sim, *Matthew and Christian Judaism*, pp. 79-92.

15. Sim, *Matthew and Christian Judaism*, pp. 92-100.

16. For discussion of the evidence and the various scholarly views, see Sim, *Matthew and Christian Judaism*, pp. 100-03 and literature cited there. Cf. too a number of later studies which argue that Paul's opponents in Galatia represented the Jerusalem church; so J.L. Martyn, *Galatians: A New Translation with Introduction and Commentary* (AB 33A; New York: Doubleday, 1997), pp. 126, 459-66 and P.F. Esler, *Galatians* (London: Routledge, 1998), pp. 74, 137-8.

17. In this section I am following to a large extent an earlier study on this theme. See D.C. Sim, 'The Defensibility of Christian Judaism', in B. Neal, G.D. Dunn and L. Cross (eds), *Prayer and Spirituality in the Early Church. III. Liturgy and Life* (Sydney: St Paul's, 2003), pp. 57-72.

18. For a more detailed reconstruction of the role of the Abraham narrative in the gospel of Paul's Christian Jewish opponents, see Martyn, *Galatians*, pp. 302-06.

19. See, for example, J.M.G. Barclay, *Obeying the Truth: Paul's Ethics in Galatians* (Minneapolis: Fortress Press, 1991), p. 53; F.J. Matera, *Galatians* (SP9; Collegeville: Liturgical Press, 1992), pp. 172-3 and J.L. Martyn, *Theological Issues in the Letters of Paul* (SNTW; Edinburgh: T & T Clark, 1997), pp. 162-3.

20. Barclay, *Obeying the Truth*, p. 53.

21. The most detailed recent discussion of Jesus' view of the Law in the Gospels and other traditions is W.R.G. Loader, *Jesus' Attitude Towards the Law: A Study of the Gospels* (WUNT 2/97; Tübingen: Mohr Siebeck, 1997).

22. See the recent discussion by J. Marcus, 'Mark - Interpreter of Paul', *NTS* 46 (2000), pp. 473-87. Cf. too J. Svartvik, *Mark and Mission: Mk 7:1-23 in its Narrative and Historical Contexts* (CBNTS 32; Stockholm: Almqvist & Wiksell, 2000), pp. 344-7.

23. See Sim, *Matthew and Christian Judaism*, pp. 123-39.

24. So correctly, R.N. Longenecker, *Galatians* (WBC 41; Dallas: Word Books, 1990), p. 171 and J.D.G. Dunn, *The Epistle to the Galatians* (BNTC; London: A & C Black, 1993), p. 216. For a contrary view, see B. Witherington, *Grace in Galatia: A Commentary on St Paul's Letter to the Galatians* (Edinburgh: T & T Clark, 1998), p. 288. Witherington argues that, while Gal. 4:4 tells us that Jesus was a Jew, it does not tell us how he related to the Law. This contention, however, overlooks the meaning of 'under the Law' in the Pauline corpus.

25. This is rightly argued by the Jewish scholar I.M. Zeitlin. See his *Jesus and the Judaism of His Time* (Cambridge: Polity Press, 1988), pp. 52-60. Cf. too E.P. Sanders, *Jesus and Judaism* (London: SCM, 1985), pp. 249-50, 268.

26. See Luedemann, *Opposition to Paul*, pp. 50, 72-3.

27. See further Luedemann, *Opposition to Paul*, pp. 185-8.

28. For a discussion of the unreliability of the Pella tradition, see Lüdemann, *Opposition to Paul*, pp. 200-13 and S.G.F. Brandon, *The Fall of Jerusalem and the Christian Church* (London: SPCK, 1951), pp. 168-73. A defence of the Pella tradition has been argued by C. Koester, 'The Origin and Significance of the Flight to Pella Tradition', *CBQ* 51 (1989), pp. 90-106, but see the convincing rebuttal by J. Verheyden, 'The Flight of the Christians to Pella', *ETL* 66 (1990), pp. 368-84.

29. In agreement with Brandon, *Fall of Jerusalem*, pp. 184-5 and Lüdemann, *Opposition to Paul*, p. 63.

30. See Sim, *Matthew and Christian Judaism*, pp. 171-2.

31. See A.J. Overman, *Matthew's Gospel and Formative Judaism: The Social World of the Matthean Community* (Minneapolis: Fortress Press, 1990). Cf. too Sim, *Matthew and Christian Judaism*, pp. 109-63.

32. Sim, *Matthew and Christian Judaism*, pp. 211-12.

33. For detailed discussion of these later Christian Jewish groups, see

A.F.J. Klijn and G.J. Reinink, *Patristic Evidence for Jewish-Christian Sects* (NovTSup 36; Leiden: Brill, 1973) and, more recently, P.J. Thomson and D. Lambers-Petry (eds), *The Image of the Judaeo-Christian in Ancient Jewish and Christian Literature* (Tübingen: Mohr Siebeck, 2003).

34. On this literature, see F.S. Jones, 'The Pseudo-Clementines: A History of Research', *Second Century* 2 (1982), pp. 1-33, 63-96. See too the more recent statement in F.S. Jones, *An Ancient Jewish Christian Source on the History of Christianity: Pseudo-Clementine Recogntions 1:27-71* (SBL Texts and Translations Christian Apocrypha Series 37/2; Atlanta: Scholars Press, 1995).

3

Debate, not Duel: The Gospel of John and its Story of Jewish–Christian Encounter

Markus Anker

The Gospel of John tells its own story of early Christian encounter with Judaism: the harsh rejection of the representatives of Jerusalem's elite (the 'Jews'/*Ioudaioi*) on one hand is correlated with the adoption of Jewish traditions on the other. Two examples demonstrate the Fourth Gospel's ambivalent attitude:

- In John 4:22, Jesus says 'Salvation is from the Jews.'
- In John 8:44, Jesus says 'You [the Jews] are from your father the devil, and you choose to do your father's desires.'

This deliberate ambivalence is one of the main characteristics of the Johannine Jesus story (circa 100 C.E.) and gives an insight into the complex self-definition process of early Christianity. By focusing on chapters 7 and 8 I will explore the contrasting interaction between the Jewishness and anti-Jewishness of the Gospel of John. I will investigate the Johannine anti-Jewish polemic and its context in both literature and history.

1. Literary Aspects

1.1   The Plot of the Fourth Gospel

Within the narrative framework of the Johannine plot, the journeys to the Temple festivals in Jerusalem are an essential element of the tale. In the other Gospels, the protagonist's only visit to Jerusalem is part of the passion narrative and the concluding act of Jesus' ministry. In contrast, in the Johannine portrayal of the public ministry in chapters 1–12, Jesus undertakes five journeys 'going up to Jerusalem',[1] each of which is a Temple festival.[2] With regard to the Fourth Gospel's attitude toward Jews and Judaism, the description of the 'pilgrimages' to the Temple is marked by two characteristics.

Firstly, a growing hostility during consequent journeys can be observed between the Jewish authorities and the Johannine Christ. This hostility comes to its climax in the passion narrative:

- 'The Jews' are seeking to kill Jesus and his believers. (John 5:18).
- The crowd (*ochlos*) lives in fear of 'the Jews' (John 7:13).
- In the context of Jesus' arrest and execution, 'the Jews' collaborate with the devil's representatives (under the leadership of Judas, John 18:12) and with the earthly power (represented by the Roman prefect Pilate, John 18:28–40).

The author creates a threatening and fearful atmosphere, in which not only Jesus and the authorities are involved, but also the whole surrounding society. By the end of chapter 12, this 'crisis' ends with the definitive separation of believers and unbelievers.

Secondly, contrary to what we might expect from the crisis described above, the Fourth Gospel integrates important elements of Jewish tradition. In terms of its functional structure, the author integrates his Jesus story in a framework of cultic and theological traditions. By describing several journeys to the Temple, the author links time and space to the Temple cult. The author realizes the performance of specific cultic rituals through the activities of Jesus. The Fourth Gospel demonstrates a chronological and semantic combination of cultic ritual and the revelation of Christ.

This intention is illustrated by the analogy drawn between the Johannine Christ and the passover lamb.[3] In the passion narrative of the other Gospels, the Passover meal is the last supper and the execution takes place the following day. The author of John's Gospel changes this schedule of events by bringing forward the date of the execution: in his narrative the crucifixion takes places in the hours before the Passover meal. He deliberately brings together the crucifixion and the preparation of the Passover lamb.[4] This coincidence becomes evident in John 19 where the Roman soldiers do not carry out the so-called *crucifragium* on Jesus, breaking the legs of a corpse on the cross.[5] The explanation given is 'that the scripture might be fulfilled',[6] which is a reference to the instructions for

Passover given to Moses and Aaron.[7] In other words, John presents Jesus as a symbol of the Passover Lamb.

In order to understand the description of the hostility between the Jewish authorities and Jesus on one hand and an acknowledgement and adoption of Jewish traditions on the other, I shall now turn to John 7 and 8.

1.2 The Literary structure of John 7 and 8

Jesus' pilgrimage to Jerusalem at the Festival of Booths (*Sukkot*) initiates a new development in the gospel plot. Like John 19 and the Passover lamb, the Johannine Christ is the embodiment of festival rituals and their functions. The actual festival remains in the background for the readers are uninformed about the priestly activities. The narrator focusses the reader's attention onto the activities of Jesus. In his activities, the protagonist performs implicitly a number of characteristic festival rituals, such as the so-called Libation, a sort of water sacrifice (7:37–39), the teaching of the Mosaic Law (7:14–24) and the lighting of lights in the Temple (8:12).

The framework of the passage is determined by the spatio–temporal setting of the scene at the festival of Booths:

-   Temporal indications:
    7:2 the festival is near; 7:14 half-way through the festival; 7:37 last day of the festival.
-   Location of the activities of Jesus:
    7:14 going into the Temple; 7:28 teaching in the Temple; 8:20 at the Temple treasury; 8:59 leaving the Temple.

The narrative analysis of John 7 and 8 reveals a sophisticated and complex structure. The passage is dominated by a quest for the origin of the Johannine Christ (7:27ff; 8:14, 23), and his fate (7:34–36; 8:14, 21–23). From the beginning the author unfolds this quest as a controversial debate (7:12, 43, 50–52) in a hostile atmosphere (7:1, 11, 13, 25).

In chapter 7, the controversies take place in public, but the two opponents (Jesus and the Jewish authorities) are not in direct contact. It is interesting to note that a scene describing an activity of Jesus is generally followed by a scene describing the reaction of his opponents. The story switches from one group to the other, back and forth, as demonstrated in. the following table.

Temporal setting	Activity of Jesus	Reaction of the authorities
The Festival is near (7:2)	Jesus going to the Festival (7:10)	'The Jews' looking for Jesus at the festival (7:11)
Half-way through the festival (7:14)	Jesus teaching the Mosaic law (7:14-31 'My teaching is not mine but his who sent me')	Chief Priest and Pharisees sending a team to arrest him (7:32)
Last day ('Great Day') of the festival (7:37)	Jesus symbolizing the water sacrifice (7:37-39 'Let anyone who is thirsty come to me, and let the one who believes in me drink.')	An arrest team returns to the Chief Priest and the Pharisees (7:45-52)

In chapter 8, an indirect confrontation of two adversaries is transformed into a direct one. Chapter 8 contains three dialogue passages in which the Pharisees/High-Priests and Jesus are involved in a verbal exchange with sharply contrasting views.

By correlating alternating scenes in chapter 7, the author creates a narrative structure that expresses the rivalry and tensions between the two opponents. He intensifies the conflict in the dialogues of chapter 8 by transforming an indirect confrontation into a direct one. From a cinematic perspective the arrangement of scenes in John 7 and 8 creates a parallel montage. Two actions, independent in terms of scenery and characters, but correlated by content, are brought together by quickly moving from one scene of action to the other on several different occasions. This narrative technique aims to build up suspense like a Hollywood drama (like the rescue of a hero stranded on the edge of a precipice – the film generally switches back and forth from the rescue team to the hero).[8]

In John 7 and 8, as well as in chapters 5 and 20, the narrative structure is similar to that of the cinematic parallel montage and although the opponents of Jesus are not equipped with firearms leading to a gun battle, the direct confrontation consists of theological debates. This observation should lead us to question the basis of Jewish–Christian conflict in the Fourth Gospel.

2. Historical Aspects

The intention behind the narrative structure in John 7 and 8 is to manifest an escalating conflict, which results in a direct confrontation and mutual rejection.

During the last three decades, since James Louis Martyn's landmark monograph on the historical backgrounds of the Fourth Gospel,[9] scholars have been more aware that the disputes in John can not be regarded as simply symbolic. Instead it is clear that they are shaped by the direct historical experience of the Johannine community. Martyn, and after him Klaus Wengst[10] and David Rensberger,[11] saw in the expulsion from the synagogue (9:22; 12:42; 16:2) the decisive element to explain the Jewish–Christian hostility. The external evidence for this hypothesis is found in the *Birkhat ha-Minim* - an anti-heretical formula in the 12th of the *Eighteen Benedictions* (known as the *Amidah*). Thus the anti-Jewish polemics in John 7 and 8 document the history of this community, which was still coming to terms with the separation from the synagogue. However, during the last few years this scholarly consensus has been increasingly questioned and we need to explore the evidence for conflicts between Jews and Non-Jews, as well as within Jewish communities.

In his analysis of Jewish diaspora life in the Hellenistic and early Roman period John Barclay demonstrates that Jewish identity is 'based on a strong web of practice and community.'[12] Thus, Josephus[13] emphasises that it is not ethnic origin alone, but the lifestyle (*proairesei tou biou*), which constitutes the community (*oikeiotes*). These Jewish customs and habits are not only circumcision, Sabbath observance, and the rejection of idolatry, but also education, food laws and sexual behaviour. Affiliation to Judaism is a question of lifestyle, which can be adopted, neglected or preserved. Thus non-Jews could become members of ancient Jewish communities by structuring their life in a Jewish manner, and Jews could lose their Jewish identity by abandoning their ancestral traditions. A famous example of this is Tiberius Julius Alexander, a nephew of Philo of Alexandria, who abandoned Jewish lifestyle in order to make a brilliant career for himself in the Roman army.[14]

In an article on apostasy, Barclay demonstrates that the boundary-maintenance of Judaism in a Hellenistic environment consisted of the preservation of a particular way of life.[15] Not only was idolatry viewed as alienation from ancestral beliefs, but also exogamy (since it endangered the preservation of Jewish lifestyle) and the violation of Jewish food laws. 4 Maccabees demonstrates a test case for abandoning ancestral laws (4:26) and adopting a Greek lifestyle (8:7f) in the attitude towards pork and food sacrificed for the idols (5:2).[16]

However, in the Gospel of John there is no evidence that conflict centres on those Jewish habits and customs, which were a stumbling block in Jewish–non-Jewish relations. The lack of such characteristics in contrast to their prominence in the Pauline epistles[17] and the Gospel of Matthew,[18] indicates that the conflict between the Johannine Christ and the *Ioudaioi* / 'The Jews' does not refer to an immediate social conflict between the Johannine community and the Jews of its environment. There are no traces of complicating factors in the conflict in the Fourth Gospel, for instance the question of food laws, circumcision, or religious practice, as in the other gospels or in the Pauline writings.

Considering the absence of features, which formed these conflicts, what can we say positively about the Johannine controversies? The absence of issues such as circumcision and food laws indicates that in John the conflict takes place on a rather abstract level, and that it represents a chapter in the history of Christian dogmatics rather than a chapter in the social history of early Christianity.

It is important to understand that the disputes in John are a literary genre (as described in chapter 8). The disputes are shaped as dialogues as illustrated by this ancient quotation: 'A dialogue is a conversation on a political or a philosophical topic, consisting of question and answer'.[19] In order to express his theological views, the author of the Fourth Gospel decided to create a fictitious dialogue, the literary genre par excellence of intellectual exchange in Antiquity. That means, that the narrator depicts the debates in John 7 and 8 not as a social, but as an ideological conflict. Thus, John 8 does not represent the type of Jewish–Christian conflict common for the first century; rather it is a prototype for Christian anti-Jewish or anti-Pagan apologetic, common in the 2nd–4th century C.E.[20]

3. Conclusion

1. By adopting this narrative strategy and following this theological argument, the Fourth Gospel offers a sophisticated interpretation of Jewish traditions. Contrary to what we find in other early Christian sources like the letters of Paul – i.e., a description of a social separation through a discussion of the status of circumcision, food laws and the Sabbath – the Gospel of John does not preserve a historical report on the so-called parting of the ways. In its carefully constructed literary framework we find story rather than history, fiction rather than description, an ideological rather than a social conflict. The Johannine controversy stories seem to belong to a later stage of the separation process, when early Christianity and Rabbinic Judaism formed two socially independent groups, interrelated and competing with each other on the basis of common traditions.

2. A narrative analysis of the passage demonstrates that the setting of John 7 and 8 is dominated by the Festival of Booths: all the scenes are located in the Temple area and coordinated according to the schedule of the festival rituals. Thus the author adapts his narrative's temporal and local structure to one of the pillars of ancient Jewish identity: the Jerusalem Temple tradition. In the course of the controversies, the author unfolds – both implicitly and explicitly – a discussion about other topics significant to the formation of Christian and Jewish religious identity, such as the Law, history of salvation and monotheism. In chapter 8, the conflict about the adequacy or inadequacy of Christian adoption of Jewish tradition finds its expression in disputes between Jesus and 'the Jews'/*Ioudaioi*. They have – and this is another Johannine particularity – the shape of dialogues, a popular genre in philosophical writings of the late classical period. The author draws a formal analogy to the style of intellectual discussions of his time. And by placing the Jewish–Christian controversies in this literary

context he expresses them as they have been seen in his eyes – as scholarly debates.[21]

3. The Gospel of John documents both a constant theological disagreement between Judaism and Christianity but also their enduring communal spirit and intricately entwined relationship. With regard to the paradoxical coincidence of anti-Jewish formula alongside Philo-Jewish statements, Wayne Meeks wrote: 'To put the matter sharply, with some risk of misunderstanding, the Fourth Gospel is most anti-Jewish just at the points it is most Jewish.'[22] What could be the reason for this paradox?

By following a dialogue style and integrating important elements of early Judaism, the narrator of the Fourth Gospel embarks on a dual strategy, similar to that of ancient Jewish apologetics vis-à-vis pagan philosophy: Initially he claims that the theology of the Fourth Gospel is the true interpretation of the Mosaic traditions and that the prophetic promises for Israel are fulfilled in the Johannine Jesus story. This claim was obviously challenged as we can see in the disputes of John 7 and 8 – and in the Jewish–Christian encounter of today. The Johannine narrative combined an exclusivism with an innovative inclusivism. The author expresses familiarity with intellectual and rhetoric standards of his time and consequently illustrates the compatibility of his theological views with their authoritative background as well as the biblical and Jewish traditions.

Notes

1. *Anabainein eis Ierosolyma* is the expression used in the Greek text, cf. John 2:13; 5:2.

2. John 2:13-3.21 – Passover; 5:1-47 – unnamed festival; 7.1-8.59 – Booths/*Sukkot*; 10:22-39 – *Hanukkah*; 12:22-20; 12:29 – Passover.

3. Another example can be found in John 6 which draws a parallel between the feeding of the 5000 and the manna miracle in Exodus 16.

4. The author has already made an analogy between Jesus and the Passover lamb in John 1:29: 'The next day he [John the Baptist] saw Jesus coming toward him and declared, "Here is the Lamb of God who takes away the sin of the world."'

5. 19:33: 'But when they came to Jesus and saw that he was already dead, they did not break his legs.'

6. 19:36: 'These things occurred so that the scripture might be fulfilled, "None of his bones shall be broken."'

7. Exodus 12:46 [Directions for the Preparation of Passover]: 'It shall be eaten in one house; you shall not take any of the animal outside the house, and you shall not break any of its bones.'

8. Another well-known example of a parallel montage is the duel scene in a 'Western': the arrangement of scenes often switches from protagonist to protagonist as they slowly move toward each other. In addition to the effect of suspense, the parallel montage creates the impression that the conflict is inevitable.

9. J Louis Martyn, *History and Theology in the Fourth Gospel* (Nashville: Abingdon, 1979 [first edition: 1968]).

10. Klaus Wengst, *Bedrängte Gemeinde und verherrlichter Christus. Ein Versuch über das Johannesevangelium* (München: Kaiser, 1992 [first edition: 1981]).

11. David Rensberger, *Johannine Faith and Liberating Community* (Philadelphia, Westminster, 1988).

12. John M.G. Barclay, *Jews in the Mediterranean Diaspora. From Alexander to Trajan (323 BCE – 117 CE)* (Edinburgh: Clark, 1996), p. 443.

13. Flavius Josephus, *Contra Apionem* 2.210.

14. Julius Tiberius Alexander was Roman procurator of Judaea (46–48 C.E.), and governor of Egypt (66–69 C.E.) when he suppressed a Jewish revolt. During the siege of Jerusalem (70 C.E.) Tiberius was chief of staff of the Roman legions under the command of Titus.

15. John M.G. Barclay, 'Who was considered an apostate?' in Graham N. Stanton, and Guy G. Stroumsa, (eds.), *Tolerance and Intolerance in Early Judaism and Christianity* (Cambridge: Cambridge University Press, 1998), pp. 80–98.

16. 4 Macc. 5:1–3: 'The tyrant Antiochus, sitting in state with his counselors on a certain high place, and with his armed soldiers standing around him, ordered the guards to seize each and every Hebrew and to compel them to eat pork and food sacrificed to idols. If any were not willing to eat defiling food, they were to be broken on the wheel and killed.'

17. Gal. 5:2–4: 'Listen! I, Paul, am telling you that if you let yourselves be circumcised, Christ will be of no benefit to you. Once again I testify to every man who lets himself be circumcised that he is obliged to obey the entire law. You who want to be justified by the law have cut yourselves off from Christ; you have fallen away from grace.'

18. Matt. 5:17–20: 'Do not think that I have come to abolish the law or the prophets; I have come not to abolish but to fulfill. For truly I tell you, until heaven and earth pass away, not one letter, not one stroke of a letter, will pass from the law until all is accomplished. Therefore, whoever breaks one of the least of these commandments, and teaches others to do the same, will be called least in the kingdom of heaven; but whoever does them and teaches them will be called great in the kingdom of heaven. For I tell you, unless your righteousness exceeds that of the scribes and Pharisees, you will never enter the kingdom of heaven.'

19. Diogenes Laertius (born first half 3rd century C.E.), *Lives of Eminent Philosophers* (Vitae Philosophorum) III.48.

20. The first preserved anti-Jewish apologetic dialogue is Justin Martyr's *Dialogue with Trypho*. Other anti-Jewish dialogues of this era are: Ariston of Pella, *Dialogue of Jason and Papiscos* (older than Justin's dialogue, but only a foreword of a translator is preserved); *Consultationes Zacchaei et Apollonii* (unknown author).

21. For a closer look on the interaction and competition between ancient religions, especially between early Judaism and non-Jewish religions, cf. P. W. Van der Horst, M.J.J. Menken, J.F.M. Smit, and G. Van Oyen, (eds.), *Persuasion and Dissuasion in Early Christianity, Ancient Judaism, and Hellenism, Contributions to Biblical Exegesis and Theology* 33 (Leuven: Peeters, 2003) and Jonathan Goldstein, *Peoples of an Almighty God: Competing Religions in the Ancient World* (New York: Doubleday, 2002).

22. Wayne A. Meeks, '"Am I a Jew?" Johannine Christianity and Judaism', in Jacob Neusner (ed.), *Christianity, Judaism, and Other Greco-Roman Cults. Studies for Morton Smith at Sixty: Vol. I. New Testament* (Leiden: Brill, 1975), pp. 163–185, 172.

4

Religious Intolerance and Toleration in the Middle Ages[1]

Marc Saperstein

I want to emphasize that I approach the contemporary Jewish-Christian dialogue not as a theologian but as a historian. I shall be speaking today not so much about what I consider to be the burning issues in the current relations between Christians and Jews, but rather about the baggage we bring with us in facing each other. Now I certainly believe that knowledge of the past is important; otherwise, I and my colleagues would be out of a job. Nevertheless, I believe that many Jews nurture an overly simplistic, almost mythic view of the history of Jews and Christians in the Middle Ages, and that the impact of this view on the present is not always beneficial. I therefore take it as my task to present a story rather different from the one that is so widely prevalent.

Ask most educated Jews – and many Christians as well – about their associations with the phrase 'Jewish life in Christian Europe during the Middle Ages', and they will paint an extremely bleak picture. The first word that comes to mind may well be 'intolerance', or 'persecution'. If pushed to exemplify, they might mention the Crusades: religious emotion raised to a peak and then spinning out of control, bands of warriors under the sign of the cross attacking Jewish communities in the Rhineland, giving a choice of baptism or death, killing thousands of Jewish men, women and children, producing a wave of Jewish martyrdom unprecedented in Europe.[2]

Or the charge of 'ritual murder', the outrageous accusation that Jews nefariously plotted to kidnap and kill Christian children, whether in a ritual re-enactment of the original torture and crucifixion of Jesus, or in order to use the blood of these children for their own purposes, including– incredibly – the preparation of *matzot* for Passover.[3]

Or the accusation that Jews schemed to get possession of the consecrated host, which Christians believed to have been transformed into the actual body of Christ, so that by stabbing the host they could once again inflict torture on the rejected messiah.[4]

Or the accusations that the Black Death, which devastated Europe in the mid-fourteenth century, leading to the loss of one third of the population in many areas, was caused by Jews who poisoned the wells of their cities, accusations that led to violent attacks against Jewish communities and many deaths in addition to those caused by the Plague itself.[5]

Or the Inquisitions established under papal or national auspices, those special courts that investigated and brought to trial men and women defined by the Church as Christians who were suspected of the heresy of 'Judaizing', namely, continuing after baptism to profess a Jewish belief or observe a Jewish practice. The image of Jews massacred under the sign of the cross, Jewish books or Jewish martyrs burned at the stake, retains significant power in the minds of many Jews.[6]

If one pushes them to go beyond the rubric of 'persecution', they may well think of 'disputation'. The spectacular public disputations of Paris and Barcelona and Tortosa, in which Jewish leaders were compelled to defend their faith against the attacks of Christian intellectuals in a contest where there was no chance of them winning. The ground-rules prevented the Jewish participant from attacking the Christian faith, and so the best they could hope for was to avoid the public perception that they had lost and humiliated their people. No Jews sought out such disputations, for they were well aware of the dangers if they appeared to be doing too well; some, reportedly, attended them with burial shrouds under their clothes.[7]

Beyond the public spectacles, there was a large polemical literature, which Jews felt constrained to write in every generation in order to defend their faith against the constant pressure by Christian intellectuals. The Hebrew word *almah* in Isaiah 7:14 did not mean 'virgin', and the context could not predict the birth of a messiah seven centuries in the future. There was no proof of a triune God in the Hebrew Scripture. The covenant with the Jewish people and its commandments had not been rescinded by God. The suffering and scattering of the Jewish people did not mean that God had abandoned them. The Messiah had not yet come.[8]

In addition to 'persecution' and 'disputation', many might think of the word 'isolation'. That unlike the Jews living in the Islamic world, who shared a literary and cultural language – Arabic – with their neighbors,

Jews and Christians in medieval Europe had no common culture, no common language of discourse. That Jews were physically isolated from Christians, forced to live in 'ghettos', cramped and dismal areas surrounded by walls, the gates locked every night.[9]

That Jews were compelled to wear something that would immediately identify them at a glance – a badge affixed to their clothing, a special kind of hat – a policy intended not only to identify but to isolate and humiliate them.[10]

That Jews were increasingly imagined to be allies of Satan, collaborators with the demonic forces of evil, engaged in a constant battle to subvert and destroy all that was sacred in medieval Christian Europe.[11]

Persecution, Disputation, Isolation, largely because of the Church and its 'teaching of contempt'. (Indeed, the Vatican document on the 'sins of the past' issued in the spring of 2000 mentioned some of these themes, including the Crusades, forced conversions, and the Inquisition.) Let it be clear: I am not suggesting that the image of Jewish life based on these negative components of our collective memory is a myth with no basis in fact. There is truth in all that I have mentioned above, though these issues are commonly misunderstood, and many are unaware of basic historical data, for example, that the 'ghetto' was formally imposed only in the sixteenth century, or that the Inquisition had jurisdiction not over Jews but only over Christians (the rampant misconception can lead at times to the absurdity of the scene in a Mel Brooks movie called *History of the World, Part I* (1981), depicting Jews in Hasidic dress being burned at the stake by the Spanish Inquisition).

For years, along with a number of my colleagues, I have been arguing that this image – what the great historian Salo W. Baron dubbed the 'lachrymose conception of Jewish history' as a series of unending persecutions by Christians[12]– is not the entire story. If it were, it would be impossible to understand how Jewish communities were able to survive for more than 1000 years under Christian rulers, who had the power to destroy them completely if they had so chosen. And how they were able not only to survive but in many cases to flourish, to prosper, to produce important works of scholarship and culture.[13]

I would like, therefore, to raise with you a different question. Not why was there so much intolerance, violence and persecution. That model of inter-group relations is characteristic not only of the Middle Ages but of our own, much more 'enlightened' era as well, as we are all too painfully reminded by the breaking news.[14] Rather, I would like to explore whether the concept of religious toleration is at all applicable to the medieval context.

Well certainly not in the modern, post-Enlightenment sense.[15] This was not tolerance based on ideas of the inviolable freedom of the individual conscience. It was not rooted in the claim that the state had no right to interfere in the private beliefs of the individual living under its jurisdiction, that those in a position of power were not entitled to use force in order to compel a uniformity of faith or to discriminate against those who held a minority belief, that the state and the church were entirely independent realms which should not interfere with each other. It was not derived from the argument that human beings by their very nature have no access to ultimate truth, and therefore have no grounds for even claiming possession of such truth, let alone imposing its acceptance upon dissenters. It was certainly not justified by the assertion that there is an inherent value in diversity, in multi-culturalism, in a rainbow coalition of alternative approaches to God. All of these ideas, which seem to many so self-evident today, are the legacy of the post-Reformation Enlightenment; they are anachronistic for the Middle Ages. If we are to understand that period, we must not judge the relations between Christians and Jews by the standards of contemporary 'political correctness' thinking.

If, however, we try to apply the term 'tolerance' to the relations between Christians and Jews in a medieval context, I believe that it is appropriate to employ the term and the concept.[16] In other words, in assessing medieval Church policy regarding the Jews, we should not condemn and dismiss it because it does not measure up to the discourse of *Nostra Aetate* and subsequent Vatican statements. Rather, we must look at the realistic, plausible alternatives at the time we are examining. It is clear, for example, that the Church historically did not hold a doctrine of toleration toward dissent within its own ranks. Once a theological position had been formally established by the leadership of the Church, all Christians were expected to respond, Credo. Those who refused were defined as heretics, and Church doctrine, first articulated by St. Augustine, justified the use of force to compel the heretic to abandon false belief and adhere to the saving truth. The entire sordid history of the various Inquisitions is based on this principle.

In dramatic contrast, the same Augustine developed a theological and exegetical rationale for the continued existence of the Jewish people in a

Christian empire. He insisted that it was in accordance with God's will for the Jewish people to live among Christians and continue to observe their distinctive religious traditions. He insisted that it was a violation of God's will for Christians to kill Jews, or to attack them violently.[17] The actual arguments that led to these conclusions need not detain us here; I will stipulate that they reveal little if any appreciation of anything positive in the Jewish religion or any indication of a love for the Jewish people. But we should not be overly concerned with the negative language about Jews and Judaism; what medieval Jews thought crucial were the positive conclusions.[18]

The same theologian who justified the use of force against pious Christians who dissented from the tiniest nuance in the understanding of the Trinity or the Incarnation ratified by a Church Council, perhaps somewhat paradoxically prohibited the use of force against the Jews, who repudiated the Trinity and the Incarnation with disdain, and who figured in Christian collective memory as the Christ-killers and murderers of the first Christian martyrs.[19] The Church launched Crusades against Muslims, against pagans, and even against Christian 'heretics'; it never launched a Crusade against the Jews.[20]

This doctrine of medieval toleration for Jews was accepted and re-asserted by the leaders of the Church throughout the centuries. To take just one example, when Christian mobs in panic over the devastation of the Black Death in 1348 began to attack Jewish communities, Pope Clement VI issued a bull, citing ten predecessors, which said unambiguously, 'Let no Christian dare to harm or kill these Jews.' (This papal precedent and tradition, it seems to me, provides the strongest foundation for questioning Pope Pius XII's failure to say publicly what Clement VI did: 'Let no Christian dare to kill Jews').[21]

There were, to be sure, ground-rules for this protection. One was that Jews were not supposed to speak blasphemy against the sancta of Christian faith; we will return to this later. Another was that they were not supposed to flourish or prosper too much; they were to live under conditions that would demonstrate that they were a reprobate people, condemned to suffer by God for their sin of rejecting the Messiah when he came. The same popes who insisted that the Jews must be protected from violence, and that they should not be compelled to accept baptism, also intervened when kings or nobles allowed the Jews in their realm to prosper.[22] While the Jewish community of Rome is the one great European community that never experienced an expulsion, tracing an unbroken presence back to ancient times, some of the popes who had political authority over Rome subjected its Jews to humiliating conditions, well into the nineteenth century.[23]

Furthermore, it should come as no surprise that Christians did not always follow the official teachings of the Church about violence (to be honest, not all medieval Jews lived every moment in accordance with every teaching of their rabbis). The massacres and forced conversions perpetrated by one of the crusading armies in the Rhineland in 1096 is a notorious example of behavior that spun out of control in violation of Church doctrine. Kings, opposed to violence against Jews for other, non-theological reasons, did not take the Church doctrine to imply that they were obligated to allow Jews to remain on their soil, and Jews were expelled en masse from England, France, and Spain. Yet within the medieval context, by contrast with the position taken toward heretics and pagans, I believe it is justified to conclude that the official doctrine of the Church toward the Jewish people and the Jewish religion deserves to be understood as a doctrine of tolerance.[24]

So much for the Christian view. What was the Jewish understanding of Christian toleration? Here, of course, I am generalizing, for there was no official leadership of European Jewry to formulate a response. Yet it seems clear that medieval Jews accepted their status under the doctrine of the Church as compatible with their own understanding of the nature of Jewish life in exile. As far as we know, no medieval Jews claimed that there was something inherently wrong with being consigned to what we would consider a second-class status – especially since they were well aware of serfs and peasants who lived under legal conditions and at a standard of living inferior to their own. When – responding to a shifting balance of economic and political forces – kings decided to expel their Jewish communities, the Jews mobilized their economic resources and political allies to try to convince the king that it would be in his interest to reverse the decision, but they never challenged the king's right to expel them.[25] They knew that they lived where they did not as a matter of innate right but at the discretion, the pleasure, of the king.

On the other hand, when zealous Christians forced Jews to the baptismal font, the Jews knew this was wrong and protested. Local Jewish leaders prevailed upon Jews in Rome to go directly to the top, and the result, in the case of Pope Gregory I, was an unambiguous official papal condemnation of this practice.[26] Jews expected the kings to protect them, to punish those responsible not only for murder but for incitement to violence, and this expectation was generally fulfilled. In short, on the whole, medieval Jews understood that their rival religion, the religion of power in Europe, had a doctrine that would make it possible for them to live among Christians—not a guarantee that they would be permitted to remain where their ancestors had lived and died, not a basis for acceptance as equals, but a doctrine of toleration.

In the thirteenth century, as the Church and Christian society became more intolerant of all deviant groups,[27] this doctrine was tested by new developments on two fronts, and I would like to review these episodes briefly and assess the Jewish responses to them. The first was the campaign against the Talmud, that small library of treatises produced in Babylonia that, together with the Bible, became the foundational text of medieval Jewish life. In the thirteenth century, Jewish converts to Christianity began to lodge formal complaints about the Talmud: that it contained theological absurdities about God (an internal problem of Jewish thought as well), that it contained hostile and hate-filled statements about Gentiles, and – most dangerous – that it contained blasphemous assertions about Jesus and Mary – as Pope Gregory IX put it, 'matter so abusive and so unspeakable that it arouses shame in those who mention it and horror in those who hear it.'[28]

A further accusation pertained not just to the specific content of the Talmud but to its general character. Judaism was tolerated as the religion of the Old Testament, but now it became known that Jews viewed this other, newer text as also revealed by God and having even higher status than the Bible itself, for sometimes Jews ignore the Bible completely and follow what the Talmud states. Pope Gregory IX therefore ordered that all copies of the Talmud be seized by the 'secular arm' and investigated by the representatives of the Church to see whether it should be tolerated. In France under Louis IX, the order was enforced, and – after a public investigation where Jewish leaders tried to defend it – all known copies of the Talmud were consigned to the flames.

But that was not the end of the story. To be sure, the Jewish response, at the Disputation of Paris, addressed the specific passages at issue. The Gentiles mentioned in the Talmud were idolaters of antiquity; you contemporary Christians are not included. The Jesus and Mary in the Talmud were not the Jesus and Mary you worship, but other individuals with the same names who lived several generations earlier. But Jews also raised the large issue of toleration. We see evidence of this in a 1247 letter by Gregory's successor, Pope Innocent IV, a fascinating passage well worth citing:

> When, therefore, the Jewish masters of your kingdom recently asserted before us and our brothers that, without the book which in Hebrew is called 'Talmud,' they cannot understand the Bible, and their other statutes and laws in accordance with their faith, we then, bound as we are by the divine command to tolerate them in their law, thought fit to have the answer given them that we do not want to deprive them of their books if as a result we should be depriving them of their law.[29]

Here is a kind of syllogism, its two premises taken from two different theological traditions. First, the claim that the Talmud, the 'oral law,' is absolutely essential for a proper understanding of the Bible, especially the legal components of the Bible that govern Jewish behavior. This is a familiar Jewish claim used internally against the Karaites, who repudiated the idea of an 'oral law' and rejected the authoritative character of the Talmud that embodied it. Second, the claim that divine command binds the Church to tolerate the Jews in their law – a premise from Christian theology. Ergo, the Church must not deprive the Jews of the Talmud. The result was therefore a practical compromise: the Talmud was to be investigated, blasphemous passages were to be removed – and Jewish scribes began indeed to alter or eliminate them – but the Talmud as a whole was to be allowed. Toleration of the Jews entailed toleration of the Talmud.

If the Talmud was the intellectual foundation of medieval Jewish life in Christian Europe, moneylending was its economic foundation. The story is all too familiar in its general contours: Jews – who in the early Middle Ages had owned land and participated in agriculture, especially the production of grapes and wine – forced off the land by the feudal system with its religious oath of fealty, crowded out of the artisans' crafts by guilds that were religiously exclusive, pressured into the role of providing credit on interest, a function that was essential for a newly invigorated economy yet prohibited to Christians by canon law. The Church recognized that it had no jurisdiction to prohibit Jews from this economic activity, yet it saw that the flow of capital from Christian debtors to Jewish creditors seemed to violate the ground rules of toleration.[30]

Many kings encouraged this enterprise not only because it provided capital for economic enterprise but also because it provided a ready source for their sometimes confiscatory taxation.[31] Yet they were also sensitive to the resentment of their subjects who were happy to have money loaned to them but unhappy to have to pay it back with compound interest. Once again, Louis IX, 'St. Louis', the most anti-Jewish monarch of the thirteenth century, took the lead in a campaign to prohibit not only excessive interest, but interest in general, a measure that would have made Jewish life in France all but impossible.

Jews recognized this as something new, a violation of precedent, a challenge to the toleration they had come to expect. One of the most interesting responses was a Hebrew text written in southern France, addressed to the king. Again, I will cite a key passage:

> It would be better for the king to allow the sin of usury on the part of the Jews, who are not of his faith and whom he has no obligation to force into his faith, rather than to bring [spiritual] death to men of his faith by causing them to transgress in public. For if he were to order an investigation throughout his kingdom he would find that from the time he forbade usury to the Jews, many members of his faith, the Christians, have become usurers far harsher than the Jews.... For it is *impossible for society to exist* without lending. Indeed the king himself, whose wealth is very great, has been forced to borrow at high interest a number of times.... Therefore, it would be better for the salvation of the king's soul that he permit the Jews to lend at usury ... rather than causing Christians to transgress their faith, since ... the sins which they commit because of him are attached to his soul.[32]

Let us unpack this curious yet compelling mixture of theology and economics. The economic argument is straightforward: no society beyond a rudimentary level of economic sophistication can survive without credit.[33] If Jews are prohibited from lending money on interest, economic pressures and opportunities will drive Christians to do so. Furthermore, because the constraints of a tolerated minority do not apply to them, the Christians will drive a harder bargain than do the Jewish creditors.[34] Then comes the theological claim: the Christian king has an obligation to care for the eternal salvation of the souls of his Christian subjects, but only to protect the bodies of his Jewish subjects. From the Christian perspective, usury is a sin. To prohibit Jews from lending money is to drive Christians into this enterprise, to cause them to sin,[35] to endanger their salvation, and – somewhat audaciously – thereby to risk the salvation of the king's own soul. In short, better to allow the Jews to do this dirty work than force the Christians to do so.

We have no record that this letter ever arrived at the court of Louis IX. Yet in one of the medieval biographies of this king, we find the very same argument placed in the mouth of his advisors:

> The Jews, odious to God and men, he detested so much that he was unable to look upon them. . . . He wished that they not practice usury, but rather that they earn their food by labor or by proper commerce, as used to be done in other areas. Many of his counselors advised him to the contrary, claiming that, without lending, the populace could not exist nor the land be cultivated nor labor and commerce be pursued. They said that it was better and more tolerable that the Jews, who were damned already, exercise this function of damnation, rather than Christians, who under these circumstances oppress the populace with heavier usury.

This good Catholic responded to these contentions:

> The matter of Christian usurers and their usury seems to pertain to the prelates of the Church. The matter of the Jews, who are subjected to me by the yoke of servitude, pertains to me, lest they oppress Christians by their usury and lest, under the shelter of my protection, they be permitted to do this and to infect my land with their poison. Let those prelates do what devolves upon them concerning their subject Christians. I wish to do what pertains to me concerning the Jews. Let them abandon usury, or let them leave my land completely.[36]

The king in this passage does not contest the economic argument, that credit and therefore loans on interest is necessary for society, and that if Jews are prohibited from this enterprise Christians will take their place, perhaps even more harshly. What he rejects is the theological argument that he is responsible for the souls of his Christian subjects. That, he says, is the concern of the prelates of the Church. His responsibility is for the behavior of the Jews. If Christians economically oppress other Christians at risk to their own salvation, that is for the Church to address. If Jews oppress Christians, that is the king's business. He does not repudiate the principle of toleration, as he proposes an alternative model of Jewish economic behavior (to 'earn their food by labor'). But he defines Jewish usury as a violation of one of the ground rules of toleration, where the Jewish writer presented it as one of the strongest arguments in its favor.

We have been speaking to this point about toleration by Christians and the Jewish understanding of this doctrine. I now turn briefly to the question of tolerance for diversity within the Jewish community. How does this compare with their Christian neighbors? Once again to generalize: on the whole, to the extent that the Jewish community was able to exercise control over its members, it tended to do so more in the realm of behavior than in the realm of belief. A medieval Jew would get into real trouble with his own community if he tried to open his market stall on Shabbat, or ate pork in public, or failed to have his baby son circumcised. So long as his behavior was according to community standards, his theology was generally not a matter of concern.

A Jew who believed naively in the anthropomorphisms of Biblical and Talmudic language about God could stand in the synagogue next to a sophisticated philosopher whose God was pure spirit, pure intellect, and on the other side of him a Kabbalistic mystic for whom divinity was a dynamic plurality-within-unity, constantly changing in response to stimuli from human actions on earth – and all three of them could say the same words of the liturgy from beginning to end. I doubt that such theological diversity in a single church existed in medieval Christendom.

There were times when Jewish leaders tried to draw boundary lines and declare that certain views were beyond the pale. The Karaite rejection of the oral law was an obvious example, and Karaites became a separate community. Other efforts by some to ban specific books or beliefs were notoriously unsuccessful. The instrument of the herem or ban could be brutally effective when it was exercised by a cohesive community against an individual, such as Uriel da Costa or Baruch de Espinosa in seventeenth-century Amsterdam. But the ban in the 1230s of the philosophical texts written by Moses Maimonides was a fiasco; it may have set a precedent for involving the Mendicant friars in an investigation of Jewish 'heresy', and it was denounced by the supporters of Maimonides as the cause for the burning of the Talmud a few years later.[37] When in 1305 a ban was proclaimed by the leading rabbinic authority in Barcelona against the study of non-Jewish (Greek and Arabic) texts by anyone less than 25 years old, its provisions were simply ignored by its opponents.[38]

Yet these issues were debated on the substance of the doctrines in question – is philosophy harmful to Judaism or helpful? are philosophical doctrines about the nature of God or creation inconsistent with Scripture? – not on the principle of freedom of inquiry. It is rather sobering to discover that the rabbinic scholar who promulgated the ban in Barcelona, Rabbi Solomon ben Adret (RaSHBA), speaking of the danger of heretical philosophical ideas being spread by preachers in their sermons, actually invoked the papal Inquisition as a model of how to respond:

> Observe how the Gentiles punish their heretics, even for a single one of such heresies as these men expressed in their books. Why, if anyone [i.e., any Christian] would dare say that Abraham and Sarah represented matter and form, they would wrap him up in twigs and burn him into cinders.[39]

Perhaps aware of the condemnation of Aristotelian and Averroist doctrines in Paris a generation earlier, he insists that they – the Christians – would never tolerate this kind of theological sedition, and we should not either.[40] This was a kind of competition and emulation between the two communities that does not seem especially edifying.

Not until the late-sixteenth century do we find a Jewish defence of intellectual openness and pluralism in principle. This was written by Rabbi Leib ben Bezalel, the MaHaRaL of Prague, printed in 1598:

> It is wrong to disqualify any matter that is opposed to one's view when expressed for the sake of enquiry and knowledge; especially if the author did not intend to be provocative, but merely to voice his conviction. Even if such words run counter to the belief and religion of the one who is in power, it is wrong for him to say to the other, 'Do not speak, hold your tongue.' For if this were to be done, there could be no investigation of religion. Rather, the one in power should declare, 'Say whatever you wish, . . . and do not say, 'If only it were possible for me to speak, I could say more.' Whoever seals the other's mouth and prevents him from speaking only betrays the weakness of his own religion. . . . The philosophers, in line with their enquiries, have insidiously and falsely maintained that the universe was uncreated. . . . Nevertheless their books are being consulted. . . . For it is necessary for the determination of the truth to listen to the arguments that they put forward.[41]

This moving and impressive statement may remind us of Milton's celebrated 'Areopagitica', written two generations later. Prof. Hayim Hillel Ben-Sasson described it as 'one of the earliest and most fundamental declarations opposing the institution of the ecclesiastical censorship of the press.'[42] Unfortunately, following the debacle of the movement proclaiming that Sabbatai Zevi was the messiah, the Jewish community went through a period of contraction, suspicion of the innovative, an energetic pursuit of heretical doctrine in the writings of some of the most respected rabbis.[43] New books could not be published without the imprimatur of well-known sages. There were attempts to excommunicate adherents of the new movement of Hasidism in the eighteenth century, the first Reform synagogue of Britain in the nineteenth, Rabbi Mordecai Kaplan in the twentieth. The road between the Maharal's clarion defence of openness to alternative viewpoints and the present is not direct. While never in a position to establish a formal Inquisition, Jews also have had to struggle to establish the freedom of inquiry and expression, even within their own communities – as the current furor over the defence of religious pluralism by the Chief Rabbi reminds us.[44]

I would like to conclude with a statement of Rabbi Hugo Gryn, printed near the end of his extraordinary memoir (so beautifully edited by his daughter, Naomi), drawn from his experience as a victim of the horrors of Nazi persecution: 'That I spend much of my time working for better understanding between religious groups and fighting racism as hard as I can is partly because I know that you can only be safe and secure in a society that practises tolerance, cherishes harmony and can celebrate difference.'[45] (Parenthetically, I would suggest that a good part of the Chief Rabbi's new book, *The Dignity of Difference*, can be viewed as a midrash or expansion of this one sentence.)

The terrorist bombings in the United States, Israel and Bali that have targeted ordinary civilians for destruction because they were different from the bombers, because they represented a culture, a society, a political system built upon different values, remind us with excruciating agony that it is not always obvious how much progress we have made since the medieval order. At times like this that can be so discouraging, it is important to remember a man like Rabbi Hugo Gryn, who – having experienced and witnessed at first hand the inferno to which fanatical intolerance can lead – could devote his life not to the pursuit of revenge, but to building a society 'that practises tolerance, cherishes harmony and can celebrate difference.' Not that these values can guarantee a world of peace. But surely they are our best hope.

Notes

1. This paper was originally presented as the 2002 Alma Royalton Kisch lecture, during Professor Saperstein's time as Hugo Gryn Visiting Fellow in Religious Tolerance at the Centre for the Study of Jewish-Christian Relations, Cambridge. In the introduction to his lecture, Professor Saperstein spoke of his sense of privilege at being able to pay tribute to the late Hugo Gryn, who had been a friend of his parents, and had welcomed him into his home when Professor Saperstein was studying in Cambridge in the 1960s.

2. See 'Bibliographical Additions' in Jacob Marcus, *The Jew in the Medieval World*, revised edition with introduction and updated bibliography by Marc Saperstein (Cincinnati: HUC Press, 1999), p. 134; David Malkiel, 'Destruction or Conversion? Intention and reaction, Crusades and Jews, in 1096', *Jewish History* 15 (2001), pp. 257-80; Jeremy Cohen, 'A 1096 Complex? Constructing the First Crusade in Jewish Historical Memory, Medieval and Modern', in Michael A. Signer and John Ban Engen, eds., *Jews and Christians in Twelfth-Century Europe* (Notre Dame: Notre Dame University Press, 2001), pp. 9-26. (The 'Bibliographical Additions' include references to scholarship in English since Marcus's original bibliographies of 1937, and I will include reference to these bibliographies where relevant.)

3. See 'Bibliographical Additions' in Marcus, p. 141, and R. Po-Chia Hsia, *The Myth of Ritual Murder: Jews and Magic in Reformation Germany* (New Haven: Yale University Press, 1988), and *Trent 1475: Stories of a Ritual Murder Trial* (New Haven: Yale University Press, 1992).

4. See 'Bibliographical Additions' in Marcus, p. 177.

5. See 'Bibliographical Additions' in Marcus, p. 55.

6. See 'Bibliographical Additions' in Marcus, p. 201.

7. On these disputations, see (for the Disputation of Paris) 'Bibliographical Additions' in Marcus, p. 168; Robert Chazan, *Barcelona and Beyond: The Disputation of 1263 and Its Aftermath* (Berkeley: University of California Press, 1992); Hyam Maccoby, 'The Tortosa Disputation, 1413-1414, and Its Effects', in *The Expulsion of the Jews and Their Emigration to the Southern Low Countries (Fifteenth-Sixteenth Centuries)*, ed. by Luc Dequeker

and Werner Verbeker (Leuven: Leuven University Press, 1998), pp. 23-34.

8. On polemical literature, see David Berger, *The Jewish-Christian Debate in the High Middle Ages* (Phildelphia: JPS, 1979); Hanne Trautner-Kromann, *Shield and Sword: Jewish Polemics Against Christianity and the Christians in France and Spain from 1100-1500* (Tübingen: J. C. B. Mohr, 1993); Anna Sapir Abulafia, *Chrisitans and Jews in Dispute: Disputational Literature and the Rise of Anti-Judaism in the West (c. 1000-1150)* (Brookfield, Vt.: Ashgate, 1998).

9. On the first ghettos, see Benjamin Ravid, 'New Light on the Ghetti of Venice', in *Shlomo Simonsohn Jubilee Volume* (Tel Aviv: Tel Aviv University, 1993), pp. 149-76; idem, 'From Geographical Realia to Historiographical Symbol: The Odyssey of the Word Ghetto', and Kenneth R. Stow, 'The Consciousness of Closure: Roman Jewry and Its Ghet', both in *Essential Papers on Jewish Culture in Renaissance and Baroque Italy*, ed. David B. Ruderman (New York: NYU Press, 1992), pp. 373-400.

10. On enforced distinctive Jewish dress, see the relevant 'Bibliographical Additions' in Marcus', p. 158.

11. The classic treatment of this theme is Joshua Trachtenberg, *The Devil and the Jews*, with new Foreword by Marc Saperstein (Philadelphia: JPS, 1983). See also Robert Bonfil, 'The Devil and the Jews in the Christian Consciousness of the Middle Ages', in *Antisemitism Through the Ages*, ed. by Shmuel Almog (Oxford: Pergamon Press, 1988), pp. 91-125.

12. For a summary of an alternative view, see my *Moments of Crisis in Jewish-Christian Relations* (London and Philadelphia: SCM-Trinity Press, International, 1989), and 'Christians and Jews: Some Positive Images', *Harvard Theological Review* 79 (1986), pp. 236-46, reprinted in my '*Your Voice Like a Ram's Horn*' (Cincinnati: HUC Press, 1996), pp. 45-54. For Baron's formulation, see his *History and Jewish Historians* (Philadelphia: JPS, 1964), pp. 84, 96, and frequently elsewhere in his work.

13. Compare, most recently, the challenge to the lachrymose conception as formulated by Ivan Marcus, 'A Jewish Symbiosis,' in *Cultures of the Jews*, ed. David Biale (New York: Schocken, 2002), pp. 450–52. Cf. also Joseph Shatzmiller, *Shylock Reconsidered: Jews, Moneylending, and Medieval Society* (Berkeley: University of California Press, 1990), p. 123.

14. A reference in the oral address to the terrorist bombing in Bali, October 12, 2002.

15. The key texts in this regard are Spinoza's *Theological-Political Treatise* and Locke's *Letter Concerning Toleration*. See, for the latter, John Locke, *Political Writings*, edited with an introduction by David Wootton (New York:

Mentor, 1993), and (appearing after the lecture), Perez Zagorin, *How the Idea of Religious Toleration Came to the West* (Princeton: Princeton University Press, 2003), esp. pp. 179-87 (on Spinoza) and pp. 256-88 (on Locke and Pierre Bayle).

16. In the discussion following the oral address, there was a challenge to my terminology based on an understanding of the word 'toleration' as simply putting up with something one does not approve of, while 'tolerance' implies a commitment to the value of diversity. In that sense, there would be little, if any, 'tolerance' in the Middle Ages. In accordance with general American usage, I employ the two terms in relation to the pre-Enlightenment period interchangeably. Cf. the recent book, *Beyond the Persecuting Society: Religious Toleration Before the Enlightenment*, ed. by John Christian Laursen and Cary J. Nederman (Philadelphia: University of Pennsylvania Press, 1998), where 'Toleration' appears in ten chapter titles and 'Tolerance' in three, but without any attempt to distinguish between them. Similarly, no such linguistic distinction is made in the book by Perez Zagorin on 'the idea of religious toleration' (n. 15).

17. On Augustine's doctrine, see the recent discussion by Jeremy Cohen, *Living Letters of the Law: Ideas of the Jew in Medieval Christianity* (Berkeley: University of California Press, 1999), pp. 23-65.

18. The central justification is that Jews should be preserved because they serve as witnesses (against their will, as it were) to the truth of Christian faith. The importance of rationale or motivation came up in the discussion. I argued that for Jews living in a medieval Christian realm, it was not crucial how the doctrine that Jews were not to be physically attacked was rationalized, but only whether it was accepted and enforced. Rabbi Julian Sinclair, Jewish Chaplain at the University of Cambridge, who had challenged my position on this issue, then suggested an analogy in Jewish law, which holds that it is not permissible to violate the Sabbath in order to save the life of a Gentile who has fallen into a pit. Rabbinic authorities did permit this, however, *mipnei darkhei shalom*: in order to promote peaceful relations between Jews and their neighbors. While one might theoretically imagine a knowledgeable Gentile down in the pit shouting up to his potential Jewish rescuer, 'I don't want you to save me for that pragmatic reason, I only want you to save me because you recognize that I am a human being whose life is every bit as important as yours is,' we concluded that this distinction would probably not weigh very heavily on the person in danger.

19. Perhaps the greatest medieval Pope, Innocent III, near the beginning of his papacy, issued a strong reaffirmation of the principle that Jews must be protected from violence; a few years later (1199, *Vergentis in senium*) he issued the strongest condemnation of Christian heretics to date, asserting that they were guilty not just of a sin but of a crime against Christian society, like traitors guilty of treason against the state, whose lives were forfeit; see Beverly Mayne Kienzle, *Cistercians, Heresy, and Crusade in Occitania, 1145-1229* (Rochester: New York Medieval Press, 2001), pp. 52-53. Under his leadership, the Albigensian Crusade against heretics in the south of France was begun, including a massacre of some 20,000 Christians ('heretics' and orthodox, without differentiation) in Beziers.

20. By this I mean that the call to the First Crusade by Pope Urban II contained no anti-Jewish element, the largest armies passed through the Rhineland without incident, and the Christians who attacked and killed Jews did so without the sanction of the Church and against its own doctrine. For a papal text explaining why it was permissible to go to war against Muslims in Spain but not to kill Jews, see Robert Chazan, *Church, State and Jew in the Middle Ages* (New York: Behrman House, 1980), pp. 99-100.

21. On Clement and the Black Death, see 'Bibliographical Additions' in Marcus, p. 55.

22. See, for example, the fascinating letters from Pope Innocent III to King Philip Augustus of France and to the Count of Nevers, in Solomon Grayzel, *The Church and the Jews in the XIIIth Century*, revised edition (New York: Hermon Press, 1966), pp. 105-9 and 127-31.

23. See on nineteenth-century material on policy in the territory under papal jurisdiction, brought by David Kertzer, *The Popes Against the Jews* (New York: Alfred A. Knopf, 2001), especially Part One.

24. See, for example, the fascinating letters from Pope Innocent III to King Philip Augustus of France and to the Count of Nevers, in Solomon Grayzel, *The Church and the Jews in the XIIIth Century, revised edition* (New York: Hermon Press, 1966), pp. 105-9 and 127-31.

25. Jews in the generation of the Expulsion seem to have understood the logic expressed in the Edict of Expulsion and even endorsed the principle that it was the duty of the Christian monarch to impose religious uniformity in his realm. See Haim Hillel Ben Sasson, 'Dor Gerush Sefarad al 'Atsmo'', *Zion* 26 (1961), pp. 53, 59; Yosef Kaplan, 'Political Concepts in the world of the Portuguese Jews of Amsterdam During the Seventeenth

Century', in Kaplan, H. Mechoulan and R. H. Popkin, eds. *Menasseh ben Israel and His World* (Leiden: Brill, 1989), pp. 49–50.

26. See Marcus, *The Jew in the Medieval World*, pp. 124-25.

27. See the now classic though brief and not uncontested treatment by R. I. Moore, *The Formation of a Persecuting Society* (Oxford: Blackmore, 1987).

28. Grayzel, *Church and Jews*, p. 241; Robert Chazan, *Church, State and Jew*, pp. 222, 223. See the 'Bibliographical Additions' in Marcus, p. 168.

29. Grayzel, *Church and Jews*, p. 275.

30. A decree of the Fourth Lateran Council began, 'The more the Christian religion is restrained in the exaction of interest, the more does Jewish in this matter increase, so that in a short time they exhaust the wealth of Christians' (Marcus, *The Jew in the Medieval World*, p. 153; Chazan, *Church, State, and Jew*, p. 198 [slightly different translations]).

31. Indeed, many authors have employed the image of the Jews as a sponge used by the medieval kings to soak up free capital in the economy; the kings would then squeeze the sponge through taxation so that much of the money ended up in the royal treasury, while the resentment of the population was directed against the creditors, the Jews. One of the first was the Dutch jurist Hugo Grotius; see the passage cited by Ralph Melnick, *From Polemics to Apologetics: Jewish-Christian Rapprochmenet in 17th-Century Amsterdam* (Assen: van Gorcum, 1981), p. 14. Note also Lester K. Little's more psychological conceptualization of the economic role played by medieval Jews: 'the main function of the Jews in the Commercial Revolution was to bear the burden of Christian guilt for participation in activities not yet deemed morally worthy of Christians.' Little, *Religious Poverty and the Profit Economy in Medieval Europe* (Ithaca: Cornell University Press, 1978), p. 56.

32. Chazan, *Church, State, and Jew*, p. 199 (my italics). For a fuller discussion of this fascinating text, see Chazan, 'A Jewish Plaint to Saint Louis', *HUCA* 45 (1974), pp. 287-305.

33. Cf. the discussion of the premise by Shatzmiller, *Shylock Reconsidered*, pp. 79-84.

34. We find this assertion made by St. Bernard: 'I will not mention those Christian moneylenders, if they can be called Christians, who, where there are no Jews, act, I grieve to say, in a manner worse than any Jew.' See S. W. Baron, *A Social and Religious History of the Jews, vol. 4* (Philadelphia: JPS, 1957), p. 121 and p. 301 n. 42 on the novel use in this passage of the

verb 'judaizare' ('to Judaize,' or perhaps equivalent to the verb 'to jew') as a synonym for improperly extorting money); Chazan, *Church, State, and Jew*, p. 103; Cohen, *Living Letters of the Law*, pp. 224-25. Shatzmiller presents archival evidence of Christians in need of credit who preferred Jewish to Christian moneylenders, not only for the religious consideration noted below, but because they found they could get a better deal from the Jews: *Shylock Reconsidered*, pp. 97-98.

35. As Chazan notes (*HUCA* article, p. 297, n. 37), in addition to the sins of the Christian moneylenders, some Christian thinkers held that it was more sinful for Christians to pay usury to a fellow Christian than to a Jew; cf. also Shatzmiller, *Shylock Reconsidered*, p. 95.

36. Chazan, *Church, State, and Jew*, p. 217.

37. See the review of the events in Yitzhak Baer, *A History of the Jews in Christian Europe. Vol 1*. (Philadelphia: JPS, 1961-1966), pp. 96-110, and Daniel J. Silver, *Maimonidean Criticism and the Maimonidean Controversy, 1180-1240* (Leiden, E.J. Brill, 1965).

38. On this conflict, see 'Bibliographical Additions' in Marcus, p. 217.

39. Yitzhak Baer, *A History of the Jews in Christian Europe. Vol. 1* (Philadelphia: JPS, 1961), p. 295.

40. On March 7, 1277, the Bishop of Paris issued a decree condemning 219 philosophical and theological errors that he claimed were espoused by faculty of the University of Paris, and excommunicated all who taught and who listened to such errors. One scholar characterizes this as 'the most serious censure of the Middle Ages,' which had 'far-reaching repercussions on the movement of ideas.' F. van Steenberghen, *Aristotle in the West: The Origins of Latin Aristotelianism* (Louvain: Nauwelaerts Publishing House, 1970), p. 235.

41. Hayim Hillel Ben Sasson, 'The Reformation in Contemporary Jewish Eyes', *Proceedings of the Israel Academy of Sciences and Humanities* 4.12 (1970), pp. 310-11 [72-73].

42. Ben Sasson, 'The Reformation in Contemporary Jewish Eyes', p. 311 [73]. Ironically, Maharal of Prague was himself involved in efforts to ban Azariah de' Rossi's Me'or Einayim. It is not clear to what extent he would apply this principle to freedom of expression within the Jewish community itself, as distinct from the government's suppression of Jewish opinions.

43. Admirably documented by Elisheva Carlebach, *Pursuit of Heresy Rabbi Moses Hagiz and the Sabbatian Controversies* (New York: Columbia

University Press, 1990).

44. Referring to the controversy in October 2002, when the lecture was given, over the newly published book by Rabbi Jonathan Sacks entitled, *The Dignity of Difference: How To Avoid the Clash of Civilisations* (London: Continuum Publishing Group, 2002).

45. Hugo Gryn, with Naomi Gryn, *Chasing Shadows* (London: Penguin, 2001), p. 257.

5

Jewish Tales on Converts and Conversion in Early Modern Germany

Maria Diemling

Introduction

'When we have made an experience or a chaos into a story we have transformed it, made sense of it, transmuted experience, domesticated the chaos.'[1] Acclaimed novelist Ben Okri suggests in this well-known quotation that in order to understand what happened to us, we tell stories. Narratives endow meaning to events and experiences and provide a sense of orientation to our lives. Narratives are the common vehicles we use to understand and communicate the value of our actions and social practices. Furthermore, they serve an important cultural function for collectives. Culturally shared narratives, such as popular stories or folk tales, provide helpful frames for interpreting collective experiences, clarifying and resolving conflicts, and affirming moral values.

In this paper I want to examine Jewish stories told in the Early Modern Germanic Lands that deal with Jewish converts and conversion to Christianity.[2] The fact that to this very day active Christian mission is restricted by law in the State of Israel[3] clearly shows Jewish sensitivity to Christian attempts at proselytising. Jewish conversion, voluntary or forced, has been one of the most painful chapters in Jewish-Christian relations. Christians often found it hard to accept that Jews would not acknowledge the obvious and apparent truth of the Christian faith and blamed them for their obstinacy and perfidy and even accused them of being deliberate unbelievers who knew the truth, but denied it out of sheer stubbornness. In contrast, Jews throughout their history in Christian lands were exposed to constant pressure, sometimes applied by sheer force and brutal violence, to get baptised and accept a religion that contradicted their religious laws and beliefs.

Jewish history in the Early Modern Period is still a rather young research subject. Until recently the period from the 16th to 18th century was traditionally seen as part of the Jewish Middle Ages which was thought to have continued without major changes in traditional Jewish society until the mid-18th century. Nowadays scholars of Jewish history recognise that the Early Modern Period includes not only medieval features, but also shows modern characteristics as well. Research on contacts and communication between the Jewish minority and the Christian majority is one reason for this important shift in perspective.[4] The study of conversion provides valuable insights in the nature of these relations.

There is no doubt that Jews converted in the Early Modern Period to Christianity in much larger numbers than previously thought.[5] We still lack a comprehensive analysis of archival sources that could provide us with information on ordinary people who just led a normal life after their conversion without attracting much public attention. Painstaking research done so far for several geographical entities shows quite clearly how valuable information on individuals can be retrieved from previously unknown sources.[6]

For the Jewish community in the Early Modern Period, however, the act of conversion to Christianity was much more than the private decision of an individual. Leaving Judaism and joining the Christian society was experienced, just as in the Middle Ages, as a considerable weakening of the community and treated with disapproval, mistrust and sorrow. The medieval ethical book *Sefer Hassidim* (The Book of the Pious) reflects this spirit by stating that one should mourn for a baptised Jew just as one mourns for a dead one, since body and soul are lost.[7] Nonetheless, we should keep in mind that in a society where the whole culture was pervaded by Christian thought and symbolism, the appeal of Christianity must have been strong. The late eminent Israeli historian Jacob Katz has reminded us that to convert to Christianity meant accepting the whole scale of values which prevailed in the ruling society: 'As medieval civilization was expressed almost entirely in religious terms, it is very likely that a Jew who was captivated by the values of Christian society experienced this process subjectively in the form of religious conversion.'[8] This was a huge challenge for Jews.

In order to be able to survive as a religious minority, the Jewish community had to develop strategies to protect its religious and cultural identity and to fight the temptation of conversion to Christianity . Telling tales is one way of dealing with internal and external conflicts and, as I will show, also a powerful means of social control within the community.

Sources

My main sources for the following comments are Early Modern compilations of Jewish tales and accounts of Jews who converted to Christianity which include the odd example of a tale dealing with conversion.[9] The printing revolution of the Early Modern Period stimulated the publication of books in Jewish communities and only a short time after printing was introduced in Rome in 1473, Jews adopted it for their own use. Soon books for Jewish readers were not only printed in Hebrew, but also in Yiddish, which opened the world of letters to a considerably larger audience.[10]

Yiddish collections of folk tales were printed in considerable numbers during the second half of the 16th century. The most widely read of these were, among others, the *Teitsch-chumesh* or *Seynah ureyna* as it was commonly called, a kind of 'women's bible', because its main target group were female readers. The *Mayse bukh*, the 'book of exempla', first published in Basle in 1602 by Jacob ben Abraham of Mezhirech (who was also known as Jacob Pollak) was another very popular collection.[11] These books were printed first and foremost for the use of the ordinary man and woman who did not have a scholarly education and whose Hebrew was not sufficient for following a text written in the Holy Language.[12] The style and language of these tales are simple, but quite endearing even to today's reader, and one can easily imagine how they were read or told during a few precious hours of rest on a *Shabbat* afternoon. These compilations were supposed to provide a proper Jewish alternative to the popular secular literature with non-Jewish themes that rabbinical authorities did not approve of.[13] The stories are permeated with the spirit of piety to strengthen the reader's faith and to teach proper conduct and ethical principles and are as such similar to Christian exempla with their clear didactic and moralising message.[14] They are certainly also supposed to be - and actually are! - entertaining and, with references to demons and spirits, kings and beggars, sages and beautiful women, miracles and mysteries quite gripping. Christians appreciated their edifying value as well, since they do not include 'ugly gossip that corrupts morality' and they 'drive away worries, heavy thoughts and sorrow'.[15] Although printed for the first time only in 1602, the origins of these stories are much older and they have a long oral tradition. More than half of the 254 tales of the *Mayse bukh* were adaptations of *Midrash* and *Aggada* with a biblical and talmudical background. Many feature medieval sages,[16] such as Rabbi Judah the Pious, and some were even variants of Christian stories.[17]

Despite the fact that these stories are generally perceived as popular folk tales, they are not necessarily a product of folklore, but rather 'an outstanding mediating factor between the elite, educated culture and the broad strata of the people'. As Eli Yassif has pointed out, Christian theologians and preachers recognised early on that lively exempla influenced powerfully through concrete examples and proved to be more comprehensible than abstract ethical rules. In a parallel process, Jewish scholars, such as Rabbi Judah the Pious (who himself features in many of the exempla of the *Mayse bukh*) realised that they could transmit religious and social values most efficiently by the use of stories. In both societies a transfer of concepts from the educated elite to the broader population took place via tales.[18]

From about the same time, the early 16th century onwards, Jews who had converted to Christianity (both Catholicism and Protestantism) began to write about their former Jewish religion and the rituals they had observed. They described in great detail Jewish customs, translated Jewish prayers, and provided a kind of introduction to Judaism for a Christian audience. Although their accounts tend to be biased and are often a continuation of medieval anti-Jewish polemical writings, they do provide us with valuable insights into Jewish life of that time. These authors do not only describe customs and observances, but also tell us what Jews thought of Christians and give details on Jewish-Christian relations.[19] As former Jews and baptised Christians, they saw themselves sometimes as mediators between the two cultures, even if they were often regarded with suspicion by both sides.

For this study I wish to focus on two main examples from both genres: the *Mayse bukh* and the *Juden Büchlein*, a 1508 book on Jewish customs written by the Jewish convert Victor of Carben (1423-1515) who became a priest and lived in Cologne after his baptism.

Young Souls in Danger
The danger of losing members who belonged to the intellectual and socially established stratum of society was an underlying threat to the Jewish community, one that caused the community to be in 'a state of permanent

defence against Christianity' (Jacob Katz). Young people seem to have been perceived as particularly vulnerable to the temptations of Christian society.

Rabbi Judah the Pious, who died in Regensburg in 1217, was a dominant figure in the Hasidism of Ashkenaz and held in the highest regard as a great teacher, leader, mystic, and magician by subsequent generations.[20] He was not only the author of the influential *Sefer Hasidim*, but also features prominently in stories of the *Mayse bukh*. In the following three exempla from the *Mayse bukh*, Rabbi Judah the Pious combats by his firm action the seductive allures of Christianity for young men.

> It happened in the time of R. Judah, the Pious, that a child was born in the city of Regensburg, where R. Judah lived. When the child was brought into the synagogue for circumcision and the people said Baruk ha-ba ['Blessed be he that cometh!' These words are addressed to the prophet Elijah, who always comes with the child. And this is the reason also for the custom of putting a second chair.], the whole congregation rose up, as is customary, but R. Judah remained sitting. Everyone said Baruk ha-ba, while R. Judah kept quiet, for he did not see the Prophet Elijah come in, as he usually does. All the people wondered and asked him why he was so disrespectful to the child. The pious man replied: 'Because I did not see the Prophet Elijah come in with the child, nor did he sit in the chair which had been prepared for him. He must have believed that no good would come of the child.' He also said to some persons: "Look through that window yonder and you will see the Prophet Elijah, in the guise of an old man with a long snow-white beard, sitting and praying." Then the people asked R. Judah to tell them why it was that the Prophet Elijah had not taken his seat on the chair, as was his custom. He replied: 'I will tell you. An evil moment will come over the child in the future, and he will have a desire to apostatize from Judaism. That is the reason why the prophet Elijah does not wish to sit by him.' [...][21]

In this story, Rabbi Judah the Pious, who possesses magical abilities, is able to notice the telling absence of the Prophet Elijah, guest of honour at each circumcision ceremony, and to interpret it as a sign of an inauspicious future. According to Rabbi Judah the Pious, the Prophet chooses to pray for the tender baby, but does not want to sit next to him, because the infant will face a moment in the future when he will be tempted to undergo baptism. The story ends with a reference to another story in which the child reappears as a young man, but it does not give any explanation of how to provide for this unfortunate child who was not deemed worthy to be welcomed by the Prophet.

Several years later, so we learn from another story in the *Mayse bukh*,

> [...] R. Judah, sitting at the window, saw a young lad running quickly along the road. So he said to his students: 'Run after that young man and hold him by his mantle until I call you.' They ran after him and called him, but he would not listen. They overtook him and held him by his mantle and asked him why he was running, what was his object, and why did he not answer when they called him? The young man replied: 'What right have you to ask me why I am running?' They said: 'Never mind, we want to know and we have a reason for asking.' But the young man refused to tell them and was trying to run away. But the students would not let him go and kept him so long until they were about to get into a fight.
>
> When the pious man saw it, he called to one of his young men and said: 'Go and tell them to stop their fighting and bring the lad here,' which they did. When they came to the pious man, he said to the lad: 'Why were you running so fast? What necessity was there for you to run?' The boy began to cry and said: 'Rabbi, I must confess my sin. I had the intention of committing a wrong, but I was prevented by your pupils. They kept me back this time, and now the evil hour has passed. Therefore my dear rabbi, impose a penance upon me fitting a thing of this sort, so that I may atone for my sins.' The pious man imposed a penance, which he carried out most faithfully and became a very pious man. Then the students said: 'Blessed be God who grants a portion of His wisdom to those who fear Him.'[22]

A third, rather detailed story in the *Mayse bukh*, 'R. Judah Hasid saves the son of a rich man from becoming baptised', shares similar motifs and again, a young fellow is saved from his own evil passion by the foresight of Rabbi Judah:

> Once upon a time, R. Judah refuses to accept the son of a rich man as his student. After the father insists on knowing the reason, R. Judah tells him that 'in the course of the year, there will be a day when your son will have an evil moment and will conceive a desire to be converted to Christianity'. He advises him to take precautions and the rich man locks his son together with a teacher to study with him into an underground room, 'away from any temptation', in his house.

Everything goes well until the hour R. Judah had anticipated, arrives. The storyteller goes into great detail to describe the impertinent behaviour of the young lad who refused to study on that day and 'spoke many strange words, which cannot be recounted here.' After he explains to this teacher that he wants to become a Christian, the shocked teacher leaves him. The student gets more and more agitated, to the great concern of his parents who listen from outside. He shouts to bring the priest, 'for I want to join the Church. If I were outside, no one could keep me back. I would kill everyone who came near me and tried to prevent me from joining the Church.' The desperate parents tie his hands and feet and lock the door. The next morning, however, the boy has calmed down and he tells his father that the danger is over, because the evil day has passed. He apologises, asks for penance and wants to study with R. Judah. He then studies day and night and becomes a great scholar in the Law. 'And his friends rejoiced in him greatly. May God grant us joy, too.'[23]

In these three stories, the danger of leaving the Jewish fold and converting to Christianity hovers above a young and promising person like a curse. Even the Prophet Elijah does not see much hope for salvation and refuses to attend the ceremony of circumcision during which a baby is accepted to the Jewish community. Thanks to the wisdom and magical abilities of Rabbi Judah the Pious the bitter fate can be prevented and the community gains a valuable, pious and learned member.

The situation described in these stories is by no means an untypical one in the reality of Early Modern Europe. Several Jewish converts write in their autobiographical accounts how difficult the time of deliberations and 'temptations', torn between Judaism and Christianity, was for them. They speak of their desperate trying to fight these seductive voices and mention great loneliness and even psychosomatic problems when they first considered conversion to Christianity.[24] Young and intelligent men seemed to be at special risk.[25] I am not sure if this phenomenon should be interpreted as some kind of 'adolescent angst' and perhaps even as a way of protesting against the rules of a patriarchal household and community. Keeping in mind, however, that many young men from scholarly families travelled in small groups from one *yeshiva* to another, where they were not always under close supervision from adults, may have stayed in Christians hostels and travelled with Christians artisans, it is hardly surprising that they came in contact with Christian ideas and values. Due to their religious education they might also have been prone to deeper questioning than other classes of society. Adolescence was a vulnerable period of searching for one's identity and self-definition then as it is today. If we accept the idea that conversion to Christianity is a complicated process that entails not just a change of religion, but also the acceptance of the cultural norms and values of the majority society by which a young person is surrounded, we can easily understand the agitation experienced by the young men in our stories. In the Middle Ages one was well aware of this phenomenon and it was customary to keep a 'cool-off period', which lasted traditionally three days, before that usually irreversible step to another religion was made. [26]

One might also want to interpret these acts of temporary 'madness' as an initiation rite or a kind of *rite de passage* into Judaism. The elaborate Bar *Mitzvah* ceremony we know today, in which a 13-year-old boy is ritually accepted into the Jewish community and becomes obliged to observe the commandments, was only being developed in Ashkenaz society at that time.[27] The struggle for identity described in the stories related above can be read as a metaphoric death of an old, inadequate self, the self of a child who still does not grasp fully the meaning of Judaism, in order to be reborn on a higher plane of existence and to choose Judaism with full commitment to its laws and commandments.

The underlying message is clearly an optimistic one. These things can happen, they even 'happen in the best families' (wealth is usually a sign of blessing and devoutness in these stories and they go together). A young person may experience signs of crisis, even symptoms of madness, but the Jewish society has to know how to deal with it – with love and understanding, but very firmly – and the person can still, after the 'dark hour' has passed and penance is done, become a valuable member of the community and even a great and pious scholar, which is in these stories the ultimate goal a Jew can aspire to. It was important, however, to act decisively and fast, just as Rabbi Judah the Pious did. Measures have to be taken before an actual conversion takes place. In theory, there was hardly a way back, since Canon Law strictly prohibited the once Baptised to turn to another religion.

Converts as Incarnation of Evil

Sometimes, however, the endangered soul cannot be rescued from impending baptism, but this is interpreted as a confirmation of irreparable evil in this person and not seen as a great loss to the community. The following story from the *Mayse bukh* lists conversion to Christianity as just one transgression of a truly vicious person:

> Once upon a time there was a wicked Jew who lived close to the house of a rich man, who had a very beautiful wife. The wicked man conceived a passion for her and asked her to do his will, promising her a great deal of money. But she refused to listen to him and abused him for desiring to commit the grave sin of adultery. So he went away. One day her husband went away on a business trip to buy goods. And when the wicked man heard of it, he broke in the wall on a Friday night, violating the Sabbath, got into the house and, tying a towel around her neck to prevent her from screaming, he violated her in her own home, thus transgressing the commandment against adultery. After he had tortured her sufficiently and satisfied his evil passion, he killed her, so that she should not be able to denounce him, and transgressed the command: "Thou shalt not kill." It soon became known that he had killed the woman, so he was arrested and about to be executed. But he asked to be liberated, promising to embrace Christianity. His wish was granted. And when he had become converted, he was thrown into the water and thus he was punished by God.
>
> Now see how many sins that man committed because of his passion for another man's wife. First he transgressed the commandment: "Thou shalt not covet thy neighbour's wife." Then he violated the Shabbath. Then he transgressed the commandment: "Thou shalt not commit adultery." Then he violated the commandment: "Thou shalt not serve other Gods before Me," as he became an apostate. So God punished him in this world, for he was cast into the water, and he was surely punished in the world to come.[28]

The evident moral of the story is to show how many transgressions of the Divine Law the passion for another man's wife can lead the unfortunate one who is too weak to resist the evil inclination. Being interested in the depiction of conversion, we note how the change of religion is a signifier for a truly evil person. Conversion to Christianity is described as just another step in his miserable development, as despicable as rape and murder.. No pity is shown for the perpetrator. The sober ending of the story leaves no doubt about what the evil sinner had to expect after his death. Moreover, it hints to a double baptism that not only costs his life, but also, more significantly, his soul. The wicked Jew who chose Christianity in order to avoid a harsh execution was defiled by the waters of baptism and apparently also killed by drowning in water.

It is remarkable that Jewish converts living in Early Modern Germanic Lands sometimes mention in their autobiographical accounts that their family or teachers had given them up at an early age. Statements uttered by family members in the spirit of the Prophet Elijah's 'nothing good can come of him' mentioned in the first story sound like self-fulfilling prophecies. The derogatory Yiddish saying, 'Di sch'mad ligt ihm auf'n punim', the near baptism can be spotted on one's face, expresses a similar sentiment.[29] Such expressions may be interpreted as witnesses of acts of an early commitment to the religion potential converts were going to choose later. Such feelings of alienation clearly assert the element of 'otherness' within their close-knit family and community and it was perhaps sometimes just that feeling of not-belonging that made Jews opt for conversion.[30]

We must not forget, however, that Jewish converts were indeed sometimes a severe threat to their former communities. Some of them did play a most unfortunate role in accusations made against Jews, such as allegations of blood libel and ritual murder or claims that Jewish liturgy was full of hatred for Christianity. Several Spanish stories of the period tell of apostates who denounced their former community, blaming them for using blood in the Passover bread or despising Christian authority, but whose malicious attempts fail, because a miracle happens and the community is saved.[31] Such stories reflect the deeds of Petrus Alfonsi (1062-1110), Nicholas Donin (13th century), Pablo de Santa Maria (ca. 1351- 1435), or Johannes Pfefferkorn (1469-ca. 1521), to name just a few medieval Jewish converts to Christianity from different European regions. All of them denounced Jewish religion, the Talmud, or Jewish prayers to Christian authorities and prompted investigations and trials which occasionally led to the burning of Jewish books and, in the worst case, to the execution of Jews. Apprehension of former Jews who left the fold and converted to Christianity is deeply embedded in Jewish collective memory. The following beautiful, but virtually unknown story about the threat of converts to their former brethren is told by Victor of Carben, himself a convert to Christianity in late 15th century Cologne:

A blacksmith who prepared a large number of axes wants to bring them to the market to sell them there. On his way to the market, he passes through a large forest. When the young and small trees in the forest see the axes the blacksmith is carrying, they begin to tremble and shake out of great fear and worry. The old and big trees ask them what the reason for their fear is and the young trees cry out loud, 'Oh, but don't you see our enemies who walk among us in great numbers?' The old trees ask the young trees, 'But are there also of our kind among them?' The young trees reply that no, there are only iron axes. The old trees comfort them and say, 'Calm down and don't worry. They won't do you much harm. As long as these axes haven't got wooden handles, they won't be dangerous to us.'[32]

Victor uses this story to show how unsettling the notion of learned and educated converts is for Jews. Made from the 'same material' as their former co-religionists they can expertly inform Christians about the 'true' Jewish religion and thus damage the Jewish community more than any Christian, who lacks the knowledge of an insider, ever could. Needless to say, Victor, the author of a book on Jewish religion, wants to boost his own reputation by telling this story and to make it quite clear that he, as a former Jew and rabbi, is a reliable and trustworthy source on all matters Jewish. However, there is no reason to doubt the authenticity of the story as one known to and told by Early Modern Jews. This tale vividly shows the uneasiness Jews felt towards those who had left the Jewish fold for another religion and from whom, according to their experience, the worst was to be expected. Another story from the *Mayse bukh* powerfully demonstrates this suspicion against converts who cannot be trusted:

R. Judah the Pious was approached by a very evil convert who was responsible for the death of many Jews, but who wished to repent and to return to Judaism. After he had told to R. Judah all the horrible sins of his past, R. Judah refused to give him penance, because his sins were just too great. He showed him an old stick and told him that his chances for atonement are about as high as his stick has of becoming green again and sprouting leaves. The convert returned disappointed to his former evil lifestyle, but R. Judah was out for a surprise, when he saw that the stick was growing leaves again. He immediately sent for the apostate and asked him what good he had done in his past to deserve such a miracle. The convert said that 'Ever since I converted, I have never done any good to a Jew; on the contrary, I have always done them evil, except once'. Then he told him the story of how he once happened to be in a place where the Jewish community was accused of having killed a Christian child. When he as a former Jew was asked by the town council to be a witness if the Jews indeed require blood for religious purposes, he explained the dietary laws and stated under oath that Jews are by no means allowed to eat blood and that they must be accused wrongly. The people of the town then released the captured Jews and the whole community was saved. R. Judah agreed that this was indeed a very good deed, gave him a penance which the convert carried out after which he became again a good and pious Jew.[33]

In this story even Rabbi Judah the Pious is disabused when the mistrust he shows to a wicked convert is proved wrong by a miracle. The one deed the apostate was not guilty of was the dissemination of the ritual murder accusation. His truthful statement saved a whole Jewish community and this was sufficient to forgive him all his previous sins and accept him back into the fold.

The allegations of blood libel and ritual murder originated in the Middle Ages, but were being spread and believed well into the 20th century.[34] This example proves how threatening this claim was for a Jewish community. If a truly evil person does only one good deed in his career of maliciousness, denying that allegation, then there is still hope for him. The story also demonstrates the status of converts as informants on Jewish religion. Back in the 13th century, when this anti-Jewish charge was raised for the first time in Germany, the Holy Roman Emperor Frederick II had invited converted Jews to give evidence on the truth of such allegations.[35] One expected them to slander their former religion, but if they testified in favour of Jews, Christian authorities would usually believe them.

As mentioned above, it was forbidden by Canon Law to convert from Christianity to Judaism and this applied also to baptised Jews who wished to return to Judaism.[36] Despite the potential risk for the Jewish community, it would often accept a convert back (and find a practical solution for avoiding Church authorities) when he or she expressed a genuine wish to return and showed sincere remorse. One possible loophole was to move to the Ottoman Empire or to Amsterdam where a return to Judaism was possible.[37] The ambivalence of accepting a remorseful convert back into the Jewish fold is vividly demonstrated in a medieval story from the *Sefer Hasidim*. There Jews face the dilemma of being asked for advice by a convert who plans to return to the Jewish fold by stealing money from those Christians who supported him while he lived among them as a fellow Christian. The Jews are well aware that their support of the contrite, but at the same time deceitful, convert could endanger the whole community.[38]

The Misery of Converts

The life of those whose conversion to the Christian faith was sincere did not necessarily become an easy one once the baptism ceremony was over. Our contemporary view of the status of Jews after their conversion to Christianity is often influenced by Heinrich Heine's well-known statement that baptism serves as 'the entrance ticket to European society' or the fact that Gustav Mahler had to convert before he could become the director of the Viennese Opera. Conversion to Christianity in Early Modern Central Europe, however, usually meant for Jews leaving behind not only their former religious affiliation, but their family ties, business relations and social network for an uncertain future.[39] Despite ongoing efforts on the part of the Churches to attract Jews willing to convert,[40] financial support often seemed to last only a short period and many Jews were left quite destitute. Since Jews were excluded by Christian guild restrictions from learning a craft, they did not always have a profession that could easily support them and their families after becoming Christians. Apart from suffering from severe financial constraints, Jewish converts often found themselves being mistrusted and despised by their new co-religionists.[41] A number of popular sayings expressed in several European languages Christian distrust of converted Jews. As one did not expect a leopard to change its spots, one did not believe that a Jew would truly change their inherent 'Jewish character' and become a sincere Christian. Sometimes this mistrust was based on bad experiences with Jews who would wander around in the Germanic lands and abuse the small decentralised political entities to get baptised time and again in order to receive the financial reward given by the Church on the occasion of a Jewish christening.[42]

Early Modern Jews appear to have had quite realistic ideas on how difficult the integration in Christian society really was. They did not cherish illusions on how a converted Jew would be accepted within Christian society. A little rhyme in Hebrew, a condensed story, as it were, recorded and translated into colloquial German by the Jewish convert Victor of Carben mentioned previously, summarises this aptly:

Moshekh bahevel/ypol bazevel
Bahevel moshekh/ypol bahoshekh
Pulling the rope/falling into the dirt
The rope pulling/falling into the dark.[43]

What do these lines mean and how are they related to conversion? Victor explains that the rope mentioned in both lines stands for the rope that is attached to the church bells. The bells, calling the faithful to the religious service into the churches, symbolise the Jew that succumbed to their alluring pealing. He or she is, however destined to 'zevel', a dirty, miserable existence in this life and to the dark of hell, the pit of eternal damnation in the next one. No gain in this life and definitely none in the world to come for those pitiable Jews who left Judaism for the ostensible temptations of Christianity.

Another Jewish saying of that time suggests that Jewish converts are for Christians like a new white shirt which is pristine and beautiful. After being worn for nine or ten days, it gets dirty and unclean and nobody finds it desirable any longer. A similar fate awaits the newly baptised Jew whom everybody supports enthusiastically in the first days after his or her christening. After nine or ten days, however, the novelty wears off and nobody respects him or her any longer and everybody despises the convert.[44] These words, uttered by a former Jew who converted to Christianity, became a priest and expressed his sincere belief by writing theological and polemical pamphlets, are a slap in the face of his contemporary Christians. Although being deeply disillusioned by the attitude many Christians showed toward baptised Jews, he insists on the sincerity of his conversion despite his humiliating experiences in the Christian world. Victor of Carben stresses Christian lack of consideration for the bitter fate of converts as expressed in these sayings in order to change their attitude towards converts. One can assume that the same stories did have a deterring effect on potential Jewish converts whose motivations for conversion might not have been religious only.

Conclusion
Social historians are justly wary of using folk stories and tales as sources for the depiction of historical events and processes. It goes without saying that we cannot expect reliable information on actual incidents and persons, but it is perhaps surprising to realise how accurately the stories related

above echo social realities that can be verified by additional source material that is more readily established.

There is more to these stories than appears on the surface, though. We also gain valuable insights in the life and thoughts of Early Modern Jews by asking what the purpose of these stories was for the Jewish community. Why were these tales, many of them with medieval origins, told so often and proved to be so popular? Why did they survive so easily the transition from oral to written literature? Dan Ben-Amos has suggested that the transition from orality to literacy is a 'selective and purposeful process' which was controlled by scribes and their religious or political patrons, who 'tend to be self-serving or, at best, to adhere to normative cultural values'.[45] I suggest reading these stories first of all as powerful means of social control.

Social control and inner discipline were vital for the survival of the Jewish community as a minority within Christian society and over the centuries, a variety of resources to ensure control was developed. Community leaders were able to impose a temporary ban or the threat of excommunication on deviant members who did not obey the internal rules.[46] Conversion was arguably the most drastic step a Jews could take to seriously disturb the social order of the community. Conversion to Christianity was not only a transgression of Jewish law, but threatened the inner equilibrium of the community and could occasionally cause genuine danger if the convert decided, for whatever reasons, to denounce his or her former co-religionists to Christian authorities. Storytelling was one way to convey the manifold dangers of this step to an impressionable audience.

These stories, however, do not only warn those who contemplate baptism, they also provide meaning to the constant threat of conversion. By constructing an element of high drama, these stories reinforce a sense of identity. A young man who experienced the 'yetzer hara', the 'evil inclination', wins a major victory over himself and a looming temptation that provides him with an acute sense of being a Jew. This would indeed be a transformation of experience and a 'domestication of chaos' in the sense Ben Okri has suggested.

Stories are indeed a secret reservoir of normative cultural values.[47] They provoke in Jews considering leaving the fold the fear of a miserable life as a Christian and of eternal damnation by offering them a poignant foretaste of the fate awaiting them. It was essential for a religious minority to develop strategies of survival and the power of these tales announces their effectiveness.

Notes

1. Ben Okri, 'The Joys of Storytelling III', published in his collection of essays *A Way of Being Free* (London: Phoenix House, 1997), p. 113.

2. For an excellent study on the conversion of Jews to Christianity in the Early Modern Period, see Elisheva Carlebach, *Divided Souls. Converts from Judaism in Germany, 1500-1700* (New Haven-London: Yale University Press, 2001).

3. A 1977 anti-proselytising law prohibits any person from offering or receiving material benefits as an inducement to conversion.

4. See Rotraud Ries: http://www.juedische-geschichte.historicum.net/themen/period/htm [30 Dec 2003].

5. A pioneering study acknowledging this is Azriel Shohet, *Beginnings of the Haskalah among German Jewry* (Jerusalem: Bialik Institute, 1960), p. 8 (in Hebrew).

6. Gerd Mentgen, 'Jüdische Proselyten im Oberrheingebiet während des Spätmittelalters. Schicksale und Probleme einer "doppelten" Minderheit', *Zeitschrift für Geschichte des Oberrheins* 142 (1994), pp. 117-39; Wolfgang Treue, 'Aufsteiger oder Außenseiter? Jüdische Konvertiten im 16. und 17. Jahrhundert', *Aschkenas* 10 (2000), pp. 307-36; Stefan Litt, 'Conversions to Christianity and Jewish Family Life in Thuringia: Case Studies in the Sixteenth and Seventeenth Centuries', *Leo Baeck Yearbook* 47 (2002), pp. 83-90.

7. Jehuda Wistinetzki (ed.), *Sefer Chasidim* (Berlin: Wahrmann, 2nd. edn. 1924), no. 192, p. 73-4.

8. Jacob Katz, *Exclusiveness and Tolerance. Studies in Jewish-Gentile Relations in Medieval and Modern Times* (London: Oxford University Press, 1961), p. 76.

9. For a study of how conversion is dealt with in east-European Yiddish folk tales, see Esther Alexander-Ihme, "'A Yid shmadt sikh nit" - Apostasie, Judenmissionsnot und Taufe in jüdischen Volkserzählungen', *Frankfurter Judaistische Beiträge* 15 (1987), pp. 47-89.

10. Shifra Baruchson, *Books and Readers. The Reading Interests of Italian*

Jews at the Close of the Renaissance (Ramat-Gan: Bar-Ilan University Press, 1993) (in Hebrew).

11. For an English translation, see Moses Gaster (trans.), *Ma'aseh Book: Book of Jewish Tales and Legends. Translated from the Judeo-German* (Philadelphia: The Jewish Publication Society of America, 1934). It is based on an 18th-century Yiddish edition of the *Mayse bukh*. For a discussion of the literary tradition of the *Mayse bukh*, see Jakob Maitlis, *Das Ma'assebuch. Seine Entstehung und Quellengeschichte. Zugleich ein Beitrag zur Einführung in die altjiddische Agada* (Berlin: Rubin Mass, 1933) and by the same author, *The Exempla of Rabbi Samuel and Rabbi Judah, the Pious* (A Study in Yiddish Folklore) (London, Kedem, 1961) (in Yiddish with English summary).

12. Shmuel Niger, 'Yiddish Literature and the Female Reader. Translated and abridged by Sheva Zucker', in Baskin, J. R. (ed.), *Women of the word: Jewish women and Jewish writing* (Detroit: Wayne State University Press, 1994), pp. 70-90.

13. Eli Yassif, *The Hebrew Folktale: History, Genre, Meaning*. Translated from Hebrew by Jacqueline S. Teitelbaum (Bloomington-Indianapolis: Indiana University Press, 1999), p. 266.

14. Ernst Robert Curtius, *European Literature and the Latin Middle Ages*, Translated by Willard R. Trask (London: Routledge and Kegan Paul, 1979), pp. 57-61. Walter Haug and Burghart Wachinger (eds), *Exempel und Exempelsammlungen* (Tübingen: Max Niemeyer, 1991).

15. Christoph Daxelmüller, 'Narratio, Illustratio, Argumentatio. Exemplum und Bildungstechnik in der frühen Neuzeit', in Haug W and Wachinger B (eds), *Exempel und Exempelsammlungen* (Tübingen: Max Niemeyer, 1991), p. 83.

16. For a recent study on medieval Jewish scholars as protagonists in Jewish legends, see Lucia Raspe, 'Payyetanim as heroes of Medieval Narrative: The Case of R. Shim'on b. Yishaq of Mainz', in Hermann, K, Schlüter, M and Veltri, G (eds), *Jewish Studies Between the Disciplines. Papers in Honor of Peter Schäfer on the Occasion of his 60th Birthday* (Leiden: Brill, 2003), pp. 354-69.

17. For a study of some motifs shared by Christian and Jewish exempla, see Joseph Dan, 'Rabbi Judah the Pious and Caesarius of Heisterbach. Common Motifs in Their Stories,' *Scripta Hierosolymitana* 22 (1971), pp. 18-27.

18. Yassif, *Folktale*, p. 295.

19. Yaacov Deutsch, '"A View of the Jewish Religion" – Conceptions

of Jewish Practice and Ritual in Early Modern Europe', *AJR* 3 (2001), pp. 273–295.

20. For a study on the German *Hasidim*, see Ivan G. Marcus, *Piety and Society, the Jewish Pietists of Medieval Germany* (Leiden: Brill, 1981).

21. Gaster, *Ma'aseh Book*, Volume Two, pp. 391-2.

22. Gaster, *Ma'aseh Book*, Volume Two, pp. 379-80.

23. Abridged from Gaster, *Ma'aseh Book*, Volume Two, pp. 375-9.

24. Carlebach, *Souls*, pp. 101-6.

25. William Chester Jordan, 'Adolescence and Conversion in the Middle Ages: A Research Agenda,' in Signer M A and Van Engen J (eds.), *Jews and Christians in Twelfth-Century Europe* (Notre Dame, Indiana: University of Notre Dame Press, 2001), pp. 77-93.

26. Ivan G. Marcus, 'Jews and Christians Imagining the Other in Medieval Europe,' *Prooftexts* 15 (1995), p. 215.

27. See Ivan G. Marcus, *Rituals of Childhood. Jewish Acculturation in Medieval Europe* (New Haven-London: Yale University Press, 1996), pp. 122-4.

28. Gaster, *Ma'aseh Book*, Volume Two, pp. 535-6.

29. Ignaz Bernstein, *Jüdische Sprichwörter und Redensarten. Mit einer Einführung und Bibliographie von Hans Peter Althaus* (Hildesheim: Georg Olms, 1969), p. 283.

30. Carlebach, *Souls*, pp. 99-100.

31. Moses Gaster, *Exempla of the Rabbis* (New York: Ktav, 1968), pp. 357, 363, 445.

32. The title page of the original work, published 1508 in Cologne, is missing and we do not know the title of the book. It was republished in 1550 under the title Juden Büchlein. I am quoting from the 1508 edition [*Juden Büchlein*] C3v.

33. Abridged from Gaster, *Ma'aseh Book*, Volume Two, pp. 380-3.

34. For the distinction between these charges and a brief summary see Norman Roth (ed), *Medieval Jewish Civilization. An Encyclopedia* (New York-London: Routledge, 2003), pp. 119-21 and 566-570.

35. Robert Chazan, *Church, State and Jew in the Middle Ages* (New York: Behrman House, 1980), pp. 123-6.

36. Solomon Grayzel, *The Church and the Jews in the XIIIth Century* (New York: Hermon Press, 1966), p. 311.

37. Elisheva Carlebach, "'Ich will dich nach Holland schicken…'": Amsterdam and the Reversion to Judaism of German-Jewish Converts', in Popkin, R. and Mulsow, M. (eds.), *Secret Conversions to Judaism in Early*

Modern Europe (Leiden: Brill, 2004).

38. *Sefer Chasidim.* no. 199, p. 75.

39. Joseph Shatzmiller, 'Jewish Converts to Christianity in Medieval Europe, 1200-1500', in Goodich, M., Menache, S. and Schein, S. (eds.), *Cross Cultural Convergences in the Crusader Period: Essays Presented to Aryeh Grabois on His Sixty-Fifth Birthday* (New York: Peter Lang,1995), pp. 311-13.

40. Martin Friedrich, *Zwischen Abwehr und Bekehrung. Die Stellung der deutschen evangelischen Theologie zum Judentum im 17. Jahrhundert* (Tübingen: Mohr Siebeck, 1988); Christopher M. Clark, *The politics of conversion: missionary Protestantism and the Jews in Prussia, 1728-1941* (Oxford: Clarendon Press, 1995).

41. Convert Victor of Carben is only one among several converts who describe in great detail the material hardship and the daily humiliation by Christians they had to face after their conversion. Victor states that he is willing to bear this indignity as a reminder of his former sins. [*Juden Büchlein*], A5r-A6r.

42. See Shohet, *Beginnings*, pp. 27-8; Rudolf Glanz, *Geschichte des niederen jüdischen Volkes in Deutschland. Eine Studie über historisches Gaunertum, Bettelwesen und Vagantentum* (New York: Waldon Press, 1968), pp. 70-4. For an interesting case study, see Meike Bursch, *Judentaufe und frühneuzeitliches Strafrecht. Die Verfahren gegen Christian Treu aus Weener/Ostfriesland 1720-1728* (Frankfurt/Main: Peter Lang, 1996). Yacov Guggenheim, 'Social Stratification of Central European Jewry at the End of the Middle Ages: The Poor', *Proceedings of the Tenth World Congress of Jewish Studies* (division B, vol. 1, Jerusalem 1990), pp. 130-6.

43. [*Juden Büchlein*], C4r.

44. [*Juden Büchlein*], A5r.

45. Dan Ben-Amos, 'Foreword', in Yassif, *Folktale*, p. vii.

46. Eric Zimmer, *Harmony and Discord. An Analysis of the Decline of Jewish Self-Government in 15th Century Central Europe* (New York: Yeshiva University Press, 1970), pp. 90-103.

47. Okri, *Being Free*, p. 112.

Jewish-Christian Relations in Modern Hebrew and Yiddish Literature: A Preliminary Sketch

Hamutal Bar-Yosef[1]

1.

Modern Hebrew literature, namely modern Jewish literature in the Hebrew language, is about two hundred years old. Its first practitioners, at the end of the eighteenth century, were Moses Mendelssohn and his followers in Berlin. Later, toward the mid-nineteenth century, its centre moved to Czarist Russia, which was the centre of Hebrew literary activity until the 1920s. Following the October Revolution, the use of Hebrew was banned in Soviet Russia, and subsequently Hebrew literature moved to Palestine (pre-state Israel) and continued to develop in Israel. The history of modern Yiddish literature (in the nineteenth-century sense of the word 'literature') begins in the 1870s, together with the rise of Jewish national consciousness in Czarist Russia. After the Shoah the creation of Yiddish literature was continued in a limited way in Soviet Russia, the United States and Israel, while literature in the Hebrew language became part of Israeli culture.[2]

In both Hebrew and Yiddish literatures, Christians and Christianity represent the Other. Jewish-Christian relations, or better: the attitude of Jews (including the writer) to Christians and Christianity, can be looked at then as part of the wider theme of the Other in modern Jewish literature. The attitude to the Other is by definition problematic because of the Other's difference. This difference is, however, also a matter of power and status: the Otherness of the weak can be more easily ignored or forgiven than the Otherness of the powerful. Modern Jewish literature emerged in a historical context where Jews were traditionally persecuted by Christians because of their Jewish Otherness. They were not only a cultural and social minority, but also a religious enemy, whose moral value was attacked. Jewish traditional writings were busy in polemics, protecting the value of Judaism against Christianity. This situation has changed significantly during the last two hundred years, resulting in interesting changes in the attitude to Christian and Christianity in Jewish literatures.

To fully understand the changing sensitivities of Hebrew and Yiddish literature in relation to Christians and Christianity, it is also important to remember that its exponents were Jewish intellectuals born and educated in Europe, surrounded by Christian culture that was basically antisemitic. For the enlightened European Jew it was not only the lack of civil rights which resulted in debasement: with a few exceptions, over the centuries Christian attitudes toward the Jewish people have been characterised by a 'teaching of contempt'.[3] From a tender age, Christian children received a picture of Judaism as anachronistic, crude, primitive and wicked. Through liturgy and catechism they were taught that the Jews had crucified Jesus and that the New Covenant of Love had replaced the Old Covenant of stern Judgement, which God had rejected and condemned.

Modern Hebrew literature began in the wake of the Jewish emancipation, as an effort to rehabilitate Judaism in the eyes of enlightened Christians and to present it as a national culture equal to other European cultures. The whole idea of writing literature in Hebrew can be explained by examining the Jewish situation in Christian Europe. Hebrew was a language used for prayers and for holy study – Yiddish was the spoken language of the Jews in Europe. In late 18th century Germany, Hebrew was chosen as the language of modern Jewish culture because it was the language of the Bible, a text highly respected by European Christian culture.

At the same time, in the wider European context, language and literature became an inseparable part of the romantic notion of 'nation', while Jewish literature in the European sense of the word was non-existent. This is why Moses Mendelssohn and his followers in Berlin were so concerned to prove the existence of a living Jewish language and literature that grew from the ancient national roots. Unlike Heinrich Heine, who chose – in his words – baptism as an entrée into Christian society, Moses Mendelssohn, pressed to become a Christian by Johann Kaspar Lavater, refused.[4] Mendelssohn believed that by showing the moral and cultural value of Judaism, Jews like him would earn their entrance ticket to Christian society without being baptised.

The original mission of modern Hebrew literature was therefore to reflect proudly the unique history, character and spirit of the Jewish people. Paradoxically, this mission grew from the necessity to judge Judaism and

Jewish life by European norms and to defend Judaism from Christian accusations by using a language loaded with Christian connotations. This double urge – to describe Jewish life as uniquely and independently Jewish, on the one hand, and to react to the European-Christian point of view on the other – motivated modern Hebrew literature as long as it was written by Jews who were born and/or educated in Europe. Only Israeli literature and thought had been partly liberated from the polemical character of the Jewish attitude to Christianity.[5]

2.

During the nineteenth century, Hebrew and Yiddish writers seemed to ignore the physical presence of Christianity around them. Pondering why, the Yiddish poet Itsik Manger, wrote in 1937: 'Did they not see, or did they pretend not to see? I think that the second is more likely, the classic Jewish turning away of the head, or closing the eyes'.[6]

There were at least four more reasons in addition to that proposed by Manger: the first is the traditional reluctance to discuss 'Christianity versus Judaism', which was characteristic of Jews as long as they lived in a European ghetto.[7] During the nineteenth century Jews in Russia were struggling for their elementary human rights, and their writings were always under grave censorship. The second is the cultural isolation of Jewish life. Most Jews spoke their own Yiddish language and could not understand the language of the Goyim (literally 'peoples'). They were completely ignorant of Christian theology and rituals. Even if they could see churches, cavalries, funerals and other ritual processions (the latter often leading to pogroms), they preferred to turn their backs on these 'impure' and dangerous images and to drive them away from their inner world. The third was the writers' wish to focus on Jewish life and to introduce Jewish national culture as independent of the Christian world. The fourth was their belief in European liberalism and their secular world-view.

Although historically concurrent with German Romanticism, nineteenth-century Hebrew literature, moving from Germany to Russia in the mid-nineteenth century, was engaged with the ideas of the Enlightenment until the 1890s, and expressed the ideas of the Jewish Haskalah (Enlightenment) movement.[8] Haskalah Hebrew writers in Russia, influenced by contemporary Russian Positivism and 'civic' ideas, tended to treat Judaism not as a theology but as a civilisation, a way of life. They attacked traditional Jewish forms of life as well as Jewish traditional institutions. These were the 'obscurant' enemies of the 'new Jew', who was trying to hone his European education and manners through open-mindedness, aesthetic refinement and freedom of thought. Haskalah writers perceived European culture as cosmopolitan and religiously universal. Such qualities were ascribed to the 'good goyim' – enlightened Russian officers, idealistic revolutionaries – who scarcely appear in prose fiction written during the second half of the nineteenth century.

Haskalah writers ascribed the same qualities to both the 'new Jew' and the historical biblical Jew. On the one hand, the idealisation of the Jewish biblical past was a continuation of the Romantic Christian-oriented literary tradition, and on the other hand it was an indirect critique of contemporary Jewish life (for example, the excessive learning of the Talmud) from the enlightened European point of view. Historical novels and long poems on Biblical themes are characteristic of Haskalah Hebrew literature, especially during the first half of the century. Famous examples include Naftali Herz Wessely's biblical epic *Poems of Glory* (1789-1811), Avraham Mapu's first Hebrew novel *Love of Zion* (1853), and Yehuda Leib Gordon's long biblical poems written in the 1860s and 1870s. Christian characters are of course absent from these works of literature.

In the 1870s, realistic prose fiction and long poems criticising 'obscurant' Jewish life became fashionable, but even here Christian characters rarely appear, and when they do appear they represent the idealised, enlightened Christian. Parallelism between the cruel attitude towards the mentally ill in the Jewish town and in a mental asylum in Vienna, depicted by Perets Smolenskin in a story published in 1878, is a surprising exception.[9] Cruelty in this case has nothing to do with Christianity; European culture is represented by Smolenskin as liberal and secular. His criticism is directed at its social defects, without any examination of Christian values. Thus at this time Hebrew Haskalah writers chose to disregard the role of Christianity in European culture.

3.

Nineteenth-century Hebrew writers in Russia were in love with Western European – and later with Russian – culture, which they knew primarily through its literature, and they wanted to become part of it. However, from the early 1880s onwards, this love was severely disappointed following waves of pogroms encouraged by official institutions and nationalistic journalists in Czarist Russia. Antisemitism appeared rooted not only in the non-educated people, but also in the enlightened, well-educated intelligentsia. This revelation undermined the foundations of Haskalah ideology.[10]

During the last quarter of the nineteenth century, the literary conventions relating to literary prose in Russia shaped the depiction of Jewish-Christian relations in Hebrew literature no less than did historical realities. As Jews were normally barred from living in big cities, most lived in little towns in the Russian Pale of Settlement, socially disconnected from their Ukrainian neighbours, whom they met at the marketplace or for business purposes. Hebrew and Yiddish writers in the 1860s do not yet describe Jewish-Christian commercial relationships. At that time they were more interested in criticizing the traditional Jewish life. In the 1870s, however, Christian characters begin to appear as party to commercial relations or as representatives of the ruling system.[11] In this context the local non-Jew was perceived not as a person having another faith or religion, but as a person belonging to the ruling non-Jewish majority.

While in the 1860s Mendele Moikher Sforim[12] in the Yiddish novel 'Fishke the Lame' (1869: translated by him into Hebrew in 1909) and in the Yiddish play *The Tax* (1869) describes Jewish economic life in all its misery and corruption as a self-contained realm, in his allegorical *The Nag* (1873), he already hints at discrimination against Jews especially in regard to economic issues and education. In his story *Aryeh the Stout* (1899-1900) Hayim Nahman Bialik (who was for a while a timber merchant) humorously describes the superiority of the Jewish commercial talent over the Ukrainian merchant and the ways by which the Jew cheats the goy.

Jews could also meet representatives of the Russian government and the police. Ben-Avigdor (pseudonym of Shalkovich), in *Leah the Fish Seller* (1891), bitterly uncovers the struggle of survival in a Jewish market, where Jewish women-pedlars confront the Russian policeman. Mendele Moikher Sforim describes similar unpleasant meetings. For example, at the end of *Travels of Benjamin the Third* (1897), the two Jewish heroes are caught by a Russian policeman who forces them to enlist in the Russian army. Their heads and side-curls are shaved as part of the procedure.

Meetings with representatives of the Church were perceived by nineteenth-century Jewish writers not as encounters with the Christian religion, but as meetings with a social power. A humorous description of such a meeting can be found in Scholem Aleichem's Yiddish novel *Tevye the Milkman* (1895, later filmed as *Fiddler on the Roof*). Tevye, the Jewish hero, debates with the *galakh*, the local Russian priest, on the subject of Judaism versus Christianity. This happens after Tevye's daughter (youngest of seven), who is working together with Russian revolutionaries, has fallen in love with a young Ukrainian, who wants to marry her. There is no question of his becoming a Jew, so the only solution is for her to be baptised. But for Tevye, the Orthodox Jew, this would mean losing his beloved daughter. The Russian priest tries hard to convince Tevye that Christianity is a better and more truthful religion than Judaism. Tevye offers his answers and wins the debate. However, the priest 'wins' the daughter. In this way the author indirectly reminds the reader of the long tradition of medieval disputes between Jews and Christians: Jews who won the debates were sometimes killed.

For Sholem Aleichem, Christianity represented the injustice of the strong, while Judaism represented the useless justice of the innocent but weak. He presented the attractions of Christianity as leading to disaster, for Tevye's daughter is not happy with her new life. The growth of antisemitism drives her desperately back to her father's home. Again, social reality, not theology, provides the meeting ground for Christianity and Judaism. This way of evaluating Christianity – focusing on the practical practice of ethics more than on theological principles – is perhaps characteristic of the Jewish point of view.

4.

During the last two decades of the nineteenth century, unjust suffering on the part of the Jew, which Sholem Aleichem described with humour, became a dominant theme in Hebrew literature, where Jewish suffering as a result of antisemitic discrimination in Russia was dramatically portrayed. Mendele Mokher Sforim, in his novel *The Nag* (1873) transformed the tortured mare, Dostoevski's symbol of suffering in *Crime and Punishment* (1866), into a symbol of Jewish suffering caused by Russian antisemitism. Many stories and novels deal with the suffering of the kantonists. These Jewish children were recruited into the Czarist army for twenty-five years, treated cruelly and forced to become Christian.[13] In the Hebrew poetry of the 1880s and early 1890s, known as *Hibat-Tsion* (love of Zion, the proto-Zionist movement) poetry, the suffering woman - sometimes a sacred mother - was a frequent symbol of the Jewish people and its fate in the Diaspora.

It is interesting to note that the traumatic failure of Jewish hopes for acceptance into European civilisation was expressed by the use of symbols, notions, and values that were important in Christian culture, and had specific colour in Russian tradition. Martyrdom was an important sign of the divinity of Christ and of human beings in Russian culture.[14] Suffering, and especially the sacred suffering of a motherly woman and child, become a trait of Jewish identity in *Hibat Tsion* poetry. In the Hebrew Bible the value most extolled in women is their wisdom; they are never represented as victims by choice. It is only in post-Christian Judaism – which Hebrew Haskalah writers rejected - that we find developed martyrological traditions (such as Hannah and her seven sons in 2 Maccabees 7). The attraction of Hibat Tsion writers to this motif was influenced by Russian-Christian, not Jewish, literary tradition, and was motivated by apologetic needs.

Such unconscious infiltration of Christian ideas, absorbed through the European culture of Romanticism, was characteristic of Hebrew and Yiddish literatures as long as they were part of European culture, even when their writers' explicit intention was to write a uniquely Jewish literature. This does not mean that Hebrew writers consciously adopted Christian theology. They were absorbing Christian ideas which were in the European 'air', in art, literature, architecture and music, in the same way that Christian popular beliefs, customs, and ritual – together with other elements of popular culture (such as songs, dances, food, etc.) – were adopted by Jews,[15] especially by those who lived on the periphery of the Pale of Settlement, far from the Jewish urban centres. Retrospectively this phenomenon is humorously described in Shaul Chernikhovski's idylls *Dumplings* (1902) and *Berele is Sick* (1907), where the poet reflects with nostalgia on his childhood in the Crimean farm, before the outburst of antisemitism in Russia. In *Dumplings*, a Rabbi's widow and her friendly Ukrainian neighbour, who comes to visit her on Sunday, both complain about the neglect of religion among the young generation. In *Berele is Sick*, the Christian nanny reminds the four-year-old Berele that he must say his Jewish morning prayers. 'What are you – a goy?!' she rebukes him. When Berele gets sick the young mother calls for a Ukrainian *volkhovitka* (a woman sorcerer or magician who cures the possessed) to cure him of his diarrhoea. The idea is suggested by a neighbour, a Jewish woman, who visits her as a representative of a Jewish charity. The *volkhovitka* herself, after finishing the curing ritual, enjoys *khalleh*, the plaited bread Jews bake for the Sabbath. Chernikhovski describes idyllic cultural interchange taking place on a very earthy and simple level. It is a physical interaction, neither ideological nor theological.

5.

Changes in Jewish life at the turn of the twentieth century made possible a closer acquaintance between Jews and Christians. More and more Jews could read Russian, and Jewish children, although limited by a quota, could go to Russian schools. Jews started to enrol in Russian universities, and those who were not accepted in Russia went abroad, mainly to France, Germany and Switzerland.[16] In St Petersburg, where only Jews who had special rights could live, many opted for conversion to the Russian Orthodox Church in order to achieve social status or to marry a Christian.[17] More and more Jews became part of Russian culture, even without converting.

These vistas, all new for Russian Jews, changed the atmosphere considerably, and their impact, reflected in Hebrew literature, was twofold. On the one hand, the attraction of the Jew to the Christian world seemed stronger and more daring. It is not coincidental that sexual relations, love and marriage between Jews and Christians became frequent themes in Hebrew prose fiction at the turn of the century.[18] On the other hand, national consciousness became stronger, and the reaction to love when frustrated by antisemitism became more desperate and dramatic. From the turn of the twentieth century Hebrew and Yiddish writers gave vent to an awareness of the irresistible charm the Christian held for Jews, while warning the reader the price of giving in to its lures.

Erotic relationships between Jews and non-Jews is a theme characteristic of Hebrew literature during the first quarter of the twentieth century. It appears in the works of leading writers such as M. Y. Berdichevski, H. N. Bialik, Sh. Tchernikhovsky, Y. Steinberg, S. Y. Agnon, D. Vogel, and others. While in reality the Christian seduction could also have a social motivation, Hebrew literature of this period describes the attraction of the Jew to the Christian world as aesthetic, or romantic or (most often) purely sexual. This view is due to fin-de-siècle literary taste, no less than to the new conditions of Jewish life.

At the turn of the twentieth century, Christian characters begin to appear in Hebrew literature, together with their surroundings. Now we find the Church and the Cross as a natural part of the literary scene, even if they do not have any thematic function.[19] Relations between Jews and non-Jews are now described as closer: the Christian is sometimes the Jew's good friend, or his room mate, or a student in the same university, or (most often) his or her lover. The Christians are no longer necessarily enlightened and open-minded. They can also be as narrow minded and devoid of European education as any ghetto Jew, such as the hero's German landlord in Micha Yosef Berdychevski's 'Two Camps' (1900), who is an alcoholic shoemaker. Mikahel, the hero, comes from Poland to study in the German University, and finds himself in a complicated sexual relationship with both his landlady and her daughter. Berdychevski (1865-1921), who at the age of twenty-five left Russia to study in Breslau, Berlin and Bern, was a pioneer in describing the inner world of the non-Jew. His non-Jewish characters, just like his Jewish ones, are motivated by their unconscious drives, especially by sexual needs, and they behave according to their individual psycho-physiological constitution.

Chernikhovsky's long poem *Baruch of Magentsa* [Mainz] (1901) ends with the madness of the Jewish hero, who murders his Christian wife and two daughters. The story, set in the Middle Ages, describes a Jew who voluntarily converted to Christianity after being enchanted by the beauty of the church, the music of the choir and the intoxicating smell of incense. However, after realising the cruelty inflicted on his people by the Crusaders, he sets fire to the church and murders his beloved wife and daughters. In his madness he fantasises about the form of his revenge. Strangely enough, his fantasies are based on European non-Jewish folklore: he will be transformed into a vampire and suck the blood of Christians. It is perhaps worth noting that Tchernikhovsky's wife was a German Christian,[20] and that in his early poetry he was a great admirer of European 'Greek' (in contrast to Jewish) beauty.

Jewish-Christian love always has a tragic ending in early twentieth century Hebrew literature. The roots of this tragedy, however, are differently explained: the tragedy of Tevye's daughter was a result of a social class conflict. In later literary works conversion does not necessarily takes place and there is no social scandal. The relationship is purely sexual, and it is a private matter. Love is frustrated, just as it rises, because of the cruel, deterministic laws of nature.

While Tevye's daughter is an innocent victim, at the beginning of the twentieth century Hebrew writers started to examine male Jewish attraction to Christian girls, and even to consider the wrongs committed to Christian girls by their Jewish lovers.

In 'Without Her' (1899)21 Berdychevski describes a destructive love affair between a Jewish student in a German university city and a local Christian girl. He abandons her because he perceives the chasm lying between them, and the separation causes him a severe mental crisis. Three years later he learns that she has gone mad.

In 'Behind the Fence' (1910)[22] Hayyim Nahman Bialik tells about a young Jewish boy who peeps through the cracks of a closed fence into the neighbouring yard, where he can see the suffering of a Ukrainian orphan girl tortured by her stepmother. Childish games between the two leads to sexual relations and pregnancy. However, there is no question of marriage: the Jewish boy, who is brave enough to fight with Christian hooligans, finds himself too weak to overcome the big blind fence between the Jewish and Christian worlds. While the author invites the reader's sympathy for the wrong the Jew committed against the Christian girl, the idea of marriage is beyond his horizons.

The catastrophic results of Jewish-Christian sexual relations are even more dramatic in Micha Yosef Berdychevski's story 'The Two' (1912).[23] It this tale a Jewish girl travels from one of the Baltic countries in order to study in a German university, where she falls in love with a Christian student from Russia. Berdychevski stresses the complete spiritual distance between the two young people, who are attracted to each other only by blind sexual drive. They experience a short-lived idyll, and then, seemingly without cause, the young Russian begins to treat his wife cruelly, drinking heavily. When she tells him that she is pregnant, he hits and kicks her. The story ends with their inevitable separation.

For both Bialik and Berdychevski there is nothing theological or spiritual in the Jewish attraction to the Christian: it is purely physical. The failure of romantic Jewish-Christian relations seems inevitable: it is perceived as a consequence of the deterministic laws of genetics. Couching the attraction of the Jew to the Christian world in terms of sexual drive reflects not only a new historical and social reality, but also a new way of thinking about the Jewish problem. It is a metaphor, hinting at male Jewish insecurity and the search for physical vitality.

Such understanding of the Jewish problem was characteristic of European conceptions of the Jew at the turn of the century, when differences between nations and cultures were explained on the basis of racial rather than spiritual factors. In this context, sexual attraction does not represent a conscious choice, but a blind drive. It expresses the irresistible charm of the Christian world in the eyes of the European

Jewish intellectual, whose inferiority complex internalised antisemitic stereotypes. David Vogel exemplifies this understanding of Jewish-Christian relations in his novel Marriage Life,[24] which takes place in pre-Nazi Vienna. The hero, a feeble Jewish intellectual, hastily marries a huge blond woman from an aristocratic Viennese family. They share no spiritual or emotional common ground whatsoever, but he feels desperately physically attracted to her. Their married life is depicted as hell on earth, leading to the death of their baby (whom he treats with characteristically Jewish devoted fatherhood) and his complete madness.

The work of nobel prize winner Shmuel Yosef Agnon is preoccupied with the subject of erotic relations between Jews and Christians.[25] Agnon is basically a Neo-Romantic writer, so his depiction of Jewish-Christian relations is not intended to be realistic. It is a poetic expression – sometimes folkloric or balladistic, or symbolic - of Agnon's nostalgia for a Jewish reality which was deserted and destroyed, and also of his anger at the evils that was done to his people. In his story 'Ha-panas' (*The Lamp*, 1907) whose Yiddish version 'Toiten Tanz' (*Dance of Death*), was expanded into the story 'Mekholat Ha-mavet' (*Dance of Death*, 1919) Agnon describes a Polish squire who murdered a Jewish groom during his wedding and took his bride to be his wife. In 'The Lamp' their grandson converted to Judaism and came at night to study Torah in the old house of study, while the epilogue to the Hebrew 'Dance of Death' describes a nocturnal meeting between the bride and the murdered groom.

In Bialik's, Berdychevski's, Vogel's and Agnon's prose fiction individual Jews are not innocent victims: their yielding to the power of sexual seduction is seen as responsible for the suffering they bring on themselves and on their Christian partners. In literary works written in Israel after the Shoah by European-born writers, the motif of Jewish-Christian sexual relations provides a vehicle for even harsher criticism. In Agnon's The *Lady and the Pedlar* (1942)26 a Jewish pedlar arrives at an isolated house in a remote village. The mistress of the house buys something from him, then asks him to repair something in the house. He stays for the night and gradually becomes increasingly useful, ingratiating himself more and more with the mistress. Comfort convinces him to stay for good, but he notices something strange: she never eats anything. He becomes aware that this woman is a vampire, whose food is men's blood, and that the only way to escape his fate is to murder her and flee. The names of the two characters, Joseph and Helena, makes clear the allegory. Agnon on the one hand he blames the Jew for his love of comfort and for his blind naivety, and on the other hand he demonises the Christian world, thus expressing the traumatised Jewish reaction to the behaviour of European Christians during the Shoah.

Agnon's attitude to Jewish-Crhistian relations is shared by the Israeli novelist Aharon Appelfeld, born in 1932 in Chernovitz (now in Ukraine). Appelfeld experienced the Shoah as a young teenager. In his short stories, collected in *Ashan* (*Smoke*, 1962), *Ba-gai haporeh* (*In the Fertile Valley*, 1964) and *Kfor al ha-aretz* (*Frost Upon the Land*, 1964) as well as in later novels, bestial cruelty is intrinsic to the survival instincts which non-Jews possess by nature, which Jews must learn through harsh experience in order not to perish. In his *Badenheim* (1979, English: 1980, 2001) and in later novels he severely criticises the illusions of pre-Shoah Western European Jews, who were living in a fools' paradise, assuming that antisemitism would have no bearing on their highly cultured existence. In his novels *Katarina* (1989, English 1990) and *Iron tracks* (1991, English: 1998), Appelfeld continues the tradition of warning against the sexual attraction of Jews to Christian women and against the seductiveness of proselytism for the sake of social success. For Appelfeld, the Shoah represents the most bitter disappointment of the Jewish people, on account of their love for European culture. It proves that Jews should remain Jewish, and that behind the enlightened European person a bloodthirsty beast may be found. Thus both Appelfeld and Agnon express a deep suspicion of European culture and Christian morality.

6.

From what has been said so far, one might get the impression that modern Hebrew and Yiddish writers had very little interest either in Christianity as a religion or in the religious experience of Christian characters. Christians were either depicted as 'good goyim' or as 'bad goyim', and their religious inner lives were ignored. Moses Rosenson's books, published in St Petersburg during the 1870s and 1890s, where the writer recommends Jewish-Christian fraternity, were an exception and not coincidentally were strongly criticised.[27] This impression should not surprise us, literature being what it is – an emotional expression of individual and collective experience. Traditional Jewish life in Eastern Europe was disconnected with Christianity, a fact which S.Y. Agnon describes in 'Ma'aglei tsedek' (*Circles of Justice*, 1923). In this tale an old Polish Jew saves half of his meagre earnings to go to Eretz Israel. He drops the money into the charity box set at a Calvary, and after some time has passed goes to take his money by breaking open the charity box. That very day priests come from Rome to open the box and the Jew in caught in the act, stone in hand, and thrown into prison. In his novel *Bridal Canopy* (1929) the early nineteenth-century hero, Reb Yudel the Hassid, is a complete stranger to the Christian customs and rituals he encounters during his journey through the villages of Galicia. He also takes care not to look at the Christian 'images' which are scattered all along the countryside (but the narrator is well aware of their presence).[28] Even when Jews and Christians met each other as students in the same university their knowledge of each other's religion was very limited: 'They also have a religion and they pray, but they don't believe in the Cross', is the way a German student thinks of the Jewish student she meets in Bersichevski's story 'The Friend' (1902). Here Berdichevski, who in later life dedicated many years to comparative Jewish-Christian studies (in German),[29] humorously dramatized the limits to inter-religious understanding, as he experienced it during his student life in Bern.

It is, however, surprising to discover the great interest in Christianity and in the figure of Jesus, which grew in Hebrew and Yiddish literature and art in the three first decades of the twentieth century, at the same time when the movement of Jewish national revival was gaining power. In 1912 Zionism was even accused of being the cause of this phenomenon:

> Since the beginning of the twentieth century young masskilim in Russia (...) have begun to be engaged in problems of nationality and Zionism, and have found the solution by praising and flattering to Jesus the God of the Christians whom they exalted as the prophet of [our] God.[30]

But this change can better be explained as a result of both historical changes in Jewish-Christian relations and new trends more generally in European culture.

During the first quarter of the twentieth century Jewish life – even in the shtetl – became more closely acquainted with Christianity, whether this is understood in terms of contact between intellectuals and revolutionaries, or increased conversion. This change in Jewish life can be clearly traced by comparing Berdichevski's image of the shtetl in his From *My Little Town* (1900) to that in his *Miriam* (1921):[31] while in the earlier work there is no sign of Christian presence, in the latter we find a series of Jewish characters who are attracted to Christianity, marry a Christian girl or even convert without leaving their dwelling place. For Jewish intellectuals and artists, Christianity became part of their inner world. The interest of Jewish artists in Christianity and in Jesus began already in the 1860s in Russia, when Mark (Mordechai) Antokolski sculpted The *Kiss of Judas Iscariot* (1867) and *Jesus in Chains* (1874). Comparisons between the Besht (the founder of Hasidism), and Jesus appear in writings S. Dubnov and M.Y. Berdychevsky.[32] Baal-Teshuva explains Chagall's attraction to Jesus thus:

> Because Christianity was central to the European cultural tradition, it attracted many Jews in the modern period: Edmund Husserl, Gustav Mahler, Alfred Doeblin, Roman Jakobson, and many others converted to Christianity. His friends in the interwar period, Raissa and Jacques Maritain, actively propagated conversion of the Jews. Chagall was not one of them, since he was deeply connected with a Jewish folk sensibility; but culturally, the Christian world was a tangible reality in his work and life.[33]

Ecumenical trends in Europe, and especially the neo-Christian 'spiritual revolution' in Russia, gave rise to intellectual experiments to blur the borders between Judaism and Christianity.[34] Interest in the psychology of the unconscious was also a factor which diminished the importance of differences between religions. Vladimir Solovyov's (1857-1900) impressions of Jewish thought and culture contributed to the convergence of Judaism and Christianity in Hebrew and Yiddish literatures.[35] Positive interest in Judaism continued among some of Solovyov's disciples (V. Ivanov, N Berdiaev, S. Bulgakov) and among writers who were not close to him: Fiodor Sologub, Leonid Andreev and Maxim Gorky. In his short stories and dramas, Leonid Andreev described the modern Jew as the real Jesus, and severely criticised contemporary Christian bourgeois morality. In his story *Judas Iscariot* (1907) he shocked the Russian church by creating a positive literary image of Judas Iscariot.

This was a time when Jewish writers used Christian symbols and narratives to mythologize and universalise the Jewish experience. Jesus – separated from the Church and from the history of Crusades, blood-libels, ghettos and auto-da-fés – became a universal tragic figure, a symbol of human suffering, sometimes on a par with the Jewish messiah.[36] Thus writers blurred the borders between the two religions, diminishing the importance of the differences between them. By adopting a semi-Christian point of view they seemed to suggest the possibility of a Jewish-Christian experience. At the same time contemporary Christian ethics was being attacked with unprecedented boldness by Jewish writers and thinkers. This duality – deep sympathy with Jesus the Jew, on the one hand, and sharp criticism of Christian ethics in practice, on the other hand – is characteristic of Hebrew and Yiddish literatures during the twentieth century.

Erasing the borders between Judaism and Christianity became possible in an atmosphere of a 'devaluation of all values', when paradox became a worldview. Paradox was a central stylistic device in symbolist literature, which was absorbed in Hebrew and Yiddish literatures at the beginning of the twentieth century. Symbolism in art and literature, where national myths and religious symbols represented universal subconscious dream-like experiences, enabled Jewish artists and writers to adopt Christian myths and make them part of their own inner world. For them Christianity, together with Kabbala and Hassidic folklore, was a legitimate source of symbolic motifs. The symbolist trend can be seen in Efraim Lilien's 1903 painting of the Jewish victims in the Kishinev pogrom as a crucified old Jew. Marc Chagall in his painting *Golgotha* (1912) painted himself as a mythological baby-Jesus, and in later paintings (*The White Crucifixion*, 1938, *The Yellow Crucifixion* 1943 and others) he painted a Jewish Jesus, symbolising the suffering of the Jewish people in pogroms and in the Shoah.[37]

In the late 1910s and in the 1920s depictions of Jesus as a Jew, or of the Jewish experience in the Diaspora as Jesus-like, became frequent – together with other Christian images – in Hebrew literature, although to a lesser degree than in Yiddish writings. Most Hebrew writers rejected the 'cosmopolitan' identity as a dangerous illusion, and tried to build a new 'healthy' and proud Jewish spirit, liberated from the complex of inferiority to Christian culture. However, they had the same wish to be translated into Russian and other European languages, and to become equal participants in world literature. Their sensitivity to the Christian world around them was no lesser than the Yiddish writers'; they were just less ready to 'blur the borders'. Not always did they succeed, for they were more absorbed in European-Christian culture than they could realize.

Jewish-Christian interchange of myths influenced even Hayyim Nahman Bialik (1873-1934), the most influential figure in modern Hebrew poetry. He was crowned with the title 'Poet of National Revival', because his poetry was perceived as an authentic poetic expression of the Jewish soul. Bialik attacked his non-Jewish context when it threatened the continuity of Jewish culture. His poems, however, sometimes show the influence of Russian-Christian traditions. For example, the poet's mission is to suffer and sacrifice himself for his people, like Jesus; the mother and the beloved woman are depicted as a form of Madonna, merging the Kabbalistic Shekhina with the neo-Christian Solovyovian symbol. In *The Scroll of Fire* (1905), however, Bialik symbolically refutes Solovyovian ideas of redemption through love of woman or through sacrificing individuality for the sacred All-Unity, presenting these seductive but false Christian symbols as alien to the spirit of Judaism and dangerous for its future. In his story *The Legend of Three and Four* (1934) Bialik symbolically described universal peace and love between Jews and Christians in terms of poetic utopia.

Literary interest in Jesus and Christianity was accompanied by the serialized publication of Yosef Klausner's 'Jesus of Nazareth' as a supplement to He-Atid (Berlin, 1908. The book appeared in Jerusalem 1922, English: 1925), the first academic work on Jesus' life in Hebrew. A few months later H. Graetz' chapter on Christ and Christianity belatedly appeared in Hebrew translation.[38] These publications were followed by a stormy polemic on the relation between Judaism and Christianity and on the Jewishness of Christ. In 1910 Ahad Ha-Am (Asher Ginzberg), the leading and most influential essayist at that time, published his essay 'Between Two Opinions'.[39] After attacking the idea of including the New Testament in the Jewish canon,[40] Ahad Ha-am went on to explain the differences between Judaism and Christianity. This was followed by a series of polemic essays written by S.A. Horodetski and S.Y. Hurwitz, published during 1910-1914.[41] Their main theme was the acceptance of early Christianity as part of Judaism.

Jewish identification with the Jesus myth became a fashion in Yiddish literature towards the end of the first decade of the twentieth century. The Yiddish symbolist writer *Der Nister* (Pinkhas Kahanovitch) ended his collection *Thoughts and Motifs* (Vilna, 1907) with Mary's prayer for a son, despite Satan's warnings that a tragic fate would await him.[42]

Chagall's use of Christian together with Jewish imagery found its counterpart in the Yiddish poetry of Itsik Manger, where Christian symbols become inseparable from the inner world of the Jew.43 From the early 1920s onwards his poetry is suffused not only with the Hebrew Bible but also with discussions of, and references to Christianity in general and Jesus in particular. In Manger's poems, 'Christ's head sobs symbolically in our dreams…The hand of the holy St Francis of Assisi lies on our heart'.44 In his first volume of poetry, Stars on the Roof: Poems and Ballads (1929) the cross appears repeatedly, indicating the poet's loneliness and his constant inner suffering:

> Now I am alone, and night is with me,
> And a red cross burns on my door,
> My wild, sick, thought.[45]

In his early work, Manger used a wide range of Christian elements as metaphors and symbols, such as his description of the night as 'Maria Magdalena',[46] or using sankt (saint) as an epithet for Baal Shem Tov, the founder of Hassidism.[47] Manger also employed the landscape of Christianity (churches, clergymen) as a backdrop to Jewish life. The use of Christian metaphors and symbols is part of Manger's figurative language even in his later poetry, written after the Shoah, especially in poems about his childhood: e.g., the night is a 'barefoot monk' in a poem published in 1948.48 Manger labelled his poems in Stars on the Roof as 'Ballads, Poems of Christ and Poems of the Baal Shem', and in fact, this volume is filled with direct treatments of Jesus, who appears as a symbol of human tragedy. Manger does not accept the suffering of Jesus as unique. Insisting on the universality of suffering, he writes:

> All paths that stray,
> Lead to the cross.
> It's all the same – whether Jesus was crucified
> Or the night, or I, or you![49]

In his 1929 poem 'The Sacrifice of Isaac', Isaac competes with Jesus for the privilege of being sacrificed. Jesus is seen as the one who deprived Isaac of his glory, of his original right to be the personification of sacrifice and suffering.

The 'problem of Crucifixion' became central in Yiddish literature from 1909, following the publication of two symbolist stories, L. Shapira's 'The Cross' and Scholem Asch's 'In a Carnival Night' in the Yiddish monthly Dos Neie Leben in New York.[50] In Shapira's story the cross is a terrible scar on the brow of a Jew who has been tortured during a pogrom.

Asch's story tells of a Christian carnival in sixteenth-century Rome, where eight Jewish leaders are tortured as part of the show. Asch describes Jesus climbing down from the cross on St Peter's Church in order to join the persecuted, followed by Mary who joins Rachel to sew the shrouds for them. Thus Asch hints at Jewish-Christian unity. In his essay 'The Problem of Crucifixion', published in the same year in *Dos Neie Leben*, Sh. An-sky (Solomon Zainwil Rappoport) and Y. L. Peretz accused Asch of 'competition through imitation' (the term was coined by Ahad-Ha-Am), namely, giving up his 'Jewish soul' in order to win the admiration of non-Jewish readers.[51]

The traumatic Jewish experience in pre-Revolutionary Russia (as described, for example, in Isaac Babel's 'My Dovecote', 1926) did not make it easy for Jews to believe either in essential Jewish-Christian unity or in the new solidarity between enlightened Jews and Christians. Jewish critics thought Asch told the gentiles what they would like to hear. Indeed, Asch was the only Yiddish writer (before Bashevis-Singer) who enjoyed an international reputation and won literary prizes in Europe after being translated into Polish, Russian and German.

Asch dedicated most of his writing to his ecumenical mission.[52] He wished to reclaim such Christian figures as Jesus and Paul for Judaism, in order to give Jews a broader sense of their contribution to Western culture. More importantly, he wanted Christians to realise the extent to which Christianity was rooted in Jewish history and religion. He demonstrated the interdependence of the two faiths by illustrating their common heritage, and he tried to effect a rapprochement based on mutual understanding and respect. It was his belief that Christianity represented the culmination of Jewish thought, and that its rituals and concepts were rooted in Jewish ideas and practices. These ideas inspire Asch's entire work, and especially his Christian trilogy, *The Nazarene* (1939, English 1943), *The Apostle* (English 1943) and *Mary* (English 1949). The publication of these novels (the last two were published only in English translation), which became best sellers, resulted in a break between Asch and his Jewish readers. The works' Christian focus, and the fact that they were published in the time of the Shoah, caused a campaign against Asch in the American Yiddish press and in the Jewish world in general. Asch was accused of encouraging heresy and conversion by preaching Christianity.[53] He even found it difficult to find a translator to his Mary, in which the balance between Jewish and Christian points of view – which Asch tried to keep in the first two novels

– is weighted in favour of Christianity.

In a trilogy of dramas – 'The Bonds of Messiah' (written in 1907-1908), 'The Goilem' (1917-1920) and 'The Goilem Dream – A Comedy of Redemption' (1930-1932) – H. Leivik (pseudonym of Leivik Halperin) continued a tradition cultivated by modern Yiddish literature: he sought to unite the Jewish and Christian traditions by creating symbolic images of the Messiah, and to connect these with contemporary events, especially with the October Revolution in Russia.

The Yiddish and early Hebrew poetry of Uri Zvi Greenberg (1894-1981) radicalised the complex Jewish attitude towards Christianity.[54] In Albatros, a Yiddish literary almanac edited by Greenberg himself, he published long poems which expressed his attitude toward Christ with such force and audacity that the editorial office had to stop publication. Greenberg was a frontline soldier in the Austrian Army during the First World War, but deserted and lived in hiding. After a pogrom in his hometown of Lemberg (L'vov, L'viv), he became an ardent Zionist.

In early poems Greenberg often refers to Jesus as 'my brother' or 'our brother'.[55] In this context Jesus is a symbol of universal human suffering. In his long poem, 'The Mystery Man', published in 1922 in Warsaw in Albatros, Greenberg expressed his universalism with the words:

> A man, Uri Zvi, or Ivan or Mustafa
> with Shadai in his blood, or with the cross in the head
> or with half a crescent at the trembling temple.[56]

In 'In the Kingdom of the Cross' (1923) Greenberg writes: 'At the churches/ Hangs my brother/ Crucified (…) Brother Jesus, a Jewish skin and bones shrinks'.

Greenberg identified himself with the historical Jesus, whom he – like Klausner – saw as a Jewish nationalist, who had been tortured and killed by the Romans because he was a leader of an anti-Roman revolt. But he detested historical Christianity, which had gone far away from Golgotha. He described Christ as being emptied from his humanity by two thousand years of distance from Jerusalem, Bethlehem and the Galilee. Jesus, a symbol of Jewish suffering, had been crucified by Christianity, and he was still being crucified in Christian churches and cathedrals.

Greenberg gives vent to his attitude toward institutionalised Christianity with the words:

Oh Christ's bald priests!
No man has cut the veins of your hands
And no one has driven his nails in your throats
No one has brought one of you to Golgotha
And hanged him naked on a blossoming tree.
Whose is the lament?
Not yours! It is our pain, the pain of the Jewish redeemer!
Not your agonies! It is our wound.[57]

In 1922 Greenberg published in Albatros a 'concrete' poem in the form of a cross, which was entitled Uri Zvi Before the Cross/ INRI (Jesus the Nazarene King of the Jews).[58] In this poem the poet turned to Jesus, saying:

You have become inanimate, my brother Jesus. You have two thousand years on the cross. Around you the world stopped. But you have forgotten everything. Your frozen brain does not reflect...You have become inanimate, you have tranquillity on your cross. I do not have it. Not me.[59]

The poet sees the Christian cross, a symbol of sympathy with suffering, as an empty, meaningless symbol. For him Jesus becomes the representative of the Jewish fate: 'Ancient Jewish distress, Golgotha, my brother, don't you see, Golgotha is here: all around.' Pilate places phylacteries on Jesus' head, which are 'a new crown of thorns'.

In the poem 'A World on a Slope' (1922) the poet expressed his nihilistic loss of his former faith in Christian ideals. In this poem Jesus is fiercely attacked by a band of invalids and madmen who curse and mock him. They demand that he should get down from his heavenly cross and join them, the real sufferers, on earth. They cry:

Get down from the cross,
you man, in our image!
Get down! The world has chimed: thirteen![50]

Never before did any Jewish writer dare to directly attack and caricaturise the image of Christ.

At a time when many European intellectuals believed in a pacifist future,

Greenberg prophesied the destruction of Europe and its Jews. He wrote:

> But I am telling you the prophecy – the black prophecy:
> From our valleys a pillar of cloud will rise
> From our dark breaths, woe to us how bitter they are!
> And you will not realize the terror in your flesh.
> And will go on prattling from burning palates
> The Jews!
> The Jews!
> While poisonous gases will enter into palaces
> And suddenly icons will scream in Yiddish.[61]

The Jews have no chance to survive in Europe. 'Ten will remain, ten pain-stricken Jews ... in order to prove: there was such a nation, on the Christian earth of distress', he wrote in his 'In the Kingdom of the Cross' (1923). Greenberg describes the metamorphosis he went through:

> I have been long meditating in the inwardness: is it possible
> That those who kneel in Europe toward Bethlehem
> And sanctify the bible – are those, these barbarians,
> Whose dream is to annihilate the Jews completely?

Now he must admit that what the elders used to say about gentiles is true:

> Oh, true-true-true is what my elders say:
> The dead in the cloister is not my brother, he is Jesus.[62]

In 1925 Greenberg wrote scathingly, 'The land of enlightened Europe is not enlightened for the Jews. We are the most contemptible of humanity, as is well known'.[63]

Greenberg perceived Christianity to be one element of a suspicious anti-Jewish world: 'We [the Jews] are the only lonely ones in the world', he wrote.

When already in Palestine, Greenberg wrote in a Hebrew essay (in his characteristic expressionistic style):

> Hey, it should be said once and for all: the pain of the pure Christianity
> is the pain of the stabbed Judaism. The wound is in our flesh under
> the skin, not theirs. The problem: Jesus of Nazareth, who was crossed

when he was thirty-three years old – this is our problem, from us it arose.[64]

His fierce attacks on Christian Europe reach their climax in his post-Shoah collection of Hebrew poetry, *Streets of the River* (1951). Greenberg's emotional attitude toward the gentile world represents the psychologically disastrous results of the Jewish experience in antisemitic Europe. The memory of this cruel experience is still active in the collective psychology and in political decisions in Israel and elsewhere.

7.

The interest in Jesus and early Christianity did not disappear from Hebrew Zionist literature when its centre moved from Eastern Europe to Palestine during the 1910s-1920s. During this period of transition there were strong contacts and mutual interest between Hebrew writers in Palestine and the Jewish Diaspora in Europe.

'The Brenner Affair' (1910 and 1914) marked a watershed in Jewish polemical attitudes to Christianity and to Christ, this time starting in Palestine.[65] In December 1910 Yosef Hayyim Brenner, who was then the leading Hebrew writer in Palestine, published in the Zionist Socialist periodical Hapo'el Hatsa'ir an essay entitled, 'In Journalism and in Literature'.[66] Its starting point was the wave of conversions to Christianity among young intellectual Jews in Russia at that time, and with which Jewish journalism in Europe was obsessively dealing as part of the New Year's reviews. Jewish journalists were attacking the shameful and dangerous phenomenon of shemad (conversion to Christianity), while serious essayists, such as Ahad Ha-Am, were engaged in asserting the praiseworthy aspects of Judaism and its superiority over Christianity. Brenner, who considered himself to be 'a free (secular) Jew', argued, that both reactions were out of place. Jews in Russia and Germany did not convert to Christianity because of theological considerations, they simply adopted a Russian or German 'form of life', which had nothing to do with Christian moral ideals. This was why proving the superiority of Judaism would not prevent conversion. Besides, the converts had long before left their Jewish forms of life, so who cared if they converted? Brenner argued that the sacred writings of all the religions contained high moral contents, but that deeds, not theory, are the real criteria of ethics. The moral quality of a person and his adherence to Christian or Jewish morality did not depend on the writings which he has studied, but on his individual psycho-physiological qualities. Morality, said Brenner, in disagreement with Ahad Ha-am and Klausner, has not a national trait. There was no connection between contemporary European national cultures and the Christianity of 'the poor Jew Joshua of Nazareth',[67] just as contemporary Judaism was a long way from being identical with biblical Judaism. Brenner also claimed that the New Testament should not be rejected by Jews, for it was kith and kin to the Jewish spiritual tradition: 'I do not see any fundamental difference between the ascetic world view and the submission before God of the prophet of Anatoth [Jeremiah] and the prophet of Nazareth [Jesus]'.[68] The Jesus myth (Brenner used the term legenda) should be treated with suspicion, because 'like every religious lie, like every continuing tradition' it was an 'intentional illusion' invented to close up 'the terrible abyss of the difficult riddle of life'. Nevertheless, one can be a very good Jew, devoted with one's whole heart to one's nation, whilst regarding Jesus with religious awe, he argued. 'I understand that there are souls which have a yearning to other worlds, and they sometimes lift up their eyes to the 'good shepherd'... It is clear: the problem of the Christian myth is the problem of religious mysticism as a whole, and for whom there is no God in heaven there is also no one who can be his son or his disciple'.[69]

Brenner's essay was the starting point of a three years' polemic, involving many dozens of stormy reactions in Hebrew, Yiddish and Russian, most of which condemned Brenner's ideas and accused him of blasphemy. Reacting to the scandal in an unpublished essay written in late 1913 or early 1914, Brenner wrote:

> We have the right to praise Christianity or to condemn it, and for this right we are fighting! – But Europe is not Christian, and converts are not Christians. They are doing business. It is shameful, but what does it have to do with Christianity? What does it have to do with the ideals of Christianity, whether they found their place in our [Jewish] literature or not? ... Our nationality does not demand from us to curse Jesus, as it does not demand that we despise Tolstoy and all the Christian writings. ... We sometimes see in the story of Jesus a world tragedy and our heart goes to him, the tortured prophet ... and sometimes we see in the whole business of prophecy a ridiculous and comic matter, and in his disciples fools who deviated from the way of the world.[70]

Brenner's later literary works (he was murdered by Arab terrorists in 1921 at the age of 40) show sympathy for moral ideals which can be considered as Christian – asceticism, submissiveness and a readiness to be sacrificed. If Christianity was for him 'the problem of religious mysticism as a whole', then he was approaching it in his mature work. Brenner's story *From Here and There* (1911), which describes the hardships and misery of Zionist pioneer life in Palestine, ends with the image of an old man and his grandchild (whose father has just been murdered by Arabs) both carrying thorns on their clothes and heads, looking at an old woman who is baking new bread.[71] The prototype of this old man in Brenner's story was no other than Aharon David Gordon (1856-1922), who in 1904 emigrated from Russia to Palestine, where he founded 'The Religion of Labour' and the first collective settlement, Degania. Gordon himself, after having translated Tolstoy's What is Art? into Hebrew, wrote an unpublished essay under the title 'Examining the Difference Between Judaism and Christianity', where he rejected Tolstoy's anti-national preaching and tried to prove both the basic purity of Judaism and its moral superiority over Christianity.[72]

Zionist writers coming to Palestine from Russia and Poland brought with them, together with the heritage of Hebrew and Yiddish literatures, their Russian background. In this context, Jewish suffering in the Diaspora and even more so that of Zionist pioneers was interpreted – like the suffering in Russia before and after the Revolutions – as part of an apocalyptic narrative, where martyrdom and bloodshed were necessary steps to redemption.[73] The influence of A. Blok's long poem 'The Twelve' (1918), where Bolshevik revolutionaries are crowned with Jesus-like halos, was particularly conspicuous in the poetry and prose of writers who experienced the revolution in Russia.

Hayyim Hazaz in his 'Revolution Stories' cycle, portrayed young Jews participating in the Bolshevik Revolution in the image of Jesus or John the Baptist. Thus in 'From This and from the Other' (1924) Henich, the young Jewish revolutionary fighter, reminds everybody – especially when he is dying – of John the Baptist.74 In 'Shmuel Frankfurter' (1925) the hero looks like Jesus. He is also attracted to Jesus' ideals (mediated by Tolstoy), which he tries to carry out in post-Revolutionist Russia. His comrade Rabi Ber argues: 'Give your left cheek … yes, yes. These 'afters' were served by Him. Of course! Of course! But gewald [Help! In Yiddish], why should he hit me, ha? Why am I – from top to toe – nothing but a cheek? I am nothing but a cheek and he is nothing but a hand?'[75] He is finally murdered by White Russian soldiers, who while torturing him cry joyfully 'let's crucify him, let's crucify him!'.[76] His grave becomes a ritual centre for the local Ukrainian farmers who believe that Shmuel was resurrected from the dead. Thus Hazaz adds a sceptical-ironical dimension to the motif of the Jesus-like suffering Jew. A similar plot is to be found in Avigdor Ha-Me'iri's story 'On Behalf of Jesus the Nazarene: How My Hair Grew White in One Night' (1928), this time in the form of a memoir.[77] Ha-Me'iri, who during the First World War was a soldier in the Austro-Hungarian army, describes the fate of his Jewish comrade, who together with him was taken captive by Russian soldiers. He was forced to drink human blood, crucified and buried alive by a Russian commander.

Literary depictions of the extreme suffering which was part of the pioneers' experience often deployed Christian symbols, especially those of Job and Jesus. Major writers such as Uri Zvi Greenberg, Avraham Shlonsky, Yitshak Lamdan, and Yosef Hayyim Brenner all mythologized through the Jewish in these terms.

Klausner, Russian-born editor of the flagship of Hebrew literature in Europe, Ha-shiloah, and the first professor of Hebrew Literature at the Hebrew University in Jerusalem (between 1925 and 1949), devoted many years to the study of Jesus of Nazareth.[78] His *Jesus of Nazareth* (1922) emphasised the similarity between Jesus' teaching and that of early Judaism, while suggesting that Paul merged the 'pure' Christianity with Roman heathen 'lower' elements. Klausner also stressed the similarity between the original Christianity and the Zionist experience, identifying both as movements of Messianic redemption. Literary authors such as Natan Bistirtski , Avraham Kabak and Hayyim Hazaz, shared Klausner's sympathy with Jesus and his views on Jesus' Jewish sources.

Natan Bistritski's drama *Judas Iscariot* (1930), Avraham Kabak's novel *The Narrow Path* (1937) and Hayyim Hazaz's unfinished novel on Jesus (1947-1948)[79] represent the continuing interest in Jesus and early Christianity in pre-Israeli Hebrew prose and drama. Following Klausner, they portray Jesus with deep sympathy and emphasize his Jewishness. They characterize him as the founder of one of the many movements and sects into which Judaism was split in the first century. The 'good' Judaism of Jesus is distinguished from the 'bad' Christianity of his apostles, especially Paul. Paul is seen as the one who popularized the morally 'pure'

Christianity and brought it nearer to Roman (heathen) culture. The New Testament is reinterpreted in a way less injurious to Jewish feelings. Descriptions of local geography (familiar to the writer and readers as part of their everyday life) enhance the suggestion that what was told in the New Testament is part of the readers' own reality. The Hebrew speech of the characters in these novels is close to Talmudic Hebrew, mixed with Aramaic elements, thus creating the impression that Jesus' preaching was an organic continuation of post-biblical Judaism. These writers tried to change the Evangelists' legends into modern prose in the tradition of psychological realism.

In Bistirtski's drama attention is focused on Judas Iscariot, who is the leading protagonist. His introverted behaviour and other moral qualities make him appear the real messiah: he is 'poor and rides on a donkey', symbolizing the humble Jewish Messiah of the Old Testament (Zechariah 9:9). He tries in vain to convince Jesus that the only way he can preserve his integrity is to flee from his misguided followers. Judas Iscariot thus becomes the prophet of Christianity's decadence.

Comparing Kabak's *The Narrow Path* to Sholem Asch's *The Nazarene* the Jewish American critic A.D. Friedland wrote that Asch's Jesus the Nazarene failed, because it was created under the shadow of apologetics, characteristic of the Jewish psychology of the Diaspora, while Kabak's Jesus is 'Hebrew' – a creature of the free spirit of Jewish Zionist revival. While Asch expended great effort on documentary details and cited exactly gospel on Jesus, Kabak painted his characters objectively with Rembrandt's brush: in Kabak's novel there is a natural harmony between Jesus' sayings and the nature around him, says Friedland. Kabak describes Jesus' cultural-spiritual background in a more realistic way and his characters are psychologically convincing, while Asch's characters are artificial, detached from reality.[80]

Critics in Eretz Israel were unenthusiastic about Kabak's novel. They accused him of interpreting Jesus in a non-Jewish spirit – not even according to the gospel sources – but in accordance with the approach of Christian liberals, or humanist neo-Christians such as Tolstoy or Freud. One critic even expressed the opinion that any attempt by a Jew to write about Jesus by a Jew, in the Hebrew language, and in the land of the Fathers, must necessarily fail, because this subject was so loaded with bitter memory and could therefore not be treated in a merely artistic way.81 Such disagreements between the critics show that the move to a new life in Eretz Israel did not always open the gate to a new, positive, more intimate understanding of Christianity.

In Hebrew poetry written from the 1920s to the 1950s by Avraham Shlonsky (1900-1973), Natan Alterman (1910-1970) and other poets, the sacred female is a symbol, which enables the merging of Jewish mysticism with European-Christian traditions. Following Russian symbolism and Bialik's poetry these poets unite the Kabbalistic image of the Shekhina together with Russian symbolist Sophiology. In their poems the amorphous anonymous divine woman appears as a symbol of various ideals and hopes in support of which the contemporary generation believed it was necessary to fight, even unto death.

Pre-state Israeli Zionist poetry adopted the Jewish-Christian (and Muslim) apocalyptic narrative of redemption, which has its roots in the Old Testament (Isaiah, Joel, Zechariah and Daniel) and its classical model in the Apocalypse of John. In Russia, especially in the period before and after the October Revolution, apocalyptic thinking was prevalent. During the 1910s- 1930s apocalyptic motifs were used in Hebrew and Yiddish poetry as a way of understanding contemporary Jewish suffering . Zionism was often understood as a messianic apocalyptic process. This understanding was common to poets of left and right wing Zionist parties (such as Shlonski and Greenberg).[82]

Hebrew literature in the pre-state Israeli period seldom deals with local Christianity and Christians in the Holy Land.[83] An exceptional example is Menahem Ussishkin's memoir 'Four Guardians' (1905).[84] The narrator visits three Christian churches – the Russian Church on Mount Scopus, the Catholic Church on Mount Tavor, and a Protestant Church by the sea of Galilee – followed by a Sephardi synagogue in Jerusalem.Ussishkin makes it clear that the Christian churches are well kept and cared for, while the synagogue is dirty and neglected, making a bad impression on the Jewish visitor. In harshly criticising Jewish civilisation,Ussishkin continues the tradition of Hebrew Haskalah literature. A few short stories, written by minor writers, express suspicion and fear of missionary activities. Yitzhak Kumer, the hero of Agnon's novel *Only Yesterday* (1945, English 1931, 1957, 2000) shares the same fear, also indicating that migration may not be enough to change psychological mechanisms: although the novel was written in a new land, the sensitivity of the European-born writer to antisemitism remained very high.

Still, the first signs of change appear, for example, in Aryeh Lifshitz' story 'The Sister and the Nun' (written in the 1930s), in which a young nun, who takes care of the narrator, arouses his love and admiration.[85] The feeling of danger dissolves, as the narrator's love for the nun does not endanger his Jewishness. Interest in the sexual and psychological life of nuns is the centre of K. L. Silman's short story 'Pilgrims' (1929) and in a novel by Shoshana Shababo, a Yemeni writer, *Maria: A Story from the Nuns' Life in the Holy Land* (1932).[86] Conspicuous in both is the freedom from 'the Jewish problem'.

8.

Jewish-Christian relations appear less in Israeli than in pre-Israeli Hebrew literature. The interest of the Israeli reader in this theme is so limited, that he would sometimes not even notice its presence. 'Christians and Christianity were up to now missing from modern Hebrew literature', said a literary critic and an experienced teacher of literature in 1975 when talking about Amos Oz's *Unto Death*. Trying to remember literary works which have dealt with goyim, he mentioned two examples of stories which describe Arab life.[87] Such a mistake is a witness of a major change in Jewish collective psychology: Jewish-Christian relations, which was a major issue in the life of the European Jew, does not play a major part in Israeli reality, which is full of other political and cultural tensions. In Israel it is Arabs, not Christians, who are regarded as the dangerous Other. This may not be the case for pre-Israeli writers who continued to create after 1948 (Agnon and Hazaz, for example) or for those who came to Israel from Europe after the Holocaust. Their view may sometimes continue the European Jewish experience.

In Israel, as elsewhere in the Jewish world, the Shoah is understood as the climax of a long history of European antisemitism, rooted in Christianity (notwithstanding Hitler's anti-Christian policy). The non-Christian behaviour of so many Christians during the *Shoah* created a deep disappointment in and suspicion of Christianity. Among the plethora of memoirs of Jews during the Second World War, one finds many descriptions of personal Jewish-Christian relations. In this literary context, however, Christians are generally treated as different persons, sometimes with great disappointment and bitterness, sometimes humorously, not as representatives of Christian theology.[88] The only Israeli writer who continues the Agnon-Greenberg tradition of demonizing Christian cruelty and seduction is Aharon Appelfeld. Appelfeld, who often expresses his alienation to Israeli culture, expresses the experience of the Jew who cannot recover from the trauma of the *Shoah*. Appelfeld does not believe there will be any improvement in understanding between Judaism and European Christianity in the future. He views the search for such understanding as a continuation of the Jewish mistakes before the Shoah.

The reader of Israeli literature – who is in most cases a non-religious native-born Israeli – often tends to avoid Jewish rituals, but willingly encounters Christianity in music, art, and architecture, disregarding the implied theological meaning of his aesthetic experiences. 'True, for generations Jews were massacred in the name of the Gospel, but is the Gospel the necessary reason for that?' asked Y. Carmel, in an article which refutes arguments against the performance of Bach's 'Johannes Passion' and 'Mathew Passion' in Israeli concert halls in the early 1970s.[89] Having read the New Testament as a youth in pre-state Israel he observes that 'at that time our Jewish feeling was so firm. So whole, so self-evident and so romantic, that there was no place for fanaticism or for pride, and that is why we were standing above any insult or criticism [of Judaism]'.[90] For the non-religious Israeli, Christianity is neither seductive nor dangerous, it is rather a terra incognita.[91]

Israeli research on Christianity, carried out by David Flusser, Shlomo Pines, Hayyim Cohen, Yaakov Fleishman, Hayyim Cohen, Israel Yuval and others,[92] as well as the archaeological findings of the Dead Sea Scrolls, aroused interest in early Christianity as a local historical phenomenon, closely tied to the history of post-biblical Judaism. However, Christianity is less available to the average Israeli than to the Jew who lives in a Christian country. The Israeli school curriculum does not contain anything from the New Testament.

Two historical short novels, Yigal Mossenzon's *Judas Iscariot* (1962) and Amos Oz's *Unto Death* (1971, English 1992) examine the conflict between Christianity and Judaism. Common to Mossenzon and Oz is the image of the Jew as a warrior who, in terms of bravery and moral values, is superior to the Christian soldier. Such a concept would have had been inconceivable before Israeli writers had personal experience of armed self-defence and the battlefield. Nor would it have been possible without a feeling of self-assurance and justice, which belongs naturally to every normal nation. Mossenzon, born in 1917, was a commander in the 1948 War of Independence and a writer of adventure books for young adults. In his novel early Christianity is a political underground movement, very much like pre-Israeli resistance to the British Mandate. Mossenzon depicts Christianity as an anti-Roman underground organisation, whose chief commander was Bar-Abba, who commanded Judas Iscariot to extradite Jesus. In contrast to the New Testament account, Judas' crime was his inability to refuse command. In Mossenzon's novel Judas did not commit suicide: he escaped and lived on a Mediterranean island under an assumed name. Mossenzon dwells upon the difference between historical reality and the myths created by Christianity for political needs: Judas was politically expedient, he was 'the bad guy' needed for the Christian story. Like former writers (Kabak, Bistiritski) Mossenzon idealizes the character of Jesus, while his apostles appear as a band of military and political activists. The loneliness of the banished Judas Iscariot is the centre of his sympathy.

Christianity and its difference from Judaism is a constant theme in the stories and novel of Amos Oz, a native-born Israeli writer (b. 1939) and the nephew of Yosef Klausner.[93] In his early story 'The Trappist Monastery' (1962) an Israeli soldier who is fighting near the Trappist Monastery in Latrun learns about the vow of silence taken by its monks. Having experienced extreme conditions of suffering and sacrifice for the goals of life, the soldier reacts towards the asceticism of the Trappist monks with ambivalent feelings.

Oz's *Unto Death* is a symbolist psychoanalytical novel about the Crusaders. There is nothing holy in their voyage to the Holy Land, only bloodshed and corruption. The novel is written in the first person as a confession of a fanatic Crusader, whose quest for Jerusalem expresses his destructive, pathological yearning for perfect purity and his death-wish. The Crusaders cruelly torture Jews, because their Jewish vitality is an unconscious threat to their wish for purity and for death. Even their sexual sadism towards the Jews reveals their rejection of their own sensuality. Gradually they sense the secret presence of a Jew hiding among them. They find out that they carry Jewishness as part and parcel of their own Christianity. There is thus a mysterious interdependence between Judaism and Christianity. For Oz, the crusaders represent Christian antisemitic attitudes to Jews. He views antisemitism as a symptom of a deep, unconscious psychopathological complex, which lies at the bottom of Christian attitude to Jews. [94]

Oz himself, when asked by a group of famous non-Jewish writers if Unto Death is not a slap in the face of Christianity, answered:

Yes, but it is not Christianity – it's Christian Europe. My historical account with Christian Europe is bitter and more frightening than the quarrel with the Arabs and the Islam, which is just as episode. Both we and the Arabs are victims, in on way or another, of Christian Europe. And this is why it is indirectly but deeply responsible for the Israel-Arab conflict. Unto Death expresses deep genetic anger at Christian Europe, and also at fanaticism in general.[95]

In his novels from the 1980s and 1990s – *A Perfect Peace* (1982, English 1985), *Black Box* (1987, English 1988), *Fima* (1989,English: 1991), and *The Same Sea* (1999) – Oz often attributes Jesus-like traits to his main characters, as part of his thematic examination of idealism, spirituality and the irrational level of the human soul. His interest in Christianity can be witnessed also in his series of memoirs, *In the Land of Israel* (1982, English 1983), which describe a visit to Father Professor Marcel Dubois at his home in Jerusalem.[96]

The writer's affinity to Christianity is in most cases an expression of his alienation from Israeli Zionist norms. Such is the case of Pinhas Sadeh, and Nathan Zach. Pinhas Sadeh (1929-1997) was born in L'viv and immigrated to Palestine in 1933. He studied first in a religious school in Tel-Aviv and then in a kibbutz, where he was sent for high school studies by his parents whose relationships' he defined as 'hell'. In an interview from 1987 Sadeh said: 'I live in the feeling that I am completely not understood; as if during my sleep I was taken to China, where everybody is speaking Chinese while I am writing in Hebrew'. In his early poetry and prose Christianity was one of the ways to escape an unbearable reality and to live in a secluded world of beauty and spiritual love. He was also attracted to Nietzschean ideas; later, Hasidism and Jewish piety took over. In his novel *Life as a Parable* (1958) and his poetry cycle *Massa Duma* (written in the mid-1950s), as well as in later poetry Christian apostles and saints are an object of interest and admiration. For Pinhas Sadeh the search for Christianity, together with other spiritual alternatives, was a revolt against Israeli mediocrity and an expression of an extreme, almost perverse yearning for spiritual purity.

Zach was born in 1930 in Berlin to a Jewish father and an Italian Christian mother, who immigrated to Israel in 1935. His native languages were Italian and French. In the 1950s-1960s Zach became the leader of a literary movement which turned against the Israeli establishment. Allusions to the New Testament, but not religious feelings, appear in his early poems, where the poet plays the role of Jesus. In his 'One Moment'97 relationships between father and son mix biographical experiences with Christian images of Father and Son.[98] In his poem 'Talita Kumi' (*Girl, Get Up*, from Shirim Shonim, 1961), the title of which is a citation from Mark 5:42,[99] the poet reconstructs the Christian narrative by ironically speaking to a girl whom he has deserted. In later poems Zach turns to Jesus with tenderness and empathy, describing him as a suffering human being and a poet. In his poem 'Image'[100] Zach describes Jesus in his own likeness, a human poet with his useless sufferings and weaknesses. In his poems on the death of his his mother (in a monastery in Haifa), Zach describes the nurses' unprecedented mercy, compassion and love.

A similar approach can be found in Joel Hoffman's lyrical autobiographical novel *Sefer Yosef* (*The Book of Yosef*, 1988), where allusion to the New Testament and the life of Jesus construct the emotional attitude to the main character, who is the writer's father. In his stories and novels Hoffman describes the alienation of his German-speaking family from Israeli 'normalcy'. His attraction to Christianity as well as to Far Eastern cultures can be considered an example of post-modernism and post-Zionism in Israeli literature and thought.

In his novel *Kastoria* (1998) Benjamin Shvili combines an autobiographical account of a writer's pilgrimage to his mother's native town of Kastoria (Greece) and a spiritual search for his own religious identity. Throughout the journey the narrator cites the New Testament, together with Hassidic stories and excerpts from Plato, thus suggesting their commonalities. A similar mixture of sources can be found in his second novel, Hayerida min Hatslav (*Down from the Cross*, 2000), which describes the writer's journey to Serbia and Croatia. The writer visits many churches, where he prays to Jesus to get down from his cross and become part of real life. Shvili deems contemporary mass culture the 'Antichrist', and he uses both the Christian narrative and hassidic stories in order to fight it. Although charmed by Christianity, the narrator never questions his Jewish identity, as Christianity is neither a threat to his natural sense of belonging to Judaism as a nation, nor is there a possibility of Christianity tempting him to leave Judaism. He is charmed by the Christian narrative without questioning Judaism's value. For a modern Jewish writer such a complex-free attitude to Christianity has become possible only in a place where Judaism is no longer a minority religion.

There are many signs of an increasingly open attitude towards

Christianity in contemporary Israel, as well as a willingness to learn more about Christian theology and history, even in Orthodox circles.[101] This trend is associated with both the gradual decline of Jewish sensitivity to the history of Jewish-Christian relations in Europe and the increasing understanding of the need to listen to the Other. Israeli readiness for dialogue with Christianity has no need to be based on Christian feelings of guilt. It is based on a personal search for spiritual renewal in a time of dominating technology, estrangement and cruelty. The possibility to be a host, not only a guest, necessarily changes the Jewish attitude to other religions.

To conclude, modern Hebrew literature reflects the changing conditions of the Jewish-Christian dialogue. During the last fifty years, because it was written mainly in Israel, it reflects the Israeli situation. The state of Israel, although full of various tensions, enables a Jew to become interested in Christianity without ever experiencing antisemitism and without living in the midst of Christians. This is a new experience for the Jew and for writers of Hebrew literature. In a country where the visible manifestations of Christianity have a limited presence, there is no urgent need for the rehabilitation of Judaism in the eyes of Christians. The growing interest in Christianity in Israeli literature must therefore be explained by intellectual curiosity and emotional attraction, almost free from the burden of victim psychology, leaving the wounds of blame and guilt to be cured through time and good will.

Notes

1. In February-March 1999 I had the honour of being the first Visiting Fellow of the Centre for the Study of Jewish-Christian Relations at Wesley House, Cambridge. This essay is based on a lecture delivered as part of the Centre's seminar series. It does not pretend to exhaust the theme, which deserves further research.

At the Centre I was generously received by Edward Kessler and his two colleagues, Deborah Patterson Jones and Melanie Wright. I met with a small but very lively group of scholars and students, an amazing mixture of religions, ages and nationalities, all of whom have deep interest in the emerging new discipline of 'Jewish-Christian Relations'. Every one of them brought something from their own background, and the interchange of ideas and views - both during seminars and through informal meetings - was a unique opportunity for all of us to widen our horizons. My time at the Centre convinced me of the importance of promoting Jewish-Christian relations as a rich academic discipline. They inspired me with a determination to develop my research and teaching of Jewish-Christian relations in Israel and elsewhere. I would also like to deliver something of the atmosphere I found there to other places. I am very grateful to the Centre for this special experience.

2. For a history of modern Hebrew literature see 'Hebrew literature, modern', in *Encyclopedia Judaica* (Jerusalem: Keter, 1972), vol. 8, pp. 175-214; Robert Alter, *The Invention of Hebrew Prose* (Seattle:University of Washington Press, 1988); Robert Alter, *After the Tradition* (New York: E. P. Dutton, 1969), G. Shaked, *Modern Hebrew Fiction* (Bloomington and Indianapolis: Indian University Press, 2000). For a history of Yiddish literature see 'Yiddish literature', Encyclopedia Judaica, vol. 16, pp. 798-832; L. Wiener, *The History of Yiddish Literature in the Nineteenth Century* (London: John C. Nimmo, 1899); S. Liptzin, *The Maturing of Yiddish Literature*, (New York: Jonathan David, 1970); S. Liptzin, *A History of Yiddish Literature* (Middle Village, New York: Jonathan David, 1972); K. Frieden, *Classic Yiddish Fiction* (Albany: State University of New York Press, 1995); B. Harshav, *The Meaning of Yiddish* (Berkley: University of California Press, 1990).

3. Rev. C. Schoneveld, 'Dialogue with Jews' *Immanuel* 5 (1975), pp. 61-2.

4. In his letter 'Schreiben an der Herrn Diakonus Lavater in Zürich' (A letter to the Deacon Mr. Lavater in Zürich, 1760). Later Mendelssohn translated the Bible into German and wrote his book Jerusalem (1783), in which he defended the honour of his Jewish faith vis-a-vis the Christian reader.

5 On images of Christians and Christianity and anti-Christian polemics in traditional Judaism see I. Y. Yuval, *Shnei goyim be-vitnekh: Yehudim ve-notsrim – dimuyim hadadyim [Jews and Christians – reciprocal images]*, (Tel-Aviv: Am oved, 2000).

6. I. Manger, editorial, *Foroy* 1 (1937), p. 2.

7. 'And rightly so', says Yosef Klausner, 'for it was dangerous for a Jew to point out any defect in Christianity, as the laws of Christian governments included grave punishments for any trivial affront, on the one hand, and

the Jews themselves were afraid from any contact with Christianity, whether good or ill, even afraid to pronounce Jesus' name'. See his 'Bein Yahadut le-Natsrut' [Between Judaism and Christianity], *Me'asef Davar* (Tel-Aviv, 1955, p. 130). See also Y. Fleishman, *Be'ayat Hanatsrut Ba-Makhshava Hayehudit MiMendelssohn ad Rosenzweig* [*The Problem of Christianity in Jewish Thought from Mendelssohn to Rosenzweig*] (Jerusalem: Magnes, 1964).

8. On the Jewish Haskalah movement see R. Mahler, *Hasidism and the Jewish Enlightenment: Their Confrontation in Galicia and Poland in the First Half of the Nineteenth Century* (Philadelphia, New York and Jerusalem: The Jewish Publication Society of America, 1985); On Haskalah literature see Stanislawski, *For Whom Do I Toil* (New York: Oxford University Press, 1988).

9. In Perets Smolenskin's story 'Torat Ha-no'ar', in *Hamabit* 13.3 (1878), pp. 2-20. Also in *Alei Hemed* (Vilna, 1901), pp. 19-27.

10. On the Jewish situation in Czarist Russia in the early 1880s see J. Klier, *Imperial Russia's Jewish Question 1881-1885* (Cambridge: Cambridge University Press, 1995).

11. On the reflection of social Jewish-Christian relations in Hebrew literature see I. Bartal, *Ha-lo-Yehudim ve-hevratam basifrut ivrit ve-Yiddish bemizrakh Eropa bein hashanim 1856-1914* [*Non-Jews and their society in Hebrew and Yiddish literatures in Eastern Europe during the years 1856-1914*], PhD. thesis (The Hebrew University: Jerusalem, 1980).

12. This is the Yiddish pseudonym (the Hebrew pronounciation is Mendele Mokher Sfarim) of Shalom Ya'akov Abramovich (1835 or 1836-1917).

13. On the Kantonists see E. Ofek, 'Kantonists: Jewish children as soldiers in Tsar Nicholas's army' in *Modern Judaism* 13 (1993), pp. 277-308; O. Litvak, *The Literary Response to Conscription: individuality and authority in the Russian-Jewish Enlightenment* (UMI: Ann Arbor, 2000).

14. On the centrality of masochistic altruism in Russian culture and literature, see: Daniel Rancour-Laferriere, *The Slave Soul of Russia* (New York: New York University Press, 1995). On martyrdom in rabbinic Judaism see D. Boyarin, *Dying for God: Martyrdom and the Making of Christianity and Judaism* (Stanford: Stanford University Press, 1999).

15. On Christian influence on Jewish religion, see M. Hilton, *The Christian Effect on Jewish Life* (London: SCM Press, 1994); D. Boyarin, *Dying for God*, ibid.; I. Y. Yuval, 'Ha-poskhim al shtei ha-se'ipim: ha-hagada shel pesakh ve-hapaskha ha-notsrit' [The Jewish Passover hagada and the

Christian Easter], *Tarbiz* 65 (1996), pp. 5-28.

16. On Jews as university students at the turn of the twentieth century see B. Nathans, *Beyond the Pale* (Berkekey: University of California Press, 2002), pp.201-307.

17. On the history of Jewish converts see Y. D. Eisenstein, the entry 'Mumar' [proselyte] in his Jewish Encyclopedia *Otsar Israel*, vol. 6 (New York: Pardes), pp. 119-121. According to Eisenstein there were about 250,000 converts in nineteenth-century Europe, including 40.000 in Russia in 1836-1875. For statistics on Jewish converts to Christianity in different Western-European countries see Yaakov Leshchinsky, 'Hashmad Be-aratsot Shonot' ['Conversion in Different Countries'], *Ha-Olam* 5 (1911), no. 1, pp. 14-16; no. 4, pp. 5-6; no. 5, pp. 4-5; no. 8, pp. 4-8; no. 9, pp. 3-5; no. 10, pp. 5-7; no. 11, pp. 6-8. On converts in Czarist Russia see Shaul Ginzburg, *Meshumodim in Tsarishen Russland* [*Converts in Czarist Russia*], New York: Bicher Verlag, 1946); Y. Slutski, *Ha-Itonut Ha-Yehudit-Russit Ba-me'ah Ha-Esrim* [*Jewish-Russian Journalism in the Twentieth Century*] (Tel-Aviv: Ha-Aguda Le-Kheker Toldot Ha-Yehudim and the Institue for The Research of Jewish Diaspora), pp. 15-17. On Jewish proselytism in St Petersburg at the turn of the twentieth century, see B.-T. Katz, *Zikhronot* [*Memories*], (Tel-Aviv, 1963), pp. 56-60; see also Sh. L. Zitron, *Me'akhorei Hapargod: Mumarim, Bogdim, Mitkakhashim* [*Behind the Curtain: Converts, Traitors, Deniers*], 2 vols. (Vilna: Zvi Matz, 1923).

18. On love between Jews and Christians and their mixed marriages see A. Komem, 'Hagibor Hayehudi ve-hana'ara ha-goya; hadegem hagavri ve-hadegem ha-nashi' [The Jewish hero and the Gentile girl; the male model and the female one], *Ma'ariv's Literary Supplement* (22.9.1993), pp. 30-1 and, (29.9.1993), pp. 34-5.

19. Examples can be found in U. N. Gnessin's 'Ktata' ['A Quarrel', 1912], where a church is mentioned just as a part of the landscape, and in Rachel Feinberg's drama 'Soné Ha-Nashim' ('The Mysoginist'), *Ha-Olam* 17 no. 2 (11.1.1929), p.39, where 'a Christian church' in included in scene direction, without any connection with the dramatic situation, just as part the scene of a Jewish market-place.

20. Chernikhovsky's wife was of Polish-German-Ukrainian origin. Their marriage raised the anger of Orthodox circles in Palestine, who until the mid 1940s refused to name a street after him in Jerusalem. Y. Klausner, *Shaul Tchernikhovsky: Ha'adam Ve-hameshorer* [*Shaul Tchernikhovsky: the Man and the Poet*], (Tel-Aviv: Yavneh, 1947), p. 61-2.

21. M. Y. Berdychevski, 'Bil'adeiha' ['Without Her'] in *Mibayit Umihutz* (Petrokov: Tushia, 1899), pp. 77-94.

22. H. N. Bialik, 'Me'ahorei Hagader' [Behind the Fence] in *Sipurim vedivrei sifrut* [*Stories and Essays*] (Tel-Aviv: Dvir), pp.43-85.

23. M. Y. Berdychevski, 'Hashnayim' [The Two] in *Kitvei Micha Yosef Berdychevski* [*Collected Writings*] (Tel-Aviv: Dvir, 1965), vol. 1, pp. 59-62.

24. 1929-1930, English: 1988, 1998.

25. Shmuel Verses, *Relations Between Jews and Poles In S.Y. Agnon's Work* (Jerusalem: The Magnes Press, 1994), pp. 85-103.

26. S. Y. Agnon, 'Ha-adonit ve-harochel' [The Lady and the Pedlar], in Samukh venir'eh (Jerusalem and Tel-Aviv: Schoken, 1946), pp. 102-92. English: 'The Lady and the Pedlar', translated by G. Scholem , in *Twenty-One Stories* (New York: Schocken, 1970), pp. 169-181.

27. On Moshe Rosenson (? – 1896) see *The Jewish Encyclopedia* (New York: Funk and Wagnalls, 1905), vol. 10, p. 477. Rosenson was a Rabbi, a physician and a poet and also a very rich person. He wrote about 20 books in Hebrew (in some editions also in Russian and French text) all of them attempting to make peace between Jews and Christians. In his book *Shalom Tsdaka Ve-Emet* [*Peace, Mercy and Truth*] he cited Jewish, Christian and Muslim sources to prove the importance of peace. The motto was Malachi 2:10: 'But we have one Father, but one God created us'. Two of his books were translated into Russian (Vilnus, 1875; Warsaw 1892).

28. *Ibid.*, pp.74-84.

29. M. Y. Berdychevski, *In Bethlehem, in Jerusalem und in Rom: Christliche Welt* (Marburg, 1916); *Der Born Judas: Märchen und Geschichten* (Berlin, Schoken, 1934) (The introduction is dated 1916); *Jesus Son of Hanan: Researches in the History of Christianity*, translated into Hebrew from the German manuscript by Emanuel Bin-Gorion [The writer's son] (Tel-Aviv: Moreshet Micha Yosef, 1959); *Shaul and Paul: Researches in the History of Christianity*, translated from the German manuscript by Emanuel Bin-Gorion (Tel-Aviv: Moreshet Micha Yosef, 1971).

30. Y.D. Eisenstein, the entry 'Messit U-madiah' in *Otsar Israel* (see note 15) vol. 6, p.260.

31. M. Y. Berdychevski, *A Completed Novel: M.Y. Berdychevski's Miriam:Annotated Edition with Introduction* (Haifa and Tel-Aviv: Haifa University Press and Zmora-Bitan, 1997).

32. The manuscript of S. Dubnov's essay can be found in the YIVO archive, New York, record group 87: Papers of Simon Dubnov folder

1009 folios 76300-76308. I would like to thank Anke Hilbrenner for the information on this source. M.Y. Berdychevsky, 'Khasidizm' [Hasidism] *Voskhod* (June 1902), p. 11.

33. J. Baal-Teshuva, *Chagall: A Retrospective* (New York: Hugh Lauter Levin Associates, 1995), p. 301.

34. B. Glazer-Rosenthal and M. Bokhachevsky-Khomiak (eds.), *A Revolution of the Spirit in Russia 1890-1924* (New York : Fordham University Press, 1990).

35. H. Bar-Yosef, 'The Jewish Reception of Vladimir Solovyov' in W. van den Bercken, Manon de Courten and E. van der Zweerde (eds.) *Vladimir Solov'ëv: Reconciler and Polemicist* (Leuven, Paris, Sterling, Virginia: Peeters, 2000), pp. 363-392.

36. D. G. Roskies, *Against the Apocalypse: Responses to Catastrophe in Modern Jewish Culture* (Cambridge MA: Harvard University Press, 1984), p. 263.

37. Z. Amishai-Meisels, 'Chagall's 'Dedicated to Christ: sources and meanings', *Jewish Art* 21-2 (1995-96), pp. 69-94.

38. This was an addition to the ninth volume of the Hebrew translation of Graetz's *Geschicte der Juden* (originally 1855, English 1891-1892). *Divrei Yemei Ha-Yehudim*, translated by Y. E. Trivosh (Jerusalem: Makor, 1972 [1908-1909]). The book was a free gift to subscribers of Hed Hazman.

39. Ahad Ha-Am, 'Al Shtei Ha-Se'ipim' ('Between two Opinions'), *Ha-Shiloakh* 23.2 (August 1910), pp. 97-111.

40. This idea was proposed by the Jewish Reform movement in England as well as by C. G. Montefiore in his *The Synoptic Gospels* (Sheffield Academic Press, 1995 ([orig. 1909]).

41. S. Nash, *In Search of Hebraism: Shai Hurwitz and His Polemics in the Hebrew Press* (Leiden: Brill, 1980).

42. Roskies, *Against the Apocalypse*, p. 263.

43. Janet Hadda, 'Christian Imagery and Dramatic Impulse in the Poetry of Itsik Manger', *Michigan Germanic Studies* 3.2 (1977), pp. 1-12.

44. I. Manger, 'Erster briv tsu xy' [First letter to xy], editorial, *Getseylte verter* (1929), I, i: p. 1.

45. I. Manger, 'Alein' [Alone], J. Hadda (trans.) *Shtern afn dach: lid un balade* (Bucharest: Sholem-aleykhem), pp. 61-2.

46. In 'Veyse landshaft' ['White Landscape'], *ibid.*, p. 90.

47. *Lantern in vint* (Warsaw: Farlag Turem, 1933), pp. 105-7. Quoted from J. Hadda, 'Christian Imagery', p. 5.

48. 'Avent' ('Evening'), *Der shnaider-gezeln Nota Manger zingt* [The Tailor-

Lad Nota Manger Sings] (London: Farlag Ararat), p.74.

49. Quoted from J. Hadda, *ibid.*, p. 5.

50. L. Shapira, 'Der Tselem', *Dos Neie Leben* (May 1909), pp. 329-44; S. Asch, 'In a Carnaval-Nacht' [In a Carnival Night], ibid., pp. 382-90.

51. An-sky, 'Di Tselem Frage' ['The Problem of Crucifixion'], *Dos Neie Leben* (New York) 1 (1909), pp. 610-17, 665-71.

52. G. Morgentaler, 'The Foreskin of the Heart: Ecumenism in Scholem Asch's Christian Trilogy', *Prooftexts* 8 (1988), pp. 219-44.

53. On the Jewish attacks on Scholem Asch see H. Lieberman, *The Christianity of Scholem Asch* (New York: Philosophical Library, 1953).

54. In the 1910s and early 1920s Greenberg wrote expressionist poetry mostly in Yiddish, and edited the avant-guard Yiddish almanach *Albatros* (Warsaw 1922- Berlin 1923). He began writing in Hebrew after his emigration to Palestine in 1924. On Greenberg's attitude to Christ, Christians and Christianity see Noah H. Rosenblum, 'Ha-Antitetiut Ha-te'ologit-Historit Shebanatsrut Beshirat Uri Zvi Greenberg' ('The Theological-Historical Christian Antithesis in Uri Zvi Greenber's Poetry') *Prakim* 4 (1966), pp. 263-320; S. Lindbaum, *Shirat Uri Zvi Greenberg: Kavei Mit'ar* ['The Poetry of Uri Zvi Greenberg: Contours'], (Tel-Aviv: Hadar, 1984), pp. 117-159.

55 Lindbaum, *Shirat*, p. 118.

56. 'Di misterie mentsch', trans. by H. Bar-Yosef, *Albatros* 2 (1922), p. 14.

57. *Ibid.*.

58. This poem might have been the inspiration for Chagall's *The White Crucifixion* (1938) where the same letters, INRI, appear above the cross.

59. 'Uri Zvi Greenberg faren Tslav INRI', *Albatros*, 2 (1922), pp. 3-4.

60. 'Velt Borg-Arop', *Kholiastre* (Warsaw, 1922), p. 17.

61. English translation quoted from Baal-Teshuva, *Chagall*, pp. 301-302.

62. Here Greenberg uses the Polish pronunciation of the word 'Jesus' (in contrast to the Hebrew 'Yeshu'), to emphasize Jesus' otherness.

63. 'Etsleinu ba-olam' ['At our place in the world'], *Sadan* 4 (August 1925), p. 5.

64. Editorial column of *Sadan*, edited by U.Z. Greenberg, 1-2 (Jerusalem, 1935), p. 2, trans. By H. Bar-Yosef.

65. N. Govrin, *Meora Brenner* [*Brenner's Affair*], (Jerusalem, Yad Ben-Zvi, 1985).

66. Y. H. Brenner, 'Ba'itonut u'vasifrut', *Ktavim [Collected Writings]*, vol.3 (Tel-Aviv: Ha-Kibbutz Ha-me'uhad ve-Sifriyat Poalim, 1985), pp. 476-487.

67. *Ibid.*, p. 482. Here Brenner calls Jesus by the Jewish name Joshua.

68. *Ibid.*, p. 483.

69. *Ibid.*, p. 484.

70. N. Govrin, *Me'ora Brenner*, p. 196.

71. Y. H. Brenner, 'Mikan umikan' ['From here and there'], *Ktavim*, vol 2, p. 1440.

72. A. D. Gordon, 'Leveirur hahevdel bein hayahadut vehanatsrut', *Kitvei Aharon Daviv Gordon in Collected Essays*, vol. 3 (Tel-Aviv: Hapoel Hatsa'ir,1927), pp. 197-215.

73. H. Bar-Yosef, 'The Zionist Revolution as an Apocalypse in the poetry of H.N. Bialik and N. Alterman', *Trumah* 10 (2000), pp. 41-57.

74. 'Mizeh U-mizeh', *Hatkufa* 21 (1924), pp. 7-32.

75. *Ibid.*, pp. 82-83.

76. 'Shmuel Frnakfurter', *Hatkufa* 23 (1925), pp. 132-133.

77. 'Beshem Rabi Yeshu Minatseret', in *Beshem Rabi Yeshu Minatseret* (Kitvei Avigdor Ha-Me'iri vol. 5), (Jerusalem and Tel-Aviv: Lema'an Hassefer and Haktav, 1928), pp.23-47.

78. See also his *Historia Isre'alit* [Jewish History], vol. 3 (Odessa: Bletnitski, 1920), and his *Historia shel Ha-bayyit Ha-sheini (History of the Second Temple Period)*, vol. 4 (Jerusalem: Achiassaf, 1950), pp. 207-266 (On Jesus), and vol. 5, pp. 87-130 (On 'Heathen' and Pauline Christianity).

79. Shmuel Verses, 'Al Roman Histori Shelo Nigmar – Usvivav' ['On an Unfinished Historical Novel and its Context'], *Mimendele Ad Hazaz [From Mendele to Hazaz]* (Jerusalem: The Jerusalem Magnes Press, 1987), pp. 41-75.

80. Eliezer D. Friedland, 'Yeshu Hanotsri – Shtei Gishot' ('Jesus of Nazareth – Two Views'), *Niv* 4.1 (1940), pp. 7-8.

81. M. Carmon, 'Bamish'ol Hatsar', *Ha-Olam* 26 (1938), pp. 109-200.

82. H. Hever, *Bishvi Ha-Utopia* [Captives of Utopia], (Sdeh Boker, 1995).

83. On descriptions of Christians and Christianity in Hebrew literature written in Palestine see N. Govrin, 'Bein notsrim lihudim: Menahem Ussishkin' ['Between Christians and Jews: Menahem Ussishkin'], *Dvash Missela [Honey from the Rock]* (Tel-Aviv: The Israeli Ministry of Defence, 1988), pp. 53-61.

84. 'Arba'ah Shomrim' ['Four Guardians'] *Luah Ahiassaf* (1905), pp.

245-50.

85. A. Lifshitz, 'Ha'ahot ve-hanezira' ['The Sister and the Nun'], *Behemda Gdola* [*With Great Passion*] (Tel-Aviv: Tarmil, 1982), pp. 14-22.

86. K. L. Silman, 'Tsailanim' ['Pilgrims'], *Sansinim* [*Twigs of Palm Tree*], (Jerusalem-Tel-Aviv, 1929), pp. 131-147; S. Shababo, *Maria, sipur me-hayei hanezirot be-Eretz Israel* [*Maria: a Story from the Life of Nuns in the Holy Land*], (Jerusaelm: Mitspeh 1932).

87. Avraham Aderet, 'A Discussion of Amos Oz's *Ad Mavet* [*Unto Death*]', *Alei Siakh* 2 (Nov. 1975), p. 163.

88. An astonishing example of a humorous representation of the goy during the Shoah is Leib Rochman's *In Your Blood Thou Shalt Live* (Yiddish, 1961), a diary describing the experience of the author while hiding for two years in a farmer's attic together with his wife, and his brother and sister in law.

89. Y. Carmel, 'Ha-Passionim Shel Bach — Ken o Lo?' ('Bach's Passions — Yes or No?'), *Keshet* (Spring 1973), p. 58.

90 *Ibid.*, p. 51.

91. On the Israeli attitude to Christianity and Jesus see Pinchas Lapide, *Israelis, Jews and Jesus* (New York: Doubleday, 1979).

92. David Flusser's articles were collected in *Yahadut U-Mekorot Ha-Natsrut* [*Judaism and the Sources of Christianity*], (Tel-Aviv: Sifriat Poalim 1979). For a bibliography of the writings of David Flusser see *Immanuel* 24/25 (1990), pp.292-305; H. Cohen, *Mishpato Umoto shel Yeshu Hanotsri* [*The Trial and Death of Jesus of Nazareth*], (Tel-Aviv: Dvir, 1968). I. Yuval, *Jews and Christians: Reciprocal Images*, see note 4.

93. A. Balaban, 'Bein Esh Le'efer' ['Between Fire and Ashes'], *Yediot Aharonot*, 16.1.87, p. 20; L. Fux, 'A. Oz Be'ikvot Agnon O Ha-brit Ha-khadasha' ['A. Oz followes Agnon or The New Testament?'], *Ha-Do'ar*, New York, 28.7.1989, pp. 20-21; D. Zilberman, 'Oz Lagoyim' ['Oz for the Gentiles'], *Moznayim* 65/4 (January 1991), pp. 20-25; A. Holzman, 'Hosfani, Meshuasha, Metsamrer' ['Stripped, Amused, Gives the Shivers'], *Yediot Aharonot* 11.12.98, p. 26; G. Shaked, 'Vidui Va-alilato' ['Confession and its Plot'], *Ha-Aretz*, 23.12.98, pp. 4, 13, 14.

94. M. Wilf, 'Ha-Tasbikh Ha-Yehudi shel Ha-tsalbanim' ['The Jewish Crusader complex'], *Ha-uma* 10/4 (September 1973), pp. 559-561.

95. News item on the Edinburgh Arts Festival, with the participation of ten famous writers (including Amos Oz), *Yediot Aharonot*, 6.9.1991, p. 23.

96. *Po Vasham Be'Erets Israel* (Tel-Aviv: Am Oved, 1982), pp. 144-150.

97. 'Rega ekhad', *Shirim Shonim* [*Various poems*] (Tel-Aviv: Hakibbutz ha-meuchad 1984 [orig. 1960]), p. 23.

98. On this poem and on Christianity and the New Testament in Zach's poetry see R. Kartun-Blum, 'Ma atem hoshvim – she'ani elohim? Bein shirato shel Natan Sach la-brit ha-khadasha' [What do you think – that I am god? N. Zach's poetry and the New Testament], Keshet ha-khadasha 3 (Spring 2003), pp. 22-37.

99. The original (in Aramaic) reads 'talieta'. Zach uses 'Talita' as if it were a first name.

100. 'Dmut' (image), Keivan sh-ani basviva [As I am in the neighbourhood] (Tel-Aviv: Ha-kibbuts hameuchad, 1996), pp. 136-137.

101. An example is the yearly theological conferences in The Shalom Hartman Institute, where scholars from the three monotheistic religions meet for study and discussion.

'Telling the Tale': The Self-Representation and Reception of Elie Wiesel

Isabel Wollaston[1]

In this paper I explore the role Elie Wiesel - a self-proclaimed 'teller of tales' - plays in the Jewish-Christian encounter. After a brief consideration of Wiesel's significance as both a writer and a public figure, I offer a more detailed analysis of his image as a teller of tales, arguing that this is more nuanced and constructed than is often acknowledged (both by Wiesel and his listeners/readers/critics). By way of a conclusion, I offer some suggestions as to why this approach has proved to be so compelling, particularly for Christians.

I. The Reception of Elie Wiesel

For better or worse (and opinion continues to be sharply divided on this point), Elie Wiesel has come 'to embody for non-Jews as for Jews, the Holocaust's penetration of Western consciousness, if not conscience.' As such, he has come to play a central role in 'arguments about the proper place of the Holocaust in our overly commercialised culture, and about victimisation as a defining note of Judaism.'[2] He has been described variously as 'one of the most important people to have lived in the twentieth century',[3] a 'living memorial of the Holocaust', and 'the quintessential survivor' who has played 'the single most prominent role in sustaining a reverent memory of the Holocaust'.[4] For Albert Friedlander, 'Wiesel towers over his contemporaries with all the authority and profundity of a prophet'.[5] Yosef Abramovitz categorically asserts that Wiesel has 'influenced the post-Holocaust landscape more than any other contemporary Jewish thinker'.[6] In awarding him the Nobel Peace Prize in 1986, the committee's citation hailed Wiesel as 'one of the most important spiritual leaders and guides in an age when violence, oppression and racism continue to characterise the world'. Yet such adulatory comments overlook, even ignore, the complexity of Wiesel's public persona. Whilst Wiesel continues to maintain that he still has much in common with the intense, shy child from Sighet he once was, the award of a Nobel Peace Prize points to his political savvy and influence.[7]

Wiesel has exerted more influence on the non-Jewish world, and on Christian theologians, than he has on modern Jewish thought.[8] This influence is cultural, political and theological. Despite the fact that he has no formal representative leadership role within the American Jewish community – 'I don't represent anybody. I'm the president of no organisation, the chairman of no group. I'm totally alone'[9] – Wiesel has nevertheless emerged as 'the most influential American interpreter of the Holocaust'.[10] One significant marker in his rise as a cultural icon came in July 1993, when Oprah Winfrey devoted an entire edition of her talk show to an interview with Wiesel, one that significantly took place outside of her normal studio environment.[11]

If his appearance on Oprah was testimony to his stature as a recognisable and influential American cultural figure, Wiesel earlier became a formal part of his adopted country's political establishment in 1978 when he accepted Jimmy Carter's invitation to chair the President's Commission on the Holocaust (reconstituted as the United States Holocaust Memorial Council in 1980). In this capacity, Wiesel presided over the inauguration of the annual Days of Remembrance (1980) and the initial planning stages of the United States Holocaust Memorial Museum in Washington, D.C. (he resigned from this post in December 1986, but returned in April 1993 as the key speaker, alongside President Clinton, at the formal opening of the museum[12]). Wiesel continues to intercede with, advise, even occasionally publicly admonish, political and religious leaders in the US and overseas. International recognition reached a peak with the award of the Nobel Peace Prize, reflecting his growing stature as 'a conscience at large, so that wherever a major ethical issue crops up, television cameras zoom in upon him for a comment.'[13]

Despite Wiesel's insistence that he is not a theologian, and his frequently expressed rejection of theology as a credible, even feasible, enterprise,[14] Alan Berger speaks for many in insisting that 'Wiesel's writings have become an indispensable starting point for anyone wishing to think seriously about the Shoah's theological and moral implications.'[15] Wiesel's theological influence is rooted both in his writing (particularly his first 'memoir', *Night*), and in a range of personal and professional relationships with Jewish and Christian theologians and religious leaders who, in turn, promote his work and ideas with evangelical zeal. The enthusiastic advocacy of Wiesel's work by the Christian theologian John K. Roth is typical of this phenomenon. Roth insists that 'in a post-Holocaust – or pre-Holocaust? – world, Christians need to become more Jewish Wiesel-style'. He begins his book on Wiesel with the confession, 'this writer has changed my life.... His story, his stories, are so crucial for our times, so lasting in their significance for the human future. They should make a difference to Christian life in America and my aim is to help make them better known in that setting.'[16]

Although *Night*, Wiesel's first book published in English (1960), was slow to make an impression (he had initial problems finding a US publisher, then the book only sold 1046 copies in the first 18 months[17]), it has since been hailed as 'probably one of the dozen most influential volumes of the twentieth century'[18] and 'a classic of Holocaust literature' (on a more popular level, Oprah Winfrey claimed that she 'was not the same' after reading it, and her televised interview with Wiesel resulted in it selling out in many bookstores).[19] This text, and the child-hanging scene in particular, recurs frequently in Christian discussions of the problem of evil and the suffering of God, as well as in Christian theological responses to the Holocaust. Wiesel's impact is further evident in the numerous honorary doctorates and awards he receives, the invitations to be keynote speaker at commemorative events and conferences, and the burgeoning secondary literature devoted to the theological implications of his thought,[20] which includes a number of conference proceedings (often explicitly staged as Jewish-Christian encounters), such as Harry James Cargas, (ed.), *Responses to Elie Wiesel: Critical Essays by Major Jewish and Christian Scholars* (1978), Irving Greenberg and Alvin Rosenfeld, (eds.), *Confronting the Holocaust: The Impact of Elie Wiesel* (1979), Carol Rittner, (ed.), *Elie Wiesel: Between Memory and Hope* (1990). Additional examples of his growing stature include the publication of book-length conversations with politicians (e.g. François Mitterand), religious leaders (e.g. John Cardinal O'Connor) and academics (e.g. Harry James Cargas). Such widespread influence and recognition led Arthur Hertzberg to caustically observe that one of Wiesel's greatest achievements is that he has 'forced the world of the Gentiles, the distant and not-so-distant cousins of the murderers, to pay him heed, on his terms'![21]

There are, nevertheless, dissenting voices amongst this litany of praise. Wiesel's stature as a public figure has always been significantly greater in the United States and Western Europe than in Israel.[22] In the US, his most vocal critics accuse him of being a 'professional Holocaust survivor'[23] and an uncritical apologist for the State of Israel's policies towards the Palestinians,[24] in other words, of exploiting his traumatic past for commercial and political gain. For example, Philip Lopate notes that 'sometimes it almost seems that "the Holocaust" is a corporation headed by Elie Wiesel, who defends his patents with articles in the Arts and Leisure section of the New York Times'.[25] Nevertheless, despite such comments, there is still a reluctance to challenge this 'public veneer of support and acclaim'.[26] Although there are increasingly critical rumblings about the nature and extent of Wiesel's influence, few are prepared to go on the record with their criticisms – outside of revisionist circles (who have honoured, if that is the word, Wiesel by targeting him for particular ridicule[27]). Those that do go 'on the record', such as Norman Finkelstein and Naomi Seidman, have been publicly savaged and accused of 'revisionism'.[28]

Yet, in many ways, supporters and detractors are reacting - in very different ways - to the same thing, namely Wiesel's public, carefully constructed persona as a survivor-witness who is a 'trace' or embodiment of the Kingdom of Night, and is, as a consequence, engaged in a constant daily struggle to 'make sense' of his survival and fulfil his obligation to the dead. Wiesel's influence is rooted in the literary articulation of this persona, but even more so in its ritual public enactment. Chaim Bermant perceptively noted that 'perhaps more important than his books are his public appearances. He is in immense demand as a lecturer, and attracts vast audiences, and the man, spare, cadaverous, with large, haunted eyes and sunken cheeks, is almost the message. When he begins to speak in a deep, sombre voice which seems to belong to another world, his audience is caught up in the long night of Jewish travail. One comes away with the taste of ashes in one's mouth.'[29] Samuel Freedman goes further in suggesting that 'Wiesel's appeal … sometimes borders on a cult of personality'.[30] For Wiesel's critics, these staged encounters between an audience and the survivor-witness as 'secular saint' or 'holy relic' are manipulative, generating a worryingly uncritical response, even from academics, that is more 'akin to the adoration displayed by mortals to their gods.'[31]

What is striking is how relatively little this public persona has evolved over the years despite the substantial change in Wiesel's status: there is little exploration - beyond the rhetorical question, 'I have lived a few lives. How does one relate to the other?'[32] – of the impact of his transition from an unknown struggling writer to internationally acclaimed and influential member of the establishment. There is also little engagement with developments in academic discussion of the Holocaust or Jewish-Christian relations, let alone the changing political context in which these encounters take place. Hence Arthur Hertzberg's observation that Wiesel's 'memories seem to exist frozen in time, unaffected by any of the new, radical considerations of the Holocaust. The tale he retells is like a pageant or mystery play, even an incantation. Each new book by him is a re-enactment.'[33]

II. Wiesel's Public Persona as a Teller of Tales

This is how Wiesel chose to begin his keynote lecture, 'Art and Culture after the Holocaust' (delivered at the Cathedral Church of St John the Divine, New York City, in June 1974):

> Let us tell tales. Let us tell tales – all the rest can wait, all the rest must wait. Let us tell tales - that is our primary obligation. Commentaries will have to come later, lest they replace or becloud what they mean to reveal.
>
> Tales of children so wise and so old. Tales of old men mute with fear. Tales of victims welcoming death as an old acquaintance. Tales that bring man close to the abyss and beyond – and others that lift him up to heaven and beyond. Tales of despair, tales of longing. Tales of immense flames, reaching out to the sky, tales of night consuming life and hope and eternity.
>
> Let us tell tales so as to remember how vulnerable man is when faced with overwhelming evil. Let us tell tales so as not to allow the executioner to have the last word. The last word belongs to the victim. It is up to the witness to capture it, shape it, transmit it and still keep it as a secret, then communicate that secret to others.[34]

This opening is typical Wiesel, both in terms of style (the rhythmic repetition gives the text a formulaic, almost liturgical or incantatory quality) and in content. Most of the themes and characters that permeate much of Wiesel's work are evident: the Holocaust as absolute injustice; the

155

emphasis on memory and the ethical imperative to bear witness so that the victim always has the 'last word'; the primacy given to testimony over academic study or analysis, with the fear expressed that such study risks blurring or missing the real issues; the insistence upon a plurality of response; the ineffability of the Holocaust, hence the reliance on paradox to communicate the 'impossibility' of communication; the use of the symbolism of night and fire to represent the Holocaust; the division of the Kingdom of Night into victims and perpetrators; the recurring emphasis on children and old men (key characters in all Wiesel's work, representations of [lost] innocence and wisdom); and the tendency to mystification.

Wiesel consistently portrays himself as a survivor-witness (that is, as one who has seen the worst that human beings can do to each other and has returned to tell the tale) and as a teacher, roles which, he argues, inevitably overlap.[35] In doing so, he locates himself within the traditions of midrash and Hasidic storytelling, thus paying tribute to both his teachers and a disrupted, and now forever lost childhood (symbolised, in his work, by recurrent allusions to his hometown of Sighet).[36] For Wiesel, the strength of this approach is that it allows him to focus on questions and the exploration of multiple perspectives, rather than the articulation of systematically thought out 'answers'. He claims, perhaps disingenuously, that 'I have no message – only tales'.[37] As a teller of tales, he sees himself both in opposition to, and as a supplier of raw material to, the 'scholars' who are duty bound to look for 'answers' and strive for consistency:

> I do not have to iron out ideas and give them shape and moral structure. Unlike the real philosophers I do not have to look for answers. I simply try to ask questions. Let scholars answer them. What I am trying to do is to provide them with testimony, with tales as raw material. Yes, I write books. I tell tales, and sometimes I try to impose upon them some kind of meaning, perhaps because they have none.[38]

The primary story Wiesel has to tell is that of the destruction wrought by the Holocaust, which is filtered through the prism of his personal experience (and, in particular, through his relationship with his father[39]). He consistently presents this story as one that is so traumatic that it is, by its very nature, unsayable, whilst simultaneously being of such universal significance that it demands to be told: 'to be silent is impossible, to speak forbidden.'[40] This paradox is only resolved, insofar as it can be resolved, by approaching the story tangentially, thus hinting at or implying what cannot be said or communicated directly. Thus, Wiesel insists in all seriousness that he rarely, if ever, speaks about the Holocaust. For example, he told an interviewer in 1973, 'only one of my books, *Night*, deals directly with the Holocaust; all the others reveal why one cannot speak about it. The Holocaust is a sacred subject. One should take off one's shoes when entering its domain, one should tremble each time one pronounces the word.'[41] In *And the Sea Is Never Full*, the second volume of his memoirs (published in French in 1996 and in English in 1999), he insists that he primarily speaks and writes about subjects other than the Holocaust, for example, the Bible, Talmud, Hasidism, the challenges facing Jews today, or human rights: 'I have written on diverse subjects mostly in order not to evoke the one that, for me, has the greatest meaning.'[42] Writing and talking about such subjects enables him to 'look away' from 'painful subjects'. Hence Wiesel insists that 'the tales that I tell are never the ones I would like to tell or ought to tell.'[43]

Insofar as it can be told, the story finds its definitive expression in *Night*. Yet, even here, numerous things are left unsaid because they are 'too personal, too private',[44] for example his parting from his mother and younger sister,[45] and the days following his father's death in Buchenwald prior to liberation.[46] The story, as told by Wiesel in *Night*, sets the scene by first outlining that which was lost (represented by Sighet, the template for every village 'surrounded by mountains' to appear in any Wieselean text[47]). This idyllic childhood was shattered on arrival in Auschwitz: 'the student of the Talmud, the child that I was, had been consumed in the flames. There remained only a shape that looked like me. A dark flame had entered my soul and devoured it.'[48] This trauma is reflected in the shattering effect Auschwitz has on Wiesel's childhood certainties: if memories of Sighet are characterised by a sense of security, fervour and continually bask in a warm nostalgic glow, those of Auschwitz are marked by death, darkness, and an overpowering sense of loss, dislocation, and the silence, even absence of concern, on the part of both God and the non-Jewish world.

This is the primary story Wiesel tells and retells, whatever the form. His subsequent work explores and unpacks its ramifications. Thus, Wiesel insists that *Night* contains the seeds of all his subsequent work: '*Night* was the foundation; all the rest is commentary. In each book, I take one character out of *Night* and give him refuge, a book, a tale, a name, a destiny of his own.'[49] Repetition therefore plays a significant role in this strategy. *Night* indicates the wide range of responses to the Holocaust that Wiesel witnessed among his fellow-Jews. Each subsequent novel explores one such response in more detail: 'all kinds of options were available: suicide, madness, killing, political action, hate, friendship. I note all of these options: faith, rejection of faith, blasphemy, atheism, denial, rejection of man, despair and in each book I explore one aspect.'[50] His work is therefore built around a recurring set of characters: 'one meets a Hasid in all my novels. And a child. And an old man. And a beggar. And a madman. They are all part of my inner landscape. The reason why? Pursued and persecuted by the killers, I offer them shelter. The enemy wanted to create a society purged of their presence, and I have brought them back. The world denied them, repudiated them, so I let them live at least within the feverish dreams of my characters. It is for them that I write.'[51]

For Wiesel, such repetition personalises the abstract figure of six million. If the Holocaust marks the destruction of Sighet and all it represented, then Wiesel sets himself the task of recreating this vanished universe,[52] so that those who were killed are not forgotten, and those who 'come after' may come to appreciate what was lost. For Wiesel, remembering the process of destruction is illuminated by nostalgia for the communities and individuals who were destroyed. Telling the tale therefore serves multiple purposes: it is an ethical obligation, ensuring that the victims' story remains at the forefront of Holocaust consciousness; it is an act of ritual mourning; it is a celebration of the values by which these communities lived and died; and it also serves to educate subsequent generations about this 'vanished universe'. His biblical and hasidic stories therefore play an integral role in his approach to 'telling the tale'. They do not so much provide a means of 'looking away', but rather enable him to look back beyond Auschwitz to Sighet and his pre-Holocaust family life, and to pay tribute to his teachers and formative influences.

This primary story of Sighet/Auschwitz is then set within a secondary narrative, one that relates Wiesel's own struggle to tell the tale and be true to his new vocation (as witness). The broad strokes of this secondary narrative embrace the realisation of his obligation to tell the tale; his ten-year vow of silence in order to ensure that, as a teller, he would be 'worthy' of the tale; his encounter with François Mauriac,[53] resulting in the publication of *Night* in French (one of the unintended ironies of this narrative is that Wiesel's post-Holocaust career is arguably dependent on this crucial intervention by a Catholic intellectual); the reluctance of the world to hear his message, hence the constant struggle to find an audience, a publisher and to make ends meet; then the gradual turning of the tide as Wiesel begins to find a responsive audience. Throughout this secondary narrative, the emphasis is upon the unworthiness and inadequacy of Wiesel as teller to communicate his message and the reluctance or inability of the audience to hear. Wiesel repeatedly questions whether he has succeeded, and rhetorically suggests that silence would have been a preferable option. He remains acutely conscious that the world has not fundamentally changed for the better as a result of listening to his, and other survivors' testimony. He therefore contextualises his primary narrative within this second-order account of the struggle, moral dilemmas, and perpetual anguish of the teller.

What is rarely challenged is Wiesel's assertion that both of these narratives are undiluted, unvarnished testimony. Naomi Seidman observes, 'because *Night* has nearly always been received as an unmediated autobiographical account, the complexity of Wiesel's interpretive craft, his writing, in other words, has been very nearly invisible.'[54] She goes on to explore the complex genesis of *Night*, from diaries written during the ten years of 'silence', to the 245-page Yiddish version, Un di velt hot geshvign (1956), to the much shorter and very different French version (1958). However, in the context of this paper, my focus is on Wiesel's representation of his crisis of faith in *Night* which is, after all, what has proved to be so compelling for Christian readers and theologians.

Wiesel insists that his text is autobiographical: 'Night is not a novel, it is an autobiography. It's a memoir. It's testimony.'[55] Elsewhere he describes it as 'a short, very short narrative of what happened to me',[56] and states that, prior to his memoirs, it is his 'only' autobiographical book.[57] And this is how *Night* has generally been read, as a straightforward autobiographical account. Yet, it is also, as Seidman notes, a carefully written, constructed and stylised text. This is particularly evident in its representation of the impact of Auschwitz on Wiesel's faith which provides the organisational framework of the text/tale. Yet this element of *Night* combines Wiesel's two narratives: it takes elements from the second-order account of his emergence as a survivor-witness and teller of tales, and reads them back into the primary narrative of his experiences during the Holocaust itself. For, as Wiesel has subsequently acknowledged, 'my doubts and my revolt gripped me only later'.[58] In *All Rivers Run to the Sea*, he comments 'there in the camp, I had neither the strength nor the time for the theological meditation or metaphysical speculation about the attributes of the Master of the Universe. The daily bread ration was the centre of our concerns.'[59]

In making this point, my intention is not to question the authenticity of Wiesel's 'doubt and revolt', but rather to draw attention to the ways in which Christian theologians in particular have read and then made use of *Night*. Would the text have had such an impact if it had been initially presented and read as a post-Holocaust religious response to Auschwitz, rather than one articulated in Auschwitz? *Night* has been read variously as spiritual autobiography, an encounter with the void, a version of protest atheism (in the tradition of Dostoevsky or Camus), and as a continuation of the Jewish tradition of contention with God. In each of these interpretations, Wiesel's Orthodoxy and hasidism is identified solely with his childhood and Sighet, which is then held to be found wanting and unable to cope with the challenges posed by his experience of Auschwitz. What we in fact have is a much more complex picture in which Wiesel acknowledges that in the immediate aftermath of liberation, in both Buchenwald and then Paris, 'I acted as though my faith in God and His Law and attributes were still whole and intact, even strengthened, as though my relationship with God were untarnished, unshattered.'[60] However, this part of the story is rarely if ever included in the ever-increasing secondary literature on Wiesel. It is also significant that despite his claim to explore a range of options in responding to the Holocaust, none of his protagonists retain or maintain traditional, Orthodox faith. This raises the question of whether *Night* and Wiesel's subsequent work would have such universal appeal if he had focused upon his initial, more traditional, response to the Holocaust.

III. By way of a conclusion: why do Christians find this tale so compelling?
Wiesel's influence in Christian circles initially comes as something of a surprise given that he has relatively little to say specifically either to Christians or on the subject of Christianity. As has been noted, the tale he tells has evolved relatively little over the years and retains its basic shape regardless of the immediate context. When Wiesel does specifically address the subject of Christianity, it is invariably in order to highlight the role played by Christian anti-Judaism. He admits that as a child he 'knew nothing

of Christianity, which inspired in me no curiosity, only fear'.[61] For Wiesel, the events of the Holocaust proved such 'fear' to be fully justified. He advocates the view, also put forward by Franklin Littell, Rosemary Radford Ruether et al, that there is a 'straight line' linking Christian anti-Judaism and the Holocaust: 'if you study the history of Christianity you will see that it is full of antisemitism. More than that – there would have been no Auschwitz if the way had not been prepared by Christian theology. Among the first to dehumanise the Jew was the Christian.'[62] There is no place in this analysis for grey areas or equivocation: 'if the victims are my problem, the killers are yours.'[63] 'Good' Christians are those who helped Jews at the time (Righteous Gentiles, symbolised for Wiesel by Maria, his family's servant, in Sighet), or those who have since publicly acknowledged Christian culpability (for example, he commends church leaders such as Pope John XXIII and John Cardinal O'Connor, whilst lambasting Pope Pius XII and Pope John Paul II; theologians, such as Robert McAfee Brown, Harry James Cargas, Carol Rittner and John Roth who have played a key role in disseminating his work also come into this category).

Dialogue is possible, but only if Christians first acknowledge their culpability: 'the question is: can one erase two thousand years of suspicion and persecution endured under the shadow of the cross? The answer is no, one cannot; nor should one. Only if we forget nothing shall we succeed in abolishing what divides us.'[64] A new relationship between Christians and Jews is to be encouraged, but will only be possible if Christians are willing to listen in humility, as Jews spell out these truths which will inevitably cause 'hurt'. If such an 'honest exchange'[65] leads to a Christian acknowledgement of culpability, then a new relationship may be possible. Wiesel makes no serious attempt to engage with different interpretations of the relationship between Christian anti-Judaism and the Holocaust or Nazi antisemitism, or to address the problematics of remembering and commemorating Christian victims, hence his less than constructive contributions to the ongoing controversies about the existence of a Christian presence at Auschwitz and other sites related to the Holocaust. Any one who disagrees and advocates a different viewpoint is held to be guilty of, at best, 'insensitivity', and at worst, anti-Judaism or antisemitism.

I would therefore argue that the appeal of Wiesel's work to Christians lies not so much in his occasional remarks on Christians and Christianity per se. Rather, the primary attraction lies with the man himself, the story he tells, and the way in which he tells it. First, the emphasis on questions rather than answers, and on the need to incorporate multiple perspectives, ensures that Wiesel's work is extraordinarily open-ended, if not inherently contradictory. One can find within it virtually any position one wishes to look for, save for an unquestioning endorsement of traditional Orthodoxy. This offers a Christian, or indeed any, theologian considerable freedom, so long as they meet Wiesel's a priori requirement of acknowledging Christianity's culpability (it also opens up the possibility of their work receiving Wiesel's public endorsement or imprimatur).[66] Wiesel consistently maintains that his primary aim is to help Jews become better Jews and encourage Christians to become better Christians (whilst implicitly leaving it up to them to work out precisely how this should be done). His emphasis on testimony and preserving multiple perspectives fits well with the perspectives of liberation and practical theologies and their call for theology to resist oppression and root itself in experience and praxis. The theologies of Christian 'disciples' of Wiesel, such as Brown and Roth, can be interpreted as forms of liberation theology: Christianity confesses its culpability and takes responsibility for the negative impact of its embrace of power (Constantianism). As a practical demonstration of this *metanoia*, it commits itself to the pursuit of dialogue and social justice.

Second, Wiesel's primary narrative is about suffering and what one does with and/or learns from this. As a survivor-witness he presents himself as one who 'knows' and is compelled to communicate this 'knowledge', insofar as it can be put into words, to those who were not 'there'. The Jew (and the Jewish survivor in particular) therefore comes to be seen as the only one entitled to speak of these things, consequently becoming a source of revelation for the Christian: the Jew as suffering witness indicates how it might be possible for Christianity to redeem itself and recover its true meaning. Peter Novick represents this relationship in more caustic terms in alluding to 'Wiesel's carefully cultivated persona as symbol of suffering, as Christ figure.'[67] Whilst Novick overstates his case, we need to consider seriously the ramifications of his claim that much recent Holocaust commemoration has assumed a Christian, rather than a Jewish character, in its veneration of relics, ritual re-enactment of the path of suffering, and 'the way that suffering is sacralized and portrayed as the path to wisdom.'[68] For Novick this emphasis upon suffering and victimization is fundamentally unJewish, quintessentially Christian even. Whilst one may not agree with his argument in its entirety, the recurrent controversies over the Christianization of the Holocaust, particularly in relation to the use of Christian imagery and theological categories in remembering and commemorating these events, suggests that there is a fundamental, maybe even irreconcilable, difference in Jewish and Christian responses to suffering, one that needs to be explored in much greater depth than hitherto.

Third, Wiesel's appeal lies in his ability to embody or provide a point of access to the eastern/central European *shtetl* culture largely destroyed during the Holocaust. He does this in a manner that is accessible and non-threatening. Jack Kugelmass points to the growing nostalgia for this 'lost' culture, particularly in the US, evident in the popularity of photograph albums of pre-war Eastern European Jewry, *Fiddler on the Roof*, Klezmer music, Yiddish literature and humour, and traditional Ashkenazi food.[69] Wiesel's public persona and emphasis on storytelling and arguing with God (à la Tevye the Milkman) appeal to similar feelings of nostalgia. Samuel Freedman notes that as 'a modern man versed in tradition, a scholar of Judaism without peyes (sidelocks) or a beard, Wiesel speaks of spiritual matters without alienating secular listeners.'[70] In encouraging his readers to become 'more Jewish Wiesel-style' by embracing contention with God as a religious strategy, John Roth introduces them to an example that is relatively divorced from its original setting, and is therefore universalised and accessible. Wiesel is often criticised for being ethnocentric and particularist, of being preoccupied with uniqueness at the expense of universalism. The ultimate irony could be that his appeal lies, at least in part, in this ability to tap into this market for a form of secularised, even universalised, Jewish-lite, Jewishness as remembered folklore and nostalgia, rather than as the real thing (that is, the Eastern/Central European Orthodox and/or Hasidic Jew as a very different, disconcerting and possibly even alien 'other').

Notes

1. I would like to thank Deryn Guest and Melanie Wright for their comments on an earlier draft of this paper.
2. James Carroll, 'Witness', *New York Times*, 2.1.2000.
3. Alan Dershowitz, 'Elie Wiesel: A Biblical Life' in Alan Rosen (ed.),

Celebrating Elie Wiesel: Stories, Essays, Reflections (Notre Dame: University of Notre Dame Press, 1998), p. ix.

4. Arthur Hertzberg, 'A Living Memorial', *Times Literary Supplement*, 7.6.1996, p. 12.

5. Albert Friedlander, 'Wiesel and the Silence of God', *The Times*, 13.12.1986.

6. Yosef I. Abramovitz, 'Is Elie Wiesel Happy?', *Moment*, February 1994, p. 37

7. A recurring theme in the two volumes of his memoirs published to date, *All Rivers Run to the Sea: Memoirs* (New York: Alfred A. Knopf, 1995) and *And the Sea Is Never Full: Memoirs, 1969-* (New York: Alfred A. Knopf, 1999) consists of Wiesel's concern that he remains 'true' to the boy from Sighet he once was.

8. Jack Kolbert notes that 'polls of his readers in France and the United States prove conclusively that far more non-Jews read Wiesel than Jews', *The Worlds of Elie Wiesel: An Overview of his Career and his Major Themes* (London: Associated University Press, 2001), p. 124. However, Kolbert cites no sources to back up this claim.

9. Elie Wiesel in Elie Wiesel and John Cardinal O'Connor, *A Journey of Faith Based On and Expanded from the WNBC-TV Broadcast: A Dialogue* (New York: Donald I. Fine, 1990), p. 39.

10. Peter Novick, *The Holocaust in American Life* (New York: Houghton Mifflin, 1999), p. 201.

11. For a discussion of Wiesel's appearance on Oprah and its significance, see John K. Roth, 'Helping Others to Be Free: Elie Wiesel and Talk about Religion in Public' in Rosen (ed.), *Celebrating Elie Wiesel*, pp. 143-48.

12. For an analysis of Wiesel's role on the USHMC, see Edward T. Linenthal, *Preserving Memory: The Struggle to Create America's Holocaust Museum* (New York: Viking, 1995).

13. Chaim Bermant, 'Laureate of the Holocaust Who Speaks for Mankind', *The Observer*, 19.10.86. In recent times, the universal applicability or sensitivity of this 'conscience' have been questioned, particularly in relation to Wiesel's unwillingness to criticise Israel's treatment of the Palestinians and US policy in Nicaragua and elsewhere. See, for example, Mark Chmiel, *Elie Wiesel and the Politics of Moral Leadership* (Philadelphia: Temple University Press, 2001).

14. For example, Wiesel observes, 'I don't like the word "theologian".

I find it disturbing. What is a theologian, really? Some one who knows things about God. But who knows what God is? Kafka once said, "Man cannot speak of God. If at all, he can speak to God." So I'm still trying to speak to Him. How can we speak of Him?', Henry Koppel and Gene Kaufmann, *Elie Wiesel: A Small Measure of Victory* (Tucson: University of Arizona, 1974), p. 13.

15. Alan Berger, 'Elie Wisel' in Steven T Katz (ed.), *Interpreters of Judaism in the Late 20th Century* (Washington, D.C.: B'nai B'rith Books, 1993), p. 383.

16. John K. Roth, *A Consuming Fire: Encounters with Elie Wiesel* (Louisville: John Knox Press, 1979), p. 13.

17. Samuel G. Freedman, 'Bearing Witness: The Life and Work of Elie Wiesel', *New York Times Magazine*, 23.10.83, reprinted in Robert Franciosi, (ed.), *Elie Wiesel: Conversations* (Jackson: University Press of Mississippi, 2002), p. 112.

18. Daniel Stern, 'Seeing Elie Wiesel Whole', *The New Leader*, 5.9.98, p. 20.

19. Berger, 'Elie Wiesel', p. 370.

20. Examples include full-length studies by Michael Berenbaum, Robert McAfee Brown, Ted Estess, Maurice Friedman, David Pattison, John K. Roth and Graham Walker.

21. Hertzberg, 'A Living Memorial', p. 12.

22. Wiesel's hurt at what he sees as the negative reactions to his success in Israel, including the award of the Nobel Peace Prize, is a theme running throughout both volumes of his memoirs. See, for example, In reviewing *Celebrating Elie Wiesel* in the Jerusalem Post (21.9.99), Mordechai Beck notes 'significantly, there is hardly an Israeli voice among the celebratory choir.... This may reflect the odd bias towards Wiesel, at least in official quarters, where he is still regarded as something of a traitor to the Zionist cause by choosing not to live here.'

23. Kali Tal, *Worlds of Hurt: Reading the Literatures of Trauma* (Cambridge: Cambridge University Press, 1996), p. 1. Further examples include Norman Finkelstein's acerbic comment that 'for his standard fee of $25,000 (plus chauffeured limousine), Wiesel lectures that the 'secret' of Auschwitz's "truth lies in silence"', in *The Holocaust Industry: Reflections on the Exploitation of Jewish Suffering* (London: Verso, 2000), p. 45.

24. Commenting on Wiesel's reluctance to criticise the policies of the State of Israel, Noam Chomsky observes, 'a similar stance of state-worship

would be difficult to find, apart from the annals of Stalinism and fascism. Wiesel is regarded in the United States as a critic of fascism, and much revered as a secular saint.' *The Fateful Triangle: The United States, Israel and the Palestinians* (London: Pluto Press, 1983), p. 16.

25. Philip Lopate, 'Resistance to the Holocaust', *Tikkun* 4.3 (1989), p. 56.

26. Freedman, 'Bearing Witness', p. 113. See also Edward B. Fiske, 'Elie Wiesel: Archivist with a Mission', *New York Times*, 31.1.73, in Franciosi, (ed.), *Elie Wiesel*, pp. 40-43.

27. See, for example, Robert Faurisson, 'A Prominent False Witness: Elie Wiesel', available on the Institute for Historical Review's website, www.ihr.org/leaflets/wiesel.html. David Irving's website, Action Report Online, has a section of 'Documents on Wiesel', see www.fpp.co.uk/Auschwitz/wiesel/Index.html.

28. See, for example, Eli Pfefferkorn is and David Hirsch's response to Seidman in 'Elie Wiesel's Wrestle with God', *Midstream*, 43.8 (1997), p. 20.

29. Bermant, 'Laureate of the Holocaust Who Speaks for Mankind'. Geoffrey Hartman makes a similar point, more strongly, in arguing that Wiesel's 'novels are significant, but they are not novels of great style... If you separated the fiction from the man, they wouldn't have the same impact' (quoted in Freedman, 'Bearing Witness', p. 109).

30. Freedman, 'Bearing Witness', p. 110.

31. Tal, *Worlds of Hurt*, p. 43. In this instance, she is specifically commenting on the literary critic, Terrence Des Pres' analysis of the relationship between Wiesel, the man, and Wiesel the writer.

32. Wiesel, *And the Sea Is Never Full*, p. 253.

33. Hertzberg, 'A Living Memorial', p. 12.

34. Elie Wiesel, 'Art and Culture after the Holocaust' in Eva Fleischner, (ed.), *Auschnitz: Beginning of a New Era? Reflections on the Holocaust* (New York: KTAV, 1977), p. 403.

35. Wiesel in John S. Friedman, 'The Art of Fiction LXXIX: Elie Wiesel', *Paris Review*, 26, Spring 1984, reprinted in Franciosi, (ed.), *Elie Wiesel*, p. 96. See also, Elie Wiesel, 'Why I Write' in Irving Greenberg and Alvin Rosenfeld, (eds.), *Confronting the Holocaust: The Impact of Elie Wiesel* (Bloomington: Indiana University Press, 1979), pp. 200-1.

36. Wiesel notes 'I am seeking my childhood; I will always be seeking it. I need it. It is necessary to me as a point of reference, as a refuge. It

represents for me a world that no longer exists'. In 'Making the Ghosts Speak', *Christian Century*, May 27, 1981, reprinted in Elie Wiesel, *From the Kingdom of Memory: Reminiscences* (New York: Summit Books, 1990), p. 135. Wiesel has published biblical and Hasidic essays and tales (based on public lectures) alongside his novels, see, for example, *Messengers of God* (1976), *Five Biblical Portraits* (1981), *Souls on Fire* (1973), *Four Hasidic Masters and their Struggle against Melancholy* (1978), *Somewhere a Master* (1982), *Sages and Dreamers* (1989).

37. Elie Wiesel, 'Telling the Tale' in Irving Abrahamson (ed.), *Against Silence: The Voice and Vision of Elie Wiesel* (New York: Holocaust Library, 1985), Volume I, p. 239. In *And the Sea Is Never Full*, Wiesel also insists, 'I have always rejected the notion of myself as a symbol.' (p. 6).

38. Elie Wiesel, 'Telling the Tale', p. 252. It should be pointed out that, despite this claim, Wiesel does not cede scholars total freedom in trying to 'answer' his questions. He retains a very strong sense of what constitute 'authentic' and 'inauthentic' responses to the Holocaust and interpretations of his work. For example, he states that the second volume of his memoirs 'evolves under the sign of conflict' and promises 'I shall take a stand against some of my adversaries, those who have, in my estimation, transgressed the limits of dialogue, having chosen obfuscation as their weapon and 'demonization' as their goal.' (*And the Sea Is Never Full*, p. 6).

39. In the first volume of his memoirs (published in French in 1994), Wiesel comments, 'to this day I am in mourning for my father, perhaps because I didn't mourn the day I became an orphan. The ordeals that preceded his death remain with me, in all their violence.' (*All Rivers Run to the Sea*, p. 92).

40. Wiesel, *All Rivers Run to the Sea*, p. 89.

41. Elie Wiesel in Lily Edelman, 'A Conversation with Elie Wiesel', *National Jewish Monthly*, 88, November 1973, pp. 5-15, reprinted in Franciosi, (ed.), *Elie Wiesel*, pp. 45-57, p. 53

42. Wiesel, *And the Sea Is Never Full*, p. 407.

43. Elie Wiesel, 'Making the Ghosts Speak', p. 143.

44. Elie Wiesel in Ted Estess, 'A Conversation with Elie Wiesel', *Image* 13, Spring 1996, pp. 43-58, reprinted in Franciosi, (ed.), *Elie Wiesel*, pp. 174-89, p. 178.

45. Wiesel, *And the Sea Is Never Full*, p. 301.

46. Elie Wiesel in Marty Moss-Coane, 'Interview with Elie Wiesel', Transcription of *Fresh Air with Terry Gross* interview, 14.11.95, reprinted

in Franciosi, (ed.), *Elie Wiesel*, p. 168.

47. In *All Rivers Run to the Sea*, Wiesel remarks of Sighet, 'in all my novels it serves as a background and a vantage point. In my fantasy I still see myself in it.' (p. 31). In Journey of Faith, he notes that he has a picture of his family home in Sighet on his desk, 'since I began writing, I always face that house. I must know where I come from. Whatever I write, it's always there. That picture is there.... I want to remember where I came from.' (p. 59).

48. Elie Wiesel, *Night* (London: Penguin, 1981), p. 48.

49. Elie Wiesel in Harry James Cargas (ed.), *Conversations with Elie Wiesel* (South Bend: Justice Books, 1992), p. 3.

50. Elie Wiesel in Cargas, *Conversations with Elie Wiesel*, p. 86.

51. Elie Wiesel, 'Why I Write', p. 205. See also, Wiesel, 'And Thou Shalt Teach Your Children' in Abrahamson, (ed.), *Against Silence*, Volume I, p. 310.

52. Elie Wiesel, 'A Personal Response', *Face to Face*, 6 (1979), pp. 35-7, p. 36.

53. Mauriac describes this encounter in his Foreword to *x* (pp. 7-11). Elie Wiesel's memories of Mauriac are found in 'An Interview Unlike Any Other' in *A Jew Today* (New York: Vintage Books, 1979), pp. 17-23, and *All Rivers Run to the Sea*, pp. 265-72.

54. Naomi Seidman, 'Elie Wiesel and the Scandal of Jewish Rage', *Jewish Social Studies* 3.1 (1996), p. 3.

55. Elie Wiesel in Friedman, 'The Art of Fiction', p. 72.

56. Moss Coane, 'Interview with Elie Wiesel', pp. 65-6.

57. Elie Wiesel in Harold Flender, 'Conversation with Elie Wiesel', *Women's American ORT Reporter*, March/April 1970, reprinted in Franciosi, (ed.), *Elie Wiesel*, p. 22

58. Wiesel, *All Rivers Run to the Sea*, p. 82.

59. Wiesel, *All Rivers Run to the Sea*, p. 83.

60. Wiesel, *All Rivers Run to the Sea*, pp. 119-20.

61. Wiesel, *All Rivers Run to the Sea*, p. 23.

62..Wiesel in Koppel and Kaufmann, *Elie Wiesel: A Small Measure of Victory*, p. 20.

63. Wiesel, 'Freedom of Conscience', *Journal of Ecumenical Studies* 14 (1977), p. 74.

64. Wiesel, *And the Sea Is Never Full*, p. 175.

65. Wiesel, 'Art and Culture after the Holocaust', p. 406.

66. It is worth noting the number of secondary texts on Wiesel that are dedicated to him and/or contain a preface or foreword by him. See, for example, Robert McAfee Brown, *Elie Wiesel: Messenger to all Humanity* and John K. Roth, *A Consuming Fire*.

67. Novick, *The Holocaust in American Life*, p. 274.

68. Novick, *The Holocaust in American Life*, p. 11.

69. See, for example, Jack Kugelmass, 'Jewish Icons: Envisioning the Self in Images of the Other' in Jonathan Boyarin and Daniel Boyarin (eds.), *Jews and Other Differences: The New Jewish Cultural Studies* (Minneapolis: University of Minnesota Press, 1997), pp. 30-53 and Jack Kugelmass (ed.), *Key Texts in American Jewish Culture* (New Brunswick: Rutgers University Press, 2002), NB pp. 3-21, 105-25, 147-60.

70. Freedman, 'Bearing Witness', p. 110.

8

Lights! Camera! Antisemitism? The Cinema and Jewish-Christian Relations

Melanie J. Wright

Introduction

The cinema – not just films themselves, but also the institutions that produce and distribute them, and the audiences who are their consumers - began in the 1890s in Europe and the United States. The first films were extremely brief, consisting of a single shot. Their viewers were seemingly fascinated by the recording of animate and inanimate objects. But as early as 1902 (the year of Georges Méliès' *A Trip to the Moon*) changes of scene and camera position were deployed to tell stories. From its beginnings as a fairground attraction, cinema rapidly developed, as art form and industry. Today, film is a global phenomenon. Countries in Africa, Asia, and Europe have noteworthy indigenous cinemas, although with few exceptions these generally define themselves in opposition to Hollywood, whose products have been dominant internationally since 1918. Throughout this history, cinema has been implicated in Jewish-Christian relations: 'implicated' here flags intimacy and complexity. As will become apparent, films do not simply reflect Jewish-Christian relations but actively participate in or constitute them. Moreover, a film's meaning or significance for Jewish-Christian Relations is not straightforwardly a function of its narrative or visual style. The relationships between history, theology, the cinematic text, and its reception, are highly complex.

This article explores aspects of the relationship between the worlds of the cinema and Jewish-Christian relations. What is attempted is a broad, critical survey, with a number of characteristic examples pinpointed, rather than an encyclopaedic history. Selected films which re-present either biblical texts or works of literary fiction are discussed, as are films dealing with some prominent issues in contemporary Jewish-Christian relations. The earliest work considered in detail is *Intolerance* (D. W. Griffith, 1916), and the most recent, *The Pianist* (Roman Polanski, 2002). Finally, the rhetoric surrounding the 'Jewish Hollywood' question is described, particularly in relation to the construction of Jewish and non-Jewish (including Christian) identities.

Film's potential as a form of mass communication has on occasion been exploited with the explicit aim of influencing Christian or Jewish attitudes towards one another. The most obvious examples of this approach to filmmaking are to be found in fascist Europe. The *Reichsfilmkammer* was one of the first bodies established by the Ministry of Propaganda following Hitler's accession to power, reflecting Nazi belief in the cinema as a tool for the reconstruction of German culture. Productions like Veit Harlan's *Jew Süss* (1940) and Fritz Hippler's *The Eternal Jew* (1940) were intended to shape audience perceptions of the Nazi enterprise. Distribution was carefully managed. The government bought theatres, and troops carried projection equipment with them into occupied territories. In 1941-1942, Hippler's film (a documentary about 'world Jewry') was scheduled for screening in all Dutch cinemas, whilst Harlan's (a period drama about an eighteenth century court Jew, who is sentenced to death for corruption) was shown to non-Jewish audiences in Poland, as part of the preparations for the Final Solution.[1] There were attempts to predetermine audience responses by printing synopses in newspapers, so that viewers were primed to recognise the film's message before they entered the movie theatre.[2] However, fascist cinema, whilst not totally divorced from the techniques of more 'respectable' filmmaking, is an extreme case. More commonly, the intentions behind a film are less didactic, but its subject matter may draw makers and viewers into exploration of and engagement with aspects of Jewish-Christian relations. This is perhaps most readily demonstrated in films dealing with biblical subject matter.

Biblical Films
Amongst the earliest films to participate in Jewish-Christian relations were those with specifically religious themes. In its early years, the cinema struggled to position itself as a respectable industry, and keen to appease the middle classes (especially those calling for rigorous censorship) studios and trade publications downplayed the comedies and melodramas that constituted the bulk of production output, and invested disproportionate resources in making and promoting a small number of 'quality' films with biblical-religious, literary and historical subjects. These genres have been

revived periodically, notably when the threats of censorship and restriction have again seemed acute. For example, the biggest box office draw of 1951-1960, a decade during which the film industry endured the attentions of the House Un-American Activities Committee and other investigative bodies, was *Ben Hur* (William Wyler, 1959) with Cecil B. DeMille's *The Ten Commandments* (1956) second and *The Robe* (Henry Koster, 1953) in fourth position.[3]

Pre-Holocaust, many biblical films propagated anti-Judaism. The first Jesus films were heavily dependent on Passion Plays and inherited traditions of anti-Judaism, alongside those of staging and plotting, from their predecessors. After their commercial runs, such films as *Passion Play of Oberammergau* (Henry C. Vincent, 1898) and the Horitz *Passion Play* (Marc Klaw and Abraham Erlanger, 1897) had extended afterlives in devotional-religious contexts. Customers could buy prints of one or more scenes, and then use them for entertainment in church socials, or as resources in worship and education.[4] Unfortunately, it is impossible to say how many clergy used this material, and to what extent it did (not) tap into anti-Jewish feeling in its audiences.

Whilst much of the reception history of these screened plays remains inaccessible, that of D. W. Griffith's influential *Intolerance* (1916) is well documented. The life of Jesus is one of four interwoven stories illustrating the theme of intolerance through the ages. Reflecting both the gospel texts and their usual interpretation in Griffith's day, the Pharisees are cast as Jesus' 'intolerant' opponents. There are shades of nuance in some of the intertitles: one suggests that the name Pharisee was 'possibly brought into disrepute by hypocrites among them'. Under pressure from Jewish communal organisations, footage of Jews (played by Orthodox Jews from Los Angeles) nailing Jesus to the cross was re-shot, substituting Roman soldiers.[5] But Griffith transformed the parable of the Pharisee and the tax-collector (Luke 18) into an actual event, and inserted references to Pharisees as haters of love and pleasure into the portrayal of the marriage at Cana (John 2). In doing so, he heightened the gospels' polemic against Jews who opposed Jesus, and placed anti-Judaism at the heart of the film 'canon'.

Intolerance's depiction of Pharisees, coupled with its encouragement to viewers to draw parallels between ancient and modern attitudes and personalities, is especially striking given the fact that the film was presented as a response to African-Americans and white liberals who had condemned

Griffith's *The Birth of a Nation* (1915) as racist. Indeed, within Film Studies it is commonplace to find critical interpretations of *Intolerance* as either atonement for, or defence of, the earlier film.[6] Whichever position is adopted, the implication is that *Intolerance*, with its stereotypes of Pharisees, may be read as evidencing a lack of prejudice on Griffith's part – which raises interesting questions about the assumptions of the discipline as much as it does about those of Griffith himself.

Further illustration of the ways in which early directors negotiated – willingly, or otherwise – the sensibilities of different communities is offered by the case of Cecil B. DeMille's 1927 *The King of Kings*. DeMille had Father Daniel Lord, who would later be instrumental in the formation of the Catholic Legion of Decency (a pressure group that aimed to enforce the Production Code, discussed later) say Mass on set each day. He also employed as consultants religious writer Bruce Barton, and Protestant minister George Reid Andrews.[7] The film takes a conservative approach narratively (the virginal conception and other miracles are presented as historical events) and stylistically (the synchronized score features traditional hymns; visual aesthetics are informed by the popular engravings of Gustave Doré, and Leonardo Da Vinci's famous painting of the Last Supper).[8] Like the makers of the early Passion films, DeMille struggled to separate Christian piety from anti-Judaism, and like *Intolerance*, *King of Kings* prompted protests, specifically from the Anti-Defamation League, who complained about the presentation of Jews in the trial and crucifixion sequences. Numerous bodies, including Conservative Judaism's Rabbinical Assembly, passed resolutions condemning the film. In a letter to Will Hays, head of the industry's trade association, the Motion Picture Producers and Distributors Association (MPPDA), DeMille hinted darkly that the protests would turn other Americans against Jews, with dangerous consequences.[9] Nevertheless, changes were made and the re-edited version, still in circulation today, bears the hallmarks of a deliberate, but uneven, effort to move away from the suggestion that Jews were collectively guilty of Jesus' death. The opening titles stress that first century Judea was under Roman occupation, and the trial before Caiaphas is almost totally excised. However, Caiaphas later declares that he alone is responsible for the crucifixion. This is a clumsy move. Seemingly intended to distance the film from Matthew 27:26, it does not fit convincingly with either the historical events or the film's own internal logic.

DeMille's efforts to appease his critics and rid the film of anti-Judaism concentrated on narrative. But it would be a mistake to focus on this dimension alone when considering the place of cinema in Jewish-Christian relations. For example, DeMille cast Yiddish theatre actors Rudolph and Joseph Schildkraut as Judas and Caiaphas, and used Orthodox Jews as crowd extras, a practice *The Ten Commandments* (1923) repeated. What motivated this decision is unclear. DeMille sought to associate all of his biblical films with reverential scholarship. (This was a strategy commonly deployed by directors attempting to present their films as 'high culture'.[10]) It is likely, then, that he believed the Jewish actors somehow lent 'authenticity' to *The King of Kings*.[11] However, DeMille did not cast Jews in the sympathetic roles of Jesus and his disciples. The film therefore suggests a problematic continuity (theological and/or ethnic) between Jesus' opponents and modern Jewry. This connection also seems implicit in one of the intertitles, which states that Caiaphas, 'cared more for Revenue than for Religion – and…saw in Jesus a menace to his rich profits from the Temple.' Its claim that Jesus' opponents viewed the world primarily in terms of the cash nexus resonates with anti-Jewish rhetoric current in 1920s America. In short, *The King of Kings* inserts modern antisemitic discourse, specifically its construction of Jewish acquisitiveness, into the narrative of Christian beginnings.[12]

In a Jewish-Christian relations context it might be tempting to interpret such films as translations of Christian anti-Judaism to the screen, which were sometimes modified in response to Jewish lobbying. Things are not so simple. One source of concern for critics of *The King of Kings* was Jewish participation in its production and exhibition: Sid Grauman was censured for showing the film in his Chinese Theater in San Francisco, where it played for twenty-four weeks.[13] The roles of the Schildkrauts have already been mentioned. Jewish personnel were variously associated with the films criticised for their antisemitic overtones. In a sense these works bear traces of the contradictions that their creators embodied and wrestled. (DeMille himself was a practising Christian with part-Jewish origins.) On the one hand, some Jewish film professionals desired to refute claims about Jewish responsibility for the crucifixion.[14] On the other hand, during the early and mid-twentieth century, they were mostly assimilationist, downplaying notions of Jewish particularity and conscious of a need to cater for Christian audiences. Given this context of production it is, therefore, accurate to speak of biblical films not as cinematic illustrations of anti-Jewish sentiment, nor as manifestations of the exercise of 'Jewish control' in the film industry, but as interesting, complex works that refract the ambivalence with which film-makers approached questions of biblical interpretation, religious and ethnic identity, commonality, and difference.

It is only since the mid-1960s – the era of Nostra Aetate (discussed in Eugene Fisher's contribution to this volume) and the Six Day War – that some biblical filmmakers have systematically tried to avoid or even confront anti-Judaism. In this respect *Jesus of Nazareth* (1977) is noteworthy. Its effort to portray a Jewish Jesus, and its evocation of the tragic consequences of the deicide charge, partly reflect director Franco Zeffirelli's reading of the Catholic documents re-assessing church teachings on Jews and Judaism.[15] The multi-faith panel of advisors who worked on the film included Rabbis Albert Friedlander and Marc Tanenbaum, both of whom were well-known participants in Jewish-Christian dialogue at the time. Accordingly, *Jesus of Nazareth* is the first Jesus-story film motivated by a desire to represent Jesus as a Jew, and to refute the view that Jews were responsible for his death, thereby inviting their rejection and punishment by God.

Mindful of these goals, Zeffirelli's film is more radical than DeMille's. In its efforts to exonerate Judas, around whom much anti-Judaism has developed, Jesus of Nazareth posits an additional character, Zerah, who plays a crucial role in Jesus' trial and death, performing functions Christianity traditionally ascribed to Judas and Caiaphas. Zerah is a prominent Sanhedrin member, who engineers Jesus' appearance at a hearing, which, the dialogue stresses, is irregular, being held in haste and at night.[16] Judas appears as naïve and confused, manipulated by Zerah into delivering Jesus to the authorities in order (he mistakenly believes) to give him an opportunity to meet and impress Caiaphas. For his part, Caiaphas is a reactive politician, working within a context of oppressive occupation. He is sympathetic and calls Jesus 'extraordinary', but has little room to manoeuvre once Jesus claims publicly to be God's son. These narrative innovations illustrate how changes in mainstream Christian teaching on Jesus' position within first century Judaism have informed the production of a given film. However, at times, Zeffirelli's didactic ends assert themselves to the detriment of the film qua film. The dialogue in the Sanhedrin 'trial', for example, is stilted, with too many explanatory asides about the constraints on Jewish government during Roman occupation. Moreover, it is questionable whether the introduction of Zerah – a character without scriptural basis – serves the purposes of art or

Nostra Aetate adequately. Can the fashioning of a speculative addition to the gospels form a sound basis for Jewish-Christian understanding?

In addition to a cumbersome handling of Jesus' death, *Jesus of Nazareth* struggles to realise post-war understandings of Jesus as a figure who operated within, rather than against or above, a first century Jewish milieu. Jesus' Jewishness is emphasised via the (anachronistic) depiction of his circumcision and *bar mitzvah*, and the betrothal and marriage of Joseph and Mary. Recitation of the *Shema* punctuates the film. There are deliberate efforts to break with the approach of *Intolerance*, and move away from the stereotyping of Pharisees as self-righteous hypocrites who were fundamentally opposed to Jesus. However, in these respects too, *Jesus of Nazareth* leaves questions unresolved. Figures who are depicted positively (e.g. Nicodemus) are presented as being such precisely because they support Jesus. Admittedly, it is hard to realise in cinematic terms the sentiment that 'good people can disagree'. On the screen, action defines character, and it is, for example, difficult to see how a director might differentiate (as some biblical commentators suggest) between 'guilt' and 'responsibility' for Jesus' death.[17] At the same time, scenes in which Jesus (following Luke 4) reads from the prophets to a synagogue congregation, and the crucifixion scene, where Zeffirelli has Nicodemus articulate the New Testament (John 12; Romans 10, etc.) elision of Isaiah 53 into Jesus' death, locates the drama within a context of Jewish suffering and messianic expectation, suggesting in traditional Christian terms that Israel finds its fulfilment in Jesus.

Despite his intentions to produce a qualitatively different kind of Jesus film Zeffirelli falls short of the mark. *Jesus of Nazareth* identifies goodness with recognition of Jesus' Messiahship. Images of Jesus reading Hebrew or wearing a *tallit* do not challenge the fundamental reading of the Judaism-Christianity relationship as one of prophecy-fulfilment. The un-reconciled tensions that characterise Zeffirelli's film raise questions for students of Jewish-Christian relations. (They are echoed in Zeffirelli's own professed desire to show Jesus' message as 'a continuation and a fulfilment' of Judaism.[18]) Is it possible to make a Jesus film that is recognisable to a predominantly Christian audience, and at the same time avoids supersessionism and triumphalism? Such issues extend beyond the scope of this essay, to the heart of fundamental debates in Jewish-Christian dialogue, about the status of scripture and its place in community formation, and about the congruence (or lack of it) between the Jesus of history and the Christ of faith.

Adaptations of 'Classic' Fiction

Biblical films constitute a small minority of those produced each year. A much larger number of films, including a majority of those to have collected the Academy Award for best film, are adapted from works of secular literature. Some of these become caught up in debates surrounding the presentation of Jews, Christians, and Jewish-Christian relations in their sources.

Oliver Twist (David Lean, 1948) is an important case in point. The film's famous opening sequence, in which Oliver's mother struggles to the workhouse, gives birth, and dies, is an impressive piece of expressionist noir photography, sustained over eight dialogue-free minutes. Dickens enthusiasts have praised the 'faithfulness' of Lean's adaptation (Sowerberry's coffin-shaped snuffbox is one of many memorable touches). Yet *Oliver Twist* was banned and censored in the United States, and remains controversial, because of its depiction of the fence, Fagin. The film's reception, juxtaposed with that of Dickens' novel, highlights changing definitions of anti-Jewishness, and attitudes to cinematic and literary 'classics'.

Dickens' characterisation of Fagin blended motifs from Christian anti-Judaism (he is a diabolic figure; a 'poisoner' of childhood innocence, whom Oliver first encounters in a fiery, cave-like lair) and the newer discourse of race (Fagin is referred to in reptiliar terms; descriptions focus on physiological characteristics that race theory associated with Jewishness, such as a large nose, and matted red hair). Moreover, in the novel's early (1830s) editions Fagin is repeatedly referred to as 'the Jew', suggesting that there is something essentially, generalizably Jewish about his role as a corrupter of young children and coordinator of a criminal gang. Lean depends on Dickens for his depiction of Fagin as devious and energetic, and, like the novel, the film links physiognomy with character. Alec Guinness' heavy makeup, including an enormous nose, gives Fagin's face an unnatural, mask-like appearance, which some viewers today find shocking.

Responding to Victorian critics of Fagin, Dickens defended his work, claiming that labelling Fagin as 'the Jew' was historically accurate, since fences almost invariably were Jewish. He also stressed that he had caricatured not the Jewish religion – a move, which, following the liberal view of the day, would have been regarded as being in poor taste – but Fagin's 'race'.[19] By 1948, when Lean's film appeared, liberal tastes had shifted. Any suggestion that race, rather than religion, was being scrutinised, would only exacerbate the controversy. Some favourable assessments of *Oliver Twist* reiterate Dickens' (unsubstantiated[20]) points about criminal activity by Jews, whilst others justify the presentation of Fagin on the basis that the film is simply being faithful to a 'classic'. Additionally, it is argued that viewers can distinguish art from reality, and are not likely to become antisemitic as a result of seeing a film.[21]

Lean claimed that having been raised a Quaker, he was ignorant of antisemitism, and baffled by the furore *Oliver Twist* engendered. Given the film's timing (the script was completed just months after the execution of Nazi war criminals at Nuremberg, only three years after the end of the Holocaust) this is perhaps disingenuous. Moreover, Joseph Breen (head of the Production Code Administration, which regulated film content in the United States) wrote to Lean before filming began, warning him of the text's sensitive nature.[22] In such a context, Lean's decision to present Fagin much as Dickens did appears as (at best) profoundly naïve.

Much debate surrounding *Oliver Twist* today dwells on the fact that unlike the novel, the film never uses the word 'Jew'. Does this absolve the film of any participation in antisemitism? Arguably, despite his protestations to the contrary, Lean's deletion of the word is a kind of tacit acknowledgement of the possibility of a connection between art and prejudice (which challenges the assumptions of some of his supporters). Even with this modification, it is hard not to see Fagin as antisemitic. Cruikshank's famous illustrations of Dickens' novel, produced for its 1838 edition, are an important source for the film's design. In a plate captioned, 'The Jew and Morris both begin to understand Each Other' Cruickshank depicts Fagin, Charlotte, and Morris seated at a table, on which stand a tankard and a drinking glass. Crosshatching and etching create the effect of the scene's being lit by a candle or similar undepicted light-source between them. The viewer's gaze is encouraged outwards from this, to the men's faces, as each taps his nose with his forefinger. This image illustrates a passage in which Fagin, having met the two run-aways, seeks to draw them into his power. Dickens' narrator observes that Morris tries to imitate Fagin's nose striking, 'though not with complete success, in consequence of his own nose not being large enough for the purpose.'[23] Such imagery is the basis for the organisation of several shots in *Oliver*

Twist. The episode with Morris is not in the film, but in one scene where the Artful Dodger, having just introduced Oliver to his mentor, discusses the day's 'business' with Fagin, and in another, where Fagin and Bill plot a robbery, the mise-en-scène closely resembles that in Cruickshank's illustration. In other shots, Fagin is typically shown in profile, with camera angles emphasising his facial features. (Significantly, Rank's press book for *Oliver Twist* juxtaposes Cruikshank's plate and a profile shot of Fagin/Guinness.[24]) He also speaks with a heavy accent, something that Fagin does not do in the novel. All this brings Lean's portrait of Fagin so close to the negative stereotype that simply deleting the word 'Jew' seems insignificant as a remedial move. Audiences who had previously encountered negative images of Jews, or who had anti-Jewish feelings, would have had no difficulty in drawing for themselves a connection between the retained 'signifiers' and the unspoken 'signified'. Mindful of this, some recent productions (including *Oliver!* (Carol Reed, 1968), and Alan Bleasdale's adaptation for Independent Television (1999) have tried to strip Fagin of features component in negative stereotypes of Jews.

Oliver Twist's implication in Jewish-Christian discourse is significant but incidental; neither Jews in Victorian England, nor their representation on screen, were the focus of Lean's interest. In contrast, Joan Micklin Silver's *Hester Street* (1975) based on the 1896 story *Yekl* by Abraham Cahan, is directly concerned with the processes of Jewish acculturation and assimilation in fin-de-siècle New York. Jake (formerly Yekl) is a recent immigrant, who works as a machinist in a sweatshop. His efforts to re-fashion himself as a 'regular American fella' and a developing romance with dancer Mamie Fein are disrupted by the unexpected arrival of his wife, Gitl, and son, Yossele, from Russia. In the claustrophobic environment of a Hester Street tenement, the couple's marriage disintegrates. After their divorce Jake marries the worldly Mamie, but ironically, it is 'greenhorn' Gitl who adapts best to the changing social conditions. Using Mamie's savings, which she cleverly secures in the divorce settlement, she plans to open a grocery store and marry Mr. Bernstein, a pious scholar who was previously the family's lodger.

As this summary suggests, the narrative premise of *Hester Street* is unremarkable. Nostalgia probably explains some of the (unexpected[25]) success of the film. Since it ceased to be the centre of American Jewish population in the early twentieth century, the Lower East Side has claimed a central place in Jewish collective consciousness. Today, it is as much a cultural construct as a physical space - a concrete and metaphorical place within which Jews interpret their history and make sense of the experience of being Jewish Americans.[26] *Hester Street*, shot in black and white, and using Yiddish extensively, translates the myth of the Lower East Side onto the screen, offering viewers the chance to see the past through the lens of the present. But the popularity of the film indicates that it had an appeal beyond American Jewish audiences: why is this? *Hester Street* is unusually nuanced in its approach to immigrant life. It highlights, for example, the ways in which women's and men's experiences differed, modifying Cahan's text to suggest that a strong network of emotional and practical support existed among ghetto women.[27] A scene in which Jake gives Gitl her get (divorce bill) powerfully dramatises the struggle of a religious tradition to assert its authority against modernity's onslaught.[28] Such elements may have appealed to audiences for a number of reasons, many of which are not necessarily related to perceptions of Jewish/non-Jewish relations. Works of ethnic cinema are as much about accentuating common values as they are about maintaining distinctions between groups: they speak to 'insiders' and 'outsiders'.[29] Non-Jewish Americans who first saw the film were members of a society still reeling from Watergate, Vietnam, and seemingly revolutionary shifts in the relations between the genders and ethnic groups. On the economic front, surveys indicated a widening gap between rich and poor. In such a climate, *Hester Street*'s upbeat ending, suggestive as it is of female empowerment and immigrant progress, is largely one of comfort. It reinforces conceptions of America as a land of opportunity and social-economic mobility, in which ethnic values are emotionally significant but nonetheless subsumed by broader American notions of liberation and newness, economic advancement, and marriage relations grounded in love. For non-Jewish audiences, images of Jews in films like *Hester Street* can, therefore, function as evocations of and support for the American dream.

In the 1890s the Lower East Side was predominantly Jewish, but residents would have come into contact with New York's establishment and other sizeable immigrant groups, especially Irish and Italian Catholics. Interestingly, *Hester Street* shows little of this on screen. As Gitl says, 'The Gentiles keep in another place, heh?' Yet the non-Jewish world overshadows Micklin Silver's ghetto. Significantly, the only scene to foreground non-Jewish characters is one in which, having met Gitl and Yossele at Ellis Island, Jake struggles to communicate with an immigration officer. Their inability to comprehend one another is telling. For Jake and other Jews, access to American society entails painful negotiation with non-Jewish mores. Conversely, the accommodation of immigrants requires effort from America's established residents.

Unsurprisingly, given the economic significance of the textiles industry for Jewish immigrants, *Hester Street* presents clothing as the site on to which much of the struggle between differing world-views is mapped. Jake, who has swapped his beard and side-locks for a sports cap and fashionable suit, demands that Gitl abandon her *sheitel* (wig) and the *tikhel* (headscarf) with which she first replaces it. He perceives dress to be a mark of the true 'Yankee'; distinctively Jewish clothing must be shed on the way to becoming an American. Yet the film hints that it is not simply religious conservatism that limits the choices available to Jews in the New World. When Jake boasts that Yossele (whom he renames Joey) is a future President of the United States, Bernstein correctly replies that the President must be American-born. In this way, with a realism borne of the struggles of the civil rights movement in the late 1960s, Micklin Silver suggests that the boundaries separating the immigrants from mainstream (Christian) society are not exclusively of their own construction.

Intermarriage and Identity

In keeping with the assimilationist aspirations of many American Jews in the early and mid-twentieth century, Hollywood films of the period that depicted interfaith romance and marriage between Jews and Christians did so in largely positive terms. They suggested that ethnic and religious differences ultimately mattered little: like Jake in *Hester Street*, they focussed on the American that the immigrant could become. *The Jazz Singer* (Alan Crosland, 1927) is one example. Many people know that it was the first feature film to include spoken dialogue as well as musical numbers, and that it turned Al Jolson into a star. What is less remembered is that a romance between Jewish singer Jake (Jolson) and a Christian, Mary, is central to its plot. Indeed, *The Jazz Singer* is the first Anglophone picture to use the Yiddish term for a gentile woman, shikse.[30] At the end of the film, happiness with Mary and stardom in the musical theatre are the twin prizes that Jake gains, having swapped the culture of his Orthodox parents for the values of mainstream society. Narratively speaking, *The Jazz Singer* suggests that Jewishness is a flawed or problematic state, to be resolved through assimilation to Christian norms.

Made two years later, *Abie's Irish Rose* (Victor Fleming; 1929) is similarly 'upbeat' about Christian-Jewish romance, although it admits problems and its advocacy of assimilation is less overt. Soldier Abie Levy and Rosemary Murphy (an Irish Catholic entertainer) fall in love. Each fears the wrath of their respective families, and the resulting duplicity (Abie introduces Rosemary to his family as 'Rose Murpheski') sees them undergoing multiple marriage ceremonies. The couple's eventual discovery leads to argument between the Murphys and the Levys, and a rift that is only healed when Rosemary gives birth to twins – a boy who is named after her father, and a girl named after Abie's dead mother.[31] This light-hearted comedy is noteworthy on two grounds. The name-play in the film suggests that identity – Jewish or Christian – is not fixed, but more like a garment which one can choose to wear or abandon (like Jake's and Gitl's costumes in *Hester Street*). A fake surname is sufficient for Rosemary to 'pass' as a Jew; and the given names of the babies suggest that the communities may each claim one child as their own. At the same time, the film is striking in its suggestion that offspring are the means to community reconciliation: child rearing is often a source of tension for interfaith couples.

The positive tone of *The Jazz Singer* and *Abie's Irish Rose* is not shared by most more recent films. In the past thirty years, just as interfaith marriage by Jews in the United States and elsewhere has increased, so its portrayal on screen has become less optimistic – an attitude evoked by the tagline to *Annie Hall* (Woody Allen, 1975), which proclaims it as 'a nervous romance'. This shift can be interpreted in relation to a number of ideological contexts. In current discourse ethnic difference is positioned as intrinsic to (American) identity. In the wake of the failure of assimilation to be truly inclusive, plurality has been naturalised as typically American. Within this discourse, intermarriage often functions as a synonym for the (now negatively valued) erosion of Jewish identity through assimilation.

In cinematic terms, the new interest in ethnic and other subcultural identities is played out in an increased willingness to portray Jews on the screen in less negatively stereotyped (not necessarily more realistic!) terms than was generally the case before the mid-sixties.[32] In Micklin Silver's *Crossing Delancey* (1988) the protagonist Isabella has unsuccessful relationships with two non-Jews, before finding happiness with Sam Posner, a pickle-seller (food is significant throughout the film) whom she first meets through a *shadchen* (match-maker) hired by her *bubbie* (grandmother). Although it does not explicitly locate Isabella's difficulties with her 'WASP'-ish partners in their religious or ethnic differences (one is married; the other, an egotistical novelist) the narrative's implication is that marriage to another Jew is a more natural, satisfactory state of affairs. Significantly, Isabella and Sam find romance in bubbie's apartment in the Lower East Side. Like the nostalgic American-Jewish viewers of *Hester Street*, Isabella's life journey takes her back to her 'roots'.

A more complex, ambivalent tone characterises Edward Norton's *Keeping the Faith* (2000). Whereas *Hester Street* constructs New York as a city of discrete, barely intersecting communities, and the Lower East Side as a virtual Jewish-city-within-the-city, *Keeping the Faith* depicts contemporary New York as a web of faiths and ethnicities. The drama centres on the relationship between Brian Flynn, an Irish-American Catholic Priest, and his friend Conservative Rabbi Jake Schram. In an important early sequence editing creates a montage of two scenes (Bryan preaching in his church; Jake addressing the synagogue congregation) to establish parallels between the men and their roles as progressive, charismatic leaders. This device, and the film's main sub-plot (Bryan and Jake's efforts to build a Catholic-Jewish seniors' centre) suggest that what the different communities hold in common is more significant than that which divides them. This idea is reinforced by the impact of the sudden re-appearance of Bryan, and Jake's childhood friend, Anna Riley. Both men fall in love with her: Jake and Anna begin a sexual relationship, which they hide from Bryan and Jake's synagogue. Their inevitable exposure provokes a crisis for both men until Bryan learns that his decision to be a celibate priest must be re-affirmed each day, and Jake finally assesses the relative importance of personal happiness and communal expectation. At the close of the film, all dilemmas are resolved. The three friends and their respective communities unite in a karaoke party at the Catholic-Jewish social centre, and Jake and Anna are set to marry.

From a Jewish-Christian relations' perspective, there is much of interest here. *Keeping the Faith* shows strong friendships across religious boundaries between the pre-adolescent Anna, Bryan, and Jake – something Norton and producer Stuart Blumberg describe as an 'essentially New York' experience. More significantly, Jake and Anna's relationship allows the film to touch on intermarriage. Before Anna and Jake become lovers, it is revealed that Jake's family has disowned his brother Ethan, because he married a gentile. Ethan and his wife never appear on screen. This move is evocative: they are 'lost' to the family, a haunting precursor of the fate awaiting Jake and Anna. On the other hand, it also lets *Keeping the Faith* off a difficult hook. For, whilst it celebrates pluralism, the film is ambivalent about the blurring of identities and inter-communal boundaries that is one of its inevitable consequences. Ambiguity is most apparent in the final scenes. In a set-piece speech, Jake uses his *Yom Kippur* sermon[33] to declare his love for Anna. Uproar ensues. However, the long-term implications of his love for her need not be addressed. It is soon revealed that Anna has been secretly attending conversion classes: Jake will marry a Jewish bride. Narratively speaking, the film suggests in somewhat idealistic terms that if one keeps faith with one's feelings and emotions, a rewarding dissolution of life's problems will result.

Perhaps more puzzling, even disturbing, is the presentation of Anna's journey into Judaism. Although her character is the only one to move significantly (geographically and spiritually) during the course of the narrative, the film's engagement with her is minimal. Anna's surname implies Irish Catholic antecedents, but her family history remains unexplored.[34] Whereas Jake is portrayed in familial contexts (at a *Shabbat* meal, by his mother's sickbed, etc.) and Father Havel mentors Bryan, Anna appears rootless. She is depicted several times with Jake's mother, never with her own parents. Whereas Jake and Bryan are settled in New York, Anna lives in temporary accommodation. *Keeping the Faith* thus presents religious conversion as a rather simplistic joining of a community or acquiring of an identity, with little acknowledgement of the difficulties that may be associated with leaving another one behind.[35]

In its ideological distance from *The Jazz Singer*, *Keeping the Faith* is expressive of the problematics of diversity in contemporary America. Whereas the liberal rhetoric of an earlier age advocated the image of American society as a 'melting pot', the current mood is pessimistic about this ideology's effectiveness as a strategy for managing a diverse population, preferring the 'salad bowl' metaphor of cultural pluralism. *Keeping the Faith* struggles with these competing models. In exploring the obstacles facing Jake and Anna's relationship, it recognises the existence of different communities. Yet in its treatment of Anna's conversion, it argues that boundaries are readily permeable – that identity and belonging are matters of individual choice. In this sense, *Keeping the Faith* speaks enticingly to a post-assimilationist generation of viewers, who wish to re-assert the discourse of difference, whilst continuing to reject the problematic ideology of race in which it was previously grounded.

The Holocaust

Despite the artistic and ethical challenges associated with representing the Nazi attempted genocide of Jews, the Holocaust and its aftermath has been the subject of countless films.[36] Indeed, the cinema is one of the key means by which the Holocaust has been established as a central symbol in western culture. Many people's sense of what the Holocaust is – what happened, and what this might mean – is constructed in relation to its representation on screen. Examining Holocaust films[37] provides a way into a consideration of issues such as antisemitism, Jewish and Christian identity (separately and in relation), suffering, and responsibility, during the Holocaust and in the particular contexts in which the films are produced and consumed.

Religious questions relating to the Holocaust are rarely the cinema's focus – films like *The Quarrel* (Eli Cohen, 1990), in which two men debate theodicy and survivor-guilt, are rare. More commonly, religious rituals function as visual devices to establish the identity of a character or characters. For example, *Schindler's List* (Steven Spielberg, 1993) the most significant Holocaust film of the 1990s, opens with the inauguration of the Sabbath, signalled by the lighting of candles and the making of *kiddush* over wine. Towards the end of the film, Sabbath candles are lighted in Schindler's factory, after he instructs his workers to prepare for the festival. In numerous films, such representations of (comparatively) well-known practices function as brief 'Jewish moments' enacted by people who otherwise appear to be of pretty indeterminate background.[38] Placed as they are in Spielberg's film, the candles serve partly as icons of Jewish identity, and partly as an inclusio suggestive of the extinguishing and subsequent rekindling of Jewish life in Europe (the selective use of colour in these two scenes also encourages viewers to relate them to each other). But Judaism receives scant treatment elsewhere in *Schindler's List*. Indeed, few Holocaust films feature characters for whom Judaism is significant; the experience of *haredi* Jews in particular is rarely explored.

These strategies may be borne of a desire to appeal to a mass audience, including viewers who may be party to antisemitism. Alternatively, they may reflect the view that Jews are defined, not by any intrinsic difference, but because antisemites identify them as such. Such sentiments inform films like Joseph Losey's *Mr. Klein* (1976). In this production, art-dealer

Robert Klein is mistakenly identified as a Jew by the *Gestapo*, and finds himself plunged into a Kafkaesque nightmare that leads eventually to the *Velodrome d'Hiver*, where Parisian Jews were held prior to deportation in summer 1942. *Gentleman's Agreement* (Elia Kazan, 1947) adopts a similar stance. The word 'Holocaust' never appears in the film, but its subject matter and references to the war and military service (significantly, the film's main Jewish character is a veteran, who first appears in uniform) establish it as the drama's context. Commissioned to write a feature on antisemitism, Christian journalist Phil Green poses as a Jew, and finds himself the target of middle class prejudices. Both narrative and dialogue assume a non-Jewish audience for whom Phil mediates the experience of the Jewish 'other'. The suggestion is that Jewish and Christian identities are matters of personal conviction. Phil can switch from Christian to Jew simply by announcing his identification; notions of essential Jewish difference are externally imposed. In this way, the film charts a careful path between challenge and reassurance, with some success. It did well at the box-office and won numerous awards. But *Gentleman's Agreement* was also the subject of a lawsuit in the United States and was initially banned in Spain, on moral grounds.[39]

Whilst *Gentleman's Agreement* is noteworthy for its focus on a 'non-Jewish-Jew', some films departicularise the Holocaust's victims to the point of near abstraction. Alain Resnais' documentary *Night and Fog* (1955) attempted to describe the Final Solution and in so doing, awaken the viewer's conscience in relation to other instances of atrocity. But in its efforts to universalise the Holocaust, *Night and Fog* fails to probe the victimisation of Jews, the complicity of local (non-German) populations and the connections between these events and the history of European antisemitism. The word 'Jew' is spoken only once by the film's narrator (it is absent from the English subtitles) and an image of a *gendarme* ('perpetrator'? 'bystander'?) is crudely censored.[40] Similar trends can be detected in many fictional features. *Life is Beautiful* (Roberto Benigni, 1998) portrays an idyllic marriage between a Jew and a Christian, but makes no reference to religion and essentially uses the Holocaust as a backdrop for a story about familial love.[41]

In contrast to these typical examples, a few films portray the Holocaust as a crisis of Jewish-Christian relations. Based on Hochhuth's play, 'The Representative', *Amen* (Constantin Costa-Gavras, 2002) uses the efforts of a German SS officer (a Protestant) and a Jesuit priest to expose Nazi atrocities against Jews, as an entrée into debates about Vatican silence during the war. These issues are discussion-worthy, but do not translate readily to the screen, and Costa-Gavras' attempts to generate suspense from a historic episode as familiar as the Holocaust meet with only limited success.

In a different vein, Louis Malle's *Goodbye, Children* (1987) deals subtly with Christian collaboration and resistance. Catholic schoolboy Julien Quentin (a fictionalised Malle; the film is semi-autobiographical) doesn't understand why new pupil Jean Bonnet is bullied by the other children, but fiercely protected by the headmaster, Father Jean. In the course of the film Bonnet's real name (Kippelstein) and Jewish identity gradually emerge. Eventually, Jean, two other Jewish boys, and the headmaster, are betrayed and taken away by the Gestapo.

Although unusually restrained (Malle omitted to show the real slap of a boy by a German officer) *Goodbye, Children*, with its images of Christian care for Jews, is not untypical of films touching on Jewish-Christian interaction during the Holocaust. In contrast to prevalent trends in Jewish-Christian relations (on which matter see David Herbert's contribution to this volume), few Holocaust films operate with what might be termed a Jew/innocence–Christian/guilt schema. Given that few Christians opposed the Nazis openly or covertly, a disproportionately high number of films show Christians as rescuers or protectors. Why this should be is an issue worthy of discussion. In the main, perhaps, audiences want to see their values upheld or praised, rather than questioned, on the screen. Images of rescuers are more appealing than those of suffering victims, dysfunctional survivors or cruel perpetrators, because they offer viewers characters with whom they are more likely to engage and identify.

A common strategy in Holocaust films featuring Christian protectors is the depiction of the Jew as a child or woman, or in some other way that presents him or her as weak and defenceless. These images tap into and perpetuate older notions of male and female Jews as stereotypically 'feminine' – that is, innately nervous, passive and hysterical.[42] *Black Thursday* (Michel Mitrani, 1974) depicts the Jew as child (-like). Its protagonist, Paul (a significant name) is a young Christian who tries to lead a number of Parisian Jews to safety. Much of the film is built around his relationship with Jewish girl Jeanne. Like Jews generally, she is presented as passive, aware of her likely fate and yet unable to help herself. At the end of the film, Jeanne rejects Paul's protection and joins her mother, to await deportation.

Schindler's List also perpetuates images of Jewish passivity and dependence. It was denounced by a number of Middle Eastern intellectuals as a cynical attempt to stir up feelings of guilt in the Christian West, and thereby counter criticism of Israel.[43] Certainly, the film might be criticised for its lack of reference to non-Jewish victims, and non-German Gentiles.[44] But arguably, *Schindler's List* emphasises not Christian responsibility for the Holocaust, but the role of Christian benevolence in Jewish survival. Like *Black Thursday*, it suggests that the relation between the communities is structured largely around Jewish need. The Jewish characters are generally passive, old, or ailing (Itzhak Stern shows courage and determination, but even he is short, slight, and visually impaired) contrasting with images of Oskar Schindler and Amon Goeth, each in their physical prime. Schindler is typically shot from a low angle, presenting him as tall and powerful. In relation to him and Goeth, the camera uses standard devices of character focalisation – the shot-reverse-shot, point-of-view shots, and so on. But the camera's relation to the Jewish characters is more 'omniscient' or distancing, visualising them as a mass, and granting them little subjectivity.[45] Jewish resistance is little explored. Finally, the closing scenes depict the actors and surviving 'Schindler Jews' visiting Schindler's grave in the Christian cemetery on Mount Zion, Jerusalem. Church domes and steeples are visible in the background of several shots. Thus a narrative that begins with images of Jewish ritual practices ends with multiple evocations of the Christian metanarrative.

Similar impulses emerge in Roman Polanski's *The Pianist* (2002) although this film hints that the Jew-Christian relationship is more symbiotic. Based on the story of Warsaw pianist Wladislaw Szpilman, the film attends to Jewish resistance. As a forced labourer, Szpilman smuggles food and weapons; and later, having escaped, he witnesses the ghetto uprising. The dramatic climax of the film is Szpilman's encounter with a German officer, Wilm Hosenfeld, in 1944. Szpilman is scarcely alive, scavenging for food in the war torn city. But on finding a piano in a bombed-out house, he is lifted out of this piteous state by the opportunity to play music. Metaphorically, Szpilman is transported into a previous, 'civilised' age when he performed on Polish radio; more prosaically, Hosenfeld, moved by the performance, feeds Szpilman until the Red Army's arrival. So *The Pianist* posits music as the site of existential encounter, and suggests that while Szpilman needs the German, Hosenfeld needs the Jew's presence, to remind him of his humanity.

In addition to those films presenting the Holocaust as a moment in Christian-Jewish relations, others which view Jewish experience of the Holocaust through the lens of Christian typology are relevant to our study. *The Pawnbroker* (Sidney Lumet, 1965) focuses on Sol Nazerman, a survivor and pawnshop owner in Harlem, New York. Physically alive, he is spiritually and emotionally dysfunctional, haunted by memories of the concentration camp and his dead family. Much of the film is concerned with Sol's detachment from those around him, including his customers, his Latino assistant (Jesus), and other Holocaust survivors. *The Pawnbroker*'s climax, which portrays Nazerman's transition from isolation to a new ability to connect with others, resonates with the Christian metanarrative. During a failed robbery Jesus (significantly he associates with Mabel, a prostitute, and refers to the shop's customers as 'children of God') is killed whilst attempting to protect Nazerman. As Nazerman grieves over Jesus' death, a crowd gathers, including Jesus' mother (compare John 19.25). Finally, Nazerman's own cathartic act evokes the crucifixion. Returning to the shop, he pierces his hand on a receipt spike, creating a stigma-like wound. The post Holocaust 'resurrection' of the Jew is assimilated to a tale of redemptive suffering conceived in Christian terms.

Why might filmmakers draw on Christian images and concepts in their depiction of the Holocaust? Is this a simple translation of supersessionism to the screen? Arguably, in turning to Christian-influenced schema, Holocaust filmmakers are not 'theologically driven'. The use of Christian typology and symbolism to impose meaning on Jewish suffering, highly problematic though it may be, is as much about a failure of artistic imagination[46] – perhaps also about the constraints audience expectation exercises on the film-making process – as it is about Christianity's hubristic claims to narrate or theologise 'the Jew'. However motivated though, it projects ideological themes that implicitly perpetuate notions of Jewishness as requiring resolution through Christianity. It denies the specificity of victim experiences, and obscures the role of some Christian ideologies, individuals, and institutions in facilitating the Final Solution.

The 'Jewish Hollywood' Question

Off-screen, debates about film censorship and regulation have been occasions for antisemitism and for neutral-positive contacts between Jews, Christians and others. Moreover, cineastes are well acquainted with the claim that Jews 'control' Hollywood. This accusation was established as early as the 1920s and posits a monolithic entity, 'the Jews,' whose quest for influence has led them to seek control over media such as motion pictures. However, the relation of Jews and Christians to the cinema (as individuals, as communities, and in dialogue with one another) has been little studied.

The early cinema was more accessible to immigrants than established industries (is it more meaningful to speak about 'the lack of Jewish absence' from the motion picture industry, than about the Jewish presence within it?) and Jews were among the founders of several film companies including Paramount, Metro-Goldwyn-Meyer, and Warner Brothers. As makers, distributors and consumers of film, Jews and Christians have often worked successfully together, but relations were perceptibly strained during the late 1920s and 1930s, at the height of the Cold War, and in the late 1980s and early 1990s.

In the two earlier periods, an antisemitic undercurrent permeating much American social life coloured the calls for increased regulation of film content. Despite his caution to Lean concerning Oliver Twist, Production Code Administration[47] head Joseph Breen (a Roman Catholic) believed that the salaciousness of many popular films was attributable to a Jewish preoccupation with money and sex.[48] Numerous Protestant and Catholic reformers felt that immoral films reflected the depravity of the Jews who made them. Fears that these manifestations of antisemitism would coalesce into a nationwide Nazi-type movement led the Central Conference of American Rabbis and the Anti-Defamation League to join the calls for increased regulation and reform. However, in doing so they unwittingly lent support to the notion that individual Jews bore a collective responsibility for the safety and reputation of all Jews, and that the perceived immorality of the cinema was indeed a 'Jewish problem'. Rather than challenging the beliefs of the antisemites, they effectively reinforced them. In urging producers to refrain from behaviours that could be used against the Jewish community, the CCAR blamed the victims, not the perpetrators.[49] Interestingly, the CCAR committee on film, chaired by Rabbi William Fineschriber, believed that its work had important potential for strengthening Jewish-Christian cooperation. Joint meetings were held in New York,[50] but were limited in their impact on either the industry or those who attacked filmmakers as Jews. Nevertheless, the work of Jewish film reformers constitutes an important, little-known episode in the history of American Jewish-Christian relations.

Filmmakers' assimilationist responses to antisemitism were more significant than the various institutional approaches to shaping film subject matter. Hollywood was reluctant to use the cinema to counter anti-Jewish prejudices. It was only after Pearl Harbour that films began to undermine negative stereotypes and suggest positive models of Jewish-Christian co-existence. Before 1942, Warner Brothers was alone in its production of openly antifascist films, such as *Confessions of a Nazi Spy* (Anatole Litvak, 1939). Even these works referenced Jewish persecution obliquely. *Casablanca* (Michael Curtiz, 1942), for example, made passing references to Victor Laszlo's escape from a concentration camp before his arrival in Morocco. But Laszlo makes light of the camp, referring to it as a place where 'one is apt to lose a little weight'. Moreover, he is a Czech resistance fighter, which distances him from Jewish experiences. Focussing on events in American history, *They Won't Forget* (Mervin LeRoy, 1937) followed a different strategy and used a treatment of the 1905 Leo Frank case to criticise racism. The fact that the film de-Judaised Frank[51] indicates the sensitive nature of the 'Jewish Question' so far as Hollywood was concerned.

For many years *The Great Dictator* (Charlie Chaplin, 1940) remained the only mainstream American production to confront Nazi antisemitism. Chaplin, who played both leading roles, also wrote, funded and directed the film, which he hoped would shorten the war. For the Nazis, the project confirmed their suspicion that Chaplin was a secret Jew: *The Eternal Jew* had included disapproving commentary on footage of crowds welcoming him to Berlin in 1931. But although Chaplin's wife (Paulette Goddard) had a Jewish father, his socialist sympathies and opposition to potentially dehumanising aspects of modernity (his *Modern Times* (1936) critiqued mechanised production methods) were his major motivations to anti-fascism. In *The Great Dictator*, a Jewish barber dons military uniform in a bid to escape persecution in the fictional country of 'Tonamia'. He is, however, mistaken for moustachioed dictator Adenoid Hynkel, a confusion that ultimately finds him called to make a speech at a military rally. Throughout, *The Great Dictator* makes explicit reference to Hynkel's (Hitler's) Judeophobia, and details aspects of Nazi antisemitic policy including the concentration of Jews into urban ghettos, the boycotting of Jewish businesses, and deportations. The closing address is a call for 'every one…Jew, Gentile, black man, white…to make this life free and beautiful'.

Predictably, the film was banned in Germany and German-controlled territories (although Hitler himself probably saw it privately). Surprisingly, perhaps, in America the Catholic Legion of Decency refused to recommend the film for children, because in one scene the barber fails to affirm God's existence. (When asked about his beliefs, he pauses and begins, "Well…" but is interrupted.)[52] For different reasons, Chaplin himself later regretted making *The Great Dictator*: in 1940 the Final Solution was not yet implemented, but conditions in the European ghettos had already become far worse than he imagined.

In the later twentieth century, just as few religious Jews would shun the cinema (*haredi* Jews who interpret Exodus 20.4 to prohibit any reproduction of human images are in the minority) so Christian opposition to secular film has largely issued from conservative fundamentalist circles. In the 1950s, conservative discourse no longer regarded Jews as money-grabbing capitalists but as 'Godless Communists'. Mississippi Congressman John Rankin (a conservative alluded to in *Gentleman's Agreement*) a key figure in the House Un-American Activities Committee, which placed Hollywood professionals accused of holding left-wing views on an employment blacklist, equated Jewish heritage with Communist sympathy.[53] More recently, some usually philosemitic figures (for example, evangelist Pat Robertson) have associated what they perceive to be the permissiveness of the industry with the influence of Jewish intellectuals and media activists. The making of *The Last Temptation of Christ* (Martin Scorsese, 1988) provided an occasion for antisemitism targeted against the chair of MCA, which released the film.[54] Some critics of the marginalisation of African-Americans in the cinema have also denounced Jewish filmmakers (especially Spielberg) as responsible for the suppression of black liberation – a view that overlooks the history of African-American and Jewish co-operation in lobbying against the *Birth of a Nation* (Griffiths, 1915) and for modifications to the screenplay of *Gone With the Wind* (Fleming, 1939).[55] (This discourse is also manifest in the work of some African-Americna directors: Spike Lee's *Malcolm X* (1992) sidelines some problematic aspects of its subject's life but retains, unchallenged, his antisemitism.[56])

Such debates about the role of Jews in filmmaking, the so-called 'Jewish Hollywood' question, raise issues for Jewish-Christian relations. They illustrate the changing character of American antisemitism. On the one hand, discourse about negative Jewish influence on the cinema taps into old stereotypes rooted in Christian theology: Jewish filmmakers are poisoning Christian society through their promotion of depraved images. As destructors of Christian values, they recapitulate Judas's crimes on the ideological plane. On the other hand, the early Cold War search for 'hidden Jews' in the industry echoes the modern conception of the Jew as *parvenu*, resonating with broader debates about ethnicity and national identity. The elasticity of 'Jewish Hollywood' discourse also points to larger questions beyond the scope of this piece. Some critics have hinted that the search for a dictating presence behind the movies is a distortion of the real puzzle, namely, the difficulties associated with explaining the source of film's ability to move and affect viewers. Focussing on Jewish control is an anthropomorphism of this much harder problem.[57] Alternatively, questions may be raised about the nature of antisemitism. Do the changing meanings attached to 'Jewish Hollywood' indicate that once established in the collective psyche, the negative image of 'the Jew' functions somewhat independently of actualities, and becomes a vehicle onto which more diffuse fears and longings are projected? If so, the task of undoing the legacy of Christian anti-Jewish teaching becomes a problem extending far beyond the modification of problematic theologies.

Finally, accusations of negative Jewish control over Hollywood and philosemitic explanations of a Jewish presence and contribution in Hollywood share a tendency to assume that Jews perennially act as Jews, that 'whatever a Jews is…a Jew will always behave like a Jew'.[58] This article has instead suggested that analysis should be based in an historical, rather than an essentialist conception of Jewish identity and cultural production. Studying and critiquing this aspect of Hollywood's 'Jewish Question' contributes not only to the context for interpreting cinema history, but also to fundamental debates about Jewish and other (including Christian) identities.

Conclusion: Cinema Studies and Jewish-Christian Relations

The cinema has been little studied as a locus of Jewish-Christian relations. Film Studies is only beginning to move beyond a schema that conceives of Jewish and Christian engagement in the cinema in simplistic terms of 'control' or 'protest'. Aside from oft-questionable historical treatments of 'Jewish filmmaking', and occasional acknowledgements of the antisemitic motivations behind censorship campaigns, most scholarship has focused on a small number of individual films. Conversely, activity in

Jewish-Christian relations remains focussed on (certain kinds of) written texts, and has largely failed to engage effectively with mass culture.

A brief article such as this one can only be suggestive – describing questions that future research might explore, and hinting at the conceptual tools and models that could be deployed in their study. It will have been successful if it has demonstrated that the worlds of cinema and Jewish-Christian relations have much to gain from dialogue with one another, and has prompted some reflection on the means by which such encounters might proceed. Those seeking to understand the dynamics of Jewish-Christian interaction miss much if they ignore the cinema, the modern medium par excellence. Indeed, the insights derivable from such work are not limited in their application to the present day. As they develop and describe anew relations between art and audience, commerce and culture, they may suggest insights into earlier moments in Jewish-Christian relations.[59] For its part, Cinema Studies is enriched when it reads both art and industry against the experience of Jews and Christians, individually and in relation with each another.[60]

Notes

1. David Welch, "'Jews Out!' Anti-Semitic Film Propaganda in Nazi Germany and the "Jewish Question,'" *British Journal of Holocaust Education* 1 (1992), pp. 55-73; Richard Taylor, *Film Propaganda: Soviet Russia and Nazi Germany* (London: I. B. Tauris, 1998), p. 186; Roger Greenspun, 'Cinema and Television', in Walter Laquer (ed.), *The Holocaust Encyclopedia* (New Haven and London: Yale University Press, 2001), p.120.

2. Nancy Thomas Brown, 'The Holocaust in Film: Christian Ideology, the Enigma of Indifference and the Portrayal of the Jew', in John K. Roth and Elisabeth Maxwell (eds), *Remembering for the Future: The Holocaust in an Age of Genocide. Volume Three. Memory* (Basingstoke: Palgrave, 2001), pp. 695-697.

3. Melanie J. Wright, *Moses in America: The Cultural Uses of Biblical Narrative* (New York: Oxford University Press, 2002), pp. 114-117; Bruce Babington and Peter W. Evans, *Biblical Epics: Sacred Narrative in the Hollywood Cinema* (Manchester: Manchester University Press, 1993), pp. 5-6.

4. Charles Musser, 'Passions and the Passion Play: Theatre, Film and Religion in America, 1880-1900', *Film History* 5 (1993), pp. 419-456.

5. Simon Louvish, 'Burning Crosses', *Sight and Sound* 10 no. 9 (September 2000), pp. 12-13 describes the incident.

6. William M. Drew, *D. W. Griffith's Intolerance. Its Genesis and Its Vision* (Jefferson, N. C.: McFarland, 1986) judges the film's values as being 'as old as civilisation' and its message as a relevant, 'priceless legacy', pp. 167, 168.

7. Wright, *Moses*, p. 38.

8. William R. Telford, 'Jesus Christ Movie Star: The Depiction of Jesus in the Cinema', in Clive Marsh and Gaye Ortiz (eds), *Explorations in Theology and Film* (Oxford: Blackwell, 1997), pp. 115-139 discusses *King of Kings* and other Christ films.

9. DeMille to Hays, October 13th 1927, quoted in Richard Maltby, 'The King of Kings and the Czar of All the Rushes: The Propriety of the Christ Story', *Screen* 13 no. 2 (1990), p. 210.

10. Wright, *Moses*, p. 93.

11. Discussing his use of Jewish extras in *The Ten Commandments*, DeMille suggested that their 'deep feeling of the significance of the Exodus' and 'appearance' would lend a special quality to the performance – a justification blending the discourses of 'race' and theology (Cecil B. DeMille; Donald Hayne (ed.), *The Autobiography of Cecil B. DeMille* (London: W. H. Allen, 1960), p. 213.

12. Note also the striking elision of present into past in DeMille's suggestion to Hays that the Jews who opposed his film would 'crucify Christ a second time, if they had an opportunity' (Maltby, *The King of Kings*, p. 210).

13. Felicia Herman, '"The Most Dangerous Anti-Semitic Photoplay in Filmdom": American Jews and The King of Kings', *Velvet Light Trap* 46 (Fall 2000), p. 18.

14. David O. Selznick tried to have *Golgotha* (Jules Duvuvier, 1936) banned on the grounds of antisemitism. See Steven Alan Carr, *Hollywood and Anti-Semitism: A Cultural History Up to World War Two* (Cambridge: Cambridge University Press, 2001), p. 198.

15. Franco Zeffirelli, *Zeffirelli: The Autobiography of Franco Zeffirelli* (London: Weidenfeld and Nicolson, 1986), pp. 273-74. Joanne Pearson and Steve Moyise link the characteristics of Zeffirelli's Jesus to Jewish finance in the person of producer Lew Grade. This assessment reads the film in simplistic terms, perhaps drawing unhelpfully on the rhetoric of Jewish agency, discussed later. See their 'Jesus in History and Film,' in

Gwilym Beckerlegge (ed.), *From Sacred Text to Internet* (Aldershot: Ashgate, 2001), p. 43.

16. This reflects the scholarly consensus, see Raymond E. Brown, *The Death of the Messiah. Volume 1. From Gethsemane to the Grave: A Commentary on the Passion Narratives in the Four Gospels* (New York: Doubleday, 1994), pp. 357-364.

17. See Brown, *Death of the Messiah*, pp. 391-397.

18. Zeffirelli, *Zeffirelli*, p. 274.

19. Charles Dickens, letter to Eliza Davis, quoted in Deborah Heller, 'The Outcast as Villain and Victim: Jews in Dickens's Oliver Twist and Our Mutual Friend,' in Derek Cohen and Deborah Heller (eds), *Jewish Presences in English Literature* (Montreal and Kingston, McGill-Queen's University Press, 1990), p. 42.

20. When Dickens characterises the receiving of stolen goods as a Jewish brand of villainy he is probably generalising from the example of Ikey Solomons, a London fence who was transported in the early 1830s.

21. Pointer, *Charles Dickens on the Screen*, p. 68 espouses the 'historical fact' defence, but seems uncertain as to whether Jews are a 'sect' or 'race'. See also Morris U. Schappes, 'Oliver Twist and anti-Semitism', in David Platt (ed.), *Celluloid Power: Social Film Criticism from the Birth of a Nation to Judgment at Nuremberg* (Metuchen, NJ and London: The Scarecrow Press, 1992), pp. 83-89.

22. See Al McKee, 'Art or Outrage? Oliver Twist and the Flap Over Fagin', *Film Comment* 36 no. 1 (January/February 2000), pp. 40-45.

23. Charles Dickens, *Oliver Twist* (London: Penguin, repr. 1985 [first published 1837-9]), p.382.

24. The press book (a marketing tool aimed at potential exhibitors and reviewers of the film) is available online at the British Film Institute's David Lean website, http://lean.bfi.org.uk/index.html .

25. See Joyce Antler, '*Hester Street*', in Mark C. Carnes (ed.), *Past Imperfect: History According to the Movies* (London: Cassell, 1995), p. 178.

26. Beth S. Wegner, 'Memory as Identity: The Invention of the Lower East Side,' *American Jewish History* 85 no. 1 (1997), pp. 3-27.

27. Sonya Michel, 'Yekl and Hester Street: Was Assimilation Really Good For the Jews?,' *Literature/Film Quarterly* 5 no. 2 (1977), p. 144.

28. Compare Alex Gordon, 'Descendant Dybbuks: Yiddish Cinema and The Hollywood Continuum', in Sylvia Paskin, (ed.), *When Joseph Met Molly: A Reader on Yiddish Film* (Nottingham: Fine Leaves Publications,

1999), p. 292.

29. Lester D. Friedman, 'Celluloid Palimpsests: An Overview of Ethnicity and the American Film', in Lester D. Friedman, *Unspeakable Images: Ethnicity and the American Cinema* (Chicago: University of Illinois Press, 1991), p. 19.

30. Joseph Greenblum, 'Does Hollywood Still Glorify Jewish Intermarriage?: The Case of The Jazz Singer', *American Jewish History* 83 no. 1 (1995), p. 461.

31. Alan Gevinson (ed.), *Within Our Gates: Ethnicity in American Feature Films, 1911-1960* (Berkeley: University of California Press, 1997), pp. 3-4.

32. See Alan Spiegel, 'The Vanishing Act: A Typology of the Jew in Contemporary Film', in Sarah Blacher Cohen (ed.), *From Hester Street to Hollywood: The Jewish-American Stage and Screen* (Bloomington, Ind.: Bloomington University Press, 1983), pp. 264-67. Spiegel points out that an increase in Jewish characters does not necessarily entail more 'Jewishness' on screen: contemporary films often deploy 'the Jew' as an exemplar or symbol of some wider aspect of American culture.

33. Is it coincidental that *Yom Kippur* is also the crisis moment for Jakie in *The Jazz Singer*?

34. In early versions of the screenplay, Anna is Brian's sister, supporting her identification as (lapsed) Catholic.

35. At the beginning of *Keeping the Faith*, Anna's independence and active pursuit of a career pose a threat to gender boundaries, realised visually though her slender physique and wearing of trouser suits. Her conversion domesticates her, placing her (literally and ideologically) within Jake's embrace. For Jake, the romance affirms his identity and potency (early scenes in the film problematise his inability to find a wife). A gentle style belies the film's complex approach to religion, ethnicity and gender politics.

36. Annette Insdorf, *Indelible Shadows: Film and the Holocaust*, third edition (Cambridge: Cambridge University Press, 2003) lists 170 titles of films made since 1989 alone, pp. 313-355.

37. This phrase does not imply that films dealing with the Holocaust constitute a discrete genre.

38. Compare Jon Stratton, *Coming Out Jewish: Constructing Ambivalent Identities* (London: Routledge, 2000), p. 291 on ethnic identification in sitcoms.

39. Sources close to the Board of Film Censors claimed that the

difficulty lay in what the board's ecclesiastical member had termed 'theological errors', including its claim that Christians were not superior to Jews, and its suggestion that the Christian message of love should embrace Jews. The board's President gave a different rationale, claiming that Spain had no experience of antisemitism or ethnic conflict, and that he wished to prohibit a film that would introduce to the country a disturbing, alien idea. (See Gevinson (ed.), *Within Our Gates*, p. 379).

40. Richard Raskin, *Nuit et Brouillard by Alain Resnais. On the Making, Reception and Functions of a Major Documentary Film* (Aarhus: Aarhus University Press, 1987), p. 31, reproduces the images.

41. Melanie J. Wright, '"Don't Touch My Holocaust: Responding to *Life is Beautiful*', *The Journal of Holocaust Education* 9 no. 1 (2000), pp. 19-32.

42. Judith Doneson, 'The Image Lingers: The Feminisation of the Jew in *Schindler's List*', in Yosefa Loshitzky (ed.), *Spielberg's Holocaust: Critical Perspectives on Schindler's List* (Bloomington, Ind.: Indiana University Press, 1997), pp. 140-152 discusses this in more detail.

43. Mariam Shahin, '*Schindler's List* – ghost movie', *The Middle East* 234 (1994), p. 42.

44. Clearly, one cannot expect a Holocaust film to 'do everything', but *Schindler's List* presents itself as a master narrative of the *Shoah*, as reflected in the cinematography, intended to evoke a documentary like quality in the drama.

45. Ora Gelley, 'Narration and the Embodiment of Power in *Schindler's List*', *Film Criticism* 22 no. 2 (1997), p. 22.

46. So Ilan Avisar, 'Christian Ideology and Jewish Genocide in American Holocaust Movies', in Sanford Pinsker and Jack Fischer (eds), *Literature, the Arts, and the Holocaust* (Greenwood, FL: Penkevill Press, 1987), pp. 21-42.

47. The Production Code, issued in 1930 and re-asserted in 1933, detailed subjects which filmmakers should avoid or handle only with extreme caution. The PCA was founded to enforce the Code.

48. Geoffrey D. Black, *The Catholic Crusade Against the Movies 1940-1975* (Cambridge: Cambridge University Press, 1998), p. 70.

49. Felicia Herman, 'American Jews and the Effort to Reform Motion Pictures, 1933-1935', *American Jewish Archives Journal* 53 nos. 1 and 2 (2001), p. 22.

50. Herman, 'American Jews', p. 26.

51. Frank was tried for child murder in 1913 and convicted on

inconclusive evidence (he was pardoned in 1986). In 1915 he was kidnapped from a prison farm and lynched. The event prompted the founding of the Anti-Defamation League.

52. Herman G. Weinberg, 'Chaplain's *The Great Dictator*', in David Platt (ed.), *Celluloid Power*, p. 347.

53. Wright, *Moses*, p. 116.

54. Harold Brackman, 'The Attack on "Jewish Hollywood": A Chapter in the History of Modern American Anti-Semitism', *Modern Judaism* 20 (2000), p. 6; W. Barnes Tatum, *Jesus at the Movies: a Guide to the First Hundred Years* (Santa Rosa: Polebridge Press, 1997), p. 163.

55. Drew, *D. W. Griffith's Intolerance*, p. 9.

56. Julius Lester, 'Black Supremacy and Anti-Semitism: Religion in *Malcolm X*', *Cineaste* 19 no. 4 (1993), pp. 16-17.

57. Sklar, quoted in Carr, *Hollywood and Anti-Semitism*, p. 10.

58. Carr, *Hollywood and Anti-Semitism*, p. 10.

59. Compare Colin MacCabe, *The Eloquence of the Vulgar: Language, Cinema, and the Politics of Culture* (London: British Film Institute, 1999), p. 29.

60. Bill Telford, Senior Lecturer at DurhamUniversity and editor of *Cinema Divinité* (forthcoming: SCM Press).

9

Europe and 'Abraham's legacy'

Tomáš Halik

I

The theme of 'Europe and religion' is extremely topical at the present time for at least two reasons.[1]

The first is to do with the tragic events that occurred outside the territory of Europe on the very threshold of the new millennium. The terrorist attacks on targets in the USA and America's unfortunate intervention in Iraq, confront the world with the risk of a new division and the possibility that social and cultural differences will escalate into violent conflict. A striking feature of these conflicts is that anti-Western Arab groups define themselves in religious terms.

We can only hope that people in responsibility in the West (Western leaders?) will realise in time that the existence of terrorist groups and dictatorial regimes is only a partial expression of the deeper tension between the West and a large part of the former 'Third World,' and that this tension cannot be resolved by force of arms. After the demise of the erstwhile 'Second World,' it is time to find a new model of coexistence between the former 'First' and 'Third' worlds. If countries with different political and economic systems, which came into existence in totally different historical and political contexts, are to live side by side peacefully it requires, among other things, an inter-cultural dialogue. I recently visited the Sorbonne in Paris for a meeting of representatives of the oldest European universities to discuss the mission of the university in the age of globalisation. There was immediate acceptance for the view that dialogue with Islam is a matter of great urgency. However, one of the participants posed the simple question as to who would be the proper European partner in the discussions with Islam. Would it be atheists and agnostics, or rather Christians and Jews? What sort of face does the West – and Europe, as the cradle of its culture – want to show the Muslims and what sort of language will be employed? Will it be the language of secularism or the language of religion? And what might happen were the West to acknowledge its Christian and Jewish identity more forcefully? Would it simply increase the tension, by evoking the spirit of religious wars of long ago, or would it provide scope for a meeting with Muslims on the common ground of 'Abraham's legacy'?

And is there not, perhaps, another possibility – that the West will first of all realise fully, and then prove in practice, that its secular character need not necessarily be anti-religious, and that instead, it is a legitimate outcome of the development of Christianity and Judaism that it offers scope not only for the ethical values of religion to be put into practice, but also for people of different persuasions to live together freely? Is it conceivable that, at least for certain currents within Islam, this type of division combined with partnership, and the possible co-operation between religion and politics, might be inspirational and acceptable? Why for many of us does this idea sound naively utopian? Is it because we assume that the separation of religion and politics is impossible within Islam, or because even in Europe this model continues to be an ideal rather than reality?

Is such a model more of a problem for today's believers, and for their churches and religious communities, or for the advocates of secularism?

II

This brings us to the second question about how significant religion is for Europe. The fall of Communism helped quicken the pace of European integration and enhance the process. The expansion of the European Union, as well as the drafting of a common European Constitution and efforts to bring the legislations of the member states more in line with each other, once more beg the question of the cultural and spiritual identity of Europe. Will the controversy about the wording of the European Constitution lead to superficial political skirmishes in the media about individual clauses, and a revival of the 'Kulturkampf' spirit, or will it provide, on the contrary, an opportunity to rethink the relationship between religion, politics and culture?

It would seem that in Western Europe, politics and the media are still dominated by the liberal mentality that prevailed within the Western European intellectual elites for most of the nineteenth and twentieth centuries and gave rise to various versions of the 'theory of secularisation.' Some of those theories assumed, in the light of the changing role of the major Christian churches in certain European countries during modern times, the gradual decline or even rapid extinction of religion throughout the world. Others did not go that far, but simply maintained that religion had shifted out of the public into the private sphere, but their assumption was that the process was irreversible.

When religion made a global come-back to the political stage in the last quarter of the twentieth century, many were shocked. Religion appeared to them like Samson, once blinded and chained, a laughing stock, shorn of all his strength, here he was, his hair freshly grown, a frenzied titan threatening the pillars of our houses and the survival of all. One of the first books to situate the re-Islamisation of part of the Arab world in the wider context of the return of monotheistic religions to public life and politics was French sociologist Gilles Kepel's best-selling *The Revenge of God*.[2] It is now evident that the deprivatisation and repoliticisation of religion is truly a global phenomenon and does not only concern the monotheistic religions. 'Religious terrorism' and 'fundamentalism' are its most obvious, but by no means sole expressions. We can find religious symbols and very active religious groups nowadays in every part of the political spectrum from the extreme right to the extreme left, from fighters for civil liberties, human rights and social justice to supporters of authoritarian regimes, from ecological activists to extreme nationalists, from the United States and Latin America to the new states of African, from the Balkans to the Arab countries, from Israel to India or Japan.

The assumption of the authors and advocates of the theory of secularisation that what had been happening in Europe for some time would necessarily have to happen throughout the world is now regarded as erroneous, particularly by analysts of present-day society, who view it as one of the many prejudices of an arrogant and naïve Eurocentrism. Religion has proved to be a more vital and multifarious phenomenon than it was viewed by the Enlightenment, Positivism or Marxism. In fact, the theory of secularisation had itself become a kind of substitute religious conviction for certain social groups and political currents; it no longer functioned as a scientific hypothesis but instead as an ideology in the service of power politics – in a 'soft' version in certain western countries, or Nehru's India, post-war Japan, or Egypt; in a very 'hard' version in the former Soviet empire or Communist China.

Even after the fall of Communism, and in the face of the current revival of religion in many part of the world, many stereotypical views of religion dating back to the period before the present changes in civilisational paradigms are proving hard to overcome. In the media, in the heads of many politicians and within broad sections of public opinion, the prevailing view of the role and future of religion still derives from the ideology of the anti-clerical movements from the eighteenth to the mid-twentieth century. Paradoxically, this view of religion adopted precisely the clerical view of religion – in other words, restricting it solely to phenomena confined to ecclesiastical institutions and doctrinal systems and raising its hands in horror at all 'religious innovations'. If the present transformations of religion are to be understood, it is necessary to abandon these old ideological clichés.

III

Ever since the Enlightenment, we in the West have been accustomed to regard the separation of Church and State as the ideal model for the relation between religion and politics. This model that was the outcome of an historical drama in many acts, one element of which was the critical attitude to power adopted by many Jewish prophets and Christian martyrs: – the 'papal revolution' against the emperor's monopoly of power in the struggle over the investiture, Enlightenment endeavours to protect the freedom of civil society from church interference, and the efforts of Christians to defend religious freedom in the face of totalitarian tendencies on the part of the State. There are many arguments in favour of retaining this mutually beneficial model in practical terms. However, if we are seeking to understand the relationship between religion and politics, we cannot today view it exclusively from the point of view of the relationship between Church and State.

Nowadays the State no longer has a monopoly of political life and the Church has lost its monopoly of religion. On the threshold of the modern age, the *corpus christianorum* disintegrated, ushering in the epoch of nation states and separate Christian denominations. These were to play a crucial role through modern times in Europe. For most Europeans, belonging to a nation and a religious denomination were the main pillars of their identity, and not infrequently, fanatical attachment to a particular denomination or nation combined with demonisation of others resulted in ruinous wars.

We still have nation states and individual churches, but their influence is considerably reduced. The dynamic of political life is increasingly provided by various new social movements and citizens' campaigns, often operating internationally while the dynamic of religious life is more supplied by various religious movements, often operating across the boundaries of the different denominations.

All human activity, including political and religious life, takes place within a new context, as part of the global information market created by the electronic media. Moreover, politics is increasingly in thrall to economics, which is increasingly globalised; the most important economic decisions, and therefore political decisions also, are taken at international level, in bodies that are subject minimally to the influence of democratic mechanisms operating within the framework of the national state. The tested mechanisms of political and religious influence that applied hitherto have to a marked extent been tied to the narrower framework of the nation state and church institutions and are hard to transfer into a wider context. Just as the classical model of democracy is hard to apply in broader contexts than the nation state, so also the classical form of pastoral work is hard to operate outside the traditional church structures. The media also play a major role in religion, as well as small experiential communities operating rather like psychotherapeutic groups.

People sense a decline in the importance of classical political and religious institutions, parties and churches. Political parties and churches are often subject to sharp criticism, which has an interesting psychological background. It would appear that many feel a certain nostalgia and displeasure – albeit often instinctive and covert – in the face of growing apathy in the areas of politics and religion (or, more precisely, because of the decline of previous forms of religion and politics) and blame this on the institutions. The untrustworthiness, corruption, ossification and non-transparency of churches and political parties and their leaders are allegedly to blame for the fact that society and the critics themselves are not sufficiently active in political and religious terms. Of course, there may be an element of truth in such criticism – all human institutions throughout history have been pervaded by human weakness to a greater or lesser degree. However, it is also a case of projection, of seeking a scapegoat. The reasons why the style of political and religious life that applied hitherto is in crisis must be sought much deeper; this crisis is not simply due the incompetence of institutions and their representatives. It is the social and cultural context of religious and political life that has changed.

Every change in civilisation's paradigms requires 'recontextualisation', whether in religion or in politics, and this is generally a lengthy and dramatic process of seeking new forms and a new style. (If one examines the transformations undergone by European Christianity, for instance, one can see how well the Church stood the test after the fall of Rome and during the great waves of migration in the fifth and sixth centuries, and how it did less well on the threshold of the modern era.) It is undeniable that people formerly identified more with institutions such as the nation state or a particular religious denomination. Nowadays they no longer regard institutions as their permanent home, but more like market stalls, from which they may pick and choose. Often they identify with them only partially, and generally they also have many other identities. Likewise, in the West more and more people have a similarly non-committal attitude to institutions such as marriage and the family.

Naturally this trend gives rise to a conflicting reaction. Religious and national fundamentalism (nationalism) strive to return to a time when things were not yet complicated, to return to various basic certainties – the sense of security they receive by identifying closely with a powerful institution tends to be at the cost of a tendency to demonise not only others who live and think differently, but also 'heretics' and 'liberals' in their own ranks who do not share their black-and-white view of the world. There is no way back, however, either to the mediaeval corpus christianorum or to 'modern times', the era of secularisation and nation states, when religion became a philosophy of life along with others and the church became just another institution. It would be quite erroneous to deduce that people are less religious just because they are less interested in the institutional and doctrinal aspects of religion.

The Enlightenment was an age of reason – or, more precisely, the dominance of one kind of rationality – its underlying passion being to categorise phenomena and describe them. A typical legacy of the Enlightenment are galleries and museums in which the individual exhibits are classified and labelled for our enlightenment, or concert performances with printed programmes. Paintings, statues and music were torn out of their previous natural environment – church and home – and placed in special halls. (The final stage of this development is when churches are transformed into concert halls and family homes end up as interesting exhibits in skansens or 'outdoor museums') Similarly, science in the modern age classified all knowledge; over fifty years ago, the Czech philosopher Emanuel Rádl concluded his work *The Consolation of Philosophy*[3] by comparing modern science's attitude to nature with the attitude of an autopsic surgeon to a corpse. He tells the story of a doctor who was one of the first to carry out autopsies; apparently on one occasion he had scarcely started to dissect the supposed corpse when it sat up in astonishment at the touch of the scalpel; the doctor subsequently undertook a pilgrimage to Jerusalem as penance. Rádl predicts that nature, too, is not quite dead yet and is quite capable of rising up in the course of our scientific research and protest against what is being done to it. To what 'holy land', Rádl asks, will we make our pilgrimage?

Yes, religion, too, which lay beneath the scalpels of the philosophers, psychologists, sociologists and many other experts, has suddenly come to life and revived. It is time for us to make a journey to the Holy Land.

IV

The Holy Land was the destination of Abraham, the 'father of believers', who is honoured by the three monotheistic religions as their common father. Jews, Christians and Muslims read the stories of Abraham not just as literature, or as a record of events of long ago, but also as part of God's word. However, it was just by his tomb in Hebron that one of the first major terrorist attacks arising out of the religious and political hatred between the Jewish and Muslim inhabitants of the Holy Land took place at the close of the twentieth century. In our time Israel has become one enormous battlefield – the urgent appeals for reconciliation and dialogue voiced by John Paul II during his pilgrimage at the start of the new millennium have fallen on deaf ears among the extremists on both sides. It would seem that the only way that reference to Abraham as the common father could help overcome the 'global chasm' is if we manage to find a sufficient number of the wise and just among the representatives of the three religions; let us not forget that in his negotiation with the Lord over Sodom and Gomorrah, Abraham signally failed.

The reference to Abraham could be the – now popular – reference to the 'common ethical basis of the different religions' Kierkegaard rightly interpreted Abraham's faith as the kind that cannot reduced to morality alone. It would be hard to make Abraham into a symbol of religion as a set of rituals, doctrines, precepts and proscriptions. He can be a symbol of the *dynamic nature of faith*, however. Abraham is the image of a man addressed by God and placed on the right way. Abraham's faith is one of setting out, commencing the journey: 'It was by faith that Abraham... set out without knowing where he was going.' (Hebrews 11.8). Emanuel

Emanuel Levinas contrasts Odysseus, who returns home after his journeys of adventure, with Abraham, who knows that he will never return home.[4]

In the course of history, as Karl-Josef Kuschel convincingly demonstrates in his *Streit um Abraham*, [5] proponents of all three of the Abraham-derived religions have variously reinterpreted him and often cited him as one who legitimises the antiquity and authenticity of their religion, even justifying their claim of the universality of their tradition and its superiority over others – the Jews, Abraham the Chaldean is a 'pre-Mosaic' Jew, for the Christians he is a Christian before Christianity, and for the Muslims, he is a 'pre-Islamic Muslim'.

Apart from the stories of Abraham in Genesis, the Hebrew Bible is full of references to Abraham, that represent a rich spectrum of interpretations of this figure. In Exodus, God is presented as the God of Abraham, Isaac and Jacob, who was revealed to the patriarchs as El Shaddai, but did not make himself known to them by his name Yahweh. In the books of Exodus and Deuteronomy the covenant with Abraham is recalled as a forerunner of the covenant on Sinai. In the Book of Joshua, Abraham is described as a pioneer of monotheism and the struggle against idolatory (Joshua 24). Ecclesiasticus and Psalm 105 represent Abraham as an example of loyalty to God, as well as of wisdom and moral probity. For the Maccabeans and their uprising, Abraham is the epitome of loyalty to belief in one God and rejection of all religious compromises. In contrast, two Jewish authors who sought to build bridges between the Hebrew and Graeco-Roman worlds, Philo Judaeus and Flavius Josephus, stress Abraham's non-Jewish origin – for them Abraham is a sage, well-versed in pagan teachings, who became a worshipper of the one, true God by studying nature and by choosing the path of virtue.

Mohammed, too, saw in Abraham a man who, like himself, had graduated from polytheism to monotheism, by the power of his own reason, and sought to convert his family and people from idolatory. An early Islamic traditional source describes Muhammad meeting Abraham in heaven and discovering that they are physically very similar – more similar than any two men.[6]

The name of Abraham crops up repeatedly in Jesus' sayings in the Gospels. In the Johannine and Pauline sources we come across traces of the controversy over who may be regarded as legitimate 'children of Abraham' – it is a question of establishing the relationship of Christians to the Law, to the Judaic tradition and to synagogal rabbinic Judaism after the disaster of the year 70 AD. A number of studies have shown that the overwhelming majority of the sayings attributed to Jesus of Nazareth in the synoptic gospels fitted entirely into the broad spectrum of Jewish thinking of those days.[7] The breakthrough came with Paul, who did not know Jesus or his teachings from personal experience and before hearing about him from Jesus' disciples he had adopted the attitude shared by Jesus' opponents from among the Pharisees, namely, that Jesus was a disrupter of the Law[8] After his conversion, Paul did not abandon this attitude, but simply reworked it and, above all, made a virtue of it. Paul's rejection of the Law as something absolutely binding is not directed primarily at the Jews, but at the Jewish Christians, who were preventing other Christians, those converting from paganism, from coming to Christ other than via the Law.

Paul defends freedom of belief as against a binding Law by reference to Abraham – *Abraham was before the Law* and was the father of faith because he relied on God. He was called when uncircumcised – circumcision, the Torah, the temple, sacrifice – these all came later and were not *a sine qua non* for someone to be 'an heir of Abraham'. For Paul, accepting Christ meant being the posterity of Abraham (Cf. Gal. 3.29), and the promise to Abraham applied to them also, because it *applied to all people*. Therefore 'there are no more distinctions between Jew and Greek, slave and free, male and female' (Gal. 3.28). According to Paul, Christ had broken down all barriers, had reconciled everything to himself and restored peace, when out of Jew and pagan he created 'one single New Man in himself' (Eph 2.13).

This offer of a new identity, which implicitly called into question the existing cultural, religious, geographical and social barriers, was clearly the main resource for the spread of Christianity. François Vouga provides persuasively evidence to show in how many different aspects this vision of Paul's enabled Christian communities to create a common social space.[9]

It might be said that this was the first and probably the most important 'recontextualisation' of Christianity. The Christian faith abandons the context of Judaism in favour of a space that is unified in terms of politics and law by Rome and created in intellectual terms by Hellenistic culture. The attempt by Philo to create a synthesis of Jewish monotheism and the sapiential tradition, on the one hand, and Greek philosophy, on the other, would seem to have been too sophisticated for it to become a popular force capable of influencing society; paradoxically, it was Paul who paved the way for the successful synthesis of Jewish faith and Greek philosophy, even though he warned against the dangerous folly of philosophy while also rejecting the pillars of the Jewish religious identity.[10]

Paul's vision of the Christian as 'a new creation', a new and bold 'project' of human existence, going far beyond the existing bounds of classical universalism, was a momentous and dynamic contribution to the culture that would later be described as 'European' (on the basis of a tricky geographical definition). What Paul paved the way for is fulfilled when Christian theologians read the sentence that God from the burning bush uses to rebuff Moses when asked his name: I am who I am, as a metaphysical definition of Being, identical with existence. The rich 'history of God' continues – after the Canaanite god El had been identified with the tribal god of the patriarchs, with Moses' God Yahweh from the Book of Exodus and with Jesus' Father from the New Testament, it was now the turn for the Biblical God of the Jews to be identified with the Supreme Being of the philosophers of Antiquity.

Every 'recontextualisation' gives rise to new interpretations, new understandings, and new syntheses – but whenever faith 'escapes' from a particular intellectual and cultural environment much is also sacrificed. Certain key metaphors of Christianity would soon become dead metaphors; this also applied to one of the key confessions of Christian believers: 'Jesus is the Christ'. After Christianity split with Judaism nobody was concerned any more about Jesus as the Jews' Messiah and the word 'Christ' gradually came to understood as the 'surname' of the founder of Christianity. Henceforth Jesus was for his adherents the *saviour of the world;* on the rare occasions when the title of Messiah was used it generally had negative and polemical connotations vis-à-vis the Jews, who refused to recognise him as the Lord's Annointed. Christians are prepared to regard Judaism positively solely as a 'forerunner' of Christianity – they mostly fail to realise that post-Biblical Judaism probably has as little in common with the ancient religion of Israel as Christianity has – Christianity and Judaism have rather tended to develop in parallel.[11] Christians often view Judaism in terms of Jesus' disputes with the Pharisees and see in it religious legalism and formalism; for many Christian theologians of the patristic epoch Iudaismos and *Christianismos* are not two 'religious systems', two faith families, but two kinds of faith, or even two evolutionary stages of faith: first human beings were in thrall to the Law, then through Christ they come to maturity and true freedom.12 Here too Paul's legacy is evident.

What a bitter surprise awaited the Christians on the part of the Muslims, on the one hand, and on the part of the humanists and Enlightenment thinkers, on the other, when they started applying the same model to their own faith, and started to regard it as no more than a temporary phase, which had now lapsed!

V

Europe is the scene of wide-ranging changes. The pace of political, economic, legal and administrative integration of the member and candidate countries of the EU has hotted up. As the birth-rate falls in many European countries, the number of immigrants from other continents is rising, changing the ethnic and religious structure of Europe's population, most strikingly in the capitals of the Western world. The demand is often heard from Christians: 'Give Europe a soul'. Even though I appreciate the concern expressed by this slogan, I can't help regarding it as a somewhat arrogant cliché. Is Europe really soulless? And even if it were, are any people capable of endowing Europe with a soul? Aren't those who are promising to give Europe 'a soul' actually offering a mere ideology?

Of course, in the present phase of European integration the focus is on the 'body of Europe' and the issue of Europe's spiritual identity seems secondary. However, is not the very courage to carry out this bold operation on the body of Europe that consists in widening and enhancing the European Union derived from the assumption that there is something that lends Europe meaning? That there exists and operates here some deep-seated unifying principle, the quiet intrinsic force of attraction holding Europe together in spite of all the changes? That there is something here that is hard to grasp, but which forms the basis of a European identity? Yes, the very political will to achieve European integration, however superficial its immediate motives might be, implies a belief in a 'European soul'. Europe neither needs nor expects us to 'give it a soul', but we the Europeans of today need very much to learn to understand its soul and nourish it.

My teacher, Professor Jan Patočka, the Czech philosopher and martyr in the fight for human rights maintained that the essence of Europe was 'care for the soul', that Europe came into existence at a time when in Greece 'care for the soul' was regarded as the fundamental task of human existence and the meaning of the community, the *polis*. I am of the view that the archetype that influenced the dynamic of European civilisation more effectively was that idea of 'being on a journey', the understanding of life as an answer to God's call, as symbolised by the story of Abraham, who is revered as a saint by all great faith families, whose adherents must learn to live together on the territory of present-day Europe after dramatic confrontations in the course of history.

VI

However, the Europe of today is made up not only of Christians, Muslims and Jews, but chiefly of those who have not found a spiritual home in any of these three communities of Abraham's heirs; they feel that they cannot take the path of faith that God once called Abraham to take, and which their ancestors trod for a thousand years. It would seem that their voice is heard loudest of all in and from Europe, and that it is they who determine the present face of Europe. It now seems likely that the future 'European constitution' will not contain any reference to 'Abraham's legacy' and that Europe will be defined in terms of a secular culture that prevailed following the demise of an era lasting several centuries, during which the concepts of Europe and Christianity were seen as virtually synonymous.

A few years ago, the distinguished Canadian philosopher Charles Taylor delivered a brilliant lecture at the University of Dayton in the USA,[13] in which he asked whether present-day Catholic Christianity ought not to attempt a synthesis of faith and modern culture, in the same way that on the threshold of the modern era the Jesuit missionary Ricci attempted the inculturation of Christianity into the lifestyle and way of thinking of the Asian nations. Taylor shows why it is difficult; modern culture is an odd mixture of Christianity and the values of modernity, which were often asserted in opposition to Christianity, so that what is non-Christian in European culture we often regard as anti-Christian. Nonetheless, if we look more closely, we discover something very paradoxical: some of the values that are clearly derived from the Gospel were only applied in Europe when the era dominated by Christianity had come to an end. For instance, modern liberalism pushed through the idea of the universality of human rights, thus putting into practice St Paul's vision that boundaries due to nationality, culture, social status or gender are unimportant.

Taylor maintains that what impeded the implementation of many of those values was not 'religion' or 'Christian belief' as such, but instead that 'marriage' of faith with a particular culture. Although the idea of a

'Christian community' was a noble one, based on the logic of incarnation, it inevitably gave rise to frustration and became a danger to faith. This is because every human society implies pressure to conform and the sacrifice of lofty ideals to momentary interests, as well as many compromises and imperfections. There can never ever be a total marriage of faith with one specific society The attempts to substitute other beliefs for Christianity – such as Jacobinism or Marxism – have had far more tragic consequences.[14]

Taylor is convinced that there must be careful study of the ambivalent nature of modern culture so as to identity the paradoxes that occur in the historical transformations of different currents. The times ahead of us are likely to provide scope for new alliances, meetings and co-operation; we must overcome the old boundaries of distrust.

In one text of the Babylonian Talmud we read: 'On the day, that our father Abraham departed from this world, all the luminaries of the nations of the world stood in one line and said: Woe betide a world that has lost its driver, and woe betide a ship that has lost its helmsman.' Maybe an honest endeavour to seek mutual links between the 'children of Abraham', who, in the course of history, split into various faith families, and links between them and the people who stand outside that community, will restore to Europe and the world the hope that they will not be tossed by the stormy waves of the times, like a ship without a helmsman.

Notes

1. This paper was first delivered in Prague on September 18th, 2003.

2. Gilles Kepel, *The Revenge of God: The Resurgence of Islam, Judaism and Christianity in the Modern World* (Pennsylvania:Penn State University Press, 1994).

3. Emanuel Rádl, *Útecha z filosofie* (Cin: Prague, 1946).

4. See E. Levinas, *Die Spur des Anderen* (Freiburg – München 1983), p. 211 a 215n.

5. K. –J. Kuschel, *Streit um Abraham* (München 1994).

6. See G. Rotter, *Ibn Ishaq, Das leben des Propheten* (Tübingen – Basel 1976), p.85

7. See D. Flusser, *Jesus* (Jerusalem: Magnes Press, 1998; česky Je•íš: Prague 2002)

8. See F. Vouga, *Geschichte des frühen Christentums* (Tübingen-Basel 1994; česky Dějiny ranného křesťanství Prague 1997), p. 96.

9. Ibid., in Czech edition, p. 248 onwards.

10. Kuschel believes that there is a parallel between Paul's universalism of salvation and Philo's thought. He adds: 'A Jew Paul fights against the Jewish particularism for the sake of Jewish universalism.' (K-J.Kuschel cit. Dílo, *Collected Works*, p. 117 of the Czech edition)

11. See H. –M. Haussig, *Der Religionsbegriff in den Religionen* (Berlin und Bodenheim 1999), p.133

12. See R. Treaer, *Faith, Belief and Religion* (Colorado 2001), p. 31

13. See C. Taylor, 'A Catholic Modernity?' Marianist Award Lecture 1996, The University of Dayton

14. See Taylor, 'Catholic Modernity', pp. 10-12

10

Civil Society as a Context for Jewish-Christian Relations: Perspectives from Sociology and Political Philosophy

David Herbert

I. Introduction

This essay starts from the premise that dialogue in Jewish-Christian relations will benefit from joint reflection on the contexts within which contemporary Jews and Christians interact. In this paper, therefore, I shall focus on two aspects of these contexts, aspects that are important for the structuring of inter-group relations in contemporary societies. The first relates closely to those tragic events that have been absolutely central to Jewish-Christian relations in Europe and America since World War II. For the Holocaust has stimulated much reflection on the causes of cruelty, prejudice and moral indifference to the sufferings of others, and it is the psychological and sociological theories which seek to understand these phenomena that make up the first 'context' I seek to examine here. My aim is to provide a counter-perspective to what I perceive as a tendency in Jewish-Christian relations to overplay specifically religious and ideological factors in the events of the Holocaust, and to underplay the general social psychological and socio-structural factors that are arguably equally important. Specifically, sociologist Zygmunt Bauman argues that:

> Until one or two decades ago it was common – not only among the lay public but among historians – to seek the explanation of the mass murder of European Jews in the long history of European anti-Semitism. Such an explanation required ... singling out German anti-Semitism as the most intense, merciless and murderous. ... [H]owever, ... both the explanation and its corollary have been discredited by historical research. ... the ever-growing volume of evidence proves beyond reasonable doubt an almost negative correlation between

ordinary and traditional, 'neighbourly' competition-based anti-Jewish sentiment, and willingness to embrace the Nazi vision of total destruction and to partake of its implementation.[1]

Therefore, reflection on more general social processes – general that is to human societies, but in some ways (and perhaps surprisingly) particularly dangerously present in advanced industrial societies – is necessary for the development of Jewish-Christian dialogue, if in its focus on the religious dimensions and ramifications of the Holocaust, and more generally of social relations, it is not to become divorced from the consensus of mainstream historical research.

Second, I shall introduce the concept of civil society, which both as an idea and as a descriptor of a particular 'space' in society – an arena of social activity relatively unconstrained by state influence – was associated in the 1980s and 1990s with hope for re-building shattered societies as diverse as post-Communist Eastern Europe, Africa and Latin America.[2] Civil society has also been identified as a pre-eminent site for the 'de-privatization' of religion, described by the Spanish-American sociologist José Casanova as 'a dual interrelated process of re-politicization of the private religious and moral spheres, and re-normativization of the public economic and political spheres'.[3] In other words, religious beliefs cease to be a matter of purely personal preference, but again become the subject of public argument, while concurrently public matters, like the economy and politics, are re-moralized, partly by challenges from religious groups. This re-emergence of religions into the public sphere has been a double-edged sword, sometimes providing a voice for the voiceless, but at other times appearing to encroach on secular rights and freedoms. Again, it seems that reflection on civil society as a space within which much Jewish-Christian dialogue takes place could enrich and develop that conversation.

II. Introducing Theories of Prejudice and Civil Society: the Conditions of Inter-faith Encounter

Two observations can help lead us into our discussion. Please bear with the broad generalizations that I'm about to make, at least for the time being. The first observation is that – in spite of de-privatization – Jewish-Christian relations in most Western countries occur in contexts in which the influence of religious institutions on the daily lives of most people and in various public spheres is rather limited. Certainly, religions in more dispersed form – as symbol, discourse and charity – remain significant beyond the numbers of their advocates; or in the American case involvement with religious institutions may remain high, but religious lifestyles increasingly converge with the secular mainstream.[4] But religion has been largely dispersed from the central institutions of public life, and public trust in these institutions themselves – including the government, political parties, trades unions, and public broadcast media – has also undergone decline.[5] Religion, with society, has been privatized in the sense that primary institutions – whether religious denominations or political parties – have shrunk in mass membership and participation. Secondary institutions – small groups and networks of various kinds – have done rather better, while increased levels of media use – especially television viewing and internet use – means that in some ways we are more connected with others than ever before.[6] But our religious affiliation or lack of it does not on the whole structure the context of our encounter with others.

There are some exceptions. It is true that within Western societies as a source of resistance identity (e.g. for some Muslims), and elsewhere, even in some central institutions (e.g. Iran, Egypt), religion has, in some times and some places, powerfully reasserted its social and political influence. Furthermore, cross-cultural comparison suggests that there is no inherent contradiction between fervent belief, enchantment and modernization, so we cannot anticipate any general movement towards disenchantment or further privatization.[7] Nonetheless, in the West inter-faith encounter occurs primarily not in environments overtly structured by religious beliefs or practices, but between people who happen to be adherents of religious traditions meeting in various public and private settings. Put another way, society in general, on which religion is just one of a range of influences, forms the primary context of encounter.

This seems to me to imply that to understand inter-faith relations in such a context it is important to understand more generally how societies work, and if one is concerned in particular with how conflict between groups arises, or prejudice against a particular group develops, it may be helpful to contextualize that specific example against the background of other kinds of conflict and prejudice.

My second observation concerns the concept of civil society. In attempting to understand how societies that have long been under totalitarian rule or in a state of anarchy can move towards democracy - in the fundamental sense of respect for the person and their right to participate in the political process – since the mid 1980s political activists, philosophers and social scientists in contexts as diverse as Eastern Europe, Africa and Latin America, have found the concept of civil society a useful or at least a challenging one. The basic idea is that civil society describes a relatively autonomous space between government and the governed, in which people are free to get together and pursue whatever common goals or interests they choose. The more and especially more diverse organizations there are in a society, the better its chances of democratization, partly because the combination of freedom and responsibility exercised in such settings nurtures the requisite virtues of citizenship, and partly because the pluralism of civil society is supposed to guard against extremism.

Today in development contexts it has been applied to the Non-Governmental Organization (NGO) sector – for example the Organization for Security and Co-operation in Europe's whole democratization strategy in Bosnia has been based on this identification – but its meaning can be broader than the formal NGO sector – arguably, it can include churches, synagogues and mosques, and certainly the range of religiously founded education, youth and welfare organizations. In this broad sense it is compatible with Jonathon Sacks' vision of society as a community of communities,[8] but also subject to the same criticism that the same communities can nurture fanaticism as well as virtue. Furthermore, as an idea that in its modern incarnation springs from the Scottish Enlightenment, it shares the same problem in the social sphere as Adam Smith's 'hidden hand' in the economic sphere, namely that it is unclear exactly how order and justice will somehow arise from its transactions. The idea of civil society, then, is not without its problems. But before considering it more fully, I shall turn first to theories of prejudice.

III. Theories of Prejudice

Broadly, pre-second world war theories focused on individual psychological factors – e.g. Freud's – post-war work, influenced by the Frankfurt school, on the interaction of personality type and mass society, while since the 1970s most emphasis has been placed on group dynamics. I'll pick up the story in the post-war period, beginning with Adorno et al.'s classic study *The Authoritarian Personality* (1950). Adorno had been part of the Frankfurt School, a pre-war group of German academics who developed a distinctive style of social theory combining ethnographic observation with broad cultural criticism. Many were Jewish, and most fled Germany for America in the late 1930s. Financed by the Jewish Committee, the purpose of the study was to investigate prejudice amongst various social groups in post-war America. The study identifies and seeks to explain the emergence of the 'fascist personality' as a new and distinct modern type. Max Horkheimer described the type in the preface to the study:

> In contrast to the bigot of the older style he seems to combine the ideas and skills which are typical of a highly industrialized society with irrational and anti-rationalist beliefs. He is at the same time enlightened and superstitious, proud to be an individualist and in constant fear of being like all the others, jealous of his independence and inclined to submit blindly to power and authority.[9]

The study argues that three main related factors have led to the emergence of this personality type. First, an increasingly means-end, instrumental social order, which inclined people to think of other people as objects of manipulation rather than persons in their own right. This observation draws on a tradition of sociological thinking which charts the transformation to urbanization from a social order based on face to face community to an anonymous and increasingly formally regulated society of strangers.[10] This process is sometimes called societalization. Second, the weakened family ties, in part the result of societalization, lead to unstable character formation, producing an individual who veers between lack of respect for others and a desire for total submission to authority. Third, this problematic character formation was explained in terms of psychoanalytical theory, using Freud's theory of the Oedipus complex. In this study, then, prejudice emerges as the effect of the disruption of social life mediated through dysfunctional family dynamics leading to an unstable and socially dangerous psychological condition for some individuals, manifest in prejudiced attitudes.

In later work that developed from the 1960s, however, the emphasis shifts from the background factors that contribute to attitudes, which are presumed to be relatively constant, towards seeing attitudes as highly volatile, and the product of changing micro-social conditions or group dynamics.[11] This work was more empirical in focus, more removed from critical theory, and more mainstream within social psychology, especially in America. Such a perspective suggests that in-group preferences are a normal part of identity formation. Identity is constructed through a process of social comparison, recognizing self as similar to some and different from others in particular respects. Self-esteem works by locating oneself on the favorable side of such a comparison. Studies with groups of children and adults both demonstrated how random assignment of individuals to groups and the development of group identities through relatively small markers of difference could rapidly lead to strong feelings of group identity, and hostility towards other groups.

Some of these studies are particularly alarming, and have become notorious. Zimbardo's (1973) prison experiment is one. In it American college kids – the usual subjects for psychological experiments – were allocated at random into prisoner and prison guard roles, denoted by uniforms, tight caps for the prisoners, dark glasses for the guards etc. A series of petty rules and regulations was devised, and then the groups were left in an enclosed space to act out their roles for a fortnight. The experiment had to be abandoned after a week for fear of physical and psychological damage to the subjects. What happened was that the more the guards humiliated the prisoners the more submissive the latter became, the more the guards abused them and so on in a vicious spiral, until the degradation of the prisoners forced the experimenters to intervene. The experiment suggests that individual psychological traits and even long-term social conditioning are relatively insignificant compared with the immediate social environment, or possibly that – *Lord of the Flies* style – cruelty lurks inside us all. We are either the puppets of circumstance or naturally vicious.

Another experiment is perhaps equally disturbing. Milgram (1971) required subjects to administer what they believed to be electric shocks to another person, in fact an actor, as punishment for failure in a learning task. The actor was placed in varying degrees of proximity to the subject, from in the room, to the other side of a screen but visible, to invisible but audible. The extent to which subjects were willing to administer the shocks depended principally on the degree of proximity of the actor/learner/victim. The closer the latter, the less willing the subject to administer the higher degrees of shock. What was shocking about the experiment was the extent to which apparently normal subjects were prepared to administer shocks, right up to the apparent death of the actor in the least proximate condition. The only encouragement to continue with the experiment was the experimentor's verbal instruction in a level voice: please continue with the experiment. More than sixty per cent were prepared to continue to the end when the subject was only audible – or rather, ceased to be audible.

Several points about Milgram's experiment are notable. First, as with Zimbardo, social factors emerge as more significant than individual differences. Second, physical proximity is closely correlated with moral inhibition. Responsibility diminishes quite rapidly with social distance. Third, a graduated approach makes moral resistance difficult; most subjects refuse to administer a high degree of shock straight away, but having set off down the slippery slope it is difficult to put the brakes on. Fourth, the power of a scientific, apparently rational setting, to absolve the individual of a sense of personal responsibility.

In his book *Modernity and the Holocaust* (1989) the sociologist Zygmunt Bauman argues that Milgram's experiment is important for understanding the processes that led to and enabled the Holocaust. It is not difficult to see why: industrial processes rely on a high degree of functional differentiation, that is different individuals and different groups perform different parts of a complex task. Modern bureaucracies rely on the same principle. In Nazi Germany both systems were deployed in the execution of the Final Solution, together with strict chains of command. The combined effect of such systems is to numb moral resistance, an effect further increased by the technical and euphemistic discourse deployed to describe the process.

But Bauman develops his case as part of a much wider argument. He argues that most sociological theory can only narrate the Holocaust as a deviation from the civilizing process of modernity, a failure to keep at bay the beast in all of us, as in the second interpretation offered of Zimbardo's prison experiment. Alternatively, occasionally the reverse is asserted – that the Holocaust reveals what is normal for modernity. Bauman rejects both approaches. In response to the former he argues that rather than revealing our essential evil the Holocaust reveals what happens when our normal moral impulses are thwarted through social processes. In response to the latter he argues that this approach levels all the sufferings generated by modernity.[12] Instead, he contends that the Holocaust should be considered as 'a rare, yet significant and reliable, test of the hidden possibilities of modern society'.[13]

In particular he argues that moral consciousness is transformed by the increasing complexity of social relations. Conditions in which 'physical and moral proximity overlapped',[14] as in the village-based society, or in pre-modern urban situations where rigid social barriers performed the distancing function, become no longer sustainable. The new norm of interaction became one with strangers on the doorstep, 'morally distant yet physically close'.[15] The effect of this increasingly widespread condition on moral sense is described by Bauman as 'adiaphorization', *adiaphoron* originally meaning a thing declared neutral by the early church. Thus Bauman's neologism refers to moral sense being neutralized by immersion in complex social situations. This complexity is not just the product of modern movements of population caused by the mobility of labor in the market, but also of modern technology increasing communication, and modern modes of production involving people in complex causal networks in which their actions may have consequences which are difficult or impossible to envisage.

An underlying assumption of his model is that rather than being socially constructed moral sense is biologically given, and merely shaped or attenuated by social conditioning. This is the reverse of the normal sociological assumption that we are born untamed and selfish, and become conditioned to respect others through socialization. A better conceptualization might be that we are biologically conditioned to respond positively to primary socialization (early conditioning in whatever kind of family unit), but that such small scale nurture does not equip us well for the complex stranger society that has developed. Be that as it may, Bauman develops a possible conceptualization of innate moral sense by placing the ideas of the moral philosopher and rabbinical scholar Emmanuel Levinas in a historical narrative which traces the fate of 'innate morality' from pre- to postmodern societies.[16]

Following Levinas, Bauman sees morality as operating at face-to-face level, a pre-social response to the 'face' of the 'Other'. This 'natural ethical impulse' can be described as a predisposition to feel responsibility for another person. It precedes encounter and therefore reciprocity or interest; it is unconditionally for the sake of the 'Other'.[17] Further, it is not only pre-social but pre-conscious, not a matter of choice, but an involuntary response to the presence of another person:

> The neighbour concerns me before all assumption, all contract consented to or refused ... It is not because the neighbour would be recognised as belonging to the same genus as me that he concerns me. He is precisely other. The community with him begins in my

obligation to him.[18]

Levinas' theory turns both philosophical attempts to find a rational basis for ethics, and sociological theories which view society as restraining innate 'uncivilised' behaviour, on their heads:

> The etiological myth entrenched in the self-consciousness of our Western society is the morally elevating story of humanity emerging from pre-social barbarity. ... By and large lay opinion resents all challenge to the myth. Its resistance is backed ... by a broad coalition of respectable learned opinions which contains such powerful authorities as the 'Whig view' of history as the victorious struggle between reason and superstition; Weber's version of rationalisation as a movement toward achieving more for less effort; psychoanalytical promise to debunk, prise off and tame the animal in man; Marx's grand prophecy of life and history coming under the full control of the human species once it is freed from the presently debilitating parochialities.[19]

To this list one might add Adam Smith's invisible hand of capitalism, ensuring that the market distributes goods effectively and fairly. What can be said against this impressive consensus of modernity? First of all, as Bauman argues the matter cannot be tested directly, since we do not have access to pre-social humanity. Therefore, the origin of moral sense can only be investigated indirectly, by presenting evidence relevant to the field of enquiry and demonstrating the coherence and consistency of the explanation proposed. Bauman's story is one of the demise of proximity. For this is moral reaction's sole precondition. It is a local response; it doesn't travel well. In pre-modern societies, where moral boundaries coincided with physical boundaries, it worked well enough, because, by definition, those encountered regularly were neighbours. But in modern societies we constantly meet people we don't (and because of their numbers couldn't) know. Therefore a need develops for mechanisms to deal with the presence of strangers. It has been suggested that the development of rights discourse is the foremost intellectual response to the society of strangers;[20] Bauman characterises the strategy of 'mismeeting' as the foremost practical response. This refers to ways of ignoring other people while being physically close, common examples of which would be keeping our gaze fixed on neutral space in a crowded lift or train.

But it also and especially applies at institutional levels, through bureaucratic systems, global trading systems, and indeed to money. Such systems work most effectively when individuals are severed from local attachments which might provide substantive interruptions to 'free' exchange. Thus Bauman cites Simmel's classic sociological analysis of monetary transactions:

> The significance of the stranger for the nature of money seems to me to be epitomised in miniature by the advice I once overheard: never have financial dealings with two kinds of people – friends or enemies. In the first case the indifferent objectivity of money is in ... conflict with the personal character of the relationship; in the other, the same condition provides a wide scope for hostile intentions ... . The desirable party for financial transactions — in which it is said quite correctly that business is business – is the person completely indifferent to us.[21]

Bauman interprets the Holocaust in the light of this adiaphorization thesis. His view is that the Holocaust was made possible not principally by local anti-Semitism, the peculiar character of the German nation, or the pathology of individuals. Rather, it was made possible by the division of labour, the diffusion of responsibility, and the adoption of a thorough-going problem-solving approach. Thus he argues:

> This effect is achieved through a number of complementary arrangements: (1) stretching the distance between action and its consequences beyond the reach of moral impulse; (2) exempting some 'others' from the class of potential objects of moral conduct, of potential 'faces'; (3) dissembling other human objects of action into aggregates of functionally specific traits, held separate so that the cause for re-assembling does not arise, and the task set for each action can be free from moral evaluation.[22]

An example of (3) is found in the language used by engineers responsible for the design of the gas vans used in the initial stages of the 'Final Solution' (another example), where the people in the vans are described as 'cargo', the vomit and excreta they produce in their dying moments as 'thin fluids' and 'thick fluids.'[23] As Bauman comments:

> The fact that the load consisted of people about to be murdered and losing control over their bodies, did not detract from the technical

challenge of the problem. This fact had anyway to be translated into the neutral language of car-production technology before it could be turned into a 'problem' to be 'resolved'.[24]

It is important to note that Bauman does not suggest that such social arrangements in themselves promote immoral behaviour, rather moral indifference. As we have said, they render social action 'adiaphoric', not immoral.

The power of Bauman's thesis lies in the way it enables us to see the moral greatness and depravity of modernity as two sides of the same coin. For the same impulse to universalise and abstract can be seen to underlie both the development and global penetration of the concept of universal human rights (perhaps the epitome of modern moral achievement) and the gas chambers.

What, then, can be done to counter modernity's adiaphorising effects? Bauman's conclusion is this:

> The readiness to act against one's own better judgement, and against the voice of one's conscience is not just a function of authoritative command, but the result of exposure to a single-minded, unequivocal source of authority.

And therefore:

> Pluralism is the best preventive medicine against morally normal people engaging in morally abnormal actions. ... The voice of individual moral conscience is best heard in the tumult of political and social discord.[25]

In theories of democratization, civil society has been widely seen as the social space within which such pluralism is nurtured and institutionalized, and so it is to this concept that we shall turn next. First, though, it should be noted that while Bauman is insistent that moral sense is seen as pre-social, it seems that everything he says is compatible with seeing it rather as a product of primary socialization, perhaps developing an innate but undeveloped capacity which requires the care, affection and sense of boundaries developed by primary social bonds in order to develop. All that he says about the problems of moral sense in complex societies – i.e. secondary contexts of socialization – fits also with this interpretation, which has the additional virtue of fitting better with research on developmental psychology.[26]

IV. Faith, Trust and Civil Society in the Thought of Adam Seligman: a Critique.

Religious activity in civil society has been particularly associated with three kinds of situation. First, where the state has retreated or been unable to fulfil basic education and welfare functions: examples include Hizbullah in Lebanon,[27] CEBs or base ecclesial communities in Brazil,[28] or a variety of locations in sub-Saharan Africa.[29] Second, where the state has repressed or undermined the credibility of more overtly political institutions, for example in Central and Eastern Europe, especially Poland and East Germany.[30] Third in democratic and advanced industrial societies with effective state structures, where modernization has been associated with secularization and religious decline, religious organizations have nonetheless continued to be active in civil society, and even experienced some resurgence. Diverse examples include the campaigning roles of Christian organizations in the US on life politics issues,[31] the association of religious practice with participation in voluntary work in Britain,[32] and the increasing self-organization of Muslim groups across Western Europe.[33]

However, each of these three categories also throws up examples that challenge the view that a proliferation of civil society groups is necessarily good for democracy. Thus while in Poland the church was important in democratic transition, its role in democratic consolidation has been more ambivalent. Islamist groups such as Hizbullah also have a problematic relationship to democracy, as, for different reasons, does the pro-life movement in the States. Thus the presence of diverse civil society organizations does not guarantee civility. How, then, are we to think about the relationship between religion and civil society?

The political philosopher Adam Seligman has been one of the leading theorists of civil society. In what follows I shall introduce and critique his theory of the relationship between faith, trust and civil society. Seligman shows that the modern idea of civil society has from its inception been saturated with hopes for its civilising, democratising and socially integrating influence.[34] He argues that the inventors of the early modern concept did not, unsurprisingly, envisage the extent of system differentiation and role segmentation in contemporary advanced industrial societies. As a result, they incorporated into their concept assumptions about the nature of the individual and community which are no longer valid, and hence render its application as a solution to problems of integration in contemporary societies problematic.

For Seligman, trust is understood as 'an unconditional principle of generalized exchange unique to modern forms of social organization',[35] developed to cover the 'gaps' between role expectations as these diversified. Under these conditions, trust gradually displaces the role of faith, replacing confidence in role expectations rooted in God's ordered universe, with trust in 'man' as endowed with universal qualities. Thus:

> ... while both faith and trust share the attribute of unconditionality, the object of unconditional belief is very different in each case: in one God; in the other, man.[36]

Trust is based on the same Enlightenment assumptions as civil society: explicit ones about the universality of humanity, and implicit ones about the relative homogeneity of communities. When these cease to hold good, differences can no longer be negotiated by appeal to common understandings in a shared 'lifeworld' (to borrow Habermas' term[37]), but only through instrumental systems – linguistic, legal or more directly coercive. As symptoms of this shift from shared understandings to instrumental systems of control, Seligman points to the increasing use of speech codes, litigation, and physical violence in American public life.[38] Thus we shift from a medieval world of stable roles, hierarchically organised and legitimated by faith, first to a modern world of horizontal trust relationships, and then to a late/post modern world in which roles and boundaries must once again be structured in the absence of consensus, this time by increasing recourse to law, identity politics and, as ever, violence.

However, several features of this account are questionable. Thus the image of early modern liberal societies as moving towards integration through horizontal relationships of trust and an inclusive public sphere has been challenged by feminists and Marxists arguing that vertical relationships and exclusion persisted and were even intensified during this period. Indeed, it may be argued that the neglect of this 'underside of modernity' as an ongoing feature, rather than a post/late modern re-emergence, seriously distorts Seligman's presentation. In particular, Foucault's argument that modernity was from its inception primarily defined by an intensification of disciplinary and surveillance practices provides an important counter-narrative to the 'modernity as emancipation' trajectory Seligman follows. This is especially important when considering his account of faith and faith-based organizations.

Of particular importance for our concerns is his account of faith. This is too tied to the image of faith as viewed in the Western tradition of political philosophy, which emphasises features specific to the post-medieval Christian setting from which it grew. This is not surprising, but suggests caution is needed in trans-cultural and trans-temporal applications. For example, writing of the way the human rights tradition has been shaped also emerging from this context, Galtung emphasises two features of the Western tradition: first, 'verticality', meaning that the authority for forms of interpersonal relationship tends to be conceptualized as descending 'from above', initially from God and later from the state, as opposed to growing 'horizontally' out of existing habits and customs. Second, a tendency toward individualization.[39] Here, an analogy may help: if society is imaged as a net, this tradition sees individuals as existing in the 'knots' at the intersection between strands, in contrast to some other cultural formations, in which individuals are also in the 'nets'. Now, individualization is part of the modernising process as systems and roles differentiate; but religious traditions in particular contain net-oriented aspects. Thus Galtung explains:

> Individualising Judaism/Christianity/Islam with a transcendental god emphasises the knots, the union-oriented Hinduism/Buddhism with a more immanent god-concept the nets. Transcendental religions endow human beings with individual souls as that which can attain union with god. Immanent religions depend less on that concept, which is rejected out of hand in radical Buddhism. But occidental religions also have immanent, net-oriented, collectivist aspects. ... God also speaks through the people. And the whole tradition of democracy took shape and is still taking shape.[40]

Seligman's characterization of faith as a vertical relationship in contrast to horizontal relationships of trust seems to preclude the possibility that faith could promote trust. Galtung's challenge to this vertical construction of faith opens up other possibilities. Thus it can be seen that Seligman's construction of a faith/trust, vertical/horizontal dichotomy tends to conceal the continuation of the vertical dimension in Western political traditions: as well as democracy, there is also state sovereignty. Furthermore, I suggest that in quite a range of circumstances religious traditions, including some quite conservative ones, can actually promote civility, in the sense of respect for the rights of individuals, recognition of other communities, and determination to solve differences through reasoned negotiation. Such civility may promote a general sense of trust in others in society, in Seligman's sense. This is not to say that faith cannot also lead to the opposite of civility, but this disparity of evidence argues for a careful analysis of each situation, and the abstraction of general principles only on the basis of such evidence, not for an a priori rejection of faith as a possible contributor to trust and civility.

A second problem with Seligman's work is also relevant to his account of faith. This is his America-centeredness, implied in statements such as:

> [T]his ... essay has been an attempt to provide the necessary background for understanding the interaction of our citizens from Los Angeles - and, by implication, the problematic meaning of civil society in all liberal individualist societies.[41]

However, Castells[42] argues that American socio-economic transformation is only one of a number of possible trajectories for late/post modern societies. Analogies from other spheres, such as employment and production, suggest caution about the universalisation of American experience: thus Castells has shown that the American model of post-industrialism, in which employment in manufacturing is replaced by employment in services, has not been followed by other successful advanced industrial economies such as Germany or Japan, where much of the traditional manufacturing base has been retained, although infused with new technologies and production methods.[43] This example may be more than a suggestive analogy: it may be that American civic disintegration and economic transformation are part of a wider common process.

Certainly, there would seem to be an association between extremes of inequality and civic disintegration in the cities of North and South America and elsewhere, in turn associated with the spatial juxtaposition of what Castells has called the global information elite with 'the Fourth World', the world-wide urban poor.[44] However, while Castells sees these new patterns of social cleavage as a global phenomenon, the extent of inequalities would seem to depend to some extent both on government policy and on the cultural systems through which they are mediated, questioning Seligman's assumption that Los Angeles represents the common destination of the logic of modernity.

So we have seen that for Seligman trust in defined in contrast to faith in a social evolutionary scheme, in which trust displaces faith as the source of social solidarity in modern societies. In this process the unconditionality of trust in God is replaced by that of trust in man, so that 'we are all a society of atheists now'.[45] At a literal level, this is simply not true; but Seligman's writing on Israel shows that he is fully aware of the vitality of faith groups, so what does he mean? Perhaps the point being made is that modern societies can no longer be held together by a common belief in God – either by hegemony or consent. Religious pluralism and secularization – in the restricted sense of the decline of the role of religion in the exercise of state power – would appear to support this view. Historically though, religious pluralism has been compatible with state domination exercised through civic religion (e.g. Roman and Ottoman Empires), so we need to specify what is distinctive about contemporary religious pluralism which makes this option no longer viable.

Many pre-modern societies were religiously plural, but these differences could always be resolved by subordinating minority groups – hence the Roman Empire's general insistence on sacrifice to the Emperor cult, the subordination of Jews in medieval Christendom, the subjection of Jews and Christians to the jizra under the Ottoman millet system, and the absorption of Muslims and Christians into the Hindu caste system. Under modern conditions, increased social mobility and correlative trajectories in political thought mean that this resolution is neither practically nor ideologically possible. Hence the sacred canopy can no longer be shared, and religion as a top-down system of societal legitimation becomes not viable. Yet this leaves open the possibility that a diversity of faith communities may, under some conditions, contribute to the promotion of trust both through the horizontal networks of trusting relationships which they foster within themselves, and more widely through universalist aspects of their ethical systems ('love your neighbour as yourself' etc.). Is there any evidence that this is the case? In the final substantive section, we shall explore this in a UK context by considering the vision of Rabbi Jonathan Sacks as outlined in his Reith Lectures on *The Persistence of Faith*, and developed by in a sociological direction by the Christian theologian Robin Gill.[46]

V. Religious Communities, Secularization and Civility

Sacks begins by contending that the basic problem of modern social life lies 'not with our economic and political systems, but in a certain emptiness at the heart of our common life'.[47] He argues that religions have a substantial contribution to make to solving this problem, specifically by 'creating communities', which is 'religion's special power', and also by 'charting our shared moral landscape, that sense of a common good that we need if our communities are to cohere as a society'.[48] But given the differences between religions, and the large number of people who do not follow any of them, how can religions contribute to 'a sense of the common good'? Sacks' answer is through the promotion of values common to the major monotheistic traditions (and, one may add, Eastern traditions), such as shared responsibility, mutual support, and fidelity in different kinds of relationships. While these may be nurtured by religious communities, they are also shared more widely across society (though, he contends, undermined by social fragmentation), and their discursive presence and practice within religious communities may promote them in the wider community. This may occur by participation in public life through a range of channels, including paid and voluntary work and other local activities. In this way Sacks' begins to respond to the criticism that communitarian contentions that whole societies should display virtues characteristic of small communities fail, because they fail to explain how virtues nurtured on the small scale can be transposed onto the large.

This response is further developed by Gill, whose book *Moral Communities* provides sociological support for Sacks' argument. Gill argues that religious communities help to sustain practices of 'caring beyond self-interest' in contemporary British society.[49] Some theories of secularization suggest that the ability of a religious community to sustain itself and grow may be adversely effected by its participants involvement in public life. Thus religious belief may provide 'start-up capital' for public-spirited activities, but this cannot sustain itself, so members become absorbed in the secular mainstream and lose their religious identity. Thus Gill cites Bryan Wilson's work on sectarianism, which suggests that it is those groups which erect the most rigid boundaries around their communities, and confine their charity to themselves or those they seek to convert, which best sustain their memberships. In contrast:

> ... once a sect does genuinely attempt to influence society especially in areas of care – the Salvation Army today is an obvious example – it soon becomes denominationalised in the process. By taking this step, so Wilson argues, such a sect is likely to become secularised itself.[50]

Nonetheless, Gill points to evidence that participation in Christian communities is related positively to involvement in caring activities in public settings, for example on motivation for involvement in voluntary work. Strikingly, individuals scoring high on a scale of religious commitment were far more likely to engage in voluntary work than those who scored low on the scale, such that 'attendance at religious services at least once a month was the most significant variable in predicting whether someone is involved with voluntary work.'[51]

These findings are broadly supported by the *European Values Systems* surveys.[52] However, Christians did not often mention their faith as a reason for engaging in voluntary work, a pattern that fits with a tendency for caring organizations with Christian foundations (e.g. Samaritans, Relate, Alcoholics Anonymous) to play down their religious roots. In spite of this reticence the connection between caring activities and involvement with a religious community persists. Gill suggests that the reason for this association lies in the role of worship in religious communities:

> For Judaism, Christianity and Islam it is worship that provides the link that I believe is especially crucial for effective care in society – the link between logic and structures. Within each of these traditions individuals who believe in theory there is a God who cares (and who encourages them to care) are confronted in worship with this caring God. ... any care that we show to others has already been shown to us by a God who cares. Goodness beyond self-interest is identified as the true telos of a world created by a God who acted and continues to act in creation beyond self-interest.[53]

Religious communities may fail to live up to such values, but in their worship they continue to bear witness to them. Understanding of the social processes by which religious communities may promote civility can be further strengthened by reference to the perspective of virtue ethics. In contrast to rival traditions of ethics, this emphasises character formation rather then abstract principles (deontology), or the calculation of consequences (consequentialism). This focuses attention on the differential development of individuals, and hence the social conditions under which this takes place, in contrast to the tendency to abstract individualism of alternative approaches. Such conditions include the role of family, community, and other social institutions.

VI Conclusion

All this suggests that religion can contribute to the development of civility and trust in late modern societies, not through the vertical legitimization relationship through which faith produced social cohesion in the medieval period, but rather through a network of horizontal relationships which faith communities can nurture both within themselves and with other groups. The presence of such groups is nor itself sufficient to promote civility, but must be combined with other conditions. As far as religion is concerned, positively it has been suggested that the kind of social nurture provided by religious traditions and specified in virtue ethics may be significant. Contrary to expectations created by secularist ideologies and some forms of secularization theory, conservative religious traditions may play an important role here, without necessarily liberalising themselves. Negatively, it may be added that an important factor is a strong association between religion, ethnicity and national identity (as in much of Eastern Europe, or Northern Ireland), especially in the absence of internal reform of religious tradition (compare Catholicism and Orthodoxy).

The religious factors shaping the impact of civil society on the promotion of civility, participation and social cohesion must be considered alongside and in interaction with other factors – including a range of other cultural influences, economic and political variables – such as that extremes of economic inequality militate against social cohesion, as we noted following Castells in the American case.

So, what is the relevance of all this to the study of Jewish-Christian relations? Well, I hope it opens up a number of avenues of enquiry and discussion. For example, if Bauman is right in interpreting the Holocaust not as a blip in the civilizing march of modernity, nor primarily as an outcome of Christian anti-Semitism, but as rather revealing something about the de-moralizing effects of the complex social systems characteristic of modernity, this might make some difference as to how the topic is approached in Jewish-Christian dialogue. Second, does the way that Seligman thinks about faith and trust ring true? Is the goal of inter-faith dialogue to promote trust, and if so, does the model of the relationship between faith, trust and civil society discussed here point to a re-thinking of how it might be developed further in the context of inter-faith activity and enquiry? Overall, I hope I have suggested that a focus on the social construction and context of inter-faith relations may be a helpful supplement to the more traditional emphasis on the role of ideas, ideologies and texts.

Notes

1. Z. Bauman, *Modernity and the Holocaust* (Oxford: Blackwell, 1989), p. 185.

2. A. Seligman, *The Idea of Civil Society* (Chichester: Princeton University Press, 1992).

3. J. Casanova, 'Global Catholicism and the Politics of Civil Society' *Sociological Inquiry* 66.3 (1996), P. 359.

4. G. Davie, *Religion in Modern Europe* (Oxford, Oxford University Press, 2000); S. Bruce, *Religion in the Modern World* (Oxford: Oxford University Press, 1996).

5. Davie, *Religion*.

6. W. Roof, 'God is in the Details: Reflections on Religion's Public Presence in the United States in the Mid 1990s' *Sociology of Religion* 57 (DATE), pp. 149-162; M. Castells, *The Information Age: Economy, Society and Culture. Vol. 1. The Rise of the Network Society* (Oxford: Blackwell, 1996).

7. D. Herbert, *Religion and Civil Society* (Aldershot: Ashgate, 2003).

8. J. Sacks, 'The Persistence of Faith: The 1990 Reith Lectures' *The Listener* 15 November 1990 – 3 January 1991.

9. T. Adorno et al., *The Authoritarian Personality* (New York: Harper and Row, 1950), p. ix.

10. E. Durkheim, *The Division of Labour in Society* (New York: Free Press, 1964 [1893]).

11. A. Davey, *Learning to Prejudiced: Growing Up in Multi-ethnic Britain* (London: Edwin Arnold, 1983).

12. Bauman, *Modernity and the Holocaust*, p. 6.

13. Bauman, *Modernity and the Holocaust*, p. 12.

14. Bauman, *Modernity and the Holocaust*, p. 23.

15. Bauman, *Modernity and the Holocaust*, pp. 24-25.

16. Bauman, *Modernity and the Holocaust*, pp. 182ff.

17. Z. Bauman, 'Effacing the Face: On the Social Management of Moral Proximity' *Theory, Culture and Society* 7 (1990), pp. 143-169.

18. E. Levinas, *Otherwise Than Being* (London: M. Nijoff, 1981), p. 87.

19. Bauman, *Modernity and the Holocaust*, p. 12.

20. MacIntyre in P. McMylor, *Alasdair MacIntyre: Critic of Modernity* (London: Routledge, 1994), pp. 102-3.

21. Bauman, *Modernity and the Holocaust*, p. 28

22. Bauman, *Modernity and the Holocaust*, p. 215.

23. Browning in Bauman, *Modernity and the Holocaust*, p. 197.

24. Bauman, *Modernity and the Holocaust*, p. 197.

25. Bauman, *Modernity and the Holocaust*, pp. 165-6.

26. S. White, *The Recent Work of Jurgen Habermas* (Cambridge: Cambridge University Press, 1988).

27. J. Esposito, *The Islamic Threat: Myth or Reality?* (Oxford: Oxford University Press, 1992).

28. R. Nagle, *Claiming the Virgin: The Broken Promise of Liberation Theology* (London: Routledge, 1997).

29. P. Gifford, *African Christianity: Its Public Role* (London: Hurst, 1998).

30. K. Kubik, *The Power of Symbols Against the Symbols of Power: The Rise of Solidarity and the Fall of State Socialism in Poland* (Philadelphia: Pennsylvania State University, 1994). J. De Gruchy, *Christianity and Democracy* (Cambridge: Cambridge University Press, 1995).

31. J. Casanova, *Public Religions in the Modern World* (Chicago: Chicago University Press, 1994).

32. R. Gill, *Moral Communities* (Exeter: Exeter University Press, 1992).

33. W. Shadid and P. van Koningsveld (eds), *Muslims in the Margin: Political Response to the Presence of Islam in Western Europe* (Kampen: Kok Pharos, 1996).

34. Seligman, *The Idea of Civil Society.*

35. A. Seligman, *The Problem of Trust* (Chichester: Princeton University Press, 1997), p. 171.

36. Selgiman, *The Problem of Trust*, p. 44.

37. J. Habermas, *Theory of Communicative Action Vol. 2: Lifeworld and System: A Critique of Functionalist Reason* (Cambridge, Polity/Blackwell, 1987).

38. A. Seligman, 'Civil Society: Between Jerusalem and Los Angeles', paper presented to the IJPR, London, 7 September, 1998, pp. 4-5, 10, 13.

39. J. Galtung, *Human Rights in Another Key* (Cambridge: Polity, 1995).

40. Galtung, *Human Rights*, pp. 6-7.

41. Selgiman, *The Idea of Civil Society*, p. 184.

42. M. Castells, *The Information Age: Economy, Society and Culture*. Vol. 1.(Oxford: Blackwell, 1997); M. Castells, *The Information Age: Economy, Society, and Culture*. Vol. 3 (Oxford: Blackwell, 1997).

43. Castells, *The Information Age: Economy, Society and Culture*. Vol. 1.

44. Castells, *The Information Age: Economy, Society and Culture*. Vol. 3.

45. Castells, *The Information Age: Economy, Society and Culture*. Vol. 3, pp. 44-45.

46. Gill, *Moral Communities*.

47. Sacks, 'The Persistence of Faith', p. 4.

48. Sacks, 'The Persistence of Faith', p. 10.

49. Gill, *Moral Communities*, p. 1.

50. Gill, *Moral Communities*, pp. 69-70.

51. Gill, *Moral Communities*, p. 20.

52. Gill, *Moral Communities*, p. 19.

53. Gill, *Moral Communities*, pp. 81-82.

11

Reporting Jewish-Christian Relations: the perspective of the *Jewish Chronicle*

Simon Rocker

One Sunday morning on 25th January 2004, still bleary after a lie-in, I turned on the radio and found myself listening to the Lord's Prayer on BBC Radio 4. There is nothing special about the Lord's Prayer being broadcast on a Sunday morning, except that in this case it was coming from a synagogue. How was it possible that such a quintessential act of Christian faith was being broadcast from a synagogue?[1] It was actually part of a special commemoration service organised by the West London Reform Synagogue for Holocaust Memorial Day, which fell two days later. It consisted mostly of Jewish liturgy but with the inclusion of one or two elements for a Christian audience. The Bishop of London was a guest preacher. It was in fact the first time that Radio Four's Sunday worship programme had been broadcast from a synagogue – a small but not insignificant landmark. I mention it because it is easy to overlook such events when such considering Christian-Jewish relations in the media and instead concentrate on more hardcore news stories. But I think it is a signal of how much progress has been made. Moreover it is not an isolated event. Not so long ago Songs of Praise featured the harmonica-playing principal of the Leo Baeck College – Centre for Jewish Education, Rabbi Jonathan Magonet. Another example is Rabbi Lionel Blue, probably the best-known exponent of breakfast reflection on Radio Four's *Thought for the Day*, who is more celebrated nationally perhaps than within his own community. Or the gravelly wisdom of the late Rabbi Hugo Gryn, whose appearances on the *Moral Maze* made him one of the most respected Jewish personalities in the country. Just recently, another rabbi, Dan Cohn-Sherbok, Professor of Judaism at the University of Wales-Lampeter

College, has become the first Jew to give a Lent talk for Radio 4. Only recently the Chief Rabbi was hailed as the country's most effective media spokesman for religion by none other than David Yelland, the former editor of *The Sun*. Cumulatively, this illustrates the extent to which Judaism and its representatives have become accepted as a natural part of the country's spiritual landscape. It shows that Judaism not only is still a living religion but also one which contributes to the religious life of the country. And in a way it perhaps does more to counteract some of the lingering prejudices of the past than more formal pronouncements or documents.

I thought it right to start on a positive note because it is tempting, for a journalist, at least to focus on the more dramatic eruptions of conflict. In this essay, I will review Jewish-Christian relations through a doubly parochial lens- as they are mainly in Britain, and through the eyes of the Jewish community. And to do so as they have been reflected in my own newspaper, the *Jewish Chronicle (The JC)*. Founded in 1841, *The JC* is the oldest continuously published Jewish newspaper in the world and the most widely ready in Britain. It is a forum in print, 'the medium', as its own chronicler, David Cesarani, has written in his history of the newspaper, 'through which Jews in Britain interact with, argue amongst and amuse each other.'[2]

To set the scene, let me refer to an editorial that appeared in the *Jewish Chronicle* in August 1988, which in a way is indicative of the mood of many of the community at that time. It was published the week after the historic resolution on Jewish-Christian relations at the Lambeth Conference (*Jews, Christians and Muslims: The Way of Dialogue*). It was written in response to some lively debate that had been taking place in the Letters Page the previous weeks in which some correspondents had dismissed Christian-Jewish dialogue as a waste of time. For some Jews, the photocalls of Chief Rabbis with Archbishops, the receptions, the awards of interfaith medallions etc amounted to little more than an attempt by Jewish leaders to cosy up to the religious establishment. Even though such views might be confined to a small minority, it is important to recognise that such hostility existed. Rejecting such a jaundiced outlook, the editorial went on to spell out the objectives - and boundaries – of dialogue.

> We do not need anybody's acceptance for the legitimisation of our faith. Nor, for the greater part of those Jews who participate in it, is interfaith dialogue an attempt to seek out a point of convergence

between our faith and others. There is none and there can be none, and we have no need to define ourselves in terms of any other system of belief. True dialogue can only take place between those who accept and respect the differences in the full knowledge that they cannot be bridged, other than by an acceptance of the fact that we are all children of the one God.

A prime purpose of interfaith dialogue from the Jewish viewpoint is not to engage in theological discussion. The area of joint concern…should be outer-directed, to combat the secularism, materialism and atheistic negation of religion and religious values which threaten the moral underpinnings of our society, and to co-operate with members of other faiths in all fields of human endeavour while, simultaneously, seeking to preserve our distinct integrity. Indeed, what some of our correspondents have chosen to ignore is the fact that, in order to preserve that distinct integrity in a society in which we are all a small minority, we need the co-operation of Christian friends.

What is noteworthy is a certain defiant defensiveness of tone; the rejection of theological discussion (echoing the opinion of then Chief Rabbi, Lord Jakobovits): and the stress on Jewish interest in pursuing dialogue. Perhaps interfaith encounters, particularly at local level, may be simply a way of getting to know one's religious neighbours, so to speak, without any particular agenda. For many Jews, organised contact with Christians was seen largely in terms of an act of reparation for the unhappy past. In particular, Christian respect and sympathy with Jews could be measured by progress in three areas, which I will explore in more detail:

1) Rejecting the legacy of Church teachings which contributed to anti-Semitism
2) Repudiating predatory missionary attempts on Jews
3) Recognising the state of Israel and its place in Jewish hearts

Firstly, the efforts to break with the teachings of contempt, to recognise Judaism as a living, breathing religion and to acknowledge the Jewish roots of Christianity were reflected in the media. In a 1992 article in *The JC*, Rabbi Jonathan Romain, of Maidenhead, a Reform Synagogue, observed;

Most Christian children at Sunday classes are today no longer being told that the Jews are responsible for killing Jesus. Instead, they learn that the Jews were the brothers of Jesus. Through their visits to local synagogues, interest and respect are replacing fear and hostility.

This was borne out by pictures, for example, of schoolchildren taking part in demonstration Passover seders or bathed in the light of the menorah as they learned about the festival of Chanucah.

From the late 1980s onward there was a growing interest in the Holocaust – reflected in a steady stream of TV documentaries and later in the national history curriculum – which prompted new scrutiny of the various Churches. Inevitably, raw nerves were touched and controversies flared up: the Carmelite monastery at Auschwitz – an act of desecration to most Jews - the award of a papal knighthood to Kurt Waldheim, the ill-fated commission to examine the Vatican archives and the role of Pius XII. These headline-making episodes threatened to confirm popular perceptions that nothing much had changed in the way of addressing Jewish sensitivities. On the other hand, there was recognition and appreciation of those who responded to the enormous moral challenge of the Shoah. Let me single out two individuals: Dr Elisabeth Maxwell, who organised the monumental *Remembering for the Future* conferences in 1988, 1996 and 2000 and Stephen and James Smith, who created the remarkable Beth Shalom Holocaust Memorial Centre in Laxton, Nottinghamshire. Both were presented to the Jewish community as actions of Christians who were willing to confront the past

The acclaim for these individual initiatives has to be balanced against the frustration that greeted events on an official level. The Vatican's important document *We Remember: a reflection on the Shoah* in 1998 was subjected to a lengthy critique in the *Jewish Chronicle* by Rabbi Mark Winer, who called it 'disappointing'. It was Rabbi Winer's synagogue, which was the venue for the Holocaust Memorial service I referred to earlier, so the fact that criticism came from a leading Jewish interfaith activist makes it all the more significant. He stressed the document's positive aspects: the use of Hebrew terms such as *Shoah* and *teshuvah* (repentance). However, he was critical of attempts to exonerate Pius XII, to balance Catholic rescuers against perpetrators and to distinguish between the anti-Judaism of historic Church teachings and antisemitism. 'An attempt to distinguish between anti-Judaism and anti-Semitism artificially dichotomises that which proved tragically continuous', he argued. But he went on to explain that the deficiencies of the document lay in its being the result of a committee process and to salute 'the friends of the Jewish people' in the Catholic

Church and the Pope himself.

Edward Kessler is right in warning that we have to be careful about making Jewish-Christians relations overly *Shoah*-focussed. But it is impossible not to ignore the passionate arguments over Pius XII – although he has some Jewish defenders such as Sir Martin Gilbert – and the proposal to beatify him is a public relations disaster.

Secondly, there is nothing more likely to upset Jewish readers than the word 'missionary' in a headline and few issues unite the community as much as revulsion at evangelical activity specifically targeting Jews. The actual threat in terms of the number of Jews who are persuaded to convert to Christianity may be small – but the passions aroused show how deeply any such attempts are viewed as a form of spiritual harassment. Tellingly, a 1980 interview in *The JC* with Robert Runcie shortly before his enthronement as Archbishop of Canterbury opened with his personal opinion on the subject: it was a kind of instant litmus test of his attitude towards Jews. 'I would not try to convert my Jewish friends to Christianity', he said. 'But if any of them showed any interest, I would see that they were given the right information.'

Many Jews do understand that the renunciation of mission towards Jews may pose theological challenges for Christians but believe that such overtures at least ought to have been formally suspended on compassionate grounds in a post-*Shoah* world. Nevertheless, coverage reflected that progress has been made. Not long before the Runcie interview, the Rector of Edgware had talked on television about knocking on the doors of local Jews to introduce them to Jesus, oblivious to the fact that his approaches would have been as objectionable to most of his recipients as if he had pushed slices of ham through the letterbox. Such overt proselytising, at least within the mainstream churches, appears to have declined. The 1988 Lambeth conference's condemnation of 'aggressive and manipulative' attempts to convert Jews was seen as an important step even though, as reports made clear at the time, it fell short of the outright repudiation of missionising among Jews that had originally been proposed.

Even more significant, in terms of popular impact, was the decision of Archbishop Carey's not to accept the *ex officio* patronage of the Church's Ministry among the Jewish People, a front page story in the *Jewish Chronicle* in 1992, which indicated the Church of England's growing distance from the missionaries. But despite the moves made by the mainstream Churches, the group Jews for Jesus continues to be a source of outrage to a great many Jews. Its provocative campaigning is designed to court publicity – most recently a full-page advertisement featuring a Holocaust survivor who came to Jesus was placed in a national newspaper to mark Holocaust Memorial Day. And although it is understood that *Jews for Jesus* is an independent group, there is still an expectation that the Churches could do more to dissociate themselves from it. Late last year, following a *Jews for Jesus*-organised *Rosh Hashanah* service in All Souls Church in central London, we reported a protest in the form of a strong letter signed by a number of prominent rabbis including Dame Julia Neuberger as well as Christian and Muslim activists against what they saw as 'a dark threat.' I mention it only to demonstrate how much any kind of missionary activity still rankles. In contrast, although *The JC* reported the historic resolution of the American Catholic bishops to renounce mission to the Jews in 2002 (*Reflections on Covenant and Mission*), the newspaper underplayed its significance, especially in light of the ensuing controversy.

The most fraught of the three areas I specified remains Israel. There is a widespread expectation within the Jewish community that Christians have a particular responsibility to show understanding for and sympathy towards the state of Israel. Although I am not commenting on whether such expectations are justified, I point to them as a factor that should be taken into account. It is no accident that in the full-page report in the *Jewish Chronicle* of the 1988 Lambeth conference, the lead story was not the resolution on Jewish-Christian relations but a resolution on the Middle East described as 'unhelpful' by the Israel embassy. That reflected the priorities of many in the Jewish community at that time and which remains the case today. Israel's image had suffered badly in the wake of the Lebanon War and the first intifada in the 1980s and in 1990, the then director of the Council of Christians and Jews, Canon Jim Richardson, commented; 'Where it matters, with the bishops and opinion-makers, there is no doubt that the majority have taken an anti-Israel line.'

Israel's position, nonetheless began to improve with the 1993 Oslo Accords and the optimism it engendered, and during the decade came two events of enormous symbolic importance – the Vatican's diplomatic recognition of Israel and the Pope's visit in 2000. If one were to nominate the single most significant image in Jewish-Christian relations during that period, it would be of the Pope at the Western Wall in Jerusalem: it was an image that would naturally reverberate far more immediately than any verbal declaration. The Vatican's reluctance to open diplomatic relations with the Jewish State had long been a running sore, which at times overshadowed positive Catholic-Jewish developments. This historic move was widely applauded in the Jewish press – but the more benign climate was not to endure and the onset of the second intifada has seen new tensions.

A new wave of hostility from the Churches, as viewed by many within the Jewish community, broke out against Israel. One extreme example in 2002, which was the subject of a lead story in the Jewish Chronicle was a letter published in the *Glasgow Herald* from Professor Robert Davidson, who represented the Moderator of the Church of Scotland on the Council of Christians and Jews (CCJ). Backing a campaign to boycott Israel, he referred to the Palestinians undergoing 'their own Holocaust.' The letter was roundly criticised by many including the Archbishop of Canterbury, George Carey but many Jews wondered how such views could have been held by anyone involved in the CCJ. That may have been a particularly flagrant instance, but there were increasing reports of what were considered anti-Israel activity by various Christian groups. In particular, repeated complaints have been aired in the press against Christian Aid, which is widely seen as having crossed the line from relief work on behalf of the Palestinians to politically partisan advocacy.

One of British Jewry's most senior friends in the Anglican hierarchy, the Bishop of Oxford, Dr Richard Harries, gave a candid assessment of the situation in a long interview with *The JC* on 15th August 2003, to mark the publication of his book on Jewish-Christian relations, *After the Evil*.

> Organisations like Christian Aid of which I used to be on the board traditionally work with the poor and people who are suffering…And they have seen the Palestinians as a suffering people they want to support…Sadly, there's very often a lack of understanding of the very genuine security needs of Israel and a clear affirmation of its right to exist.

Putting Israel's point of view across was an uphill task in Christian circles and the 'situation was worse than 10 to 15 years ago', he concluded.

For many Jews at the grassroots, there is the lurking suspicion that Christian identification with the Palestinian cause is a way of evading the historic burden of responsibility towards Jewish well-being in a post-

Holocaust world. The commentator Melanie Phillips has warned that displacement theology is rearing its ugly head again as a way of delegitimising the Jewish state, though her analysis is by no means universally shared. What is undeniable is that violence in the Middle East continues to cast a shadow over formal Jewish-Christian relations and has led to a sense of greater vulnerability on the part of many Jews, who blame media coverage of events in Israel in part for the rise in antisemitism.

So far I have discussed Jewish expectations of Christians and many Jews are content for discussions between the two faith communities to continue on this basis. But in the last few years, there have been attempts to shift dialogue between Jews and Christians on to new ground: not to close the door on the agenda on the past, but to take the enterprise forward. The Catholic-Jewish conference that took place in London in 2000 was reported in the *Jewish Chronicle* as a significant attempt to move the formal discussion beyond the traditional concerns with antisemitism, Israel and the role of the Church in the Holocaust: specifically to explore what was called in the follow-up conference last year, 'the theology of partnership.' Whereas theological discussion was largely avoided 20 years ago – and remains so in most Orthodox Jewish circles – this major conference suggested new possibilities.

It was now possible for Jews to re-examine their attitudes towards Christianity as has been advocated by an increasing number of Jewish voices. The Dabru Emet statement published in 2002 initially by some 180, mainly American, rabbis and scholars – there were a couple of British signatories – was a hailed as a pioneering step in that process. However, it has so far had limited impact in this country and *The JC* made only two references to it. Nonetheless, other Jews were prepared to challenge the status quo. In an article in the Jewish Chronicle on 22nd August 2001, the Liberal rabbi, Dr Sidney Brichto wrote:

> We Jews remain as negative as ever about the Christian faith. We are always alert to any Christian claim of superiority to our own faith, but without giving up our own claim to chosenness. We totally ignore the contribution of Christianity to human culture. We will not read the New Testament nor take any interest in understanding why it succeeded in conquering the Western world where we failed…

Dr Brichto is currently engaged in the ambitious bid to become the first rabbi to produce an English translation of both the *Tanach* and the New Testament. While any generalisation is subject to modification and qualification, his was a fair summary of the prevailing situation. It has often been argued that Jewish children did not need to learn about Christianity as they picked up a working knowledge through some kind of cultural osmosis. This was always a dubious proposition, but is even less plausible now that more Jewish children attend Jewish schools. A couple of years ago *The JC* highlighted a report on multicultural education in Jewish schools produced for the Institute for Jewish Policy Research, an independent think-tank. Its author concluded:

> It has to be a matter of concern that some respondents failed to realise (or refused to acknowledge) that it [the need to equip pupils for a multicultural society] also requires, as a minimum, a study of other cultures and particularly other faiths. With perhaps one exception, prior to the sixthform, secondary schools did not engage seriously with religious beliefs other than Judaism and even in the sixthform the treatment the topic received was felt by some students to be inadequate.[3]

It should be stressed that for most Jewish schools there are formidable practical and theological difficulties with teaching other faiths, particularly Christianity, as indicated by the argument that erupted in the Jewish community in 2002 over Chief Rabbi Sacks's book, *The Dignity of Difference*. Tackling globalisation and diversity, it was a passionate plea for inter-religious tolerance and was favourably reviewed in the *Jewish Chronicle* by Dr Rowan Williams shortly before he took office as Archbishop of Canterbury.

Nonetheless, a storm of criticism began to gather over certain references to other faiths: within weeks of publication, the Chief Rabbi was facing a revolt within his own rabbinate and denunciation from the Orthodox world's premier legal authority, the Jerusalem-based nonagenarian, Rabbi Yosef Shalom Eliashiv, for having compromised in their eyes the Torah's claim to uniqueness. As a result, he was compelled to amend the second edition of the book to avoid what were effectively accusations of heresy. One key passage was amended as follows. The first edition read, '... in the course of history, God has spoken to mankind in many languages: through Judaism to Jews, Christianity to Christians, Islam to Muslims.' This was revised in the second edition to '... as Jews, we believe that God has made a covenant with a singular people, but that does not exclude the possibility of other peoples, cultures and faiths finding their own relationship with God, within the shared frame of the Noahide laws.'[4]

The original passage, as phrased, held out the possibility – I put it no strongly than that – that Christianity might involve some element of revelation. The amended version removed that possibility and reasserted the traditional Orthodox position. As long as other religions abide by the Noahide laws – which include the prohibition against idolatory (by no means a simple matter) – their content from this perspective is irrelevant. To that extent, one could sum up the classical Jewish position as the dignity of indifference.

Nevertheless, certain questions cannot be avoided, even though they may be shunted aside in the desire to minimise the effects of a highly public controversy. If, for example, it is the prophetic mission for Jews to be witnesses of God, why have Christianity and Islam been historically more successful in the spread of monotheism? To answer this requires a Jewish re-appraisal of both Christianity and Islam. Although the row over the book reached the pages of the national press, by and large Christian leaders openly avoided entering the fray. This was partly the result of an appreciation that the Chief Rabbi was experiencing difficulties from his own community and it would have been ungracious to have exposed him further. Perhaps there was a more general inhibition about raising what is a delicate issue for Judaism. Dr Harries did make some pertinent points in a critique of the book in a theological journal which he avoided elaborating in his interview for *The JC*; yet he did venture the comment that despite the amendments in the book, that 'if he [the Chief Rabbi] admits that people can develop a relationship with God outside Judaism, the corollary of that is, you can't develop a relationship with God unless there is some sense in which God has made Himself known to you.' In other words, revelation by the back door.

That particular episode illuminates the problems of covering such issues. A media controversy helps flag questions, which would not otherwise be asked: yet the outbreak of controversy leads to an effort to suppress the very issues at the heart of it.

A new Jewish reappraisal of Christianity is difficult in any case because for many Jews it remains a taboo subject. But the case becomes even more difficult to argue in a climate of uncertainty and anxiety. The embattled defensiveness which many Jews feel about Israel at the present time, coupled with the perception of rising antisemitism, inevitably makes them less open to such a challenge.

Needless to say, Mel Gibson's contentious film, *The Passion of the Christ* – which at the time of writing was due to open in the UK shortly – is hardly helpful to the cause of Dabru Emet. To any journalist in search of a good story, it is a godsend, complete with an A-list celebrity. The transformation of the star of *Mad Max* and the *Lethal Weapon* series into celluloid evangelist, farfetched as it may initially seem, is fascinating material. It is hard not to think that the Jewish protests that were levelled against the film may be part of a wider reaction to contemporary events: a fear that the film's alleged depiction of Jews as violent, uncompromising and vindictive would help to reinforce the anti-Zionism that many believe is fed by hostile media portrayal of Israel.

There were some voices in *The JC*, nevertheless, which warned against adding to a snowballing publicity that might only help the film at the box office. The newspaper's media columnist, Alex Brummer, while believing that 'no one should underestimate this gory farrago to do enormous damage' suggested that the best Jewish response would be 'starving it of the oxygen of publicity.' Another of its columnists, Daniel Finkelstein, argued against 'full-on assault' against the film lest it lead to some kind of backlash from Israel's Christian allies. Yet the newspaper in its coverage of Gibson's intended epic could hardly ignore the universal revulsion it generated once representatives of different sections of the Jewish community had had the chance to see it for themselves at a preview. One senior Liberal rabbi, David Goldberg, who has been involved in interfaith discussions for years and who had recently warned against over-reaction to antisemitism, told *The JC*: 'I like to think of myself as unparanoid, but I felt it was potentially a very difficult and dangerous film…I think it will set back interfaith dialogue considerably – not on the level of scholars, but on the level of the person in the street…'.

How far *The Passion* marks a setback for those who have patiently striven for the Gospels to be taught in a more sophisticated and sensitive fashion remains to be seen. Inevitably, it will taken by some Jews as a sign that the clock is turning backwards. But in every cloud there is a silver lining, of course. While *The Passion of the Christ* may disturb Jewish-Christian relations in one sense, the controversy offers a counter-opportunity to draw attention to the genuine educational advances that have been quietly taking place over many years in churches and classrooms across the country.

Notes

1. The Lord's Prayer, I was later told, was edited into the programme after recording – although the listener would not have been aware of that.

2. D. Cesarani, *The Jewish Chronicle and Anglo-Jewry, 1841-1991* (Cambridge: Cambridge University Press, 1994), p.253.

3. G. Short, *Responding to Diversity? An initial investigation into multicultural education in Jewish schools in the UK* (JPR: London, 2002).

4. J. Sacks, *Dignity of Difference* (London: Continuum, 2002; second edition 2003), p 55 (both editions).

12

Implementation of *Nostra Aetate*, no. 4, in the United States and in England and Wales: Some Preliminary Observations

Eugene J. Fisher

This paper will attempt a comparison of the 'reception' (implementation by a local church) of the Second Vatican Council's declaration on the Church's relation with the Jewish People, *Nostra Aetate, no. 4*, in the U.S. and in England and Wales (Scotland and Ireland have their own bishops' conferences). There are enticing parallels between the Catholic and Jewish experiences in America and the Catholic and Jewish experiences in Britain but there are equally intriguing differences.

Nostra Aetate, no. 4, was promulgated by Second Vatican Council on October 28, 1965. It was originally to have been part of the statement on ecumenism, but became a statement on Catholic-Jewish relations in its own right. The bishops of the Middle East, Asia, and Africa all understandably insisted that they could more easily go home to their respective countries if the dominant religions of those countries were also addressed in positive terms by the Council. Thus, the statement on Jews and Judaism, which was only 15 sentences long in the original Latin, was augmented by statements on Islam, Buddhism, Hinduism and Native Traditions. Interestingly, however, when Pope Paul VI came to establishing in the Holy See the departments which would implement the various Conciliar decrees, he placed the Commission for Religious Relations with the Jews not under the Council for Interreligious Affairs, but 'attached to yet independent from' the Council for Christian Unity. The reason was theological: the relationship between the Church and the Jewish People is unlike any relationship the Church enjoys with other world religions. The

Catholic Church acknowledges that Judaism is founded on divine revelation in the Hebrew Scriptures. Hence, the parting of the ways in the early centuries after the destruction of the Jerusalem Temple was, as Cardinal Augustin Bea (who headed the Council for Unity and was responsible for the draft of *Nostra Aetate*) affirmed, the first schism in the history of the Church. The technical independence of the Commission for the Jews from the Unity Council reflected the desire by the Holy See to ensure that the aim of the Commission was in no way conversionist. From the point of view of the Church, the goal of Catholic-Jewish relations is not unity as it is for ecumenical relations, but rather reconciliation, which respecting the differences between Judaism and Christianity, might enable the two to witness to the world the sacred truths which they share.

Nostra Aetate, no. 4 sought to achieve two major goals, one positive and one negative. Negatively, it ended the centuries-old misunderstanding that the Jews were and are collectively guilty for the death of Jesus. With the removal of that cornerstone of the ancient 'teaching of contempt', as Jules Isaac so aptly called the deicide charge, its attendant notions, e.g. that God punished the Jews by destroying the Temple, sending the Jews into permanent exile, etc., lost their basis and have over the years been removed from Catholic religious texts, as we shall see, on all levels.

Nostra Aetate's positive goal was to replace the negative portrait of Jews and Judaism that had been part of Christian teaching since the second century with a more accurate and respectful image. Interestingly, the document, unlike most of the Conciliar texts, does not cite a single previous statement of a Council nor any of the Fathers of the Church. Rather, it goes back to the New Testament's one major reflection on the issue of how the Church is to understand that majority of the Jewish People who did not accept the Church's proclamation of the Jew, Jesus of Nazareth, as the Messiah and Son of God. This is Romans 9-11, where Paul, whose arguments against requiring gentiles to become Jews in order to be baptized into Christ had lead him to some negative judgements of his own, asks whether, after Christ, God has revoked his eternal covenant with the Jews. 'By no means!' (Rom 11:1) Paul thunders and affirms the irrevocability of the covenant, using the image of one root (biblical Israel) unto which gentile branches are engrafted through the grace of Christ. Gentile Christians are 'adopted heirs' alongside of Jews in the Covenant. Although there is, as biblical scholars have shown, some ambiguity in these Pauline texts, *Nostra Aetate*, using the full magisterial authority of an ecumenical council, determined that the Church must, now, meditate on their positive aspects, rather than emphasising only the negatives as virtually all Christians have done over the centuries.

How, then, did this renewed, indeed revolutionary, new meditation of the Church on its relationship with God's People, Israel, proceed? How did the Church in various parts of the world develop the 'dialogue of mutual esteem' with Jews mandated by the Council and articulate the its insights gained as part of her teachings? How these challenges have been met by Jews and Catholics in England and Wales and the U.S. depended very much on the respective histories of Jews and Catholics in these countries.

Demography & History: Parallel Immigration Stories

In the United States, there are at the time of writing some 67 million Catholics and 5.7 million Jews. According to *Religions in the UK: A Multi-Faith Directory*[1] there are 40 million Christians in the United Kingdom as a whole, of whom some 5.7 million identify themselves as Catholics. Though Catholic history in Britain is co-terminous with the island's Christian history, the 'Catholic Church's contemporary strength in England and Wales,' according to the Directory, 'is due mainly to the nineteenth and early twentieth century immigration of Roman Catholics from Ireland'.[2] The Catholic Church in England and Wales today has 3,701 places of worship certified with the Registrar General.

The *Multi-Faith Directory* estimates the Jewish population of the UK at around 300,000. Jews first settled in England following the Norman conquest in 1066, but were expelled by Edward I in 1290, only being allowed to return in the 17th century following the English Civil War. Sephardi Jews have the longest communal history in Britain, having an organized presence from the mid-seventeenth century, while Ashkenazi (Central and Eastern European) Jews, who form the majority of the contemporary community, migrated to England in the late 19th century, fleeing Russian pogroms, and from 1933 fleeing Nazi persecution. The Registrar General's list includes 303 synagogues in England and Wales.[3]

Jews and Catholics in both countries are essentially 19th & 20th Century immigrant groups. They are religious minorities in societies, which have treated them with relative tolerance but also posed innumerable obstacles socially, politically, and economically. These obstacles were in many ways similar in effect: keeping Catholics and Jews in both countries out of the 'better' neighbourhoods, universities, jobs, political positions, social clubs, etc. The major difference, of course, was that in Britain the discrimination was legalized, while in the U.S., whose constitution prohibits such legal distinctions and preferences among religious groups, the exclusions were less formal but no less effective. Lodging houses and businesses in the 19th century, for example, often posted signs such as 'No Irish Need Apply,' which, needless to say, would include Jews as well. In the early 20th century, the language was only slightly less explicit,with hotels advertising that were 'reserved for discriminating clientele only.' The first Hollywood film to tackle the subject, *Gentleman's Agreement*, portrays a gentile who assumes a Jewish name and is refused a room in a hotel in which he could have stayed under his own name. This portrait would also have been true if the assumed name were Italian or Polish.

In England and Wales, however, there were distinct laws enforcing religious preferences and discriminatory policies. The Anglican Church was (and is) The Established Church of England, with the reigning monarch at its head. In order to serve in Parliament, one had to acknowledge the sovereign as the Head of the Church; something neither Jews nor Catholics could do without abandoning their faiths. Thus, the emancipation of Catholics and Jews from these laws in the 19th century can be viewed in terms of legal battles fought in Parliament

American Jews and Catholics, on the other hand, speak more of gaining acceptance and the falling of barriers to full participation in the higher circles of academic, business, and social life. The term 'establishment' with regard to religion is parallel, but not the same in the two countries. In the UK, the term 'establishment' appears to be a legal category whereas in the US such a category has been abandoned. However, there exists a *de facto* 'establishment' in the US as can be seen by the dominance of the WASP (White Anglo-Saxon Protestant) community.

Another difference in the socio-political situation facing Catholics and Jews in the U.K. as opposed to the U.S. was the existence of members among the nobility. The oldest peerage in England, for example, is that the Duke of Norfolk, dating back to the 14th century and traditionally Catholic. For their part, Jews in the aristocracy such as Montefiore, who despite the necessary conversion to Christianity continued to identify with the Jewish people, also sat in the House of Lords. There were no such privileged people in 'high places', however, for the Catholics and Jews of America when they began to arrive in significant numbers.

In both US and British history, Catholics have been the largest religious/ ethnic minority. The ire of some established Christians who saw themselves as the sole exemplars of 'true' Americans or Britons, and whose intolerant world-view saw difference of belief and custom as a threat to the way things should be, tended to be more overtly concerned by the 'threat' of Catholicism than that of the relatively small (and therefore more easily handled) Jewish community.

Anti-Catholic nativism in the U.S. inspired not only movements to 'protect' Protestant America from Catholicism's decadent influence, but political parties as well, such as the No-nothing party. These parties ran candidates on explicitly anti-immigrant (anti-Catholic and also anti-Jewish) platforms, often successfully on the local level, and wielded influence within the major political parties as well. The infamous Klu Klux Klan, which was influential not only in the South but in the American Midwest as well, with one of its largest organizations being in Michigan and Ohio, opposed what it viewed as the three greatest dangers to the culture and mores of White Protestant America: Koons (Afro-Americans), Katholics, and Kikes (Jews).

The only true religious pogrom in American history, however, was perpetrated by the 'Nativists' (Protestants) of Philadelphia in 1844 against the city's Catholic population. The riots, which resulted in the burning of several churches, the murder of scores of Catholics, and the closing of all Catholic churches for some two weeks while the Commonwealth militia watched the fires from outside the city, was precipitated by a young Catholic girl who refused to pray from the King James Version of the Bible in her public school. The use of public schools by Protestants to proselytise immigrant youngsters is well attested and continued for decades afterwards. It is one reason that the American Catholic community built and maintained the largest private school system in the country, and why many Jewish parents, especially in the American South, preferred to send their children to Catholic schools rather than to the local public schools, even before the Second Vatican Council.

Britain, similarly, is quite distinctive in having instituted a day on its official calendar as an annual reminder of the threat of Catholicism – Guy Fawkes Day, which celebrates the capture of Guy Fawkes, a Catholic who, during the height of the persecution of Catholics after the Reformation, attempted to blow up the British Parliament. Amidst fireworks and bonfires, the tradition is to burn an effigy of Fawkes. In previous generations, it was common to burn effigies of the pope and even of the local bishop as well, though few celebrants do this today. I know of no parallels to this peculiar (to an American) institution, and while I presume its ominous implications have been worn away by the passing of the years, it does reflect the memory of the anti-Catholic legislation of post-Reformation history that only began to come to an end when my own ancestor, Daniel O'Connell, strode into Parliament without abandoning his Catholic faith.

The American Civil War, unlike the British, was not fought on religious lines, but geographical ones. The minority communities of Catholics and Jews in the South tended to stand side by side with their Protestant neighbours, though they were still not accepted as full citizens.

The Jewish community of Britain rejoiced in Catholic emancipation, beginning in 1829, seeing it as a precursor of their own emancipation, as indeed it was, with Jews winning the right to sit in Parliament without abandoning Judaism in 1858. In 1829 Daniel O'Connell, elected to Parliament from Ireland and bolstered by pressure from the Catholic Association and burgeoning numbers of Irish Catholic immigrants and clergy and an educated laity seeking asylum from the French Revolution,[4] brought about the repeal of the Test and Corporation Acts. This would have automatically removed the political disabilities of the Jews as well but according to Cecil Roth 'on the motion of the Bishop of Llandaff, the House of Lords insisted upon the insertion of the words 'on the true faith of a Christian' in the Declaration henceforth required on taking up public office.'[5] In 1833 O'Connell gave one of the three major speeches in support of a bill before the Reformed Parliament elected to sweep away old abuses. The bill, which passed the House of Commons, resolved 'to remove all civil disabilities at present existing affecting His Majesty's subjects of the Jewish religion, with the like exceptions as are provided with reference to His Majesty's subjects professing the Roman Catholic religion'.[6] Again, however, the House of Lords blocked the bill, which was not passed for another 25 years. Still, as the wording of the 1833 bill shows, the model for Jewish emancipation was Catholic emancipation, and Catholic legislators, such as O'Connell, strongly supported the Jewish community's efforts.

So, too, American Jewry stood alongside the Catholic community in the struggle of the immigrants of the 19th & 20th centuries to be accepted in American society. The American labour movement, for example, was largely a Catholic-Jewish enterprise, and the voting patterns of the two communities on most issues were, until relatively recently, virtually the same. Pictures of the earliest labour strikes in New York's garment district from before the turn of the 20th century, for example, show numerous signs in two languages, neither of them English. Rather, the signs the workers carry are in Italian and Yiddish! The labour movement, at its height, was very supportive of the emerging State of Israel, and Catholic representatives in the US Congress gave Israel-related causes steadfast and steady support.

In Britain and the U.S., therefore, the Catholic and Jewish communities, unlike in continental Europe, encountered each other in the main as equals under the laws of their respective lands, with neither having political power over the other and both looking at a larger religious community whose rules and regulations more or less equally limited and irritated them both.

Traditionally, English Jewish historians, like their counterparts in the U.S., have stressed the tranquillity, relative security, and uniqueness of the history of Anglo-Jewry vis à vis the continental experience since the Enlightenment. Cecil Roth,[7] for example, portrayed Jews as advancing steadily and serenely toward equality as British society moved in equally stately fashion from medievalism to modern, liberal democracy. Within this 'alembic of tolerance,' Roth noted, were none of the pogroms, blood libel trials, economic boycotts, or other flagrant persecutions that marred the history of the European continent in the same period.

More recent Jewish historians, such as Todd Endelman and David Cesarani,[8] have modified the unalloyed positive view of Roth's generation by pointing to the obstacles to Jewish emancipation, including the ongoing difficulties of British self-identity and the consequent 'fragility of the British polity' more centrally in the historical portrait. This fragility meant that Jews could be seen as a symbol of a threat to 'true' English society, just as it was in continental Europe, as the modern nation-state replaced the way people understood their own identity in a feudal society. According to contemporary British historians such as Cesarani, the reality of the threat to British Jewry through the decades of protracted struggle for emancipation better explains the timid character of Jewish culture in Britain, the exaggerated patriotism of British Jews and their ambivalent response to the mass immigration of Jews from Eastern Europe.

On can easily discern a comparable exaggerated patriotism among American Catholics and Jews, of course, both of whom were recurrently charged with dual loyalties. The strong rejection of Zionism (until World War II) among many Reform Jews, for example, goes back to this need. Similarly, one cannot imagine any American Protestant politician having to prove his political loyalty to the U.S., as did John F. Kennedy. And one can discern a certain ambivalence in the relatively well established German Jewish community to the mass immigrations of Eastern European Jews as well, though this breaks down around the time of the outbreak of World War I.

While contemporary British Jewish historians speak of a 'timid' Jewish culture in Britain, this to some extent masks a quiet assertiveness when the community's interests are at stake. In the first half of the 20th century, nationalism swept much of the Western world. Jewish nationalism, of course, took the form of Zionism, with the parallel Catholic nationalism in the British Isles centring around the cause of a free Ireland, leading to the Irish rebellion in the Easter Rising of 1917 and the establishment of the Irish state (save in the northern counties of the island) in 1921. Just as much of the established leadership of the Jewish community found Zionism something of an embarrassment, especially given the fact that Britain controlled the Palestinian Mandate and had clear interests in positive relations with the Arabs of the region, so did much of the Catholic aristocracy of Britain view Irish aspirations for freedom from English rule as an embarrassment which would lead the majority in the country to question the patriotism of Catholics. So both communities were split internally on the great issues of the time. But the leadership of British Jewry did use its influence to help bring about the 1917 Balfour Declaration, and the Catholic aristocracy used its influence to work toward a peaceful solution to ending British rule in Ireland.

The parallels in the national movements of Jews and Irish Catholics can be seen as a factor in the ongoing dialogue between the two communities. The Zionists in Palestine were fighting for what they, too, saw as liberation from the British Empire. The more radical Zionists read the works of the Irish rebels with great interest, learning ways of resistance to British rule, even as the more moderate majority supported Britain and joined its armed forces. Today, these parallel historical circumstances, complex as they were at the time, can help in one of the most crucial areas of the dialogue: the Land issue – in other words, the attachment of Jews to the Land of Israel and their need for a stake in the Land. Irish Catholics, perhaps better than most Christians, can understand something of the depth of that attachment, religiously impregnated as it is even for secular Jews.

By the turn of the century, immigrant Catholics and Jews alike, though still facing formidable organized political and informal social and economic barriers, were eager to let the Establishment know that they had arrived in large numbers. This may explain on the Catholic side why the residences of the Archbishops of America's largest cities built during this period rival in size and elegance the mansions of the wealthiest of established society. On the other hand, the wave of political anti-immigrant (i.e. anti-Catholic and anti-Jewish) sentiment crested in the 1920s with the passage of a set of draconian immigration laws intended to maximize immigration from the north of Western Europe (which was and is mainly Protestant) and minimize immigration from southern and eastern Europe. Tragically, these laws, aimed primarily at reducing the flow of Catholic immigrants, were still in place throughout the 1930s, which reduced the chances of Jews escaping the Nazi menace. For example, the steamship St. Louis, which was filled with Jewish refugees, was refused permission to disembark its passengers in America and ended up sailing back to Europe. The U.S. Holocaust Memorial Museum presents a series of pictures from newspapers of various public demonstrations against Hitler's persecution of the Jews in the late 1930s. Interestingly, several of these show demonstrations in which the placards carried by the demonstrators announce boldly, 'Catholics and Jews Against Hitler', and similar messages of Catholic-Jewish collaboration in the organization of the demonstrations. In the U.S. in the 1940s, while Europe's Christians (Catholics and Protestants alike) were turning their backs on Germany's genocidal mania against the Jews, Catholics, Protestants and Jews were working together. On a personal note, my father as head of the local Knights of Columbus (a Catholic social and charitable association), brought together counterparts from B'nai B'rith and the local Masonic Lodge to plan a joint banquet to raise money for the war effort.

The 1920s, during which anti-immigrant politics reached their most potent form and enjoyed their greatest successes, saw the rise of the American Jewish Committee and the Anti-Defamation League, along with a newly assertive National Catholic Welfare Conference, headquartered in the nation's capital to represent Jewish and Catholic needs to the government and lobby on their behalf. This sense of communal assertiveness among U.S. Jews and Catholics, despite ongoing economic and social discrimination, again, may help to explain the more aggressive implementation of Catholic-Jewish dialogue on all levels in the U.S. immediately prior to, during, and since the Second Vatican Council.

Another similarity between the US and the UK is the dominance of the established Protestant communities in the two countries. The early Christian pioneers of Christian-Jewish relations originated from the ranks of the privileged, with the National Council of Jews and Christians in the US in the 1920s and the British Council of Jews and Christians in the 1940s owing their birth and early success to Protestants who felt the time had come for change and dialogue. Interestingly, what precipitated the earlier institution of the NCCJ in the US was the flagrant anti-Catholicism that reared up during the campaign for the presidency of Alfred Smith of New York, a frightening phenomenon which was only effectively put to rest by the successful candidacy of John F. Kennedy, who not coincidentally enjoyed immense support in the Jewish community as well as his own Catholic community.[9]

Antisemitism in the Catholic Communities of England and Wales and the U.S.

Lest the reader think I am writing with rose-tinted spectacles I must note that antisemitism did exist in the Catholic communities of England and America. In both, of course, it was part of the received culture of the communities and, while not normally emerging publicly among Catholics, was pervasive. On the other hand, in the U.S. unlike Europe, antisemitism was not viewed in racial terms. The race that people wished to be superior to was, of course, a slot already taken by the descendants of American slaves. Jews in America, save for the hard-core bigots like the KKK, were not seen as a separate race, but as one among many ethnic immigrant groups. The major racial divide in the U.S. has been colour, with Blacks, Asians, and Native American Indians, constituting the other races. Jews were somewhat exotic, it is true, but in my view no more than Italians or Greeks. They were, and are, seen on the American racial spectrum as 'Whites.' This may be why antisemitism in America has never been politically successful.[10] When American politicians play the 'race card', the issue has been anti-Black racism, whereas in Europe, throughout the 20th century and into the 21st, dark hints that a politician may have 'Jewish blood' in his lineage could be played to sway voters away from a certain candidate. In the U.S., such allegations would yield no political advantage whatsoever.

Father Charles Coughlin (originally Canadian, but who flourished in Detroit, Michigan) is often presented as a case in point of the depth of antisemitism in the Catholic community. In fact, I would argue, he represents the opposite. His antisemitic radio tirades were very different in substance from the anti-Jewish prejudices common in the community. Christine Athans has shown their likely source to be the letters and writings of his friend – an Irish Catholic priest. Coughlin's antisemitism is typically European rather than American.[11]

Coughlin was already losing his radio audience and his influence, having unsuccessfully run as a candidate for president against Franklin Roosevelt by the time of his antisemitic broadcasts in the late 1930s. Coughlin was publicly condemned at the time in editorials by the leading Catholic journals, America and Commonweal, both of which, studies have shown, were virtually free of antisemitic articles themselves (which cannot be said of comparable European Catholic journals) and which, on the contrary, frequently expressed sympathy and support for the plight of the Jews of Europe under threat of Nazism. The leadership of the National Catholic Welfare Conference likewise publicly denounced Coughlin's antisemitism. The U.S. bishops, meeting in November of 1938 in Washington, D.C., devoted the entirety of their annual radio broadcast to a series of condemnations by bishops (and by the governor of New York, Al Smith) of Kristallnacht, the 'night of the broken glass'. They saw it, rightly, as an attack on Judaism as a religion as well as against the Jewish People. One bishop, describing it as an appalling atrocity, called on all people of good will of whatever faith to join together to 'offer up a holocaust of prayers' to God to protect the Jews.

Internal Obstacles to Dialogue: Fears of Indifferentism and Disputations

In both the US and England and Wales, the first Christian theologians to engage in Christian-Jewish dialogue were Protestants, with Catholics beginning to participate in the 1950s, and then rather tentatively for fear of the charge of religious indifferentism. In the U.S., for example, involvement of Catholic clergy in the National Council of Christians and Jews was always by way of the membership of individual priests, tolerated by their bishops, but not officially delegated by them. This informal approach simply avoided rather than tackled the question of syncretism.

In Britain, on the other hand, the matter had to be faced as early as 1942, since in the more stratified British society, the Council of Christians and Jews was to be presided over jointly by the Archbishop of Canterbury (Anglican), the Moderator of the General Assembly of the Church of Scotland, the Moderator of the Free Church Federal Council, the Archbishop of Westminster (Catholic), and the Chief Rabbi (Orthodox) of the United Congregations of the British Empire. This, of course, represented the highest possible representation for all of the involved denominations. Both the Chief Rabbi, Dr. J. H. Hertz, and the Archbishop of Westminster, Cardinal Hinsley, expressed reservations on grounds of the appearance of syncretism especially with regard to the teaching of religion. Because of the urgency of what was happening to the Jews of Europe in the early 1940s, the matter had to be resolved at the outset. In July 1942, the draft of the constitution of the Council was amended to recognize 'the importance of securing a fair presentation in elementary, secondary and Sunday School education of the position of the Jews,' while leaving the matter itself to the 'personal influence' of the Christian members of the Executive within their own communities. Likewise, language taken from a letter by the Archbishop of Canterbury was added to the constitution stating that the CCJ's

> ... approach to this matter is governed by the consideration that the effectiveness of any religious belief depends upon its definiteness, and that neither Jews nor Christians should . . . combine in any such way as to obscure the distinctiveness of their witness to their own beliefs. There is much that we can do together in combating religious and racial intolerance, in forwarding social progress, and in bearing witness to those moral principles which we unite in upholding.[12]

It is noteworthy that the definitive article of Rabbi Joseph Soloveitchik on the issue of dialogue with Christians, written in 1964 as the Second Vatican Council was debating *Nostra Aetate*, took the same approach, eschewing formal 'theological' dialogue (with its aura and reminiscence of the infamous medieval disputations), while urging Orthodox Jews to work together with Christians on matters of social justice and the common good. The Soloveitchik article determined how Orthodox Jews would participate in Catholic-Jewish consultations (the term 'dialogue,' despite its Buberian roots, was not acceptable). In the early 1980s the Bishops' Conference and the SCA co-sponsored a series of fruitful consultations bringing together Jewish and Catholic scholars. Two volumes of papers from the dialogues under the titles *Foundations of Social Policy in the Catholic and Jewish Traditions* (1980) and *Liturgical Foundations of Social Policy in the Jewish and Catholic Traditions* (1983) were published. These were, from a Catholic point of view, theological but avoided the appearance of theology from the Orthodox Jewish perspective.

The Soloveitchik dictum was generally ignored in joint programming between the bishops and other Jewish agencies, such as the American Jewish Committee and the Anti-Defamation League, which have since the Council worked together to produce a wide variety of joint educational materials for use in both synagogues and church schools. Since the demise of the SCA in the mid-1990's, the US Bishops have maintained separate twice-yearly dialogues with representatives of Orthodox Judaism, on the one hand, and with the National Council of Synagogues, on the other, observing the Soloveitchik dictum in the former, but not the latter, which represents American Reform and Conservative Judaism, (which include 90% of religiously-affiliated American Jews).

It may be the relatively high profile of the British CCJ that led to the startling announcement in November of 1954 by Cardinal Griffin, who had succeeded Cardinal Hinsley, that he would be withdrawing from the joint presidency of CCJ 'on instructions from Rome.'[13] This curious incident, so far as I know, has no parallel in Catholic-Jewish relations in the United States, though the Southern Baptist Convention did pull out of the National Workshops on Christian-Jewish Relations (NWCJR) in the 1990s when the NWCJR resisted the SBC's attempt to use it as a forum for Messianic Judaism. Cardinal Griffin's formal letter of resignation gave as his reason:

> Whereas in those days (the time of the formation of the Council), the emphasis of the Council's work lay on countering antisemitism and on cooperation between Christians and Jews in regard to problems arising principally from conditions created by the war, the emphasis seems now to have shifted to the educational field where the promotion of mutual understanding is being conducted in a way likely to produce religious indifferentism.

Despite official withdrawal by the Catholic Church, CCJ continued to be supported by the *Tablet*, the major lay-Catholic journal in the UK. In his history of the incident, Rev. Marcus Braybrooke notes the 1957 response of the Catholic Information Centre about the withdrawal, 'It is not the custom of the Church to share a common platform in matters which may involve religious and ethical questions.' Braybrooke comments, 'The ban does not, however, seem to have been so rigorously applied in the USA.'[14] Perhaps a reason for the difference in Vatican reaction may simply have been that Catholic involvement in the NCCJ in the US never reached so highly visible or hierarchal a level as it did (and does) in Britain. The NCCJ in the US at the present time, likewise, is no longer as deeply involved in Christian-Jewish relations as it was in its earlier decades.

In 1962, Braybrooke reports, Catholic laypeople were allowed, with permission of their bishops, to be associated with the Council. In 1964 Cardinal Heenan addressed the CCJ plenum expressing his pleasure that Catholics were again taking a full part in the life of the Council. Braybrooke passes along an observation by a Catholic bishop that Cardinal Heenan, after a visit with Cardinal Ottaviani, simply wrote to the Holy See's Congregation for the Doctrine of the Faith advising them if he did not hear from them by a certain date he would presume his participation was all right. 'He never did hear', Braybrooke comments. This vignette does ring true as to the way Catholic bishops at times need to act in order to proceed.

The involvement of Catholics in CCJ has been, in the years since the Council, far more important to Catholic-Jewish relations in England and Wales than involvement in the NCCJ in the U.S. Even before *Nostra Aetate* in 1965, the U.S. Bishops established a Bishops' Committee for Ecumenical and Interreligious Affairs and hired full-time directors for ecumenical and Catholic-Jewish relations, demonstrating their commitment to the dialogue. The Archbishop of Westminster set up the Cardinal's Commission for Catholic-Jewish relations which has functioned as a national commission for the Bishops' Conference of England and Wales. Sr. Margaret Shepherd of the Sisters of Sion, interestingly, is presently the full-time director of the CCJ, which has become both the principal organizing forum for local Jewish/Christian (including Jewish-Catholic) dialogues and a publisher of educational materials for promoting better Christian understanding of Jews and Judaism.[15]

Involvement of the Bishops' Conferences
The U.S. Catholic bishops came to the Second Vatican Council with a definite agenda. They wanted clear, strong statements in three interrelated

areas: ecumenism, religious liberty, and Catholic-Jewish relations, and exerted their influence both on the floor and behind the scenes to ensure the passage of all three documents. With reference to the Catholic-Jewish statement, *Nostra Aetate no. 4* (other religious traditions, such as Islam, Buddhism, Hinduism and Native Traditions were added to the Jewish statement to elicit the votes of Middle Eastern, Asian, and African bishops respectively), the Americans were joined by the influence of the German and the French bishops' conferences. Studies of the role of these conferences in lobbying for the Jewish statement have shown how decisive were their interventions.[16] There are no comparable studies of the role of the British bishops but some anecdotal evidence suggests that they were quiet on such matters. However, Thomas Stransky, CSP has offered a different view. Stranskey, a leading member of Cardinal Bea's Secretariat for Promoting Christian Unity (SPCU), was involved in the drafting of the statement which was originally intended to be limited to the Jews as the fourth chapter of the Council's decree on ecumenism titled, *De Iudaeis*, but which was ultimately enlarged to include other non-Christian religions in the form of *Nostra Aetate*. He suggests in private correspondence that the UK bishops were 'just as strong in supporting Nostra Aetate as the American bishops since 'in many ways they were closer to the European Nazi scene, to the Shoah and its consequences.' He judges that 'the bluntest and strongest' of all the speeches supporting the document was that of Cardinal John Heenan who also challenged Heschel's 3rd September 1963 New York Times article questioning the 'conversionary intent' of *De Judaeis*. Without mentioning Heschel's name, Heenan called the allegation 'sheer rhetoric' and insisted that the SPCU 'does not intend to use the document for an attack on the convictions of Jews'.[17]

Although I have been employed full time by the U.S. Conference of Catholic Bishops (USCCB) since 1977 to promote Catholic-Jewish relations, I am in the ironic situation of being at the same time perhaps the most and the least qualified person to make a comparison between the way the USCCB and the Bishops' Conference of England and Wales (BCEW) have fulfilled the Conciliar mandate of implementing *Nostra Aetate*.

My impression is that the two Conferences have gone about their tasks quite differently, and appropriately so given the differences in the communities and societies they serve.Successive Archbishops of Westminster, with one exception, for example, have been far more personally involved in participating in actual dialogues, such as the regular meetings of the CCJ, than have the Presidents of the USCCB. On the other hand, the U.S. Bishops' Committee for Ecumenical and Interreligious Affairs (BCEIA) and its Secretariat in our Washington headquarters is more active in producing statements, dialogues, and resources, than are their counterparts in the national offices of the BCEW. The official Guidelines for Catholic/Jewish Relations issued by the Committee for Catholic-Jewish Relations of the Bishops' Conference of England and Wales in 1994, for example, simply makes as its own the statement, God's Mercy Endures Forever: Guidelines on the Presentation of Jews and Judaism in Catholic Preaching issued by the U.S. bishops' conference in 1988.

The President of the USCCB relies on the duly appointed Episcopal Moderator for Catholic-Jewish Relations, Cardinal William Keeler, while the royal patronage of the CCJ virtually requires the personal involvement of the Cardinal Archbishop of Westminster in official interreligious meetings. And with ten times the number of Catholics in the U.S. as in England and Wales, America can more easily establish and maintain direct dialogues, while providing guidance to (and, often, receiving guidance from) local, diocesan efforts across the country.

Another difference is that in the U.S. there is no single Jewish entity, such as the Orthodox Chief Rabbinate in the U.K., which can claim to be an interlocutor, and is accepted as such by the Jewish community. The nearest American equivalent is the National Council of Synagogues (NCS), which represents the rabbinical and congregational associations of Reform and Conservative Judaism. Since this represents over 90% of religiously affiliated Jews, the bishops' twice-yearly meetings with the NCS are important, indeed. The BCEIA meets twice a year with representatives of the Orthodox community, while the Secretariat for Ecumenical and Interreligious Affairs maintains constant communication with other Jewish agencies interested in Jewish-Christian relations.

The consequent benefit is that at one and the same time the Secretariat can be engaged with the major religious rabbinic and congregational bodies and produce educational programs and resources with various Jewish agencies, such as the American Jewish Committee and the Anti-Defamation League. It is therefore in contact with different Jewish groups who provide an insight into the wide range of views and discussion within the Jewish community.

Another difference that I tentatively propose is that when American Catholics entered the dialogue around the time of the Council, they did so with an immense institutional strength, bolstered by a strong mandate of their bishops and the academic resources of Catholic colleges and universities around the country. The U.S. bishops set up a Secretariat and issued official guidelines to implement Nostra Aetate early in 1967 (revised, 1985), and major statements in 1975 and again in 1985 and 2000 to implement and to some extent anticipate statements of the Holy See's Commission for Religious Relations with the Jews.

The general guidelines put out by the bishops' national office were greatly expanded on the local level by the dioceses of New York, Long Island, and Brooklyn (working together) and by others, such as Newark, Detroit, Philadelphia and Los Angeles. These in turn influenced the revision of the national guidelines in 1985 as well as the statements of the Holy See.[18] In the U.S. much of the work of the dialogue has been carried out by laypeople and clergy, religious education professionals and diocesan ecumenical officers working together throughout the country.

In Britain, on the other hand, much of the actual, ongoing implementation of *Nostra Aetate* centred around the work of the Sisters of Sion, especially in London, while official involvement by the Catholic hierarchy appears to have waxed and waned depending on the interest of the particular Archbishop of Westminster of the time. Official Church guidelines in Britain have, and their own literature is admirably frank in acknowledging this, reflected statements already developed elsewhere, particularly in the U.S. where the Catholic community has more Catholic colleges and universities to draw on than the rest of the Catholic world combined.

In addition to the official BCEIA statements mentioned above,[19] the joint statements of the ongoing dialogue Consultation with the National Council of Synagogues has produced a series of statements, which have influenced others.

Moral Values in Public Education, 1989
Against Pornography, 1991
Against Holocaust Revisionism, 1993
Reflections on the Millennium, 1998
To End the Death Penalty, 1999
Joint Statement Condemning Acts of Religious Hatred, 2000

Children and the Environment, 2000
Filled with Sadness, Charged with Hope, 2001
Reflections on Covenant and Mission, 2002

The Bishop of Oxford (Anglican) in his excellent survey of the issues of Christian-Jewish dialogue, singles out for praise the latest of these joint statements.[20]

Measures of Implementation

The major success of implementation of the Conciliar vision in both the US and Britain can be seen in the revolution in religious educational materials. These have been analysed to show the vastly more positive and accurate portrayal of Jews and Judaism in current textbooks as opposed to those in use before the Second Vatican Council. In the UK, the Sisters of Sion have been involved in monitoring textbooks and the training of teachers.[21]   In the US, studies of Catholic textbooks were undertaken before the Council by Sr. Rose Thering, OP; a decade after the Council, by myself, and in 1992 by Dr. Philip Cunningham of Boston College. Each study has shown progressive improvement and one can be quite sanguine about the present curricula in Catholic classrooms.

Likewise, in both the U.S. and the U.K., there is direct involvement in the training of religion teachers, and a wide variety of programmes. The Bishops' Conference of England and Wales has recently mandated that two weeks of every year Catholic elementary students should study Judaism.

In both the U.S. and Britain, however, it is harder to verify progress made in seminary education and hence in the Church's other 'delivery system' for bringing its official teachings to its adherents, the pulpit. Finally, there is the liturgy itself. Both British and U.S. Catholic theologians have very helpful notions about what can be done to bring the lectionary, for example, into fuller accord with the Council's teachings. But neither the British nor the American bishops have authority to make substantive changes in the lectionary readings or virtually any other aspect of the liturgy for that matter. Such changes can only be authorized by Rome. And Rome, quite appropriately and for quite appropriate historical reasons, is extremely conservative about liturgical innovation.

Appendix: The Sisters of Sion

When the world's Anglican bishops met in Lambeth, England, in 1988, they desired to develop guidelines on Jewish-Christian relations that could be commended for study throughout the Anglican Communion. The commission drafting the statement for the Lambeth Conference devoted a section to the highly-charged question of 'the one mission and the mutual witness' of Jews and Christians.[22] While acknowledging other possible approaches within the Anglican Communion, the commission sought to explain its belief that the Church's basic approach to the Jews as the People of God should be one of shared mission, 'the sanctification or hallowing of God's name in the world', rather than conversion. Interestingly, the example of the change in orientation that they cited was not Anglican, but a Catholic religious order. The passage states, in full:

> We offer as one model of how Christian concern for the Jews remains but in a radically altered form, the work of the Sisters of Sion. The Roman Catholic Congregation of Our Lady of Sion was founded in the mid-nineteenth century with the avowed aim of the conversion of Jews. Under the impact of the ecumenical and biblical movements, the Holocaust, and for theological reasons, the aim of the congregation has completely changed. Keeping in mind the fundamental inspiration of the founders that there was a need for a congregation that would remind Christians of their Jewish roots, they moved away from the original goal to a fresh understanding of the permanent election of the Jewish people and the validity of the Jewish religion in both the past and the present. The sisters are now committed to the task of spreading among Christians an understanding of Jewish religious values and of theological issues concerning the permanent existence of the Jewish people alongside the Church.[23]

It is not surprising, on reflection, that Anglican bishops should look to the Sisters of Sion as a model. Not only in England and Wales, but in Australia, Canada, Ireland and elsewhere, the Sisters of Sion have been in the forefront of Catholic-Jewish dialogue since their own 'conversion' because of their experience hiding thousands of Jews in convents during the Second World War. So when the Second Vatican Council mandated a 'dialogue of mutual esteem' with Jews in 1965, the Sisters of Sion were ready to provide the resources and expertise to implement it. In England and Wales, for example, a group of sisters working from their London Study Centre for Christian-Jewish Relations has provided materials and courses for Catholic clergy and educators, working collaboratively with the diocese of Westminster. They also provide a continuity of Catholic presence in more formal Jewish-Christian groups such as the Council of Christians and Jews, the Rainbow Group, and the Manor House Group.[24] Indeed, Sisters of Sion were members of the Lambeth drafting committee, mentioned above, and also subsequent drafting committees for statements of the Church of England on Christian-Jewish relations, as Harries documents.

The London Study Centre was established by the sisters across the street from their school for girls on 8 September 1962. By the time the Council approved *Nostra Aetate* on 28 October 1965, the Centre already had a small specialised library[25] and two of the sisters were working on advanced degrees in the field. Through numerous talks, lectures, and courses at the Centre, students and faculty of colleges of education, teachers' organizations and Catholic seminaries studied the history of Christian prejudice against Jews and Judaism, the Jewish roots of Christianity, and how to overcome anti-Judaism present in catechetical textbooks and traditional interpretations of the Scriptures. Likewise, the sisters arranged for Catholic groups talks by Jewish scholars, visits to synagogues, demonstration seder services, and (more recently) Yom HaShoah observances.

One of the Centre's most remarkable accomplishments, given the limitations of its resources, has been its series of pamphlets for clergy and teachers, distributed to Catholics through the Westminster diocese, as well as commentaries on the lectionary readings and a 'Judaism kit' for students in secondary schools. Seminars for Catholic scholars, clergy and teachers have been organized at the Archbishop's House, Westminster, and at Leo Baeck College. The annual Cardinal Bea Memorial Lecture, normally given by a Jewish and Christian scholar sharing the platform, reaches a significant number of people, introducing the wide variety of issues involved in dialogue.

The Sisters of Sion have not influenced the dialogue in the U.S. to the same degree. Unlike England where the Sisters of Sion have been deeply involved before the Second Vatican Council, the U.S. Sisters themselves have not been as well established, having one school in Kansas City, but none in the rest of the country. The direction and work of the implementation in the US has been more directly at the hands of diocesan ecumenical officers and, on the national level, the Secretariat for Ecumenical and Interreligious Affairs.

Notes

1. Paul Weller, ed., *Religions in the UK: A Multi-Faith Directory* (Derby: The University of Derby, 1997).

2. Weller, *op. cit.* p. 217. In 1780, for example, the total number of Catholics in England and Wales was only 80,000. By 1840 the number had increased to about 300,000. While there were only 30 Catholic chapels in England and Wales in 1796, there were almost 600 registered in 1851. R. Leidtke & S. Wendehorst, *The Emancipation of Catholics, Jews and Protestants: Minorities and the Nation-State in 19th Century Europe* (Manchester: Manchester University Press, 1999), pp. 14-15.

3. Weller, *op. cit*, p. 382.

4. R. W. Linker, 'The English Roman Catholics and Emancipation: The Politics of Persuasion', *Journal of Ecclesiastical History* 27 (1976), pp. 151-180. Other studies of Catholic emancipation include: W. Hinde, *Catholic Emancipation: A Shake to Men's Minds* (Oxford: Oxford University Press, 1992); G. Machin, *The Catholic Question in English Politics* (Oxford: Oxford University Press, 1964); and D. Quinn, *Patronage and Piety: The Politics of English Roman Catholicism 1850-1900* (Basingstoke, 1993).

5. Cecil Roth, *A History of the Jews in England* (Oxford: Oxford University Press, 1964; first edition, 1941), p. 252.

6. Roth, *idem*.

7. Todd M. Endelman, *The Jews of Britain, 1656 to 2000* (Berkeley: University of California Press, 2002) discusses his differences with Roth in the introduction, *et passim*.

8. See Endelman, *op. cit.*, pp. 33-55.

9. An excellent history of the development of the Council of Christians and Jews in Britain is given in Marcus Braybrooke, *Children of the One God* (London: Vallentine-Mitchell, 1991).

10. Lloyd P. Gartner, 'The Two Continuities of Antisemitism in the

United States' in Shmuel Almog (ed.), *Antisemitism through the Ages* (Oxford: Pergamon Press, 1988), p. 312.

11. Mary Christine Athans, *The Coughlin-Fahey Connection: Father Charles E. Coughlin, Father Denis Fahey, C.S.Sp., and Religious Anti-Semitism in the United States, 1938-1954* (American University Studies, Series VII, Peter Lang Publishing, 1992).

12. Braybrooke, *op. cit.*, p. 17.

13. *Ibid.* p. 33.

14. *Ibid.* p. 38.

15. During my stay in Cambridge, I interviewed Bishop Charles Henderson, Chair of Catholic-Jewish Liaison Committee and Fr. Michael Seed, who has been involved in the dialogue on the national level, representing the Archbishop of Westminster. I was told that while there are some direct engagements of Catholic parishes and synagogues, most Catholic involvement has not been the result of official diocesan structures but the programmes and dialogues run by the CCJ.

16. See John M. Oesterreicher, *The New Encounter between Christians and Jews* (New York: Philosophical Library, 1986) and Michael Phayer, *The Catholic Church and the Holocaust, 1930-1965* (Indiana: Indiana University Press, 2000).

17. 29 September 1964, ACTA III, 37-39, 90th General Congregation; original English in *The Tablet* (3 October 1964, p. 1125). Heenan was the co-vice-president of the SPCU plenarium, which included both members and consultors.

18. Like my predecessor, Fr. Edward Flannery, I have been a Consultor to the Holy See and a member of the International Catholic-Jewish Liaison Committee virtually since I began working for the USCCB in 1977. Aside from Bishop McMahon for one quinquennial appointment, to my knowledge, the British bishops have not been so consistently represented in these bodies. Edward Kessler, reading this paper, made the cogent suggestion that such ongoing links between the US bishops and the Holy See in the area of Catholic-Jewish relations, may be one reason for the relatively greater influence of US statements on those of Rome.

19. These can be found on the website maintained by the Center for Christian-Jewish Learning of Boston College (http://www.bc.edu/research/cjl).

20. Richard Harries, *After the Evil: Christianity and Judaism in the Shadow of the Holocaust* (Oxford: Oxford University Press, 2003), pp. 132-133.

Harries states in his conclusion that 'It is the Roman Catholic Church above all that has pioneered a new approach to Judaism.', p. 231.

21. Sr. Claire Jardine, who is involved in the education of Catholic religion teachers for more accurate understanding of Jews and Judaism, told me that there is only one religion textbook series used in Catholic schools and catechetical classes, and that it is quite good.

22. Richard Harries, who chaired the drafting commission, describes the 'somewhat torturous path' of the development of this and subsequent Anglican statements on Jewish-Christian relations in *After the Evil*, pp. 118-123.

23. *Ibid.*, p. 120. Lambeth's description of the post-Holocaust history of the Sisters of Sion is quite accurate. A more thorough study, 'From Conversion to Dialogue: the Sisters of Sion and the Jews' was written by one of the Sisters, Charlotte Klein, and published in Summer, 1981 in *The Journal of Ecumenical Studies*.

24. For this paper, I interviewed Sisters Margaret Shepherd, Claire Jardine and Mary Kelly. Charlotte Klein, who was deeply involved from the beginning, is now deceased. Mary Kelly has written the history of 'The London Centre for Christian-Jewish Relations' for the *Journal Christian-Jewish Relations* 16.4 (1983), pp. 47-53. On the Manor House dialogues, see Tony Bayfield and Marcus Braybrooke, (eds.), *Dialogue with a Difference: The Manor House Group Experience* (London: SCM Press, 1992). Harries was also a member of that ongoing dialogue.

25. The larger Sion library in Rome, set up at the request of Cardinal Augustin Bea as a means of implementing *Nostra Aetate*, has recently been moved to the new Bea Centre in the Gregorian University in Rome. See www.sidic.org.

13

Reflections on Covenant and Mission

John T. Pawlikowski

The release of the study document *Reflections on Covenant and Mission* from an ongoing consultation between the National Council of Synagogues in the USA and the U.S. Catholic Bishops' Committee on Ecumenical and Interreligious Affairs on 12 August 2002,[1] caused a firestorm in sectors of the Catholic Church with Cardinal Avery Dulles taking a lead in attacking the document.[2] While no single document within mainline Protestantism has elicited quite the same vigorous response, a number of European statements such as the declaration from the Rhineland Synod[3] in Germany have caused controversy. And some evangelical Protestant groups in the United States have severely critiqued several statements, including the recent Pontifical Biblical Commission document entitled *The Jewish People and their Sacred Scriptures in the Christian Bible* and the statement *A Sacred Obligation* released in September 2002 by the ecumenical Christian Scholars Group on Christian-Jewish Relations. Clearly the discussion of the theology of the Jewish-Christian relationship and its implication for the churches' understanding of mission in relation to Jews has moved to the centre stage in recent years. In order to understand the contemporary discussion it is necessary to review recent history on this question.

In an address to the Catholic Theological Society of America's annual meeting in 1986 the Canadian theologian Gregory Baum, who served as an expert at the II Vatican Council and worked on *Nostra Aetate*, argued that 'the Church's recognition of the spiritual status of the Jewish religion is the most dramatic example of doctrinal turn-about in the age-old *magisterium ordinarium*' to occur at the Council.[4] For centuries Christian theology, beginning with most of the major Church Fathers in the second century and thereafter, was infected with a viewpoint which saw the Church as replacing 'old' Israel in the covenantal relationship with God. This replacement theology relegated Jews to a miserable and marginal status which could only be overcome through conversion.[5]

Vatican II's *Nostra Aetate*, together with many parallel Protestant documents, fundamentally changed Christianity's theological posture relative to Jews and Judaism that had permeated its theology, art, and practice for nearly eighteen hundred years. Jews were now to be seen as integral to the ongoing divine covenant. Jesus and early Christianity were portrayed as deeply rooted in a constructive sense in the religiosity of Second Temple Judaism (particularly its Pharisaic branch). Jews were not to be held collectively accountable for the death of Jesus. Vatican II did not 'forgive' Jews of the so-called crime of deicide as some newspaper headlines proclaimed. Rather it argued that there existed no basis for such a charge in the first place.

One indication of how thorough the change was on the Catholic side can be seen in the references used by the Bishops at Vatican II to justify a transformation in the Church's understanding of its relationship with the Jewish People. Dr. Eugene J. Fisher, who oversees Catholic-Jewish relations for the United States Conference of Catholic Bishops, wrote some years ago that '*Nostra Aetate*, for all practical purposes, begins the Church's teaching ... concerning a theological or, more precisely, a doctrinal understanding of the relationship between the Church as "People of God" and "God's People" Israel'.[6] Examining chapter four of *Nostra Aetate* we find scarcely any reference to the usual sources cited in conciliar documents: the Church Fathers, papal statements and previous conciliar documents. Rather, the Declaration returns to Romans 9–11, as if to say that the Church is now taking up where Paul left off in his insistence that Jews remain part of the covenant after the Resurrection despite the theological ambiguity involved in such a statement. Without saying it so explicitly, the 2,221 Council members who voted for *Nostra Aetate* were in fact stating that everything that had been said about the Christian-Jewish relationship since Paul moved in a direction they could no longer support. It is interesting to note that Nostra Aetate never makes reference to the several passages in the Letter to the Hebrews where the original covenant appears to be abrogated after Christ and the Jewish law overturned (Heb. 7:12; 8:13 and 10:9). Given the interpretive role of a Church Council in the Catholic tradition this omission is theologically significant. It indicates that the Council Fathers judged these texts from Hebrews as a theologically inappropriate resource for thinking about the relationship between

Christianity and Judaism today. I will return to this point subsequently in discussing Cardinal Avery Dulles' reaction to the study document *Reflections On Covenant And Mission*.

In reality the theological about-face on the Jews at Vatican II represents, along with such closely related statements as the affirmation of the democratic constitutional state in the *Declaration on Religious Liberty* and the depiction of the Catholic Church as 'subsisting' in the one true Church in which the other Christian churches are to be regarded as integral members in the document on ecumenism, one of the central theological developments at the Council. Unfortunately, its full significance for all of Christianity has been insufficiently recognised even until now within Catholicism. This is also largely true within Protestantism where the several ground-breaking statements on continued Jewish covenantal inclusion have not significantly impacted the course of Christian theological reflection in the last forty years.

The German theologian Johannes-Baptist Metz is one Christian scholar who acknowledged the overall theological implications of the recent documents from the Christian churches on the understanding of the Christian-Jewish relationship. Metz has insisted that these implications go far beyond the parameters of the Christian-Jewish dialogue. Especially after the Holocaust, Metz insists, they involve a 'revision of Christian theology itself'.[7] Yet we have seen little impact from these documents thus far on theology as such. One looks in vain for citations to *Nostra Aetate* and subsequent papal/Vatican documents on Christian-Jewish relations or to the major parallel Protestant statements in books or documents reflecting on Christian theological identity outside the context of the dialogue with Jews. Yet, historically, Christian identity, including in particular Christological affirmation, has been rooted in the notion of the Church as the replacement for the Jewish People in the covenantal relationship with God.

Jewish participants in the dialogue with Christians have sometimes noted the above reality with dismay. They are right in expressing their concern. Do these declarations on the Church's relationship with the Jewish People have relevance only when Christians are actually speaking with Jews? Or are they brought into the picture when Christians are conversing among themselves in terms of theological identity. Only if we begin to see a development of the latter can we say that there has been genuine reception of *Nostra Aetate* and the Protestant declarations within the

Christian community.

Let me cite two examples where I have seen a failure to understand the profound implications of *Nostra Aetate* and similar Protestant statements. The first was in the process leading up to the international ecumenical gathering held at Santiago de Compostela, Spain in 1993. In the preparatory drafts of the major statement to be issued from that gathering, the vision of Christian self-identity was dangerously close to displacement theology. Yet little objection was initially raised to this perspective either by Protestant or Catholic church leaders involved with the process until some of us connected with Christian-Jewish dialogue raised a fuss. Eventually, the final document backed away from the displacement theme but did not fully embody the recent Christian statements on the Church's relationship to the Jewish people. For me, this experience illustrated how far we are from integrating the recent documents on Christian–Jewish relations into mainstream Christian theological thinking.

A second example occurred during the October 1997 meeting at the Vatican on the Church and anti-Judaism. I was one of three American scholars participating in this meeting, part of the Vatican's preparation for the new millenium and specifically for the anticipated papal apology for antisemitism which took place on the first Sunday of Lent, 2000, and shortly thereafter during the papal visit to Jerusalem. Throughout the meeting I was often dismayed at the lack of acquaintance with the theological vision of *Nostra Aetate* displayed by some of the participants, including high curial officials. One bishop argued that the primary purpose of the Jewish People from a religious perspective was to teach Christians how to suffer. This gathering further convinced me that much work remains if the profound implications of chapter four of *Nostra Aetate* are to be realised within Catholicism and lead to the about-face in Christian theology that Gregory Baum suggested they would inaugurate.

Nostra Aetate and the concomitant Protestant documents have given rise to several attempts by theologians to restate the basic understanding of Christianity's relationship to Judaism. I have summarised these theological developments in a number of my own writings.[8] They include

(1) an appreciation that the Jewish covenant remains valid after the coming of Christ;

(2) Christianity is not automatically superior to Judaism, nor the simple

fulfillment of Judaism as traditionally claimed;

(3) the Sinai covenant is, in principle, as crucial to Christian faith expression as the covenant in Christ. There was no 'Old' Testament for Jesus nor should there be for us; and

(4) Christianity needs to reincorporate dimensions from its original Jewish matrix in its contemporary faith expression.

I realise that most, if not all, of these assertions may appear controversial. But I believe they are demanded by the revolution in theological thinking about the Christian-Jewish relationship represented by chapter four of *Nostra Aetate* and its companion documents from the Protestant churches. To repeat Metz, the new theological understanding of Jewish–Christian relations affects the basic face of Christian theology. That it may also do so with respect to Jewish theological self-understanding is something upon which Jewish scholars need to reflect. Some have begun that process as the recent Jewish statement on Christianity *Dabru Emet* and its accompanying theological volume have shown.[9]

The Christian theologians who moved to reexamine Christianity's theological understanding of Judaism just prior to and following Vatican II tended to focus on Paul's reflections on the post-Easter Jewish–Christian relationship which he articulated in Romans 9–11. These chapters, indicated above, served as the basis for Vatican II's approach to the Jewish–Christian issue. And they have been central to Protestant re-evaluations as well, including the recent statement from the Leuenberg Fellowship of Reformation Churches in Europe in 2001, entitled *Church and Israel*.

The first Christian scholars in modern times who tackled Jewish-Christian Relations viewed Romans 9-11 – and its assertion that God remains faithful to the original people of the covenant – as the basis for a reconsideration of Christology. They argued that 'newness' in Christ cannot be stated in a manner that relegates Jews to covenantal removal. Some of these pioneering scholars, after considerable reflection, were forced to conclude that it is not possible for the Church to go beyond saying what Paul himself said, i.e., that reconciliation between an assertion of redemptive 'newness' in Christ and the concomitant affirmation of the continued participation of the Jewish People in the ongoing covenant remains a 'mystery', presently understandable to God. Only at the end time might we come to see the lack of contradiction in these twin theological statements. Associated with this line of thought were scholars such as Kurt Hruby, Jacques Maritain and Jean Danielou. This was also the perspective of Cardinal Augustine Bea who initially was suspicious of such new theological thinking about the Christian–Jewish relationship,[10] but eventually played a central role in Vatican II's approval of *Nostra Aetate* and its initial implementation immediately following the close of the Council.

These early attempts to eradicate a Christology rooted in Jewish covenantal displacement continued to insist on a central role for Christ in all human salvation as well as on a fulfillment dimension in Jesus' Incarnation and Resurrection. No effort was made to erase the apparent contradiction between the affirmation of Jewish covenantal continuity and fulfillment in Christ. Rather these scholars argued for a dual proclamation of Jewish covenantal inclusion and salvific fulfillment in Christ as integral to Christian faith expression.

In these scholars' perspective, God remains Sovereign both of Jews and Christians. Therein is to be found the basis for the reconciliation of these two seemingly contradictory assertions. As we shall see subsequently, this tension is still far from being overcome even in more recent theological writings on the Christian understanding of the encounter with Judaism.

Scripture scholars in particular have played a major role in the process of revising Christianity's theological approach to Judaism. We are in the midst of a revolution in New Testament studies and our understanding of the early church, as well as the development of Judaism (or as some scholars such as Jacob Neusner would suggest, the 'Judaisms' of the time). The dominance of the 'Religionsgeschichte' approach within Christian biblical scholarship, notably in the writings of Rudolf Bultmann and also some of his disciples such as Ernst Kasemann and Helmut Koesster, has significantly receded. Their exegetical framework undercut any notion of Jesus' concrete ties to, and dependence upon, biblical and Second Temple Judaism. This in turn tended to produce an excessively universalistic interpretation of Jesus' message, which harboured the seeds of theological anti-Judaism and reinforced the traditional supersessionist interpretation of the Christian–Jewish relationship.

There have been a number of leading biblical scholars, some with a continuing transcontinental influence, who have attempted to remove Judaism from the heart of the Christian faith, an image that has been central to Pope John Paul II's numerous writings on Christianity and Judaism.[11] One of the most prominent, Gerhard Kittel, is the original editor of the widely used *Theological Dictionary of The New Testament*.[12] Kittel viewed postbiblical Jews as forming a community in dispersion. 'Authentic Judaism', he wrote, 'abides by the symbol of the stranger wandering restless and homeless on the face of the earth'.[13] And the prominent exegete Martin Noth, whose *History of Israel* became a standard reference for students and professors alike, spoke of Israel as a strictly 'religious community' which experienced a slow, agonizing death in the first century C.E. Noth argues that Jewish history reached its culmination in the arrival of Jesus:

> Jesus himself no longer formed part of the history of Israel. In him the history of Israel had come, rather, to its real end. What did belong to the history of Israel was the process of his rejection and condemnation by the Jerusalem religious community.[14]

After this condemnation the history of Israel moved quickly to its end.

The implication of Noth's perspective is that the Jewish People and its tradition no longer have a role to play in the Church's theological understanding of Jesus' ministry. Such a view has not altogether disappeared in Christianity, even if redefined within a wider global context. Prominent Asian Christian theologian S. Wesley Ariarajah who worked for many years in the interreligious office of the World Council of Churches has termed the effort to return Jesus to his Jewish context in such documents as *A Sacred Obligation*[15] a 'futile attempt' in terms of creating Christian faith expression in a non-European context. He acknowledges Jesus' connections with the Jewish community of his day but in his view these carry no theological significance. He feels much closer to the Eastern religions in terms of Christian theology.[16]

I am not suggesting that Noth and Ariarajah hold the same theological views of Judaism. Noth regarded Judaism as spiritually dead after the coming of Christ while Ariarajah views Judaism as an authentic religion, but of no significance for understanding Christian faith, particularly in a non-European context. However, there does exist a similarity. Neither sees the Jewishness of Jesus as theologically significant for the interpretation of his message today. I find this perspective quite troubling. While I strongly support the contextualisation of Christian theology in differing cultural settings, understanding the Jewish context of Jesus remains indispensable for an accurate understanding of his basic teachings. This point has been strongly emphasised by scholars such as James Charlesworth and Cardinal Carlo Martini, SJ, the retired Archbishop of Milan, a prominent biblical scholar in his own right. Cardinal Martini has written that 'Without a sincere feeling for the Jewish world, and a direct experience of it, one cannot fully understand Christianity. Jesus is fully Jewish, the apostles are Jewish, and one cannot doubt their attachment to the tradition of their forefathers'.[17] And the 1985 *Vatican Notes* on preaching and teaching about Jews and Judaism declares that 'Jesus was and always remained a Jew.... Jesus is fully a man of his time, and his environment—the Jewish Palestinian one of the 1st century, the anxieties and hope of which he shared'.[18] Fortunately not all Asian theologians share Ariarajah's perspective. The prominent Vietnamese–American scholar Peter Phan has been outspoken in terms of the Jewish context of Jesus' message. He is in fact one of the signatories of the statement *A Sacred Obligation*. Scholars such as Phan, while trying to integrate Christ and his message into Asian cultural traditions understand that such integration cannot authentically take place without an effort to understand the original message of the New Testament. Such understanding is impossible without a deep appreciation of Jewish religious thought at the time of Jesus during the New Testament's composition.

Another example of a biblical scholar whose writings attempted to undercut Jesus' ties to Judaism is Rudolf Bultmann. He has exercised a decisive influence over Christian biblical interpretation for many years although this influence has begun to wane in recent years. Arthur Droge has spoken of a recent liberation of biblical scholarship from the Bultmannian captivity on the question of Jesus and Judaism.[19]

For Bultmann a Jewish People cannot be said to exist with the onset of Christianity. In his perspective Jewish religious expression removed God to a distant realm. In contrast, the continued presence of Christ in prayer and worship enabled individual Christians to draw closer to God. Bultmann's view stands contrary to the position of most contemporary biblical scholars and church documents which depict Jesus and his disciples as profoundly intertwined with the Judaism of the time.

There is little question that the dominant exegetical approach during most of the twentieth century continued to sustain the classical covenantal displacement theology with respect to Judaism. It is only in the latter part of the twentieth century and into the present century that scholars such as James Charlesworth, W. D. Davies, E. P. Sanders, Douglas Hare, Daniel Harring, Clemens Thoma and Robin Scroggs, to name but a few, have moved New Testament interpretation in the opposite direction to Bultmann and Kittel. This new exegesis is gradually forcing theologians to rethink significantly the theology of the Christian-Jewish relationship, redirecting it away from the long dominant supersessionist approach. There is now an emphasis on a continuing interrelationship, rooted in the affirmation of ongoing Jewish covenantal inclusion after the Christ Event.

The Leuenberg Church Fellowship, an association of the Reformation churches in Europe, takes this new exegesis as a starting point for its theological reflections on the Christian-Jewish relationship. Its 2001 document *Church And Israel* argues that the interrelationship between the Church and Israel is not a marginal issue for Christianity but rather represents a central dimension of ecclesiology. The relationship with Israel is viewed as an indispensable foundation of Christian faith. The Church is required to reflect on its relationship with Judaism because of its profound linkage to the Jewish community in its beginnings. The document states that 'the biblical texts referring to these beginnings do not only speak of the historical origin of the Church and thus of the historical relation with Israel; they also form the starting point and critical point of reference (fons et iudex) for all theological reflection.[20]

Thus, recent biblical scholarship alongside official church teaching now teaches that any portrayal of Jesus that separates him from the Judaism of his time in the manner of Bultmann, Noth or even Ariarajah represents a truncated and distorted presentation of his message and mission. It is ironic that, at least in the case of Ariarajah, he would want to inculturate the gospel by de-inculturating Jesus himself. Certainly it is legitimate to present the image of Jesus through various cultural symbols and images but Jesus the Jew is not one among manifold ways of presenting Jesus. It forms the base for authentically interpreting his fundamental message. Without it, efforts to translate the meaning of Jesus' message into a variety of cultures, a quite legitimate and necessary undertaking, will likely eviscerate an important dimension of this message.

One of the best contemporary summaries of Jesus' relationship to the Judaism of his time, and its implications for a theology of Christian-Jewish covenantal bonding, can be found in the writings of Robin Scroggs. His view was accepted by the late Cardinal Joseph Bernardin of Chicago, a leader in promoting Jewish–Christian reconciliation.[21]

Scroggs emphasises the following points:

(1) The movement begun by Jesus and continued after his death in Palestine can best be described as a reform movement within Judaism. Little or no evidence exists to suggest a separate sense of identity within the emerging Christian community.
(2) Paul understood his mission to the Gentiles as fundamentally a mission out of Judaism which aimed at extending God's original and continuing call to the Jewish People to the Gentiles.
(3) Prior to the end of the Jewish war with the Romans in 70 C.E., it is difficult to speak of a separate Christian reality. Followers of Jesus did not seem to understand themselves as part of a separate religion from Judaism. A distinctive Christian identity only began to develop after the Romano-Jewish war.
(4) The later parts of the New Testament do exhibit the beginnings of a sense of separation between Church and synagogue, but they also retain a sense of continuing contact with the Christian community's original Jewish matrix.[22]

While not every New Testament scholar subscribes to each and every point made by Scroggs, a consensus is definitely developing that the process of church–synagogue separation was longer and more complex than was once believed. This picture significantly challenges how most Christians have previously been taught. They were raised, as was I, with the notion that by the time Jesus died on Calvary the church was clearly established as a distinct religious body apart from Judaism. This understanding was subsequently expanded, especially by the Church Fathers, into what is known as the adversos Judaeos tradition which had as a theological foundation a total displacement of the Jewish People from the covenant.[23] But more and more, thanks to such scholars as Robin Scroggs, we are coming to see that many people in the very early days of Christianity did not interpret the significance of the Jesus movement as inaugurating a new, totally separate religious community that would stand over against Judaism.

It does not appear that Jesus conveyed to his disciples and followers a clear sense that he meant to create a new and distinct religious entity called the Church which was to be totally independent of Judaism. This separate identity only emerged gradually well after his death. We now know through the research of scholars such as Robert Wilken, Wayne Meeks, Alan Segal and Anthony Saldarini that this development was of several centuries duration in a number of areas of the Christian world.[24] Evidence now exists for regular Christian participation in Jewish worship, particularly in the East, during the second and third centuries and, in a few places, until the fourth century.

The challenge now facing Christianity in light of this new research on the origins of the Church is whether the creation of a totally separate religious community was actually in the mind of Jesus himself. Cardinal Martini has addressed this and reintroduced the idea of 'schism' into the discussion of the basic theological relationship between Jews and Christians, a notion that first appeared in the early part of the twentieth century. Martini applies the term 'schism' to the original separation of the church and synagogue. For him the break between Jews and Christians represents the fundamental schism, far more consequential in negative terms than the two subsequent ruptures within Christianity itself. In introducing the notion of schism, Martini has interjected two important notions into the conversation. Firstly, schism should ideally not have occurred and secondly, should be seen as a temporary situation rather than a permanent reality. So schism, which had been applied previously to the two inter-Christian separations, implies a certain mandate to heal the rupture that has ensued.

There is legitimate room for debate as to the appropriateness of the term 'schism' in reflecting on the nature of the Christian-Jewish theological relationship today. I myself do not think it will take us too far but for Martini its strength is that Christians cannot forge a meaningful theological self-identity without restoring the profoundly Jewish context of Jesus' teaching. Clearly the Church will not return to an understanding of itself as one among many Jewish groups but in light of recent biblical scholarship, it needs to reassess how its self-identity is rooted in Judaism. This is the challenge of Ariarajah's contention that Judaism is inconsequential for Christian theological self-understanding. Christian theology has to respond in the coming years to this challenge. Is Ariarajah or is Johannes-Baptist Metz correct? In opposition to Ariarajah, Metz has argued that 'Christians can form and sufficiently understand their identity only in the face of the Jews'.[25] For Metz such a vision involves a definite reintegration of Jewish history and Jewish beliefs into Christian theological consciousness and statement. Jewish history is not merely Christian pre-history; rather, it forms an integral, continuing part of ecclesial history.

As biblical scholars and theologians have begun to probe the implications of this new vision of Jesus as being profoundly intertwined with the Jewish community, two new approaches, which emphasize covenantal inclusion in the theological relationship between the Church and the Jewish People, have emerged. Although offering different nuances, both affirm a central linkage between Judaism and Christianity. We can characterise the two trends as 'single covenant' and 'double covenant', although a few scholars also call for an understanding of the Jewish–Christian relationship within a multi-covenant framework.[26]

The 'single covenant' perspective sees Jews and Christians as basically united within one covenantal tradition with its origins at Sinai. This one ongoing covenant was in no way ruptured through the Christ Event but rather the coming of Christ represented the decisive moment when the Gentiles were able to enter fully into the special relationship with God already enjoyed by Jews, a relationship they continue to maintain. Some scholars suggest that the decisive features of the Christ Event impact all people, including Jews, but not in a way that results in the breaking of already existing Jewish covenantal ties. Others argue that the Christian appropriation and reinterpretation of the original covenantal tradition in and through Jesus apply primarily to non-Jews. This would seem to be the opinion of Cardinal Walter Kasper, President of the Pontifical Commission for Religious Relations with the Jews. Kasper argues that Jews represent an altogether special case in the history of salvation from the Christian perspective. This view has also been expressed by Cardinal Kasper's colleague at the Vatican, Archbishop Michael Fitzgerald who heads the office for relations with peoples of other faiths except for the Jews. This is essentially a view shared by Pope John Paul II as well. One major Protestant theologian who promoted the single covenantal perspective was Paul van Buren, although towards the end of his career he seemed to return to a more classical outlook rooted in the thought of his mentor Karl Barth.[27]

There are several problems with the single covenant approach. In the first instance it is dependent on a linear understanding of the Jewish-Christian relationship. Even if the linear notion is expressed in positive terms ('mother–daughter' or 'elder brother–younger brother') it still masks a form of theological fulfillment in Christianity that renders Judaism a second class religion. I fear that such an attitude lies behind Cardinal

Avery Dulles' assertion that there are not two independent covenants for Jews and Christians. Dulles insists that Jews are not saved through the Sinai covenant alone but only through the completion of the one covenant through Christ's death and resurrection.[28]

The linear thrust of single covenant perspective therefore appears increasingly problematical in light of new scholarship. An increasing number of scholars, such as Daniel Boyarin, are emphasizing what he terms the 'co-emergence' of Judaism and Christianity today from a common religious revolution in Second Temple Judaism. While the parallel approach still preserves a common Jewish/Christian core, it tends to stress their distinctive responses to the fundamental covenantal relationship. Such an outlook renders any simple notion of a single covenant, especially in terms of theological fulfillment, increasingly difficult to sustain. Yet I believe that Boyarin and others have made a strong case for their parallel approach.[29]

The 'double covenant' theory begins at more or less the same starting point as its single covenant counterpart. Jews and Christians continue to remain bonded despite their somewhat distinctive appropriation of the original covenantal tradition. But it prefers to highlight the distinctiveness of the two communities and their traditions particularly in terms of their experiences after the final separation of the church and synagogue. I personally favour this view though it certainly needs qualification.

Christians associated with this perspective insist on maintaining the view that through the ministry, teachings, and person of Jesus a vision of God emerged that was distinctively new. Even though there may well have been important groundwork laid for this emergence in Second Temple or Middle Judaism, the understanding of the divine-human relationship, and hence the covenantal relationship, through the Christ Event has to be seen as distinctive.[30]

An important example of the double covenant approach can be found in the writings of the German theologian Franz Mussner.[31] Mussner highlights Jesus' deep, positive links to the Jewish tradition of his day. He likewise rejects any interpretation of the Christ Event over against Judaism in terms of Jesus' fulfillment of biblical messianic prophecies. Rather, for Mussner, the uniqueness of the Christ Event arises from the complete identity of the work of Jesus, as well as his words and actions, with the work of God. As a result of the revelatory vision in Christ, the New Testament speaks about God with an anthropomorphic boldness not found to the same extent within the biblical or postbiblical tradition of Judaism.

For Mussner, the disciples' experience through their close association with Jesus, indicates 'a unity of action extending to the point of congruence of Jesus with God, an unheard of existential imitation of God by Jesus'.[32] But this imitation, Mussner insists, is in keeping with Jewish thinking, a contention that many Jewish scholars would certainly challenge, though Elliot Wolfson has argued that the rabbinic corpus does reveal some evidence of a modified incarnational theology.[33] For Mussner, the uniqueness of Jesus arises from the depth of his imitation of God. Consequently, the most distinctive feature of Christianity in contrast to Judaism is the notion of Incarnation rather than the fulfillment of messianic prophecies. And even this Christian particularity, he insists, represents an outgrowth of a sensibility profoundly Jewish at its core.

I have offered a somewhat similar approach, suggesting that the distinctive identity of Christianity vis-á-vis Judaism primarily resides in the notion of the Incarnation. And, with Mussner, I point to Jewish roots for this notion in the Pharisaic understanding of God's proximity to humanity. Ellis Rivkin has argued this represents the core of Pharisaism, the Jewish movement to which Jesus, according to the 1985 *Vatican Notes* on Jewish–Christian relations, stood closest.

There is another aspect to the ongoing relationship between the Church and the Jewish People from the perspective of covenantal theology, suggested by Metz and myself. A theology of the covenant cannot be oblivious to the contemporary problem of God, especially in light of the Holocaust. Irving Greenberg, for example, has maintained that the covenant now becomes voluntary in the shadow of Auschwitz. Today we must grapple with the issue of what kind of understanding of God can sustain a covenantal theology. We cannot glibly endorse biblical or classical theological categories without confronting this central question.[34]

In recent years it has become evident that neither the single nor double covenantal perspectives adequately address all the important issues, at least from the Christian side. Clearly we cannot forge a new covenantal theology in terms of the Christian–Jewish nexus without explicitly considering the Christological question. This lies behind the affirmation in the ecumenical statement *A Sacred Obligation* mentioned earlier which underlines that 'Affirming God's Enduring Covenant with the Jewish People has consequences for Christian understandings of salvation'. The accompanying paragraph spells out further the challenge facing the Church regarding Christology:

> Christians meet God's saving power in the person of Jesus Christ and believe that this power is available to all people in him. Christians have therefore taught for centuries that salvation is available only through Jesus Christ. With their recent realization that God's covenant with the Jewish people is eternal, Christians can now recognize in the Jewish tradition the redemptive power of God at work. If Jews, who do not share our faith in Christ, are in a saving covenant with God, then Christians need new ways of understanding the universal significance of Christ.[35]

Today a theology, which interprets the Christ Event as the fulfillment of Judaism and the inauguration, in Jesus' own lifetime, of a new religious community to replace the 'old Israel', no longer meets the test of historical accuracy. We need to find new ways of expressing Christological distinctiveness that acknowledges at the same time the ongoing participation of Jews in the salvific covenant.

Because Christology stands at the very nerve centre of Christian faith, re-evaluation of Christological affirmations cannot be undertaken superficially. There is a trend found especially among those most open to general interreligious understanding, that the Christ Event is only one of several authentic revelations with no particular universal aspect. Such a starting point is not acceptable to myself nor to many people who have championed a significant rethinking of the Church's theology of the Jewish People such as Cardinal Walter Kasper or the biblical scholars and theologians associated with *A Sacred Obligation*. We must maintain from the Christian side some understanding that the Christ Event carries universal significance.

It seems to me that Incarnational Christology provides the best possibility for preserving the universalistic dimensions of the Christ Event while also creating theological space for Judaism (a term proposed by Cardinal Joseph Bernardin of Chicago).[36] Cardinal Walter Kasper has insisted in several essays that any reconsideration of Christology in response to new biblical scholarship and official church documents must include some understanding of Christ's mission as universal. I wholly agree with Cardinal Kasper.

An important contribution to the Church's ongoing reinterpretation of the meaning of the Christ Event, in light of its new understanding of covenantal theology, appears in a document issued by the Pontifical Biblical Commisison in 2001. The document carries a supportive introduction by Cardinal Joseph Ratzinger under whose jurisdiction the Commission falls. Released without much fanfare, this new document offers several new possibilities of understanding the significance of the Christ Event while maintaining theological space for Judaism.[37]

Despite some significant limitations in the way it portrays postbiblical Judaism, the document makes an important contribution to the construction of a new Christology in the context of Jewish covenantal inclusion. Developing *Nostra Aetate*'s assertion that Jews remain in the ongoing covenant after the Christ Event, the document includes two statements that are particularly relevant for any discussion of Christology.

Firstly, Jewish messianic hopes are not in vain. This is coupled with a recognition that Jewish readings of the Hebrew Scriptures in terms of understanding human redemption represent an authentic interpretation of these texts. Here are the seeds of what appears to be a recognition of a distinct salvific path for the Jewish People as a theological principle. In this connection Cardinal Kasper has said that 'if they (i.e. the Jews) follow their own conscience and believe in God's promises as they understand them in their religious tradition, they are in line with God's plan'.[38]

Secondly, when the Jewish Messiah appears he will have some of the same traits as Christ. Though this statement is rather oblique in its formulation and probably would not elicit strong applause from Jewish scholars, its importance for covenantal theology lies in opening up the possibility for authentic messianic understanding within Judaism that is not totally dependent on Christianity's use of the Christ symbol for such understanding. It likewise retains a profound link between the two messianic visions, reaffirming the theological bond between Jews and Christians which Pope John Paul II has made so central in his many writings on the subject.[39]

The Pontifical Biblical Commission document is a study rooted in biblical exegesis, not a work of systematic theology which lies outside of the commission's mandate. Hence the commission did not draw out the full theological implications of the above statements. But these affirmations certainly can provide building blocks for developing such implications. They create the space for exploring whether the Church can speak about the universal significance of the Christ Event through Jewish religious symbols not directly connected with Christology. This may prove a most fruitful way of developing a Christology that remains open to covenantal pluralism, particularly with respect to Jews who, as Cardinal Kasper has pointed out, have an authentic revelation from the Christian theological perspective.[40]

Some may say that the above approach is a version of the 'anonymous Christian' notion proposed by the renowned German theologian Karl Rahner who profoundly shaped the theology of Vatican II. I do not believe this to be the case. Rather, it suggests that the process of human salvation revealed in the Christ Event goes beyond its articulation within the Church through symbols solely associated with the Christ Event. Hence Jews, and perhaps some other religious people, do not have to apprehend it directly through Christological symbolism. It suggests that while the salvific reality behind the Christ symbolism is indeed universal, the specific symbolism associated with this salvific reality within the churches may be more limited in scope.

In my judgment, this goes considerably beyond what Rahner proposed under the rubric of 'anonymous Christian', where the Christ Event remained the dominant religious symbolism. The proposal certainly remains a hypothesis that primarily aims to help Christians come to a new self-understanding in light of recent biblical scholarship and magisterial pronouncements regarding the Christian–Jewish relationship. This approach follows the suggestion of Luke Timothy Johnson [41] and enables Christians to think about themselves with reference to Jews, rather than focusing on a theology of Judaism and the Jewish People from the Church's perspective. While, unlike Johnson, I believe both avenues of reflection need to be pursued, he is correct in claiming that a certain priority should be given to Christian self-understanding. It is also true to say, and Christians need to recognise this, that Jews and other religious communities may not feel any necessity for theological confirmation of their faith perspective from the churches.

Cardinal Joseph Ratzinger has also recently entered this discussion. Besides giving overall approval to the Pontifical Biblical Commission document (though he does not specifically reference the two key passages in the text), he addressed the issue of the covenantal relationship between the Church and the Jewish People from a theological perspective in his own writings. It would appear that he would exempt Jews from the framework presented in Dominus Iesus, the controversial document issued by his doctrinal commission. Cardinal Walter Kasper in commenting on the question of Jews and Dominus Iesus cites Cardinal Ratzinger's statement that Jews are an altogether special case in terms of their relationship with the Church. Ratzinger describes Judaism as the foundation of Christian faith, a perspective which Kasper takes to mean Dominus Iesus is not applicable to the Jews.[42]

According to Cardinal Ratzinger the Jewish community will move to final salvation through obedience to its revealed covenantal tradition. But at the end time, Christ's Second Coming would confirm their ultimate salvation. It is not clear whether Cardinal Ratzinger would require explicit recognition of Christ as the Messiah from Jews as a condition for their salvific confirmation. In my judgment this 'delayed' messianism of the Christ Event is not as fruitful a starting point for rethinking Christological understanding today as the direction proposed by the Pontifical Biblical Commission. It is interesting to consider whether Cardinal Ratzinger would adapt his position in light of the recent Pontifical Biblical Commission document.

We are thus at a very early stage in the process of rethinking Christology and its impact on a theological understanding of covenant in terms of the Christian–Jewish relationship. As Christians, we may never be able to affirm a Christology leading to a theology of religious pluralism which is in agreement with the basic faith affirmations of Judaism or other world religions. But I believe we have a continuing obligation to continue this process. In today's globalised world, interreligious understanding is not merely confined to the realm of theological ideas but directly impacts on peoples' lives. A noticeable shift is presently emerging towards a double covenant theology but maintaining a Jewish–Christian bonding. This shift has produced strong disagreement from some, such as Cardinal Avery Dulles. Church leaders such as Cardinals Kasper and Ratzinger need to develop a synthesis of their perspectives which at the moment represent only fragments of meaning. This is also necessary for scholars who have been discussing reimaging the Christian–Jewish relationship by using terms such as 'siblings' or 'fraternal twins', which are rooted in Daniel Boyarin's co-emergence project. These images and their distinctiveness need to be drawn out further.

Before completing this chapter, I would like to discuss the role of the Old Testament or Hebrew Scriptures in forging Christian theological self-identity, the necessity of a Jewish matrix for fully comprehending Christian teaching and the controversial issue of Christian mission to the Jews.

Some years I ago I become involved in a debate regarding the title Christians ought to use for the first part of our Bible. I suggested that Hebrew Scriptures was a more appropriate term than 'Old Testament' but the name itself is not key. Rather, it is rather how we use this biblical resource in terms of Christian theological self-identity that is key. This discussion has continued for more than a decade with no clear resolution[43] and surfaced again on the Jewish side with the appearance of *Dabru Emet*, the Jewish statement on Christianity, which asserted that Jews and Christians take authority from the same book. This statement occasioned both harsh and more sober criticism from scholars such as Jon Levinson and David Berger. As a result, *A Sacred Obligation* offered a moderate statement, suggesting that 'The Bible Both Connects and Separates Jews and Christians'. (#5)

In the past the Hebrew Scriptures were not generally valued highly as a resource for Christian self-identity. The ancient Christian writer, Marcion, represents an extreme rejectionist position urging their total elimination from the Christian version of the Bible. There are some exceptions to this trend, such as Calvinism. Overall Christians have used the Hebrew Scriptures as a foil or for the New Testament. There even develop a strong sense that one could find glimpses of Christian revelation, including Christ and Mary, in these books.

While it is not possible to elaborate on this issue in a short essay, it must be said that any Christian covenantal theology which deals with the Church's relationship with the Jewish People will need seriously to reconsider the place of the Hebrew Scriptures. Some years ago A. Roy Eckardt, a pioneer in reinterpreting the Christian theological tradition in terms of Judaism, wrote that the covenant forged at Sinai is in principal no less important than the covenant renewed through Jesus Christ.[44] I have always regarded Eckardt as fundamentally correct on this point. The Hebrew Scriptures cannot serve merely as a prelude for Christian self-understanding. They did not fulfill that function for Jesus for whom they clearly served as a framework for his religious outlook. Whether we regard them as absolutely 'coequal' in defining Christian theological identity is open to discussion. But if Jews remain part of the ongoing covenant after the Christ Event, and if they remain bonded with Christians, consequently, their sacred books, as well as their interpretations of these books, become an undeniable resource for Christian theology. Yet rarely do they serve this function even today.

Reincorporating the Hebrew Scriptures as a primal resource for Christian theology will not come easy because of the history of their (mis)use by Christians. It is simplistic however to assert that Christians do not really rely on the Hebrew Scriptures because they have used them in different ways. Historically this may be true but the historic change in Christianity concerning the inclusion of Jews in the covenant after the Christ Event over the past forty years, forces Christians to re-evaluate their role in formulating Christian doctrine.

One cautionary note needs to be sounded here. There is some danger that Judaism as a theological resource for Christianity will become solely and exclusively identified with the Hebrew Scriptures. The Judaism of Jesus' time was already postbiblical and we need to come to understand its perspectives if we are accurately to interpret Jesus' teachings. Scholars such as Cardinals Ratzinger and Kasper seem to fall into this trap. We shall have to ask not only how the Hebrew Scriptures function as a continuing theological resource for Christianity but how postbiblical Jewish thinking ought to impact on Christian thinking. Although the 1985 *Vatican Notes* do emphasise the importance of Christians becoming familiar with postbiblical Jewish thought, they imply that this will help Christians better understand contemporary Judaism. It is additionally important we appreciate that, given Jewish–Christian covenantal bonding, present-day Jewish interpretations of Scripture and tradition should impinge not only on overall Christian doctrine but also on specific religious and ethical issues.

Regarding the reincorporation of Christianity into its original Jewish matrix I turn to the words of Cardinal Walter Kasper, 'Christianity therefore cannot be defined without reference to biblical Israel and to Judaism'.[45] This means that an understanding of Judaism is integral to an authentic interpretation of Christian doctrine as such, not merely for a theology of Christian-Jewish relations. Both Cardinal Kasper and I have emphasised Jesus' sense of ethics, ecclesiology and spirituality was profoundly conditioned by his Jewish religious background.[46] It is not possible to comprehend his vision in these critical areas without a deep grounding in Judaism.

Finally, let me briefly take up the issue of mission. This is certainly one of the most difficult issues in the contemporary Jewish–Christian dialogue. The proposed rejection of any notion of mission to the Jews in documents such as *A Sacred Obligation* and *Reflections on Covenant and Mission* has encountered strong opposition in sectors of Christianity. Cardinal Avery Dulles took strong exception to *Reflections On Covenant And Mission* on this point and the Southern Baptists attacked these documents as well as the Pontifical Biblical Commission document.

Mission to Jews has been a longstanding contested issue within Protestantism. In 1989, 15 Evangelical scholars met in Willowbank, Bermuda under the auspices of the World Evangelical Fellowship and drafted a two-page declaration on the need for Christians to evangelize Jews because Jews need Jesus to be saved. Within Catholicism where the concrete effort to convert Jews has never been quite as strong as within Protestantism the issue was pretty much kept under wraps since the time of the Council as I emphasised in an address to an international conference held at Cambridge University in 2001.[47] But in the same address I stressed that the issue might surface at any moment within Catholicism. It remained in my view a central, unresolved question in the Christian–Jewish dialogue. A Catholic lay scholar Tomasso Federici spoke to it in a paper delivered at the 1978 Vatican–Jewish International Dialogue held in Venice. In that paper he called for the formal termination of any Catholic mission to the Jews on the grounds that the Jews, in light of *Nostra Aetate*, were now recognised as standing within the divine covenantal framework and possessing authentic revelation from the Christian theological perspective. The same points have been used by Cardinal Kasper to argue against any organised effort to convert Jews within Catholicism. Federici s paper was subsequently altered in its final form, to read that 'undue' proselytizing of Jews is to be avoided. And Kasper has not further developed his thinking on the matter.[48] *Reflections On Covenant and Mission* represents in fact an effort to develop further the ideas Kasper has put forth on mission to the Jews, something he himself urged in in talks at Sacred Heart University and at Boston College.[49]

There is no easy resolution of the issue as mission has been at the heart of Christian self-understanding. To renounce it for Jews is to touch the very nerve centre of the Christian faith. Some Christians have argued that it represents a failure to love Jews because there is no greater love a Christian can offer anyone than the love made present in the life of Jesus. Certainly we must leave open the possibility of individual conversion in either direction—Jew to Christian or Christian to Jew. But as a theological principle I would support Cardinal Kasper's argument that the Church has no formal obligation to espouse the conversion of Jews to Christianity through organised missionary efforts. I recognise that this affirmation can open a pandora's box in terms of mission and other world religions. That is something we need to discuss but for the moment we should simply follow *A Sacred Obligation*, #7:

> Christians should not target Jews for Conversion…In view of our conviction that Jews are in an eternal covenant with God, we renounce missionary efforts directed at converting Jews. At the same time, we welcome opportunities for Jews and Christians to bear witness to their respective experiences of God's saving ways. Neither can properly claim to possess knowledge of God entirely or exclusively.

In light of the above discussion, I have confirmed the view of Gregory Baum cited at the beginning of this essay. By restoring Jews to the divine covenant from a Christian theological perspective, *Nostra Aetate* began a radical rethinking of Christian faith identity. Over forty years the major dimensions of this fundamental re-definition have begun to unfold as scholarly research leads to institutional restatement. But clearly a backlash has arisen in some quarters of Christianity. How quickly this process will continue in the coming years, if it continues at all, remains an open question.

Notes

1. Cf. 'Reflections on Covenant and Mission, by participants in a dialogue between the United States Conference of Catholic Bishops' Committee on Ecumenical and Interreligious Affairs and the National Council of Synagogues', *Origins* 32:13 (5 September 2002), pp. 218-224.

2. Cf. Avery Dulles, 'Evangelization and the Jews', with a Response by Mary C. Boys and Philip A. Cunningham and John T. Pawlikowski, *America* 187:12 (21 October 2002), pp. 8-16.

3. Cf. 'Towards renovation of the relationship of Christians and Jews: A statement of the Evangelical Church of the Rhineland', in Allan Brockway, Paul van Buren, Rolf Rendtorff, and Simon Schoon (eds.), *The Theology of the Churches and the Jewish People: Statements by the World Council of Churches and its Member Churches* (Geneva: WCC Publications, 1988), pp. 92-94 . Also cf. K. Hannah Holtdschneider, *The 1980 Statement of the*

Rhineland Synod: A landmark in Christian–Jewish Relations in Germany (Cambridge, UK: CJCR Press, 2002).

4. Gregory Baum, 'The social context of American Catholic theology', *Proceedings of the Catholic Theological Society of America* 41 (1986), p. 87.

5. Cf. Edward Flannery, *The Anguish of the Jews* (New York: Macmillan, 1965), and Marvin Perry and Frederick M. Schweitzer (eds.), *Antisemitism: Myth and Hate – From Antiquity to the Present* (New York: Palgrave/Macmillan, 2002). Also cf. John T. Pawlikowski, *Sinai and Calvary: A Meeting of Two Peoples* (Beverly Hills, CA: Benzinger, 1976), pp. 129-161.

6. Eugene J. Fisher, 'The evolution of a tradition: From *Nostra Aetate* to the Notes, in International Catholic-Jewish Liaison Committee', *Fifteen Years of Catholic–Jewish Dialogue: 1970-1985* (Rome: Libreria Editrice Vaticana and Libreria Editrice Lateranense, 1988), p. 239.

7. Johannes-Baptist Metz, 'Facing the Jews: Christian theology after Auschwitz', in Elisabeth Schussler-Fiorenza and David Tracy (eds.), *The Holocaust as Interruption. Concilium 175* (Edinburgh: T & T Clark, 1984), p. 27.

8. Cf. John Pawlikowski, *Christ in the Light of Christian–Jewish Dialogue* (Eugene, OR: Wipf and Stock, 2001); *Jesus and the Theology of Israel* (Wilmington, DE: Michael Glazier, 1989); 'Christology, Anti-Semitism, and Christian–Jewish bonding', in Rebecca S. Chopp and Mark Lewis Taylor (eds.) *Reconstructing Christian Theology* (Minneapolis: Fortress Press, 1994); and 'The Christ event and the Jewish People', in Tatha Wiley (ed.), *Thinking of Christ: Proclamation, Explanation, Meaning* (New York/London: Continuum, 2003), pp. 103-121.

9. *Dabru Emet* can be found (with commentaries by Jewish and Christian scholars) in Tikva Frymer-Kensky, David Novak, Peter Ochs, David Fox Sandmel and Michael A. Signer (eds.), *Christianity in Jewish Terms* (Boulder, CO: Westview Press, 2000).

10. Michael Phayer, *The Catholic Church and the Holocaust, 1930-1965* (Bloomington and Indianapolis: Indiana University Press, 2000), pp. 206-215.

11. Cf. Eugene J. Fisher and Leon Klenicki (eds.), *Pope John Paul II on Jews and Judaism* (Washington: United States Catholic Conference, 1987) and Eugene J. Fisher and Leon Klenicki (eds.), *Spiritual Pilgrimage: Texts on Jews and Judaism 1979-1995-Pope John Paul Ii* (New York: Crossroads, 1995. Also cf. Byron L. Sherwin and Harold Kasimow (eds.), *John Paul II and Interreligious Dialogue* (Maryknoll, NY: Orbis, 1999).

12. Gerhard Kittel, *Die Judenfrage* (Stuttgart: Kohlhammer, 1933), p. 73.

13. Martin Noth, *History of Israel* (Edinburgh: Oliver and Boyd, 1966).

14. Rudolf Bultmann, *Theology of the New Testament* (New York: Scribners, 1951).

15. *A Sacred Obligation: Rethink Christian Faith in Relation to Judaism and the Jewish People: A Statement by the Christian Scholars Group on Christian-Jewish Relation, 1 September 2002* (Boston: Center for Christian–Jewish Learning, Boston College).

16. S. Wesley Ariarajah, 'Towards a fourth phase in Jewish–Christian relations: An Asian perspective', unpublished paper, Conference on Christian-Jewish Dialogue Temple Emmanuel, New York, co-sponsored by the Center for Interreligious Understanding and the Office of Interreligious Affairs of the World Council of Churches, November 2003.

17. Carlo Maria Martini, S.J., 'Christianity and Judaism: A historical and theological overview', in James H. Charlesworth (ed.), *Jews and Christians: Exploring the Past, Present, and Future* (New York: Crossroad, 1990), p. 19.

18. The Notes may be found in Helga Croner (ed.), *More Stepping Stones to Jewish–Christian relations: An Unabridged Collection of Christian Documents 1975-1983* (New York: Paulist, 1985).

19. Arthur J. Droge, 'The Facts about Jesus: Some Thoughts on E. P. Sanders' JESUS AND JUDAISM', *Criterion* 11 (Winter 1987), p. 15.

20. Cf. The Leuenberg Church Fellowship, *Church And Israel: A Contribution from the Reformation Churches in Europe to the Relationship Between Christians and Jews* (Frankfurt am Main: Verlag Otto Lembeck, 2001) 1.3 and 3.1

21. Robin Scroggs, 'The Judaizing of the New Testament', *Chicago Theological Seminary Register* 75 (Winter 1986), p. 1.

22. Cf. Wayne A. Meeks and Robert Wilken, *Jews and Christians in Antioch in the First Four Centuries* (Missoula, MT: Scholars Press, 1978); Robert Wilken, *John Chrysostom and the Jews: Rhetoric and Reality in the Late 4th Century* (Berkeley, CA: University of California Press, 1983); and Anthony J. Saldarini, 'Jews and Christians in the first two centuries: The Changing Paradigm', *Shofar* 10 (1992), pp. 32-43.

23. Cf. Rosemary Ruether, *Faith and Fratricide: The Theological Roots of Anti-Semitism* (New York: Seabury,1974); and David P. Efroymson, 'The patristic connection', in Alan T. Davies (ed.), *Antisemitism and the Foundations of Christianity* (New York/ Ramsey/Toronto: Paulist, 1979), pp. 98-117.

24. Cardinal Carlo Martini, S.J., 'The relation of the Church to the Jewish People', *From the Martin Buber House* 6 (1984), pp. 3-10.

25. Cf. Johannes-Baptist Metz, *Facing the Jews*, p. 33, and Johannes-Baptist Metz, *The Emergent Church* (New York: Crossroad, 1981).

26. Rosemary Ruether and Paul Knitter are two examples of this perspective. Marcus Braybrooke in a volume entitled *Christian–Jewish Dialogue: The Next Steps* (London: SCM, 2000), has argued for further reflection on how we might relate Jewish–Christian covenantal thinking to the wider dialogue of world religions. I myself have taken up this important theme as well: John T. Pawlikowski, 'Toward a theology of religious diversity', *Journal of Ecumenical Studies*, 11 (Winter 1989), pp. 138-153.

27. Franz Mussner, *Tractate on the Jews: The Significance of Judaism for Christian Faith.* (Philadelphia: Fortress, 1984); also cf. Franz Mussner, 'From Jesus the "Prophet" to Jesus the "Son"', in Abdold Javad Falaturi, Jacob J. Petuchowski and Walter Strolz (eds.), *Three Ways to the One God: The Faith Experience in Judaism, Christianity and Islam* (New York: Crossroad) pp. 76-85.

28. Avery Dulles, 'Evangelization and the Jews', p. 10.

29. Two of Boyarin's recent books have amplified his theme of 'co-emergence': Daniel Boyarin, *Dying for God: Martyrdom and the Making of Christianity and Judaism* (Palo Alto, CA: Stanford University Press, 1999); and *A Radical Jew: Paul and the Politics of Identity* (Berkeley, CA: University of California Press, 1997).

30. On my Christological writings, cf. #8.

31. Franz Mussner, *Tractate on the Jews*, p. 226.

32. *Ibid.*

33. Cf. Elliot R. Wolfson, 'Judaism and Incarnation: The Imaginal Body of God', in Tikva Frymer-Kensky, David Novak, Peter Ochs, David Fox Sandmel, and Michael A. Signer (eds.), *Christianity In Jewish Terms*, pp. 239-254.

34. Cf. Johannes-Baptist Metz, 'Facing the Jews'; John T. Pawlikowski, 'Christology after the Holocaust', in T. Merrigan and J. Haers (eds.), *The Myriad Christ* (Leuven, Paris and Sterling, VA: Uitgeveru Peeters and Leuven University Press, 2000), pp. 381-397 and Irving Greenberg, 'Judaism, Christianity and Partnership After the Twentieth Century', in Tikva Frymer-Kensky, David Novak, Peter Ochs, David Fox Sandmel and Michael A. Singer (eds.) *Christianity in Jewish Terms*, pp. 25-36.

35. Cf. *A Sacred Obligation* #6.

36. Cf. #8.

37. Cf. The Pontifical Biblical Commission, *The Jewish People and Their Sacred Scriptures in the Christian Bible* (Vatican City: Libreria Editrice Vaticana, 2002). Also cf. Donald Senior, 'Rome has spoken: A new Catholic approach to Judaism', *Commonweal* 130 (31 January 2003), pp. 20-23. Joan E. Cook, 'The new PBC document: Continuity, discontinuity, and the progression revisited'. Unpublished paper presented to the Annual Meeting of the Catholic Biblical Association, San Francisco, California, 5 August 2003; also cf. the articles by Mary Boys, Leslie Hoppe, Michael O'Connor, John T. Pawlikowski and Amy-Jill Levine in *The Bible Today*, 41:3 (May 2003), pp. 141-172.

38. Cardinal Walter Kasper, 'Christians, Jews and the thorny question of Mission', *Origins* 32:28 (19 December 2002), p. 464.

39. Cf. #11.

40. Cf. Cardinal Walter Kasper, 'The good olive tree', *America* 185:7 (17 September 2001), 12-14; 'Spiritual and ethical commitment in Jewish–Christian dialogue', in Ruth Weyl (ed.), *From the Martin Buber House*. 30 (Summer 2002),pp. 12-20; and 'Christians, Jews and the thorny question of mission', pp. 457; 459-467.

41. Johannes-Baptist Metz, 'Facing the Jews', p. 27.

42. Cf. Cardinal Walter Kasper, 'The Church and the Jews', America, 185:7 (17 September 2001); and Cardinal Joseph Ratzinger, 'The heritage of Abraham, the gift of Christmas', *L'osservatore Romano* (29 December 2000); *Many Religions—One Covenant* (San Francisco: Ignatius Press, 2000); and *God and the World: Believing and Living in our Time* (San Francisco: Ignatius Press, 2002). For a Jewish response, cf. David Berger, 'Dominus Iesus and the Jews', *America* 185:7 (17 September 2001), pp. 7-12.

43. Cf. Roger Brooks and John J. Collins (eds.), *Hebrew Bible or Old Testament?* (Notre Dame, IN: University of Notre Dame Press, 1990). Also Cf. *Dabru Emet*, #2 and A *Sacred Obligation* #5. For a critical Jewish response, cf, Jon D. Levenson, 'How not to conduct Jewish–Christian dialogue', *Commentary* (December 2001), pp. 31-37. It is followed by a spirited exchange of letters. I briefly address this issue in 'Jews and Christians: The contemporary dialogue', *Quarterly Review* 4:4 (Winter 1984), pp. 26-28.

44. A. Roy Eckardt, *Elder and Younger Brother* (New York: Schocken, 1973), p. 142.

45. Cardinal Walter Kasper, 'Issues concerning future dialogue between Jews and Christians'. Unpublished Paper delivered at The Catholic Theological Union, Chicago, 17 April 2002, p. 3.

46. See ibid., 10; also cf. John T. Pawlikowski, *Christ in the Light of the Christian-Jewish Dialogue*, pp. 76-107 and 'The Jewish covenant: Its continuing challenge for Christian faith', in Joseph A. Edelheit (ed.), *The Life of Covenant: The Challenge of Contemporary Judaism: Essays in Honor of Herman E. Schaalman* (Chicago: Spertus College of Judaica Press, 1986), pp. 113-123.

47. John T. Pawlikowski, 'Maintaining momentum in a global village', In E. Kessler, J. Pawlikowski, and J. Banks (eds.), *Jews and Christians in Conversation: Crossing Cultures and Generations* (Cambridge, UK: Orchard Academic, 2002), pp. 75-91.

48. Tomasso Federici, 'Mission and witness of the church', in *International Catholic–Jewish Liaison Committee, Fifteen Years of Catholic–Jewish Dialogue, 1970-1985*, pp. 46-62.

49. Cf. Cardinal Walter Kasper, 'Christians, Jews and the thorny question of mission'.

14

Reading Violent Scripture

Edward Kessler

If you have seen evil, it was shown to you in order that you learn of your own guilt and repent; for what is shown to you is also within you. (Baal Shem Tov, 1698-1760)

This essay will offer a variety of approaches to the interpretation of violent biblical texts. This is valuable in a world where violence is often carried out in the name of religion, justified by a particular interpretation of one or more sacred texts. I will begin with a brief consideration of the traditional Jewish responses to violence in biblical, rabbinic and modern times. The survival of Judaism in the face of external attacks is not a new phenomenon and I suggest that recognition among Jews today of the ideas put forward in the rabbinic writings may provide some help in developing an appropriate response in an increasingly violent world. In addition, the realisation among Jews that there now exist partners in this exercise should strengthen our resolve to tackle these texts. Christianity, for so long an instigator of violence against and contempt for Judaism has, in recent years, become a friend who has respect and admiration for Judaism. Awareness of this transformation in Christian attitudes towards Judaism may contribute to the development of a hermeneutical principle by which both Jews and Christians can read and interpret violent texts. I hope that some of these suggestions would also be of value to Muslims in their reading of the Qu'ran.

The Traditional Jewish View of Violence
Until recently, the traditional and most common Jewish response to violence was based on Jeremiah 29:4-7:

> Thus saith the LORD of hosts, the God of Israel, unto all the captivity, whom I have caused to be carried away captive from Jerusalem unto Babylon: Build ye houses, and dwell in them, and plant gardens, and eat the fruit of them; take ye wives, and beget sons and daughters; and take wives for your sons, and give your daughters to husbands, that they may bear sons and daughters; and multiply ye there, and be not diminished. And seek the peace of the city whither I have caused you to be carried away captive, and pray unto the LORD for it; for in the peace thereof shall ye have peace.

The yielding to outside power and accepting the violence that prevailed were strategies, which ensured the survival of Judaism. By relinquishing a desire for sovereignty, Jews gained some autonomy in regulating their lives. Under the motto *dina d'malkulta dina* ('the law of the land is the law') the Jewish community based its existence on the law of the host society. 'A person must be at all times yielding like a reed', said the rabbis, 'and not unbending like a cedar'.[1] This approach ensured Jewish survival and enabled Judaism to develop and flourish in the face of violence until the rise of antisemitism in the 19th and 20th centuries when the passiveness of the rabbinic model, with its acceptance of pogroms, massacres and finally the Holocaust, offered no respite.

Arthur Waskow points to the 1880s as the time when Jews began to realise that they could no longer live by the rabbinic model[2] and desired to take control of their own destiny. Self-determination in the Land of Israel became the goal. The Zionism of the left-wing Palmach as well as the right-wing Irgun produced a military model, which aimed to protect Jews in the Land of Israel by force. For the most part, the effort to secure and defend territory on which to build a Jewish society allowed for compromise, partition and self-restraint. However, in the last few years a more aggressive response to violence has become noticeable and the military decision-making process, which had been based on the use of military force sparingly and defensively, has now changed into the use of force liberally and belligerently – for conquest as well as for self-defense.

There are many difficulties with this approach, one of which is that it is unlikely a small people living in Israel can wage a long-term ethical military effort and at the same time develop a decent society. Not even the Soviet Union, a continental super-state, could shoulder this burden. It is not altogether clear that even the richest country in the history of the world, the United States, can for generations wage continuous war – even 'a war against terror' – and remain a decent society at home.

The chances that Israel can do so are very small. It may seem implausible at first, but if we turn to some of the more violent passages from Scripture and examine the rabbinic interpretations alongside, we will find some surprisingly relevant and refreshing comments, which can provide guidance in developing a response to the issues raised by this problem.

Reading the Bible

The centrepiece of the Jewish service is the reading of the Written Torah, the 5 books of Moses. Jews traditionally read each and every verse, including the more problematic verses. These include violent passages such as Deuteronomy 20 which deals with fighting a war and the ethics of warfare and begins with a remarkably democratic, enlightened and morally topical message:

> When thou goest forth to battle against thine enemies, and seest horses, and chariots, and a people more than thou, thou shalt not be afraid of them; for the Lord thy God is with thee, who brought thee up out of the land of Egypt. And it shall be, when ye draw nigh unto the battle, that the priest shall approach and speak unto the people, and shall say unto them: 'Hear, O Israel, ye draw nigh this day unto battle against your enemies; let not your heart faint; fear not, nor be alarmed, neither be ye affrighted at them; for the Lord your God is He that goeth with you, to fight for you against your enemies, to save you.' And the officers shall speak unto the people, saying: 'What man is there that hath built a new house, and hath not dedicated it? Let him go and return to his house, lest he die in the battle, and another man dedicate it. And what man is there that hath planted a vineyard, and hath not used the fruit thereof? Let him go and return unto his house, lest he die in the battle, and another man use the fruit thereof. And what man is there that hath betrothed a wife, and hath not taken her? Let him go and return unto his house, lest he die in the battle, and another man take her.' And the officers shall speak further unto the people, and they shall say: 'What man is there that is fearful and faint-hearted? Let him go and return unto his house, lest his brethren's heart melt as his heart.' And it shall be, when the officers have made an end of speaking unto the people, that captains of hosts shall be appointed at the head of the people.

The Bible proposes a volunteer army and suggests that many groups of people should not be expected to fight in a war, particularly those who have:

· Recently moved into a new home
· Planted a vineyard but not yet reaped its fruits
· Become engaged and are shortly to be married
· Fear of war

The passage goes on to explain that the city to be attacked should first be offered terms for a peaceful surrender but if it refuses, should be besieged. Upon victory its women and children should not be harmed. So far, so enlighteningly good, but verses 16-18 are especially problematic:

> Howbeit of the cities of these peoples, that the Lord thy God giveth thee for an inheritance, thou shalt save alive nothing that breatheth, but thou shalt utterly destroy them: the Hittite, and the Amorite, the Canaanite, and the Perizzite, the Hivite, and the Jebusite; as the Lord thy God hath commanded thee; that they teach you not to do after all their abominations, which they have done unto their gods, and so ye sin against the Lord your God.

The Bible commands that the cities of the Hittites, Amorites, Canaanites, Peruzites, Hivites and Jebusites should be destroyed and that every man, woman and child (and animal) should be killed. Although these cities, from the perspective of Scripture, may symbolise the Nazis of their time, how should such verses be interpreted, particularly in today's violent world?

The rabbis decreed that military power should no longer be used. They did this by evading, nullifying, and otherwise interpreting away the genocidal commands against the Canaanites and other idolatrous people. Instead of extrapolating from these commands that it was right – even obligatory – to wipe out a people that rejected the one true God, the rabbis went in the opposite direction, ruling that the Canaanite example was null and void. Since the Canaanite peoples no longer existed – the rabbis explained that the Assyrians had scattered them as well as the ten lost tribes of Israel in 721 BCE – the rabbis ruled that the commands to use military action against the Canaanites were a dead letter.[3] If military action against the Canaanites was no longer necessary, then military action itself was no longer commanded.

The rabbis were creative in applying Torah to a new situation. They could have understood the six nations as symbols for ongoing dangers to be dealt with militarily but chose instead to annul the genocidal meaning of the text and even rejected the command to execute a rebellious Israelite child or wipe out a rebellious Israelite city.[4] This was an ethical decision not to carry out literally the command of Torah. One could argue that to a certain extent the rabbis were simply being pragmatic, given the power of the Roman and Byzantine empires, but these rulings point to an ethical rejection against the use of violence. Indeed, the rabbis mostly rejected the violent punishments prescribed in Torah, indicating that a court which sentences even one person to death in seventy years, is a court of murderers.[5]

Consequently, rabbinic Judaism constructed a non-violent way for the Jewish people to live in the world. Living as a vulnerable minority in Christian (and Muslim) society, Jewish communities in the rabbinic period abandoned the hope of overcoming oppressors. Only within ourselves, said the rabbis, can Jews overcome evil. According to one tradition, when all Jews truly observe the Sabbath twice in a row, the messiah will come and transform the world.[6] It is noteworthy that such a transformation will take place as a result of divine action rather than human interference. For almost two thousand years, with few exceptions, Jews accepted their suffering passively. They experienced expulsions, pogroms and burnings, believing that they would live beyond such events. This survival technique is illustrated by the fact that even as the Jewish lights of Western Europe were extinguished one by one – expelled from England (1290), France (1306) and Spain (1492) – new Jewish centres were being established in Eastern Europe, Turkey and the Middle East.

It is unsurprising that over the centuries a mentality permeated the minds of most Jews, which saw the Jewish community as still being utterly engulfed by enemies. The legacy of this mentality exists today and must be overcome. The need to develop friendships and build positive relations with like-minded faith communities is essential. This is increased by the danger that a small people will suffer another catastrophe in the land of Israel. Judaism needs allies for this challenge. The mindset of isolation imbued both biblical and rabbinic Judaism. It developed in the effort to conquer Canaan against what was viewed as an ocean of idolaters and grew in the effort to survive the Roman Empire. This mindset was reinforced by Inquisitions and pogroms and even by the gentler Muslim habit of treating the Jews like tolerated pets. The Shoah and the continued threats to the State of Israel fuel it even further.

Whether Jews survived by military means in the ancient land of Israel, or lived a life of non-violence among other civilizations, both biblical and rabbinic Judaism reinforced the perception among Jews that they were on their own, that no one else shared their vision and that all outsiders were enemies. For centuries, this may well have reflected considerable truth. However, in the last one hundred years Jews have begun to discover that there are other communities in the world with which they can share a vision of a decent society. The transformation in Christian attitudes towards Judaism is one example. Indeed, a positive relationship between Judaism and Christianity is one of the few pieces of good news in media reports about religious encounters in today's violent world.

Transformation in Christian Perceptions of Judaism
In the last 100 years, the need for Christianity to abandon its historical religious animosity and misleading caricature of Judaism has been overwhelming. These are now generally admitted as being wrong and their full and public rejection was required before the possibility of rebuilding good relations with Judaism. Thus, what was required was a shift from what was, for the most part, an inherent need to condemn Judaism to one of a condemnation of Christian anti-Judaism. This process has not led to a separation from all things Jewish but, in fact, to a closer relationship with 'the elder brother'. In the words of German theologian Johannes Metz, 'Christian theology after Auschwitz must stress anew the Jewish dimension of Christian beliefs and must overcome the forced blocking out of the Jewish heritage within Christianity'.[7] Social ethicist, John Pawlikowski stated that, 'the Holocaust has made it immoral for Christians to maintain any Christology that is excessively triumphalistic or that finds the significance of the Christ Event in the displacement of the Jewish People from an ongoing covenantal relationship with God'.[8]

As far as reading the Bible is concerned, this has led to the tackling of the traditional teaching of contempt of Judaism (known as Adversus Iudeaos) in Christian interpretations of Scripture. This teaching of contempt had become part of Christian identity. The extent to which this first stage has been successfully completed is subject to some disagreement among scholars – critics both within and outside the Church believe that there is more to be done. However, the changes have been dramatic and it is clear that many of the main divisive issues between Judaism and Christianity have been either eliminated or taken to the furthest point at which agreement is possible. The efforts of Catholics and Protestants towards respect of Judaism are reflected in documents, which project attitudes that would have been unthinkable a few decades ago. Christian theology has been profoundly revised at the official level - all Churches are committed to the fight against antisemitism and to teaching about the Jewishness of Christianity. This is illustrated by the recent document published by the Pontifical Biblical Commission entitled *The Jewish People and their Sacred Scriptures in the Christian Bible*, (2002) which among other things called for Christians to read and learn about rabbinic interpretations of Scripture and stated that the Jewish messianic expectation was not in vain.[9]

Few would deny that a massive change in attitude has taken place and that for the most part Christianity, in the West at least, is no longer part of the problem of antisemitism but part of its solution. As far as Scripture is concerned, Christians are now taught that the Hebrew Bible is not simply a foil for the New Testament, possessing little authority in its own right. It was necessary for some kind of balance to be restored between the Hebrew Bible and the New Testament and reverence towards the *graphai* (Scriptures) as a whole has been reasserted in Christian biblical interpretation. Jewish biblical interpretation is valued and respected by Christians to an extent, which would have caused disbelief just a couple of generations ago.

Whilst Christian biblical scholarship has rejected its former negative stereotyping of Jews and Judaism, resulting in a revised approach to the teaching of biblical studies, some Jewish writers have focussed more on how to read the Bible in light of the Shoah. In general, Jewish responses to the Shoah tend to fall into two categories, both of which impact upon the Jewish reading of the Bible. The first is represented by figures such as the philosopher Emil Fackenheim, the theologian Richard Rubenstein and the author Elie Wiesel. They have all argued that the Shoah has resulted in a 'rupture' in the relationship between Jews and God and a consequent Jewish distancing from Scripture.

Richard Rubenstein offered an 'atheistic' reaction in his 'death of God' theology. In *After Auschwitz* (1966) he stated that the *Shoah* had buried any possibility of continued belief in a covenantal God of history and that instead of interpreting the Bible in traditional terms, Jews should consider it simply in terms of an earthly existence. In his revised second edition of the same work (1992), Rubenstein offered a more mystical approach. What has not changed is his affirmation of a view of God quite different from the mainstream view of biblical and rabbinic Judaism and his rejection of the notion that the Jews are in any sense a people either chosen or rejected by God.[10]

The second response is to view events between 1933 and 1945 as one would do persecution and oppression during other periods of extreme Jewish suffering. This view is represented by Jewish scholars such as Jacob Neusner, Eliezer Berkovits, Eugene Borowitz and Michael Wyschogrod. The latter makes their position clear when he states that, 'the voices of the prophets speak more loudly than did Hitler'.[11] According to this argument, traditional approaches to Scripture provide the means by which to come to terms with the *Shoah*. But how should we read Scripture in light of the Holocaust?

Emil Fackenheim calls for a struggle with the biblical text and if need be, a fight against it. The biblical text is accepted as a primary text but is viewed as 'naked'; Jews are impelled to tackle the biblical text because they are also 'naked'.

> After the Holocaust Jews cannot read, as they once did, of a God who sleeps and slumbers not; so enormous are the events of recent history … that the Jewish Bible … must be struggled with, if necessary fought against.[12]

Fackenheim examines a number of previous approaches to the Bible and rejects them all. For instance, Martin Buber had proposed that each generation in turn 'struggled' with the Bible. Before the *Shoah* Buber stated that:

> The generations are by no means ready to listen to what the book has to say, and to obey it; they are often vexed and defiant; nevertheless, the preoccupation with this book is part of their life, and they face it in a real world.[13]

After the *Shoah*, Buber asked whether one could dare recommend to Holocaust survivors, 'thank ye the Lord for He is good, for His mercy endures for ever'? (Psalm 111:1). Adopting the phrase 'eclipse of God' (hester panim) as a means of describing the Shoah, he suggested that just as the moon can appear to block out the sun, so God was eclipsed during the Holocaust.[14]

But for Fackenheim the focus lies not with a metaphorical eclipse of God but with a more tangible struggle by Holocaust survivors:

> If these [survivors] open the Jewish Bible they are more than 'vexed' and 'defiant': the Book fills them with outrage; yet, too, more than merely 'preoccupied' with it, they clutch it as if for survival. So new, so paradoxical a relation is coming into being between the Book, then and there, and the 'generation' here and now. This is because of two events both referred to by names of places. One is Auschwitz, the other, Jerusalem.[15]

Exegetical Relativity[16]

To a certain extent, struggling with the meaning of scripture lies at the heart of rabbinic exegesis. The Rabbinic Bible, the Mikraot Gedolot, with its commentaries spanning the centuries ranged around the biblical text, is rightly regarded as a celebration of the enduring nature of the debate about meaning. The rabbinic willingness to see a multitude of different possible meanings, in marked contrast to the single 'authentic' meaning, backed by clerical or scholarly authority, provides us with the means of handling difficult biblical texts.

This approach may be described as exegetical relativity and is put forward by the rabbis as follows:

> In the School of Rabbi Ishmael it is taught: 'See, My word is like fire, an oracle of the Eternal, and like a hammer that shatters a rock' (Jeremiah 23:29). Just as a hammer divides into several sparks so too every scriptural verse yields several meanings.[17]

This approach to biblical interpretation can also be found in classical Christian exegesis. Although less well known in the West because it derives from the Syriac tradition, the following passage from the fourth century church father, St. Ephrem, is significant to our study:

> The facets of God's word are more numerous than the facets of those who learn from it. God depicted His word with many beauties, so that each of those who learn from it can examine that aspect of it

which he likes. And God had hidden within his word all sorts of treasures, so that each of us can be enriched by it from whatever aspect he meditates on. For God's word is the Tree of Life which proffers to you on all sides blessed fruits; it is like the Rock which was struck in the Wilderness, which became a spiritual drink for everyone on all sides: 'They ate the food of the Spirit and they drank the draft of the Spirit'.[18]

An acceptance of the legitimacy of a variety of different meanings, each of which claims validity, is therefore found at the heart of traditional Jewish and Christian exegesis. The existence of exegetical relativity means traditional interpretations of Scripture allow for a breadth and plurality of viewpoint. In this way, both the Jewish and Christian exegetical traditions provide a means by which to deal with texts, which run contrary to what we regard as the fundamental values of our tradition or which may be read as a license for violence or bigotry. The application of exegetical relativity is dependent upon one criterion: that biblical interpretation should reject any interpretation, which promotes hatred, discrimination or superiority of one group over another. For example, the literal application of a biblical text for the purpose of the subjugation of women to men, black to white, Jew to Christian and so on should be considered invalid, requiring reinterpretation.

This approach is justified by a hermeneutical principle shared by both Christians and Jews: humanity should live by the commandments and not die by their observance.[19] This means that in light of the Shoah biblical texts need to be examined in light of potential damage they may cause (or the real damage they have caused). The rabbis coined the term *Pikuah nefesh*, referring to the duty to preserve life, taking precedence over the commandment: simply put, when human life is at stake the biblical text needs reinterpretation.

The recognition that the biblical text can have more than one meaning is significant for contemporary Jewish and Christian interpretation of Scripture in particular and Jewish–Christian relations in general. It is no longer appropriate to search for the one and only correct meaning of a text but rather it is essential to examine a number of different interpretations, each within its own context, each worthy of consideration in its own right. The existence of exegetical relativity may leave the interpreter with an uncomfortable tension because of the presence of a number of interpretations arising out of a single biblical passage. The multitude of possible interpretations may be disconcerting to some but their existence illustrates the variety of interpretations, which can be applied to Scripture. Occasionally, even the biblical text contains an inherent ambiguity.

Consider the following opposing translations of Job 13:15:

- Behold, he will slay me; I have no hope (RSV)
- Though he slay me, yet will I trust in him (KJV).

The reason for the difference between the RSV and KJV is the result of a variation in the reading and spoken versions. The Masoretic vocalisation (spoken reading) indicates that Job has hope while the consonantal text (written text) offers the view that Job has no hope. The Mishnah acknowledges the ambiguous meaning of the biblical text and has recognised that both translations are possible 'the matter is undecided – do I trust in Him or not trust?'[20] The contradiction is meaningful as it expresses the tension of one who is torn between hope and doubt: the very tension that inhabits our mind when we read the Bible today. According to Andre Neher 'Job pronounces two words which signify simultaneously hope and hopelessness...I hope in Him, he shouts, but also do not hope in him'.[21]

Such an approach does not offer an easy or a comfortable reading of Scripture for it leaves the reader with unresolved tension and contradiction. Yet it provides a way of understanding the text to those who, like Fackenheim, are struggling with the meaning of the Bible in light of the Shoah. It can be equally applied to reading violent Scripture. The existence of ambiguity may enable Christians and Jews to realise that the plain, obvious and literal interpretation is not the final meaning of the text. The tension which arises as a result is helpful because, like the Bible and its interpretations, the Jewish-Christian encounter is full of ambiguity.

Techniques for Handling Difficult Texts

This paper has shown that although both Jews and Christians share difficult texts, each has within its own history of biblical interpretation the means by which to handle such texts. However, some polemical texts are particular to the Church.

The problem of polemic in the New Testament provides one of the major challenges in Jewish-Christian relations. The problem is exaggerated by the fact that Jesus was a Jew who taught his fellow Jews, some of whom followed his teaching and some others did not. Most of his contemporaries, of course, had never heard of him. After his death, his Jewish followers, encouraged by their experience of the resurrection – commonly called the Christ Event – argued for the validity of his teaching and their own, against their fellow Jews who had not been persuaded. To complicate the position somewhat further, Jesus' Jewish followers argued amongst themselves about the conditions under which Gentiles might be admitted to this new Jewish movement. In addition, some of the Jewish communities within the Jesus movement – with or without Gentile members – found themselves further at odds with other Jews over issues such as Torah observance and claims about Jesus.

The New Testament bears witness to all of this and many of the texts illustrate the debates and arguments, which were taking place. These disputes were serious, vigorous and often bitter. Nevertheless, what must not be forgotten – but which over time has been almost completely neglected – is the fact that the arguments were between Jews, about a Jew or about Jewish issues (even when they concerned Gentile converts!).

The problem of polemic is therefore magnified greatly when we read the polemical passages as if they were 'Christian' arguments against 'Jews'. To read them this way is to misread them. It is this misreading which has resulted in the Christian teaching of contempt. While we cannot deny that the New Testament includes many polemical texts, other than exegetical relativity, there are a number of important techniques to handle such texts.

The most important method is to contextualise them. This means to consider the implications of the fact that the mission and ministry of Jesus can only be understood in the context of first century Palestinian Judaism. Not only is it essential to emphasise that the concerns of Jesus and his followers are Jewish concerns, as we mentioned above, but that Christianity in part shares the Scriptures of the Jews and that the Jewish way of worship heavily influenced Christian modes of worship.

In addition, it is essential to read the text in light of:

• Modern statements about the Christian relationship to Jews and Judaism such as the various Vatican statements, The Anglican Lambeth 1988 Document entitled *Jews, Christians,*

Muslims: the way of dialogue and so on. For example, John Paul II's famous comment in 1980, 'the people of the Old Covenant, never revoked by God' might be cited alongside Matthew 23. A comparison of post WWII statements would be worthwhile in the interpretation of such passages.[22]

• The close relationship between Jesus and the Pharisees. For example it was a Pharisee who warned Jesus about the intention of Herod (Lk 13:1); Jesus taught and associated with Pharisees; many of Jesus' teachings are paralleled in the rabbinic writings.

• More positive biblical passages. For example, one might compare negative interpretations associated with verses such as 'No-one comes to the Father except through Me' (John 14:6) or 'nor is there salvation in any other, for there is no other name under heaven given among men by which we must be saved' (Acts 4:12) with passages such as 'Other sheep I have which are not of this fold'. (John 10:16).

• Its abuse by later Christian interpretation, most noticeable in the Adversus Iudaeos tradition. The dangers of abuse, such as the harmful consequences of Matthew 27:25, should be highlighted.

Conclusion

Abraham Joshua Heschel tells the story of a band of inexperienced mountain climbers. Without guides, they struck recklessly into the wilderness. Suddenly a rocky ledge gave way beneath their feet and they were tumbled headlong into a dismal pit. In the darkness of the pit they recovered from their shock, only to find themselves set upon by a swarm of angry snakes. Every crevice became alive with fanged, hissing things. For each snake the desperate men slew, ten more seemed to lash out in its place. Strangely enough, one man seemed to stand aside from the fight. When the indignant voices of his struggling companions reproached him for not fighting, he called back: If we remain here, we shall be dead before the snakes. I am searching for a way of escape from the pit for all of us.[23]

Heschel points out that the killing of snakes will provide security for a brief moment but not forever. The killing of snakes is also an inadequate metaphor in reading the Bible and especially those violent texts shared by our religious traditions. A successful re-reading of the texts is more likely to be achieved through partnership than in isolation. Jews and Christians share many of the same textual difficulties but also have many of the same tools within their exegetical traditions by which to tackle these problems. The story of the Jewish-Christian relationship in the last 100 years provides us with a lesson of how we can learn from and help each other.

Notes

1. Babylonian Talmud (BT), Ta'anit 20a.

2. A. Waskow 'The Sword and the Plowshare as Tools of Tikkun Olam' *Tikkun*, May 2002.

3. Based on Mishnah Yadayim 4.4.

4. Mishnah Sanhedrin 8.1-4; BT Sanhedrin 71a.

5. Mishnah Makkot 1.10.

6. BT Shabbat 118b

7. J –B. Metz, 'Facing the Jews: Christian theology after Auschwitz', E. Schussler-Fiorenza and D. Tracy (eds.), *The Holocaust as Interruption. Concilium* 175 (Edinburgh: T & T Clark, 1984), p. 27.

8. J. Pawlikowski 'Christology after the Holocaust' *Encounter* 3(1998), p. 346.

9. *The Jewish People and their Sacred Scriptures in the Christian Bible* (Vatican City: Libreria Editrice Vaticana, 2002).

10. R. Rubenstein, *After Auschwitz: history, theology, and contemporary Judaism* (Baltimore: The Johns Hopkins University Press, 2nd ed, 1992), pp. 311-2.

11. M. Wyschogrod, 'Faith and the Holocaust', *Judaism* 20 (1972), p 294.

12. E. Fackenheim, *The Jewish Bible after the Holocaust* (Manchester: Manchester University Press, 1992), pp. vii-viii.

13. M. Buber, 'The man of today and the Jewish Bible', *Israel and the World Israel: essays in a time of crisis* (New York: Schocken, 1948).

14. M. Buber, *The Eclipse of God: studies in the relation between religion and philosophy* (London: Gollancz, 1953).

15. Fackenehim, *op.cit*, pp. 16-17.

16. I am grateful to J. Magonet whose paper at a conference in London in 2000 sparked this idea. See his 'Reading our Sacred Texts Today', in T. Bayfield, S. Brichto and E Fisher (eds.), *He Kissed Him and They Wept* (London: SCM, 2001), pp. 110-119.

17. BT Sanhedrin 34a.

18. *Commentary on the Diatessaron* I:18-19.

19. E.g., compare Mark 2:27 with Mekhilta de Rabbi Ishmael on Exodus 31:12 or BT Sanhedrin 74a.

20. Mishnah.Sotah 5:5.

21. A. Nehr, *L'Exil de la paraole: du silence biblique au silence d'Auschnitz* (Paris: Editions du Seuil 1970) p. 215.

22. See www.jcrelations.net for a selection of the main statements issued by the Churches and Jewish community.

23. Delivered in March 1938 at a Quaker conference in Frankfurt-am-Main, Germany and published in. E. Kaplan, *Holiness In Words: Abraham Joshua Heschel's Poetics Of Piety* (Albany: State University of New York Press, 1996), pp. 145-51.

Printed in the United Kingdom
by Lightning Source UK Ltd.
107113UKS00001B/66